Health Management Information Systems

Methods and Practical Applications

Second Edition

Joseph K. H. Tan, PhD
Associate Professor
Division of Health Policy and Management
Department of Health Care and Epidemiology
Faculty of Medicine
University of British Columbia
Vancouver, British Columbia

AN ASPEN PUBLICATION®
Aspen Publishers, Inc.
Gaithersburg, Maryland
2001

Library of Congress Cataloging-in-Publication Data

Tan, Joseph K. H.
Health management information systems:
methods and practical applications/
Joseph K.H. Tan—2nd ed.
p. cm.
Includes bibliographical references and index
ISBN 0-8342-1777-5
1. Information storage and retrieval systems—Health services administration.
2. Management information systems.   I. Title.
RA971.6.T36 2000
362.1'068'4
00-040602

Orders: (800) 638-8437
Customer Service: (800) 234-1660

About Aspen Publishers • For more than 40 years, Aspen has been a leading professional publisher in a variety of disciplines. Aspen's vast information resources are available in both print and electronic formats. We are committed to providing the highest quality information available in the most appropriate format for our customers. Visit Aspen's Internet site for more information resources, directories, articles, and a searchable version of Aspen's full catalog, including the most recent publications: **www.aspenpublishers.com**
Aspen Publishers, Inc. • The hallmark of quality in publishing
Member of the worldwide Wolters Kluwer group.

Editorial Services: Joan Sesma
Library of Congress Catalog Card Number: 00-040602
ISBN: 0-8342-1777-5

Printed in the United States of America

1 2 3 4 5

To my most beloved wife, Leonie, and my dearest son, Joshia,
for all their love and inspiration; and
To all other loved ones in my family whose lives have or had been
dear to me.

Table of Contents

Chapter 8—Communications System Architecture: Networking Health Provider Organizations and Building Virtual Communities **179**
J. Michael Tarn, H. Joseph Wen, and Joseph K. H. Tan

PART IV—MANAGING DOMAIN AND CONTROL ARCHITECTURE OF HEALTH MANAGEMENT INFORMATION SYSTEMS **205**

Chapter 9—Health Management Information System Strategic Planning and Managerial Accountability: Specifying Domain and Control Architecture **207**
Joseph K. H. Tan

Contributors

Monica Adya, PhD
Assistant Professor of Information Systems
University of Maryland Baltimore County
Catonsville, Maryland

Ashok Bhatkhande, MD, DPH
Director (Administration)
Breach Candy Hospital
Bombay, India

Mark L. Corley
Vice President of Operations
Abbott Ambulance, Inc.
St. Louis, Missouri

Albert S. Dexter, MBA, PhD
Professor
Faculty of Commerce and Business Administration
University of British Columbia
Vancouver, British Columbia

Guisseppi A. Forgionne, PhD, MBA, MA
Professor of Information Systems
University of Maryland, Baltimore County
Catonsville, Maryland

Aryya Gangopadhyay, PhD
Assistant Professor of Information Systems
University of Maryland Baltimore County
Catonsville, Maryland

Henry J. Groot, MS
Director, Information Resources
Holy Cross Health System
South Bend, Indiana

Charalambos L. Iacovou, PhD
Assistant General Manager
Management and Information Services
Cyprus Popular Bank
Nicosia, Cyprus
Research Fellow
McDonough School of Business
Georgetown University
Washington, DC

Rajiv Kohli, PhD
Project Leader, Decision Support Services
Holy Cross Health System
South Bend, Indiana
Adjunct Assistant Professor
Management Department
University of Notre Dame
Notre Dame, Indiana

Liam O'Neill, PhD
Assistant Professor
Policy Analysis and Management
Cornell University
Ithaca, New York

N. Jane Prater, RN, BSN
Nurse Manager
University of Iowa Hospitals and Clinics
Iowa City, Iowa

Wullianallur Raghupathi, PhD
Professor
Graduate School of Business
Fordham University
New York, New York

Glenn H. Roberson, MD
Professor and Vice Chairman
Chief of Neuroradiology Section
Radiology Department
University of Alabama at Birmingham
Birmingham, Alabama

Homer H. Schmitz, PhD
Professor
Department of Health Administration
Saint Louis University
President and Chief Executive Officer
Abbott Ambulance, Inc.
St. Louis, Missouri

Yao-Yang Shieh, PhD
Professor
Radiology Department
Texas Tech University Health Sciences Center
Lubbock, Texas

Joseph K. H. Tan, PhD
Associate Professor
Division of Health Policy and Management
Department of Health Care and Epidemiology
Faculty of Medicine
University of British Columbia
Vancouver, British Columbia

J. Michael Tarn, PhD
Assistant Professor of Computer Information Systems
Department of Business Information Systems
Haworth College of Business
Western Michigan University
Kalamazoo, Michigan

H. Joseph Wen, PhD
Associate Professor
Management Information Systems
New Jersey Institute of Technology
Newark, New Jersey

Foreword

In this age of exploding technologies and information superhighways, students, health professionals, and managers need more than ever to understand health management information systems. To do so they need to understand the theories and methods underlying their structures and limitations, and the range of their applications not yet tapped in most places. Take the seemingly simple example of word processing software. It has insinuated itself into virtually every desktop computer. Nearly every desktop of health professionals now sports a computer with at least this software if none other. Health professionals use few of the capabilities of these word processors, even those who use them daily for routine writing tasks. If word processing software is so underemployed, consider spreadsheets, database management packages, statistical packages, and other generic productivity software. All these productivity tools await a new fifth generation of user-friendliness to put their wider range of capabilities to work. That new generation is here.

Joseph Tan describes the generations of health management information systems and the latest generation of expert systems that could change this underutilization. He takes pains in the early chapters to convey an appreciation of the health management information systems that have built the platform for new technologies. Artificial intelligence and expert systems software hold promises for taking information systems to new heights of decision-making support for managers. Health informatics and telematics hold the parallel prospect of integrating health information systems in more seamless and accessible ways.

One platform on which Dr. Tan builds his account of the oncoming information era is systems theory. His development of insights from the systems perspective puts this book in the forefront of both health care and information science. He uses the perspective to examine data systems and subsystems, management functions and roles, and systems development methodologies.

Tan outlines some of the issues for the future on the basis of projections and assumptions concerning the reform or renewal of health care systems. These include new criteria of effectiveness, and the fate of the total quality management paradigm.

The graphics in this book demonstrate a feature of desktop information technology. Combining new information systems and concepts with new communications technology has opened new horizons in management productivity, mobility, independence, and competitiveness. Those who have been the early adopters of these systems, technologies, and concepts have opened the doors of the health care system to new possibilities, new efficiencies, and new accountability.

—Lawerence W. Green, DrPH
Professor and Director
Institute of Health Promotion
University of British Columbia
Vancouver, British Columbia

Preface

Health Management Information Systems was first published in 1995 and quickly became a widely distributed, internationally recognized text. A number of significant developments in the field of health care computing and network technologies have occurred over the past few years, which lead to the justification of this new edition. This is not surprising, given that the field of health management information systems (HMISs) is still very young and is growing at an accelerating pace.

Key revisions in this edition include but have not been limited to (1) the use of a more practice-based approach than the previous edition to improve and widen the appeal of this work to instructors, students, health professionals, and practitioners; (2) the use of scenarios at the beginning of each chapter to motivate and assist readers in developing a critical appreciation of important informatics concepts in health services delivery and in reflecting on the practical uses of these concepts; (3) the revision of entire chapters throughout the text and the addition of case studies at the end of the text to fill the need for an expanded knowledge and understanding of issues affecting the strategic, tactical, and operational implementation of an HMIS; and (4) the streamlining and integration of related concepts from various chapters appearing in the previous edition. In this sense, this new edition may indeed be construed as a new text altogether.

In this edition, an HMIS is viewed as a mix of information, technology, and domain and control architecture. Briefly, these concepts are captured in this new edition in five major parts. Part I (Chapters 1 and 2) provides an overview of the HMIS field. Part II (Chapters 3 through 5) focuses on building HMIS information architecture, whereas Part III (Chapters 6 through 8) concentrates on integrating HMIS technology architecture. Part IV (Chapters 9 through 11) moves on to issues relating to managing HMIS domain and control architecture. Finally, Part V (Chapter 12 and Cases 1 through 5) provides major HMIS cases to illustrate how the various concepts discussed in Parts I through IV can be applied in real life scenarios.

More specifically, Chapter 1 shows why an integrated management perspective is needed for health care information systems. This chapter also provides a discussion of the PUSH-PULL framework to organize the entire HMIS field and to provide an organizing framework to the various parts of the text. Indeed, HMISs must be conceived, planned, designed, developed, and tested within the context of a guided paradigm, and the PUSH-PULL framework provides such a paradigm. Systems theory, the underpinning theory explaining key concepts of planning, designing, and developing HMISs, is discussed in Chapter 2. It is important to note that the major emphasis found in these chapters is specifically written to fit in with today's evolution of integrated delivery systems.

The theme about integrated delivery systems, their role in defining health care data requirements clearly and accurately, and their need to build appropriate information architecture is carried through from Part I to Part II. The fundamental concepts of health care data and databases as providing the building blocks for HMIS design and development are reviewed in Chapter 3. The evolving standards for HMIS data, technologies, and methodologies to integrate modern health care delivery systems are presented in Chapter 4. The subject of HMIS development methodologies and their historical evolution from systems development life cycle to prototyping to end user computing are detailed in Chapter 5.

The emergence of newer forms of HMIS technologies is surveyed and richly illustrated in Chapter 6. Examples of HMIS technologies surveyed include virtual patient records, document management, data warehousing, networking and asynchronous transfer mode networks, medical informatics, and telematics, as well as the Internet, intranets, and extranets. Data warehousing, data mining, and integrated health decision support system architecture are further elaborated on and illustrated in a comprehensive cancer surveillance system in Chapter 7. Chapter 8 concentrates on communications system architecture and shows how the use of such architecture can be applied to network among health provider organizations and to build virtual communities. Because of accelerating changes in HMIS technologies, substantial revisions have been made in this new edition for this part of the text. The resulting effort is a series of contributions and collaborations from both academics and practitioners primarily situated in the United States, where the text currently is being used actively and extensively.

On the challenge of HMIS strategic planning and management, Chapter 9 advocates the use of various techniques for defining information requirements within the context of a macro-micro view as presented in Chapter 1. The challenge of HMIS resource management is the subject of Chapter 10, whereas the challenge of HMIS implementation is carefully detailed in Chapter 11. These chapters have been generally revised from the previous edition with new emphasis placed on relating these challenges to managing domain and control architecture for integrated delivery systems.

Finally, Chapter 12 provides a general discussion of the various cases to bring together HMIS concepts discussed in the earlier parts of the text. It also presents a comparative analysis for the different cases to show how each case study would fit into the PUSH-PULL framework presented in Chapter 1. It should be noted that contributors to these cases wrote them based on real-life scenarios and use them to illustrate HMIS applications in operational, tactical, and strategic management contexts for health facilities and hospitals functioning within an integrated delivery system.

Acknowledgments

Above and beyond those to whom I feel indebted in putting together the first edition of this text, I would like to thank the many professional and academic contributors, several of my research assistants and students, as well as those associated with Aspen Publishers, all of whom have worked together to make this substantially revised second edition a reality.

First, I am especially indebted to each of our contributing authors for the collaborative spirit and cheerful participation that each has provided throughout the lengthy duration of this project. Their willingness to direct their contributions to a common theme, to conform to a set format or a particular layout, to restrict themselves to a particular topic or area of research, to revise earlier drafts, and to make extensive changes when these were necessary and they were asked to do so is highly admired and greatly respected. Most important, their strong commitments to quality of thought and concise expression have ensured the readability and integrability of the finished product.

Second, special acknowledgment is due to all others who have contributed to make this project possible, including the reviewers and our colleagues, secretaries, students, and academic and research assistants. To name each of them would run the risk of missing someone important, but the abilities and selfless contributions of several such individuals should be especially recognized: Kamran Kheirani, who assisted selflessly in reading much of the revised materials and providing feedback from the point of view of a student taking a course with this text; Kenneth Tang, who assisted in the drafting of a few chapter outlines for the new edition and coordinating the contributing authors; Alan Chiu and Egidio Spinelli, both of whom assisted in the production of several new graphics not available in the previous edition; Michael Wong and Kelly Lee, who assisted in reviewing Parts I and II of the work; and Fanny Liu, who willingly helped out in some of the literature search and the library work involved. Without the help of these individuals, I am certain that the current work would not have been completed in a timely fashion.

Third, I am also very grateful to the staff of Aspen Publishers, Inc., for their support and guidance throughout the project. I greatly appreciate and thankfully acknowledge all of their assistance, encouragement, and understanding in the various production stages of this work, from beginning to end.

To all these individuals and to my family members, friends, and relatives, I offer my many thanks for the support provided to me throughout the germination and compilation of this new edition. Much of the value of this work is due to their contributions and assistance.

Part I

Overview of Health Management Information Systems

Chapter 1

Health Care Information Systems: An Integrated Management Perspective

Joseph K. H. Tan

SCENARIO

You have just been hired as the chief information officer (CIO) to advise Metropolitan General Hospital and Health Sciences Center on the strategic management and operational deployment of advancing computer-based information technologies. Currently, Metropolitan represents a newly formed network of seven previously independently governed hospitals, health centers, and physician-owned health clinics. Over the years, these organizations have developed their own health data registries and clinical information systems. Among other applications, general administrative and financial management systems, patient care systems, clinical and ancillary department clinical systems, and practice management systems are those that need to be integrated as a result of the merger. In fact, some of the partners have even begun talking about sharing a common data warehouse and implementing data mining applications. Even so, the lack of a shared strategic vision, a sound data architecture, an integrated communication policy, and a linked technology infrastructure among the partners have caused unnecessary barriers to accessing and sharing critical but confidential patient data and images throughout Metropolitan.

Mr. CEO, the newly appointed chief executive officer who has had very little formal training in health care information systems (HCISs), has been receiving complaints on patient care services from board members, physicians, other health professionals, and patients. He advises you to set up a triage and utilization care plan solution for effective patient data management. However, you see a more urgent need to build a central pool of administrative and technical support resources to cope with the design of various architectures for integrating information system (IS) services at Metropolitan. Think about how you would manage these pressing needs while keeping Mr. CEO informed of the current HCIS status at Metropolitan. Contemplate what Mr. CEO needs to know regarding HCISs and how you can effectively communicate to him about the steps needed to address the complaints and the challenges ahead.

INTRODUCTION

In this chapter, a broad conceptualization of HCISs from an integrated management perspective is provided. The underlying architecture and basic functions of an integrated health management information system (HMIS) are laid out with emphasis on the need for health administration students to learn to apply information technology (IT) in integrated health services environments. More generally, students will be introduced to a macro-micro framework that encompasses the planning, designing, and developing of strategically aligned HMIS applications in the context of evolving health services administration problems and realities. Finally, how this book is organized within the general HMIS framework is discussed.

AN INTEGRATED MANAGEMENT PERSPECTIVE IN HEATH CARE INFORMATION SYSTEMS

Over the past few decades, the evolution of IT in organizations within the health care field has been relatively slow and sporadic compared to IT development in other fields. Nolan et al. have noted that this rather appalling technological slack is the result of a failure to involve health services managers in HCIS design and development.[1] Also, they stress that hospital administrators have failed over the years to secure sufficient funding for HCIS developmental projects, in particular, projects that would have a significant effect on the cross-functioning of the organization. In addition, they found very little evidence of support among top management of health services organizations for actively involving end users in ongoing HCIS design and developmental efforts. This lack of support was attributed to the fact that many health managers were unable to perceive the benefits of applying IT in such health organizational activities as strategic planning, clinical operational decision making, health resource utilization and management, manpower planning and scheduling, and health program design and evaluation. Moreover, there was a lack of strategic IT applications in health services organizations. Largely, apart from isolated, entry-level applications such as payroll and inventory systems for improving efficiency of routine business operations, little attention was paid to applying IT to improve the strategic impact of organizational, clinical, and managerial decision making.

Soon, it was realized that this typically one-off, piecemeal HCIS approach could no longer be feasible or acceptable. The scenario described by Nolan and his colleagues has since been changed because of increased globalization, continuous health care reforms, the gradual corporatization of medicine, and other major trends such as forming new alliances and consolidations among health provider organizations. Moreover, the emergence of wireless user-friendly portables, the proliferation of powerful network-based computing, and the fact that new implementation of these network-based systems are now in the order of multi-million dollars all pressure senior management to become seriously interested in endorsing cost-beneficial, integrated HCIS solutions. Finally, as health consumers (the public) are becoming more knowledgeable and better trained in accessing computerized health information and evaluating alternative health services, they are becoming more demanding. Thus, it has been predicted that the potential growth of HCIS applications during the coming years will probably be greater than in most other industries.[2] Therefore, management should not and cannot afford to leave the job of designing, developing, and implementing network-based, integrated HCISs in the hands of specialists. By doing so, they may allow the resulting systems to center around the technology and not organizational requirements. As such, the importance of adopting an integrated management perspective in HCIS implementation should not be underestimated.

Accordingly, the term, "health management information system" is used throughout this book to convey the need for an integrated management perspective in HCISs. To familiarize health administration and health management students with this perspective of HCISs, we now turn to the architecture and basic functions of the HMIS.

ARCHITECTURE AND BASIC FUNCTIONS OF THE HEALTH MANAGEMENT INFORMATION SYSTEM

In its broadest sense, the HMIS encompasses diverse concepts and methods from many related fields. The beginning of the HMIS discipline may be traced to many roots, including general systems research, information economics, management science, information system development methodologies, computer science and communication theory, medical computing, health organization behavior, health policy, and health services research. A basic understanding of the integrated HMISs, however, includes the four major HMIS architectural components.

Four Major Architectural Components

Essentially, an integrated HMIS comprises a mix of four key architectural components and their interrelationships:

1. data-information-knowledge component (information architecture)
2. hardware-software-network component (technology architecture)
3. process-task-application component (domain architecture)
4. user-administration-management component (control architecture)

These four architectures correspond generally to those presented by Bourke.[3]

Information architecture is the fundamental building block of all HMIS design and development. It encompasses the specification of, organization on, and interrelationship among data, information, and knowledge elements required of an integrated HMIS. Building effective data, information, and knowledge resources involves specifying the precise requirements of these elements and their structures to serve as inputs, and identifying the most appropriate sources for the acquisition of these inputs. Specifically, the information architecture design largely determines how data, information, and knowledge are provided, classified, and stored as inputs within an HMIS to generate the needed outputs (solutions). In an integrated and well-designed HMIS, the goal is to distribute these information-related elements efficiently, effectively, and appropriately throughout the organization for enriching learning among end users and for enhancing the delivery of health services among providers. In Part II, various aspects of information architecture are discussed.

Technology architecture entails the effective deployment of computer hardware, software, interface, and communication networks to support HMIS integration and use. Briefly, this involves configuring various hardware, software, interface, and communication-enabling elements in such a way that best achieves efficient and effective information processing. Based on this information processing, various health organization processes are integrated to perform designated tasks and activities. In this sense, new and emerging HMIS technologies and methods play an increasingly significant role in enhancing organizational delivery of health services. Part III therefore focuses on technology architecture.

Domain architecture exemplifies the interdisciplinary nature of managing health care information services. In other words, all domains of organizational information processes must be engineered to work together for the efficient, effective, and excellent delivery of health services. This requires not only an up-to-date knowledge of the structure and changing characteristics of the health care industry, but also a detailed understanding of organizational task processes and how these processes should be designed to fit well with the other architectural components of an integrated HMIS. In fact, as early as 1980, Lincoln and Korpman recognized the difficulties with computer applications in health care.[4] In their classic paper, "Computers, Health Care, and Medical Information Science," they argued that the goals for medical information science, although easy to state, are difficult to achieve for many reasons.

> First, it has proved insufficient merely to adapt information processing procedures and programs of proved success in other fields, largely because of the complexity of the medical context, the diversity of medical data, and the vagueness, disparity, and variety of health care objectives. . . .The goal of MIS [medical information science] is to resolve the apparent dissonance between the rigid structure of computer logic and the often inherently ambiguous structure of medicine. The materials are the full range of patient care data and their applications. . . . The methods employed encompass a wide range of disciplines, including not only information processing and communications but also the management, behavioral, and fundamental sciences.

Control architecture presupposes that the science and art of HMIS design and development can only be perfected through building, administering, and managing an intelligent organization-technology interface. The function of this critical component, when blended appropriately with information architecture, technology architecture, and domain architecture, is to culminate a meaningful conceptualization that absorbs the many insights and interactions inherent in any organizational HMIS application. Issues of domain and control architecture are summarized in Part IV and illustrated using a number of study cases in Part V.

An integrated HMIS approach is a holistic conceptualization of the fit among various architectural components within the context of an integrated management perspective. The relationships among these major architectural components are shown in Figure 1–1.

Figure 1–1 may be explained and illustrated in the context of designing and implementing a computer-based triage and utilization care plan solution for effective patient data management in the Metropolitan case. Here, in designing an HMIS to provide an integrated solution to the application task at hand, considerations must be given to the following:

- the content, structure, and standardization of patient data requirements and management report format (information architecture)
- the specification, configuration, and support required of computer hardware, software, interface, and communication networks to transmit, process, and distribute the input data, information, and knowledge elements into a useful utilization care plan (technology architecture)

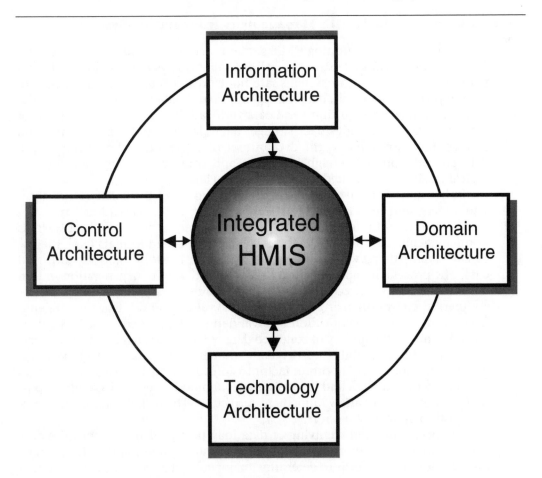

Figure 1–1 An Integrated Health Management Information System (HMIS) Architecture

- the need to analyze, design, and map out computerized information processes to support the task application at hand (domain architecture)
- the need to manage, train, and educate Metropolitan personnel so that the integrated HMIS can be applied beneficially to aid end user decisions on health services delivery (control architecture)

Ultimately, the human users are the ones who must determine whether these architectural components fit together for better or worse. If inaccurate or unreliable data result, if the technology is too cumbersome to use, if the underlying task processes interface poorly, and if there is lack of support from top management to end users, then the potential for HMIS failures will be real and consequential. Other considerations in this simple example may include how this HMIS implementation will affect the organization in terms of economic, political, and sociocultural outcomes, and possible future expansion and restructuring of Metropolitan.

Basic Functions of the Health Management Information System

It is critical that beginning HMIS students achieve a good grasp of the basic functions of an HMIS. Historically, all information systems, including health management information systems, are built on the foundation of three processing phases: data input, data management, and data output. The data input phase includes data acquisition and data verification. The data management or processing phase includes data storage, data classification, data update, and data computation. Finally, the data output phase includes data retrieval and data presentation. These eight elements and three phases together define a typical HMIS as represented schematically in Figure 1–2.

Data acquisition involves both the generation and the collection of accurate, timely, and relevant data. Data are the raw materials requiring transformation into useful information. The process of data generation in an HMIS is normally achieved through the input of standard coded formats (e.g., the use of bar codes), thereby allowing rapid mechanical reading and capturing of data. The process of data collection differs from that of data generation in that data can be entered directly at source (e.g., the use of a point-of-care bar code scanner), thereby enhancing data timeliness, validity, and integrity. Data verification involves the verification and validation of gathered data. It is generally known that the quality of collected data will depend largely on the authority, validity, and reliability of the data sources. The garbage in garbage out (GIGO) principle is an important factor to consider in this process; that is, data containing inaccuracies and inconsistencies should be detected as early as possible in the system to allow immediate correction. This will minimize the eventual costs of system data errors.

The preserving and archiving of data may be regarded as part of the data storage function. Memory (i.e., a physical storage system) and indexing (i.e., the selection of key words to determine major subject areas) are primary means of amassing data. When accumulated data are no longer actively used in the system, a method to archive the data for a certain period is usually advisable

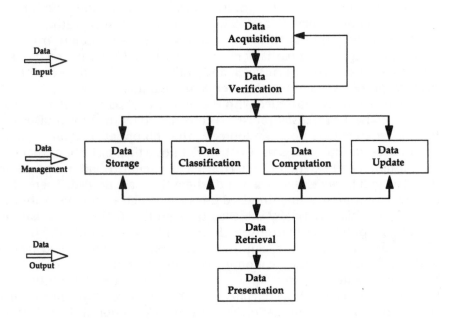

Figure 1–2 Basic Functions of a Health Management Information System (HMIS)

and may sometimes be mandatory, as when it is required by legislation. A closely related element to data storage is data classification (or data organization). It is a critical function for increasing the efficiency of the system when the need arises to conduct a data search. Moreover, imposing taxonomy on the data that have been collected and stored provides greater understanding of how the data will be used. Most data classification schemes are based on the use of certain key parameters. For example, data referring to a patient population may be classified and sorted according to various diagnostic classification schemes, such as the widely accepted International Classification of Diseases, 9th Revision, Clinical Modification (ICD-9-CM).[5] Such an organized patient data system is useful for conducting a case-mix analysis because it comprises a set of diagnostic codes of 14,000 patient classifications. Indeed, the particular taxonomy employed will have a powerful influence on the way the data subsequently may be used. This is because a high degree of semantics is implied in any particular data classification. Crowe and Avison noted that if the wrong classification is chosen, a great deal of potentially useful information may be lost.[6]

New and changing information is accounted for through the element of data update. The dynamic nature of such data changes calls for constant monitoring. Allowance for updating changes in the event of a transaction's occurring assumes that the HMIS must maintain current data. The concept of processing a transaction (i.e., whenever an event alters the current state of the system) is critical for ensuring data timeliness. Such updates can be either online (real-time) or batch processed. Data computation involves various forms of data manipulation and data transformation, such as the use of mathematical models and statistical applications, linear and nonlinear transformation, and completely or partially random processes. Computational tasks allow for further data analysis, synthesis, and evaluation so that data can be used for strategic purposes besides tactical or operational use.

Data retrieval is concerned with the processes of data transfer and data distribution. The data transfer process is constrained by the time it takes to transmit the required data from the source to the appropriate end user. A key problem in data transmission is the existence of noise (i.e., distortion) that could be both internal and external to the HMIS. The data distribution process ensures that data will be accessible when and where these are needed. There must also be ways to ensure that unauthorized users are denied access to sensitive data in the system. This is normally achieved through the institution of data security and access control mechanisms, such as the use of passwords and other forms of user identification. One significant criterion to be considered in the data retrieval function is the economics of producing the needed information. Many early systems (particularly, large mainframe hospital information systems) were far too costly to operate and the costs were simply not justified relative to the value of information that was finally produced. This situation has largely changed with advancing HMIS techniques and technologies.

Finally, data presentation has to do with how users will interpret the information produced by the system. In situations where only quantitative managerial decision making is expected, summary tables and statistical reports may be all that is needed. However, most managerial decision making involves both quantitative and qualitative components. The use of presentation graphics for qualitative managerial analysis is particularly encouraged because these appear to provide a better intuitive feel of data trend. Tan and Benbasat[7] and Tan[8] have presented a theory to explain and predict the human processing of graphical information, which is valuable to guide HMIS designers in the matching of presentation graphics to tasks.

To illustrate the three HMIS data phases, we can use the case of a computerized patient medical record system, which is also supported with bedside terminals. In this system, data acquisition comprises the generation and gathering of daily notes on symptoms, treatments, diagnoses, progress notes, discharge summaries, registration of orders for laboratory tests, operations, anesthesia, and other sources of information such as patient demographics and physicians' findings. The data to be coded and automated is usually formatted into specific and normalized elements, fields, and records.

Exhibit 1–1 illustrates an abstract of a patient medical record that could be implemented on a microcomputer system for use in monitoring patient medical conditions and treatments in a health service organization. As for data verification, the system relies on the ease with which the coded data may be mechanically processed and properly decoded. In many cases, standard forms and standard terms are used in recording patient data to ensure data integrity and consistency. Some organizations still employ data clerks to inspect and verify data input manually, but many computerized patient record systems

Exhibit 1–1 A Sample Abstract for a Computerized Patient Medical Record System

1. Patient Medical Insurance Number: _____	3. Date of Admission: / /
2. Patient Name: _____	4. Date of Discharge: / / Mo/Day/Yr:

5. Sex:
  - Male ☐
  - Female ☐

6. Birthdate: __ / __ / __

7. Tel. No.: ___ ___ ___

8. Next of Kin: _____

9. Address: _____

10. Admission Source:

  - Admitting ☐
  - Emergency ☐
  - Outpatient ☐

11. Location of Patient: _____

12. Discharge Status:

Alive:
  - With Approval ☐
  - Against Notice ☐

Death:
  - Autopsy ☐
  - No Autopsy ☐

Transfer to:
  - Other Institution ☐
  - Home ☐

13. Type of Death:
  - Anesthesia ☐
  - In Operating Room ☐
  - Postoperative ☐
  - Other ☐

14. General Remarks:
_____

PROCEDURES

15. Principal Procedure:
  a. _____ Date: / /

16. Additional Procedures
  a. _____
  b. _____
  c. _____

17. History/Physical:
_____

18. Laboratory:
_____

19. Radiology:
_____

PHYSICIANS

20. Principal Specialist: _____

Second Specialist: _____

Family Physician: _____

DIAGNOSIS

21. Principal Diagnosis: _____

22. Additional Diagnosis:
  a. _____
  b. _____
  c. _____

have built-in capabilities to reject invalid data inputs through the use of range checks (e.g., specifying a patient's age to fall within a verifiable range of classification) and other means (e.g., using batched totals).

After data input, the data are kept securely (data storage) in a database, a central data depository. This is to ensure that the data are accessible to the health service providers on any subsequent visits by the same patient. A master patient index is used to identify the exact location of a specific patient record. This type of data classification also allows for easy processing and regular updating by most provider organizations. Updating and maintenance of the data

(data update) to ensure timeliness and integrity can be carried out either on a daily basis (i.e., routinely) or interactively (real-time or online). For example, some hospitals collate their daily census through batch processing around midnight. Additional data processing functions include data analysis and synthesis to transform and combine various elements of the input data into useful and meaningful information (data computation). The data retrieval function ensures that the appropriate end users (e.g., physicians and nurses) have access to accurate, timely, and relevant information from the system. The distribution of information to end users typically occurs through the imposition of a system of user identification and authentication. Ultimately, data presentation in the context of the preceding example is concerned with generating reports that are easy to read and interpret for use in patient care–related decision making.

CLASSES OF HEALTH MANAGEMENT INFORMATION SYSTEM APPLICATIONS

An HMIS exists as part of a larger system to support one or more of a combination of administrative, financial, clinical, or managerial activities occurring within the health organization. More generally, existing HMIS applications may be classified as belonging to one of four groups: administrative and financial applications, patient care applications, clinical decision support and expert system applications, and strategic applications.

On one hand, administrative and financial applications support routine administrative and financial activities; on the other, patient care applications support routine clinical and patient care activities. Applications in the administrative and financial areas include admission, discharge, and transfer (ADT) registration, scheduling, materials management, patient billing, accounts receivable and accounts payable (AR and AP), payroll, general ledger, purchasing and inventory control, quality assurance/utilization review (QA/UR), human resources, and others (e.g., office automation). Applications in the clinical and patient care areas include the medical record, order entry and results reporting, bedside terminals, nursing, utilization care planning, and departmental information systems to support clinical activities (e.g., laboratory information systems, radiological information systems, and pharmacy systems). These early systems focus mainly on efficiency of routine business and clinical reporting. Changes in costing procedure and advances in specialized clinical knowledge and technologies lead to developments in integrated patient care, clinical decision support, and expert system applications.

Clinical decision support and expert system applications are designed to support intelligent clinical diagnostic, therapeutic, and treatment activities of health care organizations. Unlike traditional HMIS applications driven mainly by efficiency concerns, the development of these systems was driven by the need for better clinical management and greater support for clinical decision effectiveness.[9] Examples include the following: computer-aided diagnostic systems, drug dispensing and interaction alert systems, medical expert systems, automated medical instrumentation, imaging systems for use in operating rooms, intelligent monitoring systems, clinical process improvement, clinical robots, integrated patient care and group decision support systems, and information systems to support clinical education and research. Many of these applications have been discussed in Tan with Sheps.[10]

New and emerging strategic HMIS applications are the result of sweeping changes and growing competition in health care, in particular, the growth of managed care and multi-provider organizations. These applications include provider managed care systems, health plan managed care systems, home health systems, executive information and executive support applications, strategic and group decision support systems, and electronic networking. Examples of these applications have been presented in Tan and Raghupathi.[11]

In Part V, we will present a number of study cases for which various classes of HMIS applications will be used to stimulate class discussions. These cases illustrate in some detail many of the key concepts, issues, and challenges that are briefly introduced in Part I and discussed throughout Parts II through IV. It is hoped that instructors will find these cases helpful in preparing students to think critically about the type and nature of HMIS problems encountered in real life. At this point, it is useful to introduce a generic framework, the PUSH-PULL framework, to integrate the concepts discussed so far and to provide a lead to the overall organization of this book.

THE PUSH-PULL FRAMEWORK

Although many suggested frameworks exist to organize the HMISs field, the emphasis of these frameworks has mostly been skewed toward either a micro-view of HMIS problem-solving activities, or a more macro-view of the need for strategic alignment between corporate and HMIS plans. Unfortunately, both of these perspectives provide only partial views and the need for a comprehensive understanding of the complex interface between the two views remains. A linked macro-micro perspective of HMIS framework, the PUSH-PULL framework, is depicted in Figure 1–3.

As shown in Figure 1–3, the rationale for the PUSH-PULL framework is that all planning, programming, and evaluation activities relating to HMIS must not only transpire at two levels (i.e., the macro organization problem-finding level and the micro IT problem-solving level), but also there must be continuous monitoring of strategic business–IT alignment and a need for continuous quality improvement to serve as a feedback loop. We use the "PULL" acronym to denote *p*lanning *u*ncertain *l*inkages and *l*evels as key steps underlying the series of macro-planning phases and the "PUSH" acronym to denote *p*rogramming *u*nique *s*olutions and *h*ousekeeping as key activities representing the series of micro-programming stages. The details for these two grouping of activities are now discussed.

The macro-planning phases entail the following:

- planning, that is, gathering knowledge about the environment and the industry
- uncertainty, that is, identifying the variables and articulating those key factors influencing and driving the organization's vision and strategies

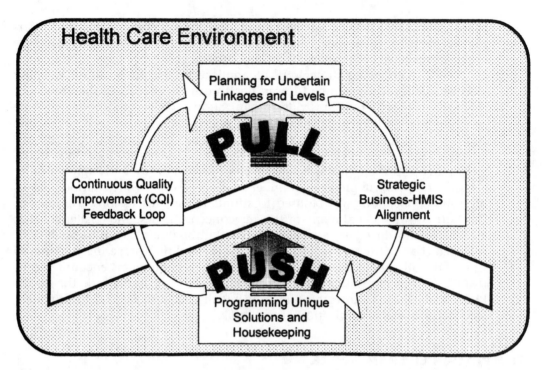

Figure 1–3 The PUSH-PULL Framework for a Macro-Micro Integrated Health Management Information System (HMIS) Approach

- linkages, that is, specifying the links between organizational strategies and values (critical success factors), and between organizational values and its system processes
- levels, that is, aligning the planning process from one level of the organization to the other, more particularly, aligning the business goals and objectives with IT goals and objectives

The first phase in macro-planning is assessing the broader external environments, including reviewing data on economic trends, sociocultural and political issues, demographics, competitor performance, and actions. This macro-planning exercise is also critical in assisting management to gain knowledge about the nature and characteristics of the industry. For example, accelerating changes within the health care industry over the past several years may warrant this kind of assessment if a health provider organization or system is to succeed in today's increasingly competitive environments. Michael Porter's five-factor model provides an excellent tool for this sort of assessment.[12] Briefly, the model submits that knowledge about the environments is derived or "pulled" from the most current environmental assessments of suppliers, industry rivals, customers, new entrants, and substitutes. This knowledge will provide the meta-level context for meaningful strategic planning in any health service organizational system.

Based on these environmental assessments, the second phase involves top management attempting to articulate a clear vision for the organization in the face of the uncertain future. In other words, management must define and articulate a vision and some general strategies for the system as a whole. Hopefully, the result of this process is a clear statement of the system's mission and a series of related goals based on many hours of brainstorming and discussions among members of top management. Often, this process can be facilitated by the use of a knowledgeable and well-trained consultant who can provide objectivity to the entire exercise. It is critical that top management not be detracted from the chief intent of this strategic planning session, and a retreat is typically recommended. Every word in the mission and goal statements is carefully selected to convey the trends and directions of the organization. In many cases, the goal statements are further translated into general strategies to guide the organization in the strategic planning process. Again, Porter's concepts of price differentiation, product differentiation, and market differentiation can be applied to guide these discussions. These concepts have now been applied in some detail for the strategic use of computers in the health care industry.[13,14]

Having articulated these strategies and goals, the next phase of macro-level planning typically involves carefully linking these strategies/goals with organizational values or critical success factors (CSFs) and generating further links between CSFs and system processes.[15] In other words, how do these goals and strategies translate into values and what HMIS vis-à-vis business initiatives should be implemented to realize these values? Here, some researchers have suggested the use of value chain analysis.[16] For instance, given that one strategy may be for nursing to work collaboratively with other care providers to offer world-class computer-aided yet humane inpatient care services, a value chain for nursing care might include computerized bedside assessment of patients, use of automated care plans, digital charting and tracking of routine nursing care, electronic monitoring of daily interactions with patients and family members, computerized discharge planning for patients, and other computer-aided general nursing activities. For each value, the following questions may be asked: Does each of the current activities add value to the overall achievement of the stated strategy for patient care? What are the system "bottlenecks" and what processes (and activities in the value chain) are seen as "value detractors" and should be given special attention? At the end of this planning phase, management should be able to answer the question of what and how programs or services should be delivered in order to best achieve the system's vision, mission, goals, and objectives in light of the identified CSFs and given all of the constraints (value detractors). Also, this analysis may beg the question of how the system's resources as a whole should be reallocated.

The final phase on the PULL side of the framework is to take this strategic planning process at the macro-level and "align" it through every subsystem level of the organization, thus essentially achieving a "leveled" alignment of system–subsystem mission, goals, strategies and objectives. In particular, for HMIS implementation to succeed, achievement of business–IT alignment is critical. This brings us to the micro-level stages where specific IT problem-solving activities can be programmed and implemented.

As observed, the "PUSH" acronym denotes micro-programming stages. These stages entail the following:

- programming, that is, detailing the strategies, design, programming, and development activities to meet the enterprise information needs
- uniqueness, that is, fitting various architectural components so as to uniquely support the proposed IT initiatives
- solutions, that is, rolling out of the IT strategies, design, programming, and development activities to achieve solutions for the problems on hand
- housekeeping, that is, maintaining the fit between programmed HMIS solutions and current realities

Metaphorically, these stages correspond neatly to the Simon's classic stages of problem solving: analysis, design, choice, and implementation/maintenance.[17] At the programming (analysis) stage, the information needs are identified at micro levels based on the previous value chain analysis at the macro level. The intent of this exercise is to achieve strategic alignment of system initiatives with subsystem initiatives. This can then provide both top and middle management with a common understanding of where the problem-solving activities should be concentrated. Defining the information requirements clearly and reaching consensus among departmental personnel and management as to which problems are amenable to computerized solutions is key for designing HMIS architecture at both the micro and macro levels. At this stage, therefore, it is imperative to relate back all of the micro-level views with the macro-level understanding to achieve an integrated HMIS.

At the uniqueness (design) stage, the architecture pieces that we discussed earlier, including the data, information, and knowledge requirements (information architecture); the hardware, software and communication network configurations (technology architecture); and the management and use of technical experts and other human resources (control architecture), are designed to tailor fit the various application tasks (domain architecture). The key here is to ensure that all of these architectural components fit in a way to ensure HMIS integration. Various alternatives can be proposed; for example, outsourcing of IS services such as the use of consultants and full vendor support, in-house design and own customization of software, or a mixed arrangement of these models.

The solution (choice) stage involves appropriating the most practical HMIS solutions to solving the problems at hand. It is not unusual to pilot test a certain alternative and then drop it altogether when there are enough signs to show its eventual rejection among end users. Total reliance on top management to drive these solutions is a mistake because these activities are supposedly at the micro-level. However, it is known that without top management commitment and support, most HMIS solutions will fail. One of the alternatives that people tend to forget at this stage is "doing nothing." Indeed, if none of the presented solutions appear to be supportive of an integrated HMIS, waiting may be wiser because a better alternative may be just round the corner, given the highly changing nature of the current health computing and technological marketplace.

Finally, the housekeeping (implementation/maintenance) stage ensures that the chosen solution (results) can be worked smoothly into realities and maintained through active testing, training, and education. A continuous quality improvement feedback loop is again provided between the micro-programming stages and macro-planning phases to ensure that changes in the system are duly accommodated by the HMIS implementation.

Logically, the macro problem-finding phases should precede the micro problem-solving activities, as these have to do with goal-setting activities at the system level. These activities are, by nature, more uncertain and longer term focused. Similarly, it appears that the micro-programming activities should proceed with active feedback from the macro-planning phases, as these have to do with goal-achieving, shorter-term activities using IT solutions at lower organizational hierarchies. This natural sequence, however, may be reversed in practice and therefore it is possible for macro-planning to begin when the need for system or organizational renewal is strongly felt. Further, the need for constant feedback between the two levels warrants a periodic and forced review at the macro-planning level every 5 to 10 years.

In summary, top management should employ a PULL strategy at the macro-planning phases because of the presence of risks and uncertainties in the system decision processes, whereas lower management should employ a PUSH strategy at the micro-programming stages as HMIS solutions are analyzed, designed, programmed, and implemented. Within the context of this broader framework, the underlying HMIS architecture of information, technology, application domain, and human control must interact actively in various combinations, generating integrative and satisfying HMIS solutions for health care organizations. The following definition of an integrated HMIS is therefore advanced as representing an "applied" view of this broad and complex field:

> An integrated HMIS is the application of a total systems approach in linking information architecture, technology architecture, domain architecture, and control architecture for the efficient, effective, and appropriate delivery of health services within the context of evolving health care environments.

ORGANIZATION OF THE BOOK

Figure 1–4 provides a visual representation of how this book (i.e., Parts I through V) can be organized in the context of the broader framework, and more specifically, with respect to the underlying integrated HMIS architecture.

In terms of the HMIS framework, the macro-planning phases are the subjects of Parts I and IV, whereas the micro-level problem-solving stages are covered primarily in Parts II and III. Part V, which comprises the study cases, provides insights into the complex link between the macro- and micro-level activities. More specifically, Part I serves as an introduction to HMIS architecture, Part II focuses on HMIS information architecture, Part III directs attention to HMIS technology architecture, and Part IV deals with the diversity encountered in HMIS domain and control architecture.

Part V brings together all of the HMIS concepts, perspectives, methods, and issues discussed in the book's earlier parts. By emphasizing the critical role human resources play in integrating the complex HMIS equation, the study

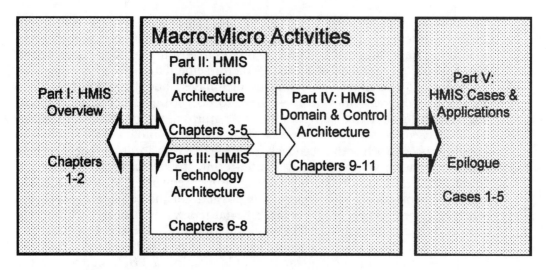

Figure 1–4 Relationships among Various Parts of This Book

cases presented in this part provide the link between understanding existing implementation barriers and developing future designs of HMIS architecture.

Part II: Health Management Information System Information Architecture

Part II, consisting of Chapters 3 through 5, focuses on HMIS information architecture. These chapters, placed near the beginning of the book, provide the fundamental principles for conceptualizing, building, and integrating HMIS methods and applications.

Chapter 3 concentrates on the relationship between data, information, and knowledge. This chapter discusses concepts of health care data and databases, information and communications, and demonstrates the application of health information system modeling through the use of data flow diagrams, flow charts, and entity-relationship models. Chapter 4 concentrates on the structuring of data requirements. It discusses traditional methods and presents a fresh approach to organize and manage data as an enterprise resource for today's health provider organizations. Chapter 5 focuses on HMIS design and development methods from classical system development life cycles and prototyping to contemporary models (e.g., CASE). Issues of accessing organizational and external data are also covered.

Part III: Health Management Information System Technology Architecture

Part III, consisting of Chapters 6 through 8, focuses on HMIS technology architecture. This part provides a general survey and more specific detailing of current HMIS technology architecture and landscape.

Chapter 6 provides an introduction to many existing and emerging HMIS technologies and discusses their proliferation within the health service delivery sector. It surveys the different cutting-edge HMIS technologies and their applications in today's integrated delivery systems. Chapter 7 focuses on decision support and expert system technologies as applied to the health service industry. It also covers HMIS technologies for assisting clinical research, managerial decision making, and complex administrative problem solving. Chapter 8 concentrates on electronic communication network technologies and demonstrates how these technologies may be applied in enhancing health service delivery today. Together, Chapters 6 through 8 in sequence show how HMIS technologies and applications may be changing over time and how these emerging forms of HMIS solutions and others may be combined for future integrated HMIS design.

Part IV: Health Management Information System Domain and Control Architecture

Part IV, which consists of Chapters 9 through 11, focuses on HMIS domain and control architecture. Part IV begins with a chapter on HMIS strategic planning and managerial accountability (Chapter 9) followed by a discussion on HMIS resource management (Chapter 10) and HMIS implementation (Chapter 11). These chapters deal with concepts and issues of managing HMIS domain and control architecture. They are placed near the end of the book to extend our understanding of HMIS management in a health informational, technological, and organizational context.

Part V: Health Management Information System Cases

As noted, these study cases should enhance student understanding of key concepts and issues presented not only in Chapters 9 through 11 of Part IV, but throughout Parts I and III of the book. No readings can replace the experience gained through real-life participation in HMIS design, development, and evaluation. Nevertheless, in a classroom setting, study cases provide a good alternative to real experience because they are an effective way to elicit and promote critical analysis. In writing these study cases, the contributors have tried to draw on real-life scenarios where HMISs play a critical role. Therefore, health management students are encouraged to use these cases to stimulate further thoughts and discussions on how the underlying concepts and issues presented may relate to the PUSH-PULL framework and the total HMIS architecture.

CONCLUSION

This chapter started out with a brief introduction of underlying architectural components and basic functions of a health management information system and then gradually arrived at the analysis of a PUSH-PULL framework for the HMIS field. This broad framework and the architectural components are the bases on which parts of this book are organized. It is hoped that the reader will find this work invaluable, not only as a reference tool, but also as a comprehensive text to accommodate and organize all of the current insights and fundamental concepts when preparing oneself for a rewarding career in the field of health management information system.

CHAPTER QUESTIONS

1. Distinguish HCIS from HMIS.
2. Discuss the need for an integrated management perspective of HCIS.
3. Discuss the four architectural components of integrated HMIS and provide examples of these in the context of your work.
4. List and illustrate the basic functions of an HMIS. How may these basic functions be extended to accommodate complex health information processing tasks such as medical diagnosis and teleconsultation?
5. Depict an HMIS framework that is built upon similar concepts suggested in the book and discuss the implications of this framework to future HMIS deign, development, and evaluation.

NOTES

1. R.L. Nolan, et al., Computers and Hospital Management: Prescription for Survival, *Journal of Medical Systems* 1, no. 2 (1977): 187–203.
2. W. Raghupathi and J.K.H. Tan, Strategic Uses of Information Technology in Health Care: A State-of-the-Art Survey, *Topics in Health Information Management* 20, no. 1 (1999): 1–15.
3. M.K. Bourke, *Strategy and Architecture of Health Care Information Systems* (New York: Springer-Verlag, 1994).
4. T.L. Lincoln and R.A. Korpman, Computers, Health Care and Medical Information Science, *Science* 210, no. 4467 (1980): 257–263.
5. ICD9 is a U.S. Public Health Service official adaptation of a system for the classification of diseases and operations. The original system was developed and updated periodically by the World Health Organization (WHO) for indexing hospital records. See T. C. Timmreck, *Dictionary of Health Services Management* (Owings Mills, MD: National Health Publishing, 1987): 306.
6. T. Crowe and D.E. Avison, *Management Information from Data Bases* (Basingstoke: Macmillan Press, 1980).
7. J.K.H. Tan and I. Benbasat, Processing Graphical Information: A Decomposition Taxonomy To Match Data Extraction Tasks and Graphical Representation, *Information Systems Research* 1, no. 4 (1990): 416–439.
8. J.K.H. Tan, Graphics-Based Health Decision Support Systems: Conjugating Theoretical Perspectives To Guide the Design of Graphics and Redundant Codes in HDSS Interfaces. In J.K.H. Tan with S. Sheps, *Health Decision Support Systems* (Gaithersburg, MD: Aspen Publishers, 1998): 153–173.
9. J.K.H. Tan, et al., Utilization Care Plan and Effective Patient Data Management, *Hospital & Health Services Administration* 38, no. 1 (1993): 81–99.
10. J.K.H. Tan with S. Sheps. *Health Decision Support Systems* (Gaithersburg, MD: Aspen Publishers, 1998).
11. J.K.H. Tan and W. Raghupathi (eds.). Strategic Relevance and Impact of Health Information Technologies, *Topics in Health Information Management* (entire issue). 19, no. 4 (1999).
12. M.E. Porter, *Competitive Advantage* (New York: Free Press, 1985).
13. Ibid.

14. R. Kropf, *Service Excellence in Health Care through the Use of Computers* (Ann Arbor, MI: Health Administration Press, 1990). A review of this book by J.K.H. Tan has been published in *Hospital & Health Services Administration* 38, no. 1 (1993): 159–161.

15. J.K.H. Tan, The Critical Success Factor (CSF) Approach to Strategic Alignment: Seeking a Trail from a Health Organization's Goals to Its Management Information Infrastructure (MII), *Health Services Management Research* 12 (1999): 1–13.

16. M.K. Bourke, *Strategy and Architecture of Health Care Information Systems.*

17. H.A. Simon, *The New Science of Management Decision* (New York: Harper & Row, 1960).

Chapter 2

Systems Thinking: Toward a Systems Perspective of Today's Integrated Delivery Systems

Joseph K. H. Tan

SCENARIO

In the previous chapter, you were exposed briefly to the concept of systems; more specifically, integrated health management information systems (HMISs) and organized health delivery systems. Imagine that you have just been funded to aid the Capital Health Region to plan a multi-community health promotion project (MCHPP). Several health promotion programs and activities are to be developed for community residents through the mobilization of an interdisciplinary team of health professionals including physicians, administrators, social workers, public health officers, nurses, and other volunteer participants. The efficient and effective sharing and use of information is therefore crucial to the success of MCHPP. To document the stakeholders who will share information, and to illustrate their perceived concerns and problems, you came up with a rich picture as shown in Figure 2–1.

The rich picture[1] is a convenient tool for documenting themes or issues for an ill-defined problem situation, specifically for soft and fuzzy issues. This innovative diagramming tool does not subscribe to any standards (or a particular convention). It uses the language and terminology of the environment and shows how various pieces of a problem situation are perceived as relating to each other by those who developed the picture. The aim here is to record the problem situation as a whole, that is, in a holistic fashion without limiting it to the agenda or biases of key actors and decision makers.

Figure 2–1 illustrates the various parties who share the information pool, and some of the tasks and concerns encountered in the MCHPP project. Based on the information provided in this picture and your further investigation of other available health services programs in Capital Health Region, you are asked to present to the various MCHPP project stakeholders a sense of where and how the different proposed health promotion programs and services can be situated and fitted appropriately into the larger picture of the present health services delivery system of Capital Health Region. To do this, contemplate on how you can apply systems concepts and systems thinking to provide a lead to solving MCHPP problems.

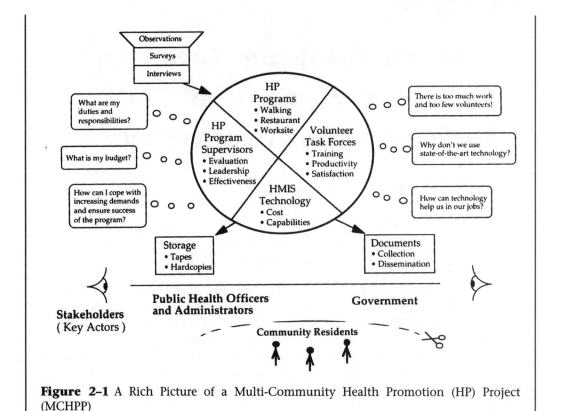

Figure 2–1 A Rich Picture of a Multi-Community Health Promotion (HP) Project (MCHPP)

INTRODUCTION

In this chapter, we discuss general systems concepts and the role systems thinking plays in augmenting our understanding of the health service delivery sector and HMISs. Viewing the health service industry from a systems perspective provides valuable holistic insights into the functioning and structure of the present system. This perspective also helps better define the changing role and functions that HMISs might need to shift in order to fit strategically with the future health service delivery trends. Upon completion of this chapter, the reader will be able to distinguish between concrete versus abstract systems, closed versus open systems, deterministic versus probabilistic systems, and to understand the basic structure, interactions, and behaviors of systems. This knowledge will in turn enable the reader to apply systems thinking when developing HMIS models for health service delivery organizations. More broadly, the application of general systems concepts on a contemporary health organizational system model, the integrated delivery system (IDS), will be elaborated. In this model, three organizational levels are identified:

1. organizational environments
2. organizational fields and populations
3. organizational sets and organizations

Conceptually, major changes that took place during the past few decades can be rationalized on different levels of organizations within the IDS context.

DEFINITIONS

By definition, a *system* is a set of interrelated elements. It is a unified or integral reality in its own right, composed of at least one other element in the set. Each element connects to every other element, directly or indirectly, and no subset of elements is unrelated to any other subset.

As a direct consequence of the inherent concept of unity within systems theory, a system must have a unity of purpose in the accomplishment of its goals, functions, or desired outputs. In other words, a system must have its own identity and be able to differentiate itself from external events, objects, or other such subsystems outside certain definable boundaries. For example, a bed allocation system should be differentiated from other systems in a health service facility by its unified goals and defined boundaries. This constitutes an independent system, whereas an assemblage of people waiting in the lobby of the health service facility normally do not, because these people do not have a unified purpose and are themselves not much different from, say, others walking into and out of an office building.

Outside the definable boundaries of a system is its environment. This environment has a set of elements with relevant properties that are not part of the system, but a change in any part of the environment can effect a change in the state of the system. For example, a decrease in transfer payments from any private or public funding agency has a resultant effect on the functioning and quality of services provided by a health service facility. This is similar to the human anatomy, where insulin and glucose can effect a change in the biological state of the system.

One cannot ignore the dynamic nature of systems. An important point to remember is that the state of a system at any moment in time contains a set of relevant properties restricted to that time frame. For example, a bed allocation system functions in the environment of a health service facility. However, other systems of the health facility, such as an outpatient clinic, may affect the bed allocation system, which, in turn, may affect the pharmacy department and the laboratory unit.

CONCRETE VERSUS ABSTRACT SYSTEMS

A concrete system is one in which at least two elements are tangible objects, and an abstract system is one in which all the elements are concepts. For example, languages and philosophical systems are abstract systems, whereas the bed allocation system is concrete. In an abstract system, the elements are created by definitions and the relationships between them by assumptions. These abstract systems are subjects of study of the "formal sciences." On the contrary, in a concrete system, the establishment of the existence and properties of elements, and the relationships among them, are empirically observed. These systems are subjects of study in the realm of "nonformal sciences." HMISs, because their study involves the establishment of the existence and properties of elements that are empirically observed, can be considered a concrete system in the context of a nonformal science.

At this point, we turn our focus on to general systems concepts to help us gain a better appreciation of the potential application of systems thinking to HMISs in particular, and to health service delivery systems in general.

GENERAL SYSTEMS CONCEPTS

General systems theory has been around for decades.[2] It originated in studies in communication and cryptography spawned in the desperate and frenzied atmosphere of World War II and grew into a powerful conceptualization tool. Essentially, it provided insights into everything from the structure of the ball-peen–hammer assembly line to the interactions of states and nations. The concept of systems has since played an increasingly critical role in contemporary science. During the post–World War II period, considerable research has been conducted on systems theory and its potential applications in all segments of our society,[3] including health service delivery systems and HMISs.[4]

Accordingly, it is important to consider how previous work in systems theory has impacted our understanding of the health service delivery system to date.[5] The evolution of the traditional health service delivery facility into a highly complex system, with many new ideas, organizational arrangements, structures, processes, and supporting entities, such as the MCHPP project introduced earlier, requires one to view this entire order by using a systems approach. This allows one to exert a valuable holistic perspective on the structure, process, and outcome of the present and ever-evolving health services delivery system. Through such a broad understanding, the role of HMIS as related to today's integrated delivery systems will become more defined (i.e., in terms of its effects on various facets of the health service industry).

A popular view of the general systems theory is given by combining the analysis of individual parts of the system with the study of the interactions among these parts. The theory begins from the empirical observation that all systems, in whatever disciplinary domain, share certain important similarities in their underlying structure and exhibit some common behavioral patterns. Moreover, in every system, the whole is greater than the sum of its parts.

All systems have objects and attributes. Objects constitute the components of a system, whereas attributes are the properties of these objects. Specifically, an attribute is an abstract descriptor that characterizes the component parts of the system. For instance, in a health service facility, objects of the bed allocation system can include actual beds, patients, health service providers, and the computer that stores, analyzes, and provides the bed allocation information. The attributes describing the object "patient" may include, for example, the patient's condition, gender, age, and the time the patient needs a bed. Figure 2–2 shows the basic objects of a bed allocation system and their interactions in a health service delivery institution.

A system combines all the objects and their attributes and defines the relationships among these objects, enabling the parts to add up to some greater

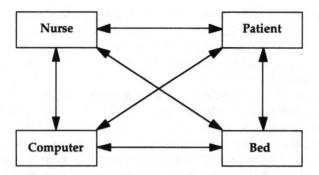

Figure 2–2 Basic Components of a Bed Allocation System in a Health Service Facility

unity rather than simply constituting an unplanned assemblage of objects. For example, the combined action, as in human-machine interaction, is more significant in total emergent effect than the sum of the separate effects. Relationships of objects may also be planned or unplanned. For instance, in our bed allocation system, the percentage of beds allocated to children, adults, and older adults is a planned relationship; conversely, the percentage of beds allocated to children immediately after an unexpected measles outbreak among children in the community is an unplanned relationship.

Systems Structure and Systems Interactions

The structure of a system ranges from simple to very complex. An example of a simple system may involve the input of a single resource, a conversion process, and the output of a single product or service. Figure 2–3 shows the patient admission process of a nursing home as an example of a simple system. Inputs to the system consist of elective admission requests from physicians, current bed availability, admitting department resources, and other emergency admission requirements. The conversion process includes a set of actions in which the admitting clerks collect information from referred patients, match

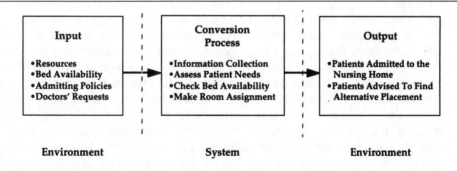

Figure 2–3 Patient Admitting Process of a Nursing Home

patient requirements to available beds, and make room assignments. Output of this simple system comprises patients admitted to the facility or patients who are asked to go elsewhere. This output may then become the input for the planning of several other functional systems, such as nursing care and diagnostic services.

In contrast, the relationships among system components in multi-provider health organizations tend to be very complex. The intricate network of complex relationships that constitutes most social systems often makes it difficult to describe simple causal (i.e., cause-and-effect) relationships among individual components of the system. This phenomenon of system complexity aptly captures the statement that the whole (system) is greater than the sum of its parts. Moreover, causal relationships are subjected to the definer's perspective. The same phenomenon may be viewed in terms of different systems and environments by different observers. For example, the patient admission process of a nursing home system may be described from an information resource management perspective, as was illustrated by our simple example. If the same system were viewed from a governmental program funding and regulatory perspective, however, it would be necessary to collect utilization and cost data and to determine the costs associated with the different processes involved during the admission and other stages of the nursing care program. Outputs of the system would have comprised some sort of periodic program reports generated to serve as feedback to the government on the effectiveness of the program in order to justify its continued funding.

In addition to the difficulty of establishing causal relationships, complex systems are also defined by their hierarchical or nested structure of subsystems, each having some meaningful function while interacting to produce the overall system. Large systems in health service organizations can be divided into multiple subsystems, and these in turn can be subjected to further subdivision in a nested fashion. For instance, the MCHPP system discussed at the beginning of this chapter can be broadly divided into health promotion programming subsystem, support services, and community relations. As shown in Figure 2–4, the health promotion programming subsystem may in turn be composed of a walking program subsystem, a healthy food catering program subsystem, and a smoking cessation program subsystem.

Parallel to the macro-micro view discussed in Chapter 1, the hierarchical or web-like structures of subsystems will reflect a hierarchy or network of goals embedded in the total system. The goals of a community health delivery system, for example, are dictated by the platform of the presiding government who represents the voice of the people in that community. On the contrary, the goals of the MCHPP may be specified by its governing board members. Moreover, there may not be clear distinctions between the goals within a system hierarchy. In effect, the narrower goals of the subsystems may be viewed as subsets of the broader goals of the entire system. In the context of health services management and HMIS, the narrow subsystem goals are mainly goal seeking (i.e., they relate to actualizing preset objectives), whereas the broader goals of the entire system are primarily goal setting (i.e., they relate to setting and aligning total system-subsystem goals and objectives).

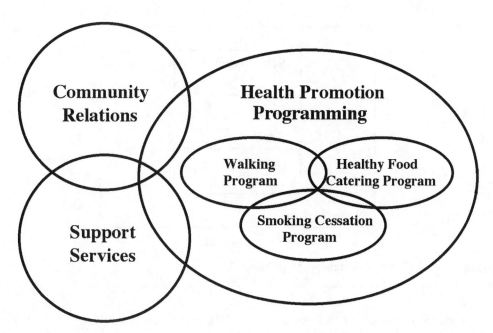

Figure 2–4 Boundaries of Various Subsystems within a Multi-Community Health Promotion Project (MCHPP)

Open versus Closed Systems

A major element identifying the holistic behavior of a system is the nature of interactions among its subsystems and between the system and the environment. Systems whose only goal is to maintain self-viability are called closed (autotelic) systems.[6] A closed system is one that is not affected by its environment: It is completely self-contained. In a closed system, elements in the system do not interact with elements in the environment in which they are immersed. Hence, they are autonomous. Figure 2–5 shows that the internal processes of a closed system are not generally affected by the larger system (i.e., social context of the system). An open system is one that is influenced by the external environment, that is, elements in an open system do interact with, and are influenced by, factors outside the system. Typically, open systems may be described as those exhibiting the standard input-process-output triad. The output from the system may be classified as either intermediate or final; intermediate output is needed to produce the final output, but itself is not the final output, whereas final output is the end-product of a system or subsystem. Even so, the output at any one stage may serve as input at another, essentially repeating the same process cycle at a different level.

In summary, an open system is one that has an environment and interacts with it. Every living organism is essentially an open system. It maintains itself in a continuous inflow and outflow, a building up and a breaking down of components, never in a state of absolute or static equilibrium. Our bed allocation system is an example of an open system because it interacts with the

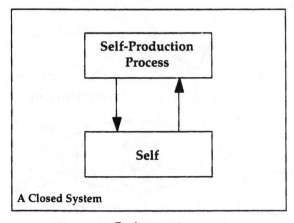

Figure 2–5 A Closed (Autotelic) System Model

many facets of its environment and its functioning depends on the health needs and well-being of its surrounding community.

Open systems are often referred to as intelligent systems because they can be drastically influenced by external factors. In extending the scheme to include several subsystems, we then get a "network" consisting of nodes (representing subsystems) that are connected by arrows (representing process flows). The integration of both open and closed system views is depicted in Figure 2–6. Complex systems are those systems that result when a closed and open system are combined. The term "heterotelic model" may sometimes be used to describe such a system.[7]

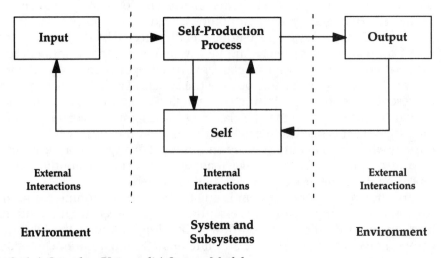

Figure 2–6 A Complex (Heterotelic) System Model

Feedback

In an open or a complex system, the output may be used to regulate the input of the same system. This is typically achieved by comparing the actual output with a reference standard (or a desired output). Any resulting discrepancy or error discovered by this comparison could then be used to determine the corrective or regulatory action necessary to return actual performance to the desired level. This whole process is then repeated with the corrected input. The homeostatic mechanism of the body to regulate temperature is a prime example. This mechanism, termed feedback control, is illustrated in Figure 2–7 for our bed allocation system.

The logic of the functioning of the feedback control system is similar to the homeostatic mechanism in humans whereby blood glucose levels are regulated by secreting glucagon when sugars are decreased or by secreting insulin when they are increased. Positive feedback is the process by which a difference between actual and desired (or reference) output is increased through repetition. This type of process is relatively rare in biological systems and is generally of little concern in systems theory. Negative feedback, the process by which discrepancies between the desired and the actual output are reduced or eliminated through adjustments of the conversion process, is prevalent in biological systems. Through the use of this feedback, resource utilization and output production can be constantly adjusted or adapted to the desired level.[8] In our MCHPP system, for example, the government and third-party payers can act as a feedback control mechanism by gathering information about resource utilization and outputs. This control feedback will then help decide whether and how the system should be changed in the future to achieve the desired outcomes.

Systems Behavior

A system event (transaction) is a change in one or more structural properties of the system (or its states) over a period of specified duration. System events can also be classified as either static or dynamic. A static (one-state) system is one that lacks events, whereas a dynamic (multi-state) system contains various events whose states change over time (i.e., transactions occurring over time). For example, the utilization rate of certain diagnostic devices in a health maintenance organization (HMO), an establishment that is designed to help maintain wellness through early detection and prevention of health problems with predetermined fees, may exhibit dynamic behavior over time. A homeostatic system is a static system whose elements and environments are dynamic, that is, a system that retains its state in a changing environment through internal adjustments.

Three common patterns of time-behavior in systems are of major practical importance in health services. These are statistical constancy, growth and decay trends, and rhythmic or oscillatory behavior. Statistical constancy, or steady-state (equilibrium), refers to a time-varying behavior characterized by a functional constancy with a superimposed randomness. Such patterns may be caused by complex self-regulatory, or homeostatic, mechanisms. For example,

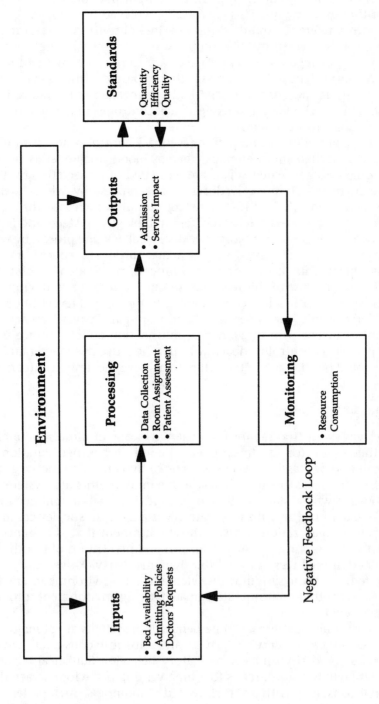

Figure 2–7 The Bed Allocation System: An Open System with Feedback and Control

an intravenous drip represents a functionally constant addition to a patient's system on a macroscopic scale but when examined microscopically exhibits momentary changes of data that may be the result of stochastic variations.

The increase in the proportion of people over 65 years of age is a growth trend that carries significant utilization implications for the health service delivery industry. In recent years, incidence of acquired immune deficiency syndrome (AIDS) has increased because of irresponsible use of contaminated hypodermic needles, frequent casual and unprotected sexual contacts, and uncontrolled transmission of tainted blood products. Such trends can often be characterized, over time, by an exponential curve, which is well known for its constant double-time (in the case of growth), or half-life (in the case of decay). Over a longer time, however, there is usually a "softening" of the exponential growth or decay trend, resulting in a sigmoid curve (or S curve). Oscillatory or rhythmic behaviors occur throughout the health service system in examples ranging from heartbeat to patient admissions cycles, from diurnal body temperature changes to nursing duties. These oscillations can arise as a result of external environmental factors or from within the system itself because of contributory forces inherent in the system's components and structure. Furthermore, when examined in detail, the periods of these oscillations seldom stay exactly the same. These periods tend to fall in close ranges in very dynamic systems.

Deterministic versus Probabilistic Systems

The behavior of systems objects can be broadly classified as either deterministic or probabilistic. The objects of deterministic systems function in completely predictable or definable relationships, whereas those of probabilistic or stochastic systems do not. Such completely predictable relationships are characteristic of certain mechanical systems but never of human or most biological systems. For example, in a hospice, an establishment that provides services for the terminally ill, the bed allocation system becomes probabilistic because bed availability cannot be entirely predicted. Predictions for probabilistic systems are based on probability laws and are therefore meaningful only for long-term trends.

Even so, the behavior of a system must still be characterized by some stability and equilibrium if it is to continue functioning in a changing environment. For instance, a sudden outbreak of childhood diseases such as mumps and measles in a community requires hospital bed allocation systems to adapt to this sudden change. This adaptation must retain the basic rules and defined relationships within the system's elements to prevent its collapse. In other words, the procedures involved must be general enough to accommodate a variety of unexpected environmental changes but must also retain basic characteristics of structural and functional integrity.

SYSTEMS THINKING

According to Senge, systems thinking is a conceptual framework, a body of knowledge and tools, that has been developed over the past 50 years to help us see the total system and how to change the pieces within the system more effectively and intelligently.[9] An important step in the systems approach to decision making is the development of models that are used to obtain valuable insight into the behavior of a system.

The meaning of the term "model," and the usefulness of models in decision making, are best understood through a number of important considerations that focus on model classification. First, models attempt to imitate systems by capturing their major components and interactions. By referring to a model, valuable insights into the behavior of the system being modeled can be obtained. Second, models are representations or abstractions of actual objects or situations. They show the interrelations of actions and reactions and of cause and effect in operational situations. Third, models can be regarded conceptually as substitutes for the real systems. Thus, instead of investigating and experimenting with the real system, the model can be studied and interrogated, usually with less risk, less time, and fewer resources. Finally, models are caricatures of reality. If the models are good, then they should portray, though perhaps in a distorted manner, some of the features of the real world. Thus, the main role of a model is not to explain and to predict, but to formulate thinking and to pose sharp questions. Models, by definition, are not expected to be complete substitutes for real systems.

Models can be broadly classified into several types, as depicted in Figure 2–8: conceptual models, iconic models, analog models, and symbolic models. At an administrative level, however, several different kinds of models may coexist to assist or support decision making.[10]

Briefly, conceptual models are those formed through our experience, knowledge, and intuition. These may be mental, verbal, or descriptive in form and are essentially abstractions based on our experience. Mental models are deeply ingrained assumptions, generalizations, or even pictures or images that

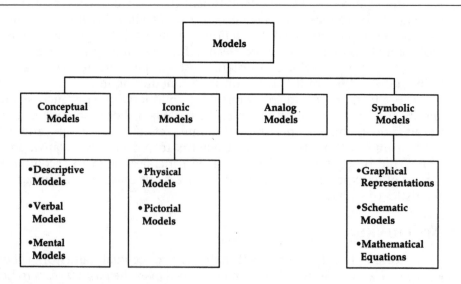

Figure 2–8 A Classification of Models

influence how we understand the world and how we take action. Mental models are normally ill-defined and not easy to communicate. Verbal models are better structured than mental models but are still difficult to transmit. Descriptive models represent a higher level of conceptualization and may be articulated and communicated. For example, a crude conceptual model of a hospital visit from a patient's point of view may involve steps such as referral by the primary physician, admission by the hospital, further diagnosis (or confirmation of diagnoses), treatment, and release. Iconic models are those that resemble what they represent, although the properties of an iconic model may not be the same as those of the real system it represents. Iconic models include physical and pictorial models. Physical models are constructed from concrete, tangible materials. Pictorial models are images of objects and provide description rather than explanation. The three-dimensional architectural prototype of a hospice agency is an example of a physical model; an artist's drawing of the hospice agency is a pictorial model.

Analog models are those that are built to act like real systems, although they look different from what they represent. An artificial kidney dialysis machine that provides life support is an example of an analog model. These models employ one set of properties to represent some other set of properties possessed by the real system. Symbolic models use symbols to designate the components of a system and relationships among those components. They are abstract models in which symbols are substituted for systems characteristics. These models usually take the form of graphs, schematics, and mathematical equations. Graphical models are used normally to represent growth, flow, or activities. Schematic models are obtained by taking an idea or an event and reducing it to a chart. Mathematical models are symbolic models that employ the language of mathematics. They differ from all other "natural" models in that they are informational models expressed solely in a logical, mathematical, analytical, or numerical relation. For instance, a mathematical equation that attempts to simulate the amount of utilization of an HMIS in a typical day for an HMO may be regarded as part of a mathematical model. Furthermore, mathematical models often employ variables, constants, and parameters. Constants, as the term implies, always have fixed values, whereas parameters can have arbitrarily assigned values. Variables assume different values while the model is run or calculated. A variable is exogenous when it is determined by conditions in the environment, and endogenous when it is determined by the system.

Our focus on models is important because an integrated HMIS may be conceived as an enterprise model, comprising a combination of various computerized information flow models. Because models are attempts to imitate systems, and HMISs are essentially models to support rational decision making, the close relationship between HMISs and organizational decision making cannot be overemphasized. HMIS models are, therefore, sometimes simply referred to as decision models. On this basis, the most important levels at which organizational systems should be modeled for analysis of their information resource and processing needs are at the problem-finding (macro) and problem-solving (micro) levels. These two levels involving application of systems thinking challenge us to a greater appreciation of its significance in decisions relating to health services planning and management.

PROBLEM FINDING AND PROBLEM SOLVING VIA SYSTEMS THINKING

The general systems approach to problem diagnosis focuses on systems as a whole, as opposed to their individual parts. This approach is concerned with the total system performance (i.e., from a holistic perspective) rather than with the performance of individual components. Therefore, the relationships among parts of systems, that is, how the parts interact and fit together, are of great interest and importance. The rationale is that in an imperfectly organized system, even if every part performs to its potential, there is no guarantee that the total system will meet its overall objectives.

As a direct result of continuing specialization over the years, provision of health organizational services has created some very fundamental problems that need to be addressed. These basic problems arise essentially from the duplication and fragmentation of services. For example, an individual with a particular ailment will first contact a family physician. The physician will proceed with history taking, perform a general examination, and arrive at an initial diagnosis. Given the hypothetical complexity of the ailment, the physician will order specific tests in an attempt to confirm the diagnosis. In all probability, the patient will be requested to visit another center (Referral A), where the ordered tests will be conducted. Upon arrival at the testing center, the patient will probably be required to undergo a similar type of preliminary medical history check. Already, we see the duplication of a service that has previously taken place, as shown in Figure 2–9. This duplication is both costly and time consuming. Moreover, a second visit to the physician may be required just to follow up on the test results. Under certain circumstances, the physician may not have the expertise to treat this patient further, and a referral to a specialist may be required (Referral B). At this point, another cycle of patient-physician interaction has thus been created.

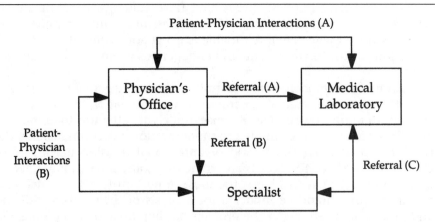

Figure 2–9 Life Cycles of Patient–Physician Interactions and Referrals

Many components of our current system are therefore still serviced by inefficient and ineffective information gathering and reporting systems, which in turn have resulted in fragmentary clinical and managerial decision making. In the system described, it is rather clear that the impediment to sharing information flow among various subsystems is a major problem. Once this is recognized, we can proceed to problem solving.

In order to reduce the problem of fragmentation and duplication of information gathering activities among various subsystems, it may be suggested that only one source should be allocated to take care of all data gathering. This suggestion is precisely optimized by the concept of information architecture, more specifically, use of advanced database technology, a centralized but distributed computerized patient record system, and an integrated HMIS methodology (see Part II). The data requirements in this instance, however, should be thorough. More importantly, in order to ensure integration of provider services, electronic networking and linkages of information must be employed (see Part III). Not only would this allow for seamless information flow in a continuum, but also it would support integration to occur multi-dimensionally: vertically, horizontally, and even diagonally.

Indeed, Gilles et al. argued that clinical integration of services is key to enhancing system and HMIS performance in our health service organizations.[11] The idea of clinical integration outlines the coordination of patient care services within the functional activities and operating parameters of a health service delivery system, as identified in the preceding example of physician-patient interactions. The ideal HMIS design takes an integrated approach to information services to support effectively the entire value-added chain of health service provision. When applying systems thinking to solving specific micro-level problems, an efficient next step is to generate as much end user involvement and participation as possible to ensure relevant feedback and to ensure that control information is continuously made available. This will prevent the development of meaningless and nonusable databases, or even worse, the costly failure of organization-wide HMIS.

With the dramatic decrease in the cost of information technology, it is not difficult to envision the possibility of integrating existing systems at multiple delivery sites. At this point, it is possible to extend our discussion of systems concepts and systems thinking from the level of a single, isolated health organization to the networks of multi-provider health organizations that are pervading the United States and Canadian health services delivery industry.

INTEGRATED DELIVERY SYSTEMS

In both local and national settings, the provision of health services in the United States and in Canada is very complex in structure and function. To understand the functioning of all individual components and their collective interrelationships, a systems approach can be employed to view all of these components as parts of an evolving system, that is, the IDS. To adopt such an approach, all the elements of systems theory must be considered. Integral components such as unity, external environment, subsystem structure interactions, and behaviors will come into play when attempting to understand and model the complexity of an IDS.

Open System

An IDS comprises a variety of continually evolving organizations. Despite an evolution into a complex structure with web-like interactions among its component organizations, the entire system does have at least one unified goal: to improve the health conditions of a defined population. Analogous to the IDS are systems that are constantly evolving and merging, such as the airline system, the financial and banking system, and the hotel chain system.

Undoubtedly, the IDS exists within the environment of our society. Accordingly, various sociopolitical factors, such as government policies or local decisions, do affect the operations of the system. For example, changes in the fiscal policies of provincial states and municipalities that arise from changing economic conditions can often bring about changes in the functioning or organization of the IDS. Taken as a whole, the IDS, with its interactions with the physical environment, is by definition an open system. As an open system, the IDS is constantly under the influence of various factors, among which organizational factors, environmental factors, and biological and behavioral factors are considered the chief determinants of population health.[12]

On the one hand, organizational factors are intrinsic to the IDS, whereas environmental factors are extrinsic and outside the realm of health management control. Organizational factors include cultural, technical, structural, psychosocial, temporal, and managerial factors. Each of these factors can again be subdivided into many other factors. For example, structural factors underlying IDS formation and development may include affiliation or merger with a centralized service organization, corporate ownership, and super IDS affiliation. These internal IDS factors and subfactors are briefly summarized in Table 2–1.

Similarly, environmental factors include politics, laws and regulations, economics, demographics, sociological factors, cultural factors, education, and technology. These external IDS factors are briefly outlined in Table 2–2.

Biological factors are the basic characteristics and processes of human biology; behavioral factors relate to a person's lifestyle. Thus, disorders such as high blood pressure and hypercholesterolemia can be inherited and are attributable to human biological processes. In contrast, disorders such as hypertension and myocardial infarction may often be attributed to an unhealthy lifestyle, which is behavioral. High cholesterol food intake, smoking, and excessive drinking are examples of an unhealthy lifestyle.

Together these diverse and often unpredictable factors influence the functioning and continual evolution of the IDS. The IDS is therefore inevitably dynamic in nature, and a stochastic or probabilistic component of this dynamic nature of the system that should not be unheeded is self-evident.

Subsystems Interactions

Regardless of the particular organizational design within subcomponents, the IDS typically has a complex structure. When viewed from a systems approach, each of these broad factors or subcomponents of the system may be viewed as either an independent subsystem or a narrower component of other

Table 2–1 Organizational Factors Underlying an Integrated Delivery System (IDS)

Organizational Factors	Description
Cultural factors	Goals and values of the IDS, comprising not only the cultural values and goals of internal IDS members but also a merging of these values and goals with those of the broader external environment described below
Technical factors	Know-how and technologies of the IDS to carry out tasks in achieving its goals and objectives
Structural factors	Subfactors may include affiliation or merger with a centralized service organization, corporate ownership, and super IDS affiliation
Psychosocial factors	Informal corporate linkages and the informal interaction between IDS members and groups, thus contributing to a "people climate," which dictates psychosocial differences
Temporal factors	Incidental or sudden occurrences arising at any point in time with unpredictable outcomes that must be resolved in order to avert major problems or collapse such as temporary labor disputes, breakdown of electrical and water suppliers, and food poisoning in the cafeteria
Managerial factors	Managerial roles, responsibilities, and accountabilities that are the central factors of the IDS because these affect the coordination of the different parts of the organization members to ensure its efficient and effective functioning

sub-subsystems. The linkages among the components can be either hierarchical, network, or matrix.

In particular, the affiliation or merger of health service institutions has now been a general trend for some years. The functions of the traditional government-funded hospitals are now increasingly being performed by ambulatory care institutions, nursing homes, hospice agencies, and home health services and, in the case of IDS formation, supplemented by HMOs, preferred provider organizations (PPOs), and individual practice associations (IPAs). HMOs have been described earlier. A PPO has a network of providers under contract to offer services to policyholders for a prenegotiated fee schedule, but, unlike HMO patients, PPO policyholders are only *encouraged* to use, and are not locked into, the preferred provider. The IPA functions similarly to the HMO and the PPO, but IPA providers are reimbursed on a "fee-for-service" basis, and the subscriber is restricted to using only these providers in the IPA.[13] Although IDS development is more prevalent in the United States than in Canada, a modified version of managed care is conceptually operative throughout Canada, and in particular, a regional model of merged health services institutions (regionalization) can be found in the Canadian province of British Columbia.

Depending on the extent of affiliation, each subsystem or organization within the IDS may or may not have its own goal or purpose that is distinct from the goals or purposes of other such subsystems. The interactions among the various subsystems often arise primarily to supplement the functioning of the individual subsystems. However, the unified goal of the entire system should also be reflected in the interactions among the various subsystems.

Table 2–2 External Factors that Influence the Integrated Delivery System (IDS)

Environmental Factors	Description
Politics	Governmental initiatives, policies, and changes in political interests and orientations because of changes in government such as the U.S. President's health care reform policies
Laws/regulations	Governmental rules and regulations and the enforcement of federal and provincial legislative acts, such as the Freedom of Information Act and Protection of Privacy Act
Economics	Government fiscal policies and changes in economic climate of countries, such as recessional and anti-inflationary pressure. Examples include fiscal restraint and lowering of the prime lending rates to encourage economic growth
Demographics	Changing population demographics from growth and an increase in older adults, as well as changing institutional direction as seen with mergers and new forms of IDS arrangements within the Canadian and U.S. health service industry
Sociological factors	Reforms in the health care industry, such as greater privatization, regionalization, globalization, and general changes in management thinking across the North American society as seen in the North American Free Trade Act
Cultural factors	Changes in North American culture, such as pressures for greater patient involvement and improved quality of care
Education	The need for more information to be made available to providers and purchasers of health services, such as the Canadian Freedom of Information Act and growth and expansion in health promotion education
Technology	Technological advances and diffusion of innovative technologies, such as advancing computers automating voice systems, telemedical, and managerial technologies, for example, teleradiology services and team management approaches

Because of the trend of specialization, a patient's medical information may become disseminated in various subsystems, thus creating a problem for case management and directly threatening the unified goal of the IDS. To alleviate this problem for case management, effective communications and interactions among the subsystems become increasingly crucial. In the IDS setting, those interactions can be either vertical or horizontal, depending on the structure being adopted. Vertical interactions take place among subsystems in the same field but in different positions in the hierarchy, whereas horizontal interactions are those of subsystems of different fields. For example, decisions made in association with the administrative subsystem of the same hierarchy are vertical interactions as in the case of a merger where information systems, management consulting, payer contracting, group purchasing, and centralized business office services are integrated, but services not offered centrally are provided locally by the hospitals, physician foundation, home health agency, IPAs, and payer organizations in the IDS. The concerted effort of specialists, occupational therapists, physiotherapists, and nurses on the care of a patient is an example of horizontal interaction.

Often, such interactions function as negative feedback. A typical input to the system may be an increased demand for a particular health service program. The conversion process would then include various vertical and horizontal interactions among the responsible subsystems to produce the desired output, for example, an increase in the desired services. The amount and quality of the increased services would then be influenced by environmental, organizational, and other factors, which together would determine the degree and form for which the output should be changed.

Local Subsystems

In a local setting, the systems approach can also be applied to further our understanding of the functioning of an IDS component. According to Ackoff, an organization is a purposeful system that contains at least two purposeful elements with a common purpose.[14] The term "purposeful" here refers to the fact that the same outcome can be produced in different ways in the same state (internal or external), and different outcomes can be produced in the same or different states. A purposeful system is one that can change its goals under constant conditions, and one that can select ends as well as means to achieve its goals. In this regard, human beings are the most familiar examples of such systems.

On a local level, for example, the actual functioning of an HMO in terms of an integrated HMIS design and development can also be examined by using systems theory. Conceptually, an HMO is usually designed to help maintain wellness through early detection and prevention of health problems. Many HMOs contract with hospitals and physician groups to perform services for predetermined fixed fees that are paid in advance. When viewed within a systems perspective, as in Figure 2–10, inputs of an HMO may typically include an increased demand for services requested from the hospitals, physicians, or other funding agencies. Changes in the availability of labor, materials, or equipment may also act as inputs to the system.

These inputs normally undergo a "conversion process" through both formal and informal procedures and are then followed by management decision making. Here, the use of an integrated HMIS is likely to be most intense during the management decision-making process. For example, various kinds of information on the utilization of resources such as equipment, the availability of professional help, and the operational costs can be drawn from existing and independent HMIS applications, and this can play an important role in system-wide managerial decision making. Accurate estimates can also be made by integrating HMIS information automatically rather than relying on intuitive feelings in one case and/or computerized predictions of possible outcomes in other cases.

The output of the conversion process is usually the execution of decisions made by the managers, such as providing particular services, changing the price charged for specific services, or altering the current resource distribution pattern among the subsystems. Moreover, these outputs are by no means the end product. Very often, these outputs may signal the need for further changes

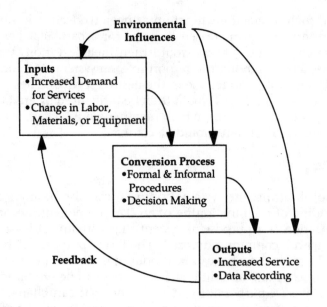

Figure 2–10 The Functioning of a Health Maintenance Organization from a Systems Perspective

in the information, technology, domain, and control architecture discussed in Chapter 1. Based on these changes, the adequacy of the services provided, the quality of care, patient impact, staff satisfaction, and efficiency of resource distribution can all be periodically evaluated if these HMIS architecture pieces are to be integrated. Put simply, the integrated HMIS should be designed to provide meaningful and comparative data throughout the HMO on structure, process, and outcome, and should be based on desirable performance indicators.

In the end, if a discrepancy still exists between the actual performance and the desired level, decisions may be required to increase the provision of the service through further changes in the designated architecture. For example, these architectural changes may involve education and training, procedural changes, personnel changes, incentive programs, or even disciplinary actions. These decisions are then converted into an actual output through a conversion process similar to the one mentioned previously or can, in turn, create additional demands for related services, thus repeating the entire cycle.

AN INTEGRATED ORGANIZATIONAL MODEL FOR THE HEALTH SERVICE INDUSTRY

Despite numerous efforts aimed at rationalizing one or more key aspects of the changing health service sector in the United States and Canada, these attempts have occurred in a rather piecemeal fashion. Although each of these rationalizations may provide a sharper understanding of a particular trend of change, few can provide a broad, comprehensive framework upon which a holistic understanding of the health service industry can be built. Richard Scott, a professor of sociology at Stanford University, recently proposed a general organizational framework within which various changes in the health service industry and within IDS may be viewed, interpreted, and explained.[15] The discussion in the following section draws largely from his work.

A THREE-TIER ORGANIZATIONAL MODEL

Figure 2–11 presents Scott's layered organizational model for the health service industry. It identifies three definable levels of organizations: organizational environments, organizational fields and populations, and organizational sets and organizations.

In this model, organizational environments constitute the most general and comprehensive level of health services delivery organizations, whereas organizational sets and organizations constitute the smaller units. Organizational environments comprise both institutional and technical environments. The institutional environment consists of the symbolic systems that we, as social beings, develop to input meaning to our world: these symbolic systems also determine the parameters within which individuals and collective forms operate. In modern societies, symbolic systems have become highly differentiated around particular sets, making it necessary to identify the "culture" of an

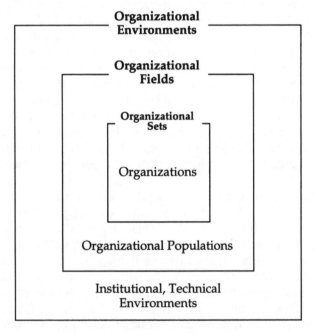

Figure 2–11 A Three-Tier Organizational Model for the Health Service Industry

institutional environment. In the most comprehensive level of organizational environments, the institutional environment of the open system of health services delivery is predicated on several fundamental theories about how these services should be organized and administered. The profit or nonprofit nature of organizations, the reliance on market conditions, and the extent to which management enhances its power at the expense of health service professionals are all manifestations of these fundamental concepts. It is also through these ideas that it is possible and useful to talk about the "culture" of health care, which, according to Scott, refers simply to "activities that surround efforts to cure and care for the ill."[16]

The technical environment refers to the network of knowledge systems and technical apparatus that supports the efficient and effective transformation of inputs into outputs. The technical environment is concerned with quality and efficiency (i.e., how well the valued activities are performed) and emphasizes outcome controls with the available technology. During the period 1950–1980, the combination of high levels of public funding for medical research and third-party reimbursement policies in North America supported the adoption of a "technological imperative," that is, the idea that advancing medical technologies, regardless of cost, questions of priority, or optimal allocation of resources, should be made available to all physicians for the benefit of their patients.[17] Although the application of new technologies does improve the quality of health services on average, increasing evidence indicates resulting ineffectiveness (or redundancy) and inappropriate diffusion of medical technologies.[18]

Organizational fields and populations are identified as the intermediate level of comprehensiveness and organizational structure. DiMaggio and Powell propose that the concept of organizational fields refers to organizations that, in the aggregate, constitute a recognized area of institutional life or social activity.[19] Organizational fields contain several diverse organizational populations. The traditional view of organizational populations focuses on the fate of a particular organizational form as it is created, is reproduced (diffused), falls into decline, and is then succeeded by a different organizational form.[20] However, population ecologists have also advocated examination of the linkages between organizations and wider systems, thus shifting the focus from the fate of a particular organization to the changing distributions of organizational forms (for example, the decreasing prevalence of the independent solo practitioner in our case).[21]

The organizational field of the health service industry includes within its domain not only the focal organizations providing core services, such as the IDS and HMO sets, but also those diverse organizational sets, such as medical associations and health services financing administrations, that support and control these activities. Organizational fields also vary in their degree of structure. The health services delivery field, in particular, has exhibited a higher level of structuring earlier than many other industrial sectors in the United States and Canada. The stability and order evident in many health services organizations reflect, in general, a professionally imposed division of occupational labor, rather than managerial design and influence. Nevertheless, structural isomorphism within the organizational field of health services delivery, and mutual awareness and interaction, has been encouraged as funding has become more centralized in recent decades.

In the most specific level of the model are organizational sets and actual organizations. Here, organizational sets refer simply to the specific collection of organizations providing the critical sources of inputs, and markets for outputs, required for organizational survival. For instance, an IDS may be regarded as an organizational set, whereas its components, in association with its medical supply companies, insurance companies, and nursing homes, can each be regarded as an actual organization within the IDS set.

In applying Scott's three-tier organization framework to model the health services industry, HMISs are expected to play an increasingly crucial role as a continuous flow linking various organized health delivery systems and health organizational sets to provide data, information, and knowledge supportive of quality care to selected populations.

CONCLUSION

Parallel to the concept of HMIS architecture as discussed in Chapter 1, Shortell et al. have noted and identified the development of an IS infrastructure for improving quality and cost performance of the IDS and for generating useful data for external stakeholders as a key challenge to achieving greater levels of integration of health services.[22] In this sense, building an integrated HMIS infrastructure supportive of the IDS is key to its successful development, future growth, and expansion within the health services delivery industry. Accordingly, an integrated HMIS infrastructure comprises HMIS information infrastructure, HMIS technology infrastructure, core HMIS application domain infrastructure, and core HMIS personnel control infrastructure.[23]

HMIS information infrastructure is essentially a data architecture for linking corporate and external HMIS data resources and databases. HMIS technology infrastructure is a technical architecture for the hardware, software, interface, and communication network facilities to support HMIS applications. Core HMIS application domain infrastructure refers to HMIS domain architecture that supports fundamental health organizational processes and strategies, and provides the basis for growing additional specialized HMIS applications. Finally, core HMIS personnel control infrastructure may be defined as the control architecture in which a pool of technical expertise is made available for building, maintaining, and integrating all the other HMIS components.

After viewing the entire health service delivery system, it is clear that an integrated HMIS should not only be able to provide a convenient tool for aiding administrative and clinical decision-making processes within a health service organization, but also should be able to generate a continuous information backbone to facilitate case management along the continuum of care. Moreover, efficient and effective information processing and HMIS design and development for the IDS cannot be realized without paying particular attention to building integrated HMIS architecture and infrastructure.

CHAPTER QUESTIONS

1. Explain in terms of the general systems theory the functioning of a state or provincial health service delivery system.
2. Distinguish between open and complex systems. Why might the IDS be more appropriately considered a complex rather than just an open system?
3. Identify critical success factors for HMIS implementation in the context of an IDS.
4. How does Richard Scott's three-tier organizational model for the health service delivery industry relate to general systems theory?
5. Discuss how systems thinking can be useful in enhancing our understanding of the PUSH-PULL framework presented in Chapter 1. How can these two approaches (PUSH versus PULL) be reconciled in designing an integrated HMIS?
6. Discuss the role of integrated HMIS infrastructure for the evolution and continuation of IDS development.

NOTES

1. D.F. Avison and G. Fitzgerald, *Information Systems Development: Methodologies, Techniques, and Tools* (Oxford: Blackwell Scientific Publications, 1988).
2. R.L. Ackoff, Towards a System of Systems Concepts, *Management Science* 17 (1971): 661–671.
3. F.E. Kast and J.E. Rosenzweig, General Systems Theory: Applications for Organization and Management, *Academy of Management Journal* (December 1972): 447–465.
4. R. Lindstorm, et al., Organizational Health Decision Support Systems: The Application of Systems Concepts, Chaos Theory, Quantum Mechanics, and Self-Organizing Systems. In *Health Decision Support Systems,* ed. J.K.H. Tan with S. Sheps (Gaithersburg, MD: Aspen Publishers, 1998).
5. W.R. Scott, The Organization of Medical Care Services: Toward an Integrated Theoretical Model, *Medical Care Review* 50, no. 3 (1993): 271–303.
6. *Random House Webster's College Dictionary* (New York: Random House, 1992).
7. Ibid.
8. C.J. Austin and S.B. Boxerman, *Information Systems for Health Service Administration,* 5th ed. (Chicago, IL: AUPHA/Health Administration Press, 1998).
9. P. Senge, *The Fifth Discipline: The Art and Practice of the Learning Organization* (New York: Doubleday Currency, 1990), 7.
10. N. Sharif and P. Adulbhan, *Systems Models for Decision Making* (Bangkok: Asian Institute of Technology, 1978).
11. R. Gillies, et al., Conceptualizing and Measuring Integration: Finding from the Health Systems Integration Study, *Hospital & Health Services Administration* 38, no. 4 (Winter 1993): 467–490.
12. B.B. Longest, *Management Practices for the Health Professional,* 4th ed. (Norwalk, CT: Appleton & Lange, 1990).
13. R.M. Hodgetts and D.M. Cascio, *Modern Health Care Administration,* 2nd ed. (Dubuque, IA: Brown & Benchmark, 1993).
14. R.L. Ackoff, Towards a System of Systems Concepts, 661–671.
15. W.R. Scott, The Organization of Medical Care Services, 271–303.
16. Ibid.

17. H. Aldrich, *Organizations and Environments* (Englewood Cliffs, NJ: Prentice Hall, 1979).

18. M.T. Hannan and J. Freeman, The Population Ecology of Organizations, *American Journal of Sociology* 87 (March 1977): 929–964.

19. P.J. DiMaggio and W.W. Powell, The Iron Cage Revisited: Institutional Isomorphism and Collective Rationality in Organizational Fields, *American Sociological Review* 38 (April 1983): 147–160.

20. I.L. Bennett, Jr., *Technology as a Shaping Force, in Doing Better and Feeling Worse: Health in the United States* (New York: W.W. Norton & Co., 1977), 125–133.

21. P.J. Neumann and M.C. Weinstein, *The Diffusion of New Technology: Costs and Benefits to Health Care, in The Changing Economics of Medical Technology* (Washington, DC: National Academy Press, 1991), 21–34.

22. S. Shortell, et al., Creating Organized Delivery Systems: The Barriers and Facilitators, *Hospital and Health Services Administration* 36, no. 4 (1993): 447–466.

23. G.B. Davis and J.D. Naumann, *Personal Productivity with Information Technology* (New York: McGraw-Hill, 1997): 59.

Part II

Building Information Architecture of Health Management Information Systems

Health Care Data and Database Concepts: Defining Information Requirements for Integrated Delivery Systems

Joseph K. H. Tan

SCENARIO

On the morning of April 29, 1999, 26-year-old David experienced intense abdominal pain and discomfort (especially on the right side) at a breakfast meeting with his friends. The pain lasted for a few hours and did not dissipate. David's friends drove him to Mount St. Joseph's Hospital in Vancouver, British Columbia. Shortly after being registered into the admission, discharge, transfer (ADT) system at the emergency department, David was examined by a physician on duty. After eliminating several other possibilities, such as food poisoning, the doctor suspected appendicitis. He then informed the relevant departments and personnel that exploratory surgery was needed. The examination confirmed the doctor's suspicion.

The doctor wanted a laparoscopic procedure performed immediately on David. The schedule showed that the surgeons on duty would be available once they finished an ongoing operation. The surgeons were then notified and agreed to complete the procedure for David rather than sending David to another facility, because it would not take them more than half an hour. Two hours later, the surgeons and nurses started operating on David. In the meantime, a bed in the acute care unit was ordered for the 2 days following surgery. The intravenous glucose solution and other medications were prepared. However, no bed was available in the acute care unit until the following morning, so David spent the first night in the surgical intensive care unit. This made coordinating of nursing care and visiting somewhat more disruptive and inconvenient for both the nursing staff and members of David's family.

Early the next morning, David was transferred to the acute care unit, and the various departments were again notified and asked to rechannel any communications about David. In particular, the dietetics department was informed not to give David any food or drinks except water until more than 24 hours after the operation. After examining David the day after the procedure, another physician on duty found that there was insufficient information to determine if David was fit to be discharged. He reordered some tests that should have been done, but somehow the data were missing. After reviewing these test results, a third physician on duty decided to release David the next morning. The other departments concerned were notified, and David left the hospital 2 days following his operation.

Imagine that for the purpose of improving future emergency procedures and bed scheduling at the hospital, you have been asked to study the flow of events (information) pertaining to David's admission, discharge, and transfer, as well as the storage, usage, and distribution of data being collected while he was under the care of physicians and nurses at Mount St. Joseph's. Think about the type of data and databases that you would need to use to encapsulate this encounter. Contemplate how the flow of information at Mount St. Joseph's and its information architecture could be reengineered to improve emergency care effectiveness for incoming patients like David.

INTRODUCTION

In earlier discussions, we saw that a health service organization may be regarded as a collection of interacting subsystems. These interactions involve communications and networking among different subsystem elements. Information was seen as the common link among these interacting elements. This flow of information is the distinguishing feature of a health management information system (HMIS). In this chapter, essential data and database concepts are discussed to augment our understanding of HMIS methods and applications. Upon completion of this chapter, the reader should be able to differentiate between data, information, and knowledge; define database and identify various external data sources for enhancing health services; emulate desirable characteristics of information for clinical and health managerial decision making; describe elements of information and communication theory; understand the significance of information architecture; and use data flow diagrams, flow charts, and entity-relationship models for depicting information architecture. The chapter closes with insights on the various facets of data requirements for a typical integrated delivery system (IDS).

DATA VERSUS INFORMATION VERSUS KNOWLEDGE

In everyday language, the terms "data" and "information" are often used interchangeably. However, these two terms tend to have very different meanings to HMIS analysts and specialists. Whereas data are perceived as unstructured, raw facts, or facts resulting from empirical observations of physical phenomena, information may be thought of as data elements that have been processed into a form that is both meaningful and useful in prospective or current decisions and actions.[1-3] Interestingly enough, the Latin origin of the word "information" is derived from the verb *informo*, meaning "to give form to."

An analogy often drawn in the discussion of data versus information is the relationship between raw material and finished products in a manufacturing context. For example, in an automobile production line, a series of processes takes place in which the parts (i.e., the raw material) are gradually assembled and eventually transformed into a car (i.e., the product). The finished products from one division (e.g., the assembly line) often go on to become the raw material for another section within the organization (e.g., the sales division). Thus, what may be considered information for one source may be raw data for another. Therefore, differentiating between data and information emphasizes the fact that some form of meaningful processing takes place before the raw data from one source (e.g., the data entry clerk) become useful information for another (e.g., the health manager).

Viewing information as "meaningful" data has its significance. First, meaningful information is a relative concept, relative to the situation, to the time when a decision is made, and to the decision maker and his or her background and expertise. Information that is considered important in one situation may be relatively useless in another, even to the same decision maker. Second, information and decision making are closely intertwined; that is, information is useful for decision making when, and only when, decision makers can have direct (or indirect) access to it. Finally, the value of information is established when it is used in the process of decision making. Figure 3–1 shows that available, relevant, and high-quality information (including knowledge) is critical to the generation of meaningful and significant decisions.

The distinction between data and information and the significance of information to decision making may be extended to explain the distinction between information and knowledge and the added significance of knowledge to insightful and intelligent decision making. Briefly, knowledge is the cumu-

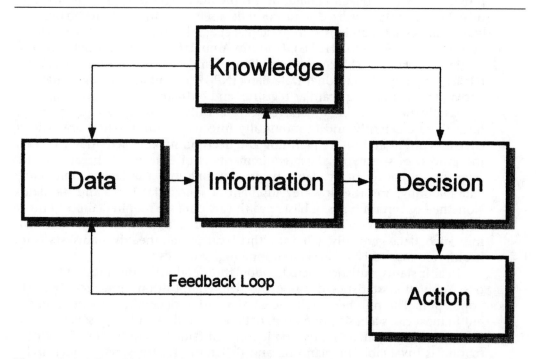

Figure 3–1 A Data-Information-Knowledge Decision System

lative experience of applying information to decisions, thereby producing "wisdom," "rules," and "associations" to be useful and insightful for future related decision situations.[4] Figure 3–1 shows knowledge as a result of insights gained from actions in the application of information to decisions and knowledge as providing a feedback to the decision-making process. Hence, the use of an HMIS should not only focus on transforming quality data into meaningful information for making particular sets of decisions, but also should incorporate, to some extent, previously learned or acquired knowledge.

HEALTH CARE DATA AND DATA SOURCES

There are many types and classes of health care data and databases. Although a detailed description of these data taxonomies is beyond the scope of this book, it is important for the reader to understand what is meant precisely by a "database." According to Kroenke, a database is a "model of a model" (i.e., a model of the user's model of the world).[5] Essentially, he viewed the database as a self-describing depository of integrated records. In this sense, any database should be designed to support its users' needs and perspectives for using the databases.

Even so, health care data and databases must support the delivery of health services. Major types of health care data include socioeconomic data (e.g., demographics), financial data (e.g., patient billing and account data), patient identification data (e.g., personal health number used for British Columbia residents), and clinical data (e.g., patient treatment data maintained by care providers). When collecting data, health provider organizations typically organize these into standardized or uniform data sets, registries, and databases. Several examples are highlighted in Abdelhak et al.,[6] including the Uniform Hospital Discharge Data Set (UHDDS), Uniform Ambulatory Care Data Set (UACDS), Minimum Data Set (MDS) for Long-Term Care, National Cancer Data Bank (NCDB), National Practitioner Data Bank (NPDB), hospital discharge databases, and other registries (e.g., cardiac registries and birth and death registries).

Ideally, health services managers can identify the data needed and transform these efficiently and economically into useful information and knowledge for current and future planning and decision-making activities. However, the process of specifying data requirements is often difficult because of the fragmentary nature of available health information, the lack of long-range data planning, and the slow development of shared databases and standards. Nonetheless, certain types of basic health care data are required almost universally by health services organizations to support planning and decision making. Such data generally fall into three categories: health status statistics, health resource statistics, and environmental statistics.[7]

Health status statistics include population and vital and morbidity statistics. Population statistics describe the size, composition, and growth of the population. The number of characteristics varies, depending on the purpose, but in most cases a basic population data set should include age, sex, race, profession or employment status, residence, and family composition. This information is invaluable in planning and delivering health services, identifying high-risk groups, locating places in need of services, flagging potential problems, and evaluating the effectiveness of existing programs.

Vital statistics are the oldest and most developed form of health statistics compiled from birth, death, marriage, and divorce information. These statistics can provide a great deal of information about a population health status. Mortality statistics, for example, provide important indicators of the prevalence of specific diseases, whereas birth certificates may provide valuable insights into maternal and child health. These records can be important for evaluating programs and determining environmental health hazards.

Morbidity statistics refer to incidence of ill health in the population, such as communicable diseases, chronic diseases, and other illnesses or ailments. Local health departments often publish statistics on communicable diseases such as tuberculosis, venereal disease, and typhoid. Statistics on other types of morbidity are more difficult to collect. The most important sources of morbidity statistics are physicians. When available, these statistics may be used to enhance our understanding of population health status. Along with vital statistics, morbidity statistics become more valuable when they can be linked to specific population groups, thus facilitating the identification of high-risk groups who can then be reached through special programs.

Health resource statistics include statistics on health care personnel, facilities, and services. The number of different professionals in the health field is immense, and it is important for policy planners and administrators to have specific information about these professionals. A basic labor force data set includes the total number of staff in a health organization, a professional population profile, licenses and certifications, facility affiliations, services provided, a patient population profile, and the number of patients served annually. A major type of labor force statistic is the doctor-to-population ratio. However, care must be taken in interpreting data, for example, an acceptable ratio is one doctor for every 1,500 people. This statistic, though frequently used, can be misleading. The type of physician must be specified, as well as the population breakdown by age and gender. A large number of females in a population, for example, indicates a higher need for obstetricians and gynecologists. Children need pediatricians, and older adults require specialized palliative services.

Health facilities statistics are collected and published by a variety of organizations, including hospital associations and government agencies. A major problem of facilities statistics is that each association tends to describe facilities in different ways. Also, the data are usually provided by facility administrators, who, for various reasons, might not accurately describe their organization's utilization of facilities. Like the doctor-to-patient ratio, the population group used in the evaluation should be known.

Health services statistics describe the delivery and receipt of health services by the population. This information facilitates the analysis of the level of services through which particular health problems may need to be addressed. The most common form of data on health services is the medical case abstract. The individual care provider, however, should not have to take the responsibility for maintaining a long historical base of detailed data from medical case abstracts. As the operational needs for data of a health provider grow with reasonable specificity, statistical abstracts of historical data will serve long-term needs more efficiently.

Environmental health statistics, formerly called public health statistics, provide data on health hazards, including noise, pollution, and deficient sanitation. These statistics are critical in the prevention of health problems through various medical and non-medical interventions by defining, more clearly, the causes of existing health problems. Statistics in this field can be obtained from government agencies that are responsible for regulating health and safety. Again, a major problem is linking environmental statistics with the populations affected, or even more difficult, with mobile populations that have been affected.

Figure 3–2 summarizes the various sources of health statistics and epidemiological data commonly used in databases that are parts of a layered HMIS. Above all, because one of the primary objectives of HMIS is to generate relevant and useful information in the context of health services planning and decision making, the quality of the information generated can also be an indicator of the system's performance as a whole.

DATA QUALITY

As we have seen, the efficiency and effectiveness of health managerial and clinical decision making depend largely on the context in which data are collected and transformed into useful information and knowledge. Nevertheless, on a broader level, certain characteristics of data quality are desirable for all useful health management information processing systems. Table 3–1 summarizes these key desirable data characteristics.

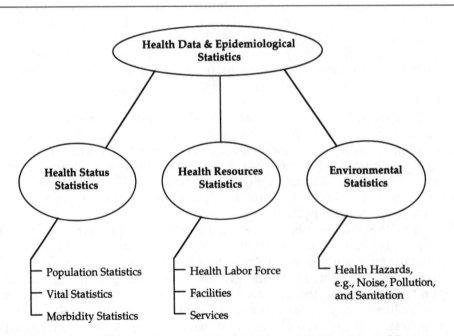

Figure 3–2 Summary of Various Sources of Health Data and Epidemiological Statistics

Table 3–1 Major Desirable Data Characteristics

Data Characteristics	Description
Accessibility	Available and can be extracted
Accuracy	Error-free
Appropriateness	Contain sufficient detail to support decision making
Comprehensibility	Easy to read and understand; well-formatted
Comprehensiveness	Inclusive and support information needs
Consistency	Not self-contradictory
Relevance	Related to decisions to be made
Reliability	Credible and valid
Timeliness	Available at the right time
Usefulness	Presented in an easy-to-use format

The desirable characteristics of information essentially imply that there are certain expectations for the functions of any working HMIS. More specifically, the HMIS must be able to:

- separate the important, relevant information from the unimportant and irrelevant
- condense the "filtered" information into even more concise form within a short period

The second function is especially important in view of the mounting evidence that information managers and clinicians in most arenas are suffering from an overabundance of irrelevant information instead of a lack of relevant information.[8] Factors that hinder these two important processes of isolation and condensation may arise for various reasons. Yet, they generally tend to reside in three broad areas: the inability of health managers and clinicians to specify their information needs, a misfit between technical and organizational designs, and errors in communications.

Clinicians and managers of health services delivery organizations who have yet to develop a working model of their decision processes or the various subsystems involved at their workplace may not be able to specify what and which information they require in order to make effective and intelligent decisions. They will likely be gathering as much information as possible, even information that is only marginally related to the domain of concern, before making a decision. In this case, the function of the HMIS of differentiating between important and unimportant, relevant and irrelevant information, is hindered. Here, understanding health care data sources and their applications is key to removing the barriers.

The misfit challenge refers to the fundamental discrepancies between the various functions and processes in the HMIS (in terms of data collection and information infrastructure) and the normal operation of the health services organization. For instance, the data computation ability of the HMIS may not be adequate to produce the kind of rigorous analysis demanded by management. This often creates additional workload for health professionals and directly affects both the perceived value and the acceptability of the HMIS to the users. In this instance, understanding information architecture and flow will offer a way to eliminate such mismatches. These concepts will be discussed later.

Finally, even if there are no problems in both information requirement specifications and mismatches, the normal functioning of the HMIS may be hindered. In such cases, the delivery of the "refined" information often breeds trouble. For example, problems may reside in the transmission of electronic signals or in some external electromechanical interfaces. Here, an understanding of information and communication theory, which are concerned with methods of coding, decoding, sorting, and retrieving information, is needed. This is the subject of our next section.

INFORMATION AND COMMUNICATION

The originator of the information and communication theory was Norbert Weiner, a well-known mathematician, who, as a result of his study of cybernetics in the late 1940s, argued that any organization is held together by the possession of means for acquisition, use, retention, and transmission of information.[9]

Accordingly, this theory supports a framework that investigates the likelihood of a given degree of accuracy in the transmission of a message through a channel, which is subject to probable failure or noise. Weiner defined information as the average number of binary digits that must be transmitted to identify a given message from the set of all possible messages to which it belongs.[10] If there are a limited number of possible messages that must be transmitted, it is possible to devise a different code to identify each message—the message may be composed of alphanumeric characters, complete sentences, or certain predefined codes. Although much of the research focused subsequently on the mathematical aspect of communications, important nonmathematical insights into the design and operation of HMISs from a communication perspective can be gained. As shown in Figure 3–3, there are five major components of all information communications systems: the information source, the transmitter, the channel, the receiver, and the destination.

The information source in a communication system has the initial role of selecting the particular piece of information, or message, to be transmitted. For a meaningful transmission to occur, the underlying language, or code, must represent the message. The set of characters used on a microcomputer keyboard and the vocal sounds of the English language for a spoken message are examples of communication codes.

The transmitter has an encoding function that converts the message into a medium that can be transmitted over the required distance. The generation of electronic signals by keyboard strokes for transmission via cabling or radio waves and the generation of muscular signals for speech production by brain activities are typical examples of transmitters within a communication system.

The communication channel provides the physical conduit or medium necessary for the information to flow over distance. Air waves and electrical cables are communication channels. A communication channel, as a physical

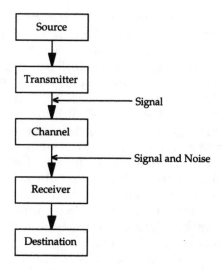

Figure 3–3 A General Model of a Communication System

process, can include the addition of noise and distortion to a signal. Distortion is caused by a known (even intentional) operation that can be corrected by an inverse operation. Noise refers to random or unpredictable interference that reduces the purity of the signal and the fidelity with which the message is transmitted. In practice, no channel can be made absolutely noise-free, although many techniques are used to reduce noise to a satisfactory extent. Examples of noise are voltage surges and meteorological disturbances in electronic transmissions and unintended sounds and echoes in speech transmission.

The receiver converts the message from its transmitted form to a state permitting its reception. Thus, a human listener converts sound waves into nerve impulses in the inner ear, whereas a microphone receiving the same sound waves converts them into electrical signals. In microwave transmission within a computer network, the receiver apparatus converts the message back into computer-compatible electronic signals for use by other computers.

The destination is the final stage of reception, in which the received form is decoded to provide a meaningful message. For instance, a patient's health record received in English sounds or written words may have little or no meaning to a practitioner who knows only French. Technically, the information is present in the message; however, given the ability of the receiver, it cannot be decoded.

Within any communication system, the transmission of any form of information essentially flows from a given source to a chosen destination. Feedback is an additional component of most systems. A feedback loop can check how successfully a message has been transmitted. If the transmission has been unsuccessful, a feedback mechanism may provide the means to have the information retransmitted. The obvious performance criterion of a communications system is the fidelity with which an encoded and transmitted message is received and decoded, and the associated reduction of any noise or distortion causing uncertainty of information. Although all communication systems are imperfect, those depending on human voice alone are perhaps especially vulnerable. As we have seen, to enhance efficiency and effectiveness in the communication of information, the noise and distortion of data should be reduced.

To illustrate these concepts, we can look at a situation involving an instructor and a student. The "source" of information may be the instructor who chooses the message to be relayed. The "transmitter" refers to the instructor's voice and hand gestures. These signals are passed through the "channels" of sights and sounds. Interference, such as background sound and voices of other students, may be considered noise within the system. The message is then converted by the eyes and ears of the listening student, who is the "receiver." The "destination" is the student's mind. Additionally, if the message is not sufficiently understood or received, the student has to reverse the communication process (feedback) to request clarification or further information. This simple example demonstrates how a relatively routine information processing system, such as a class lecture, can be mentally broken down into a manageable series of communication stages.

Typically, in a health service organization, the amount of data and information flowing through the system is enormous. A considerable amount of time and effort is therefore required to understand and document this flow. Since the advent of computer systems, many techniques and tools have been created to improve documenting organizational information flow. By using appropriate tools, HMIS designers and specialists can graphically depict organizational information flows on paper quickly and effortlessly. An important point in the application of any of these techniques is that it is the end-user's information model that is to be represented architecturally.

INFORMATION ARCHITECTURE AND FLOW

For all practical purposes, information architecture represents essentially the enterprise view of the organization's complete data flow. It is the context for depicting meaningful information flows from the user's perspective and thus the effort to be expended is analogous to the design of an architectural plan depicting the "flow" of materials and usable spaces within a building that is yet to be constructed. Information architecture may be deemed the blueprint emphasizing the data and information processes (or flows) expected to occur within an organization.[11]

In a health service context, identical information can exist simultaneously in many different formats. For instance, a physician's order may exist as a thought, a set of written words, or some electronic configuration in a computer. Yet, in transmitting information, the final form of the transmitted information is pertinent, rather than the physical means of accomplishing the transmission. Examples of transmission methods include manual or pneumatic delivery of multi-part paper form; telephone, teletype, or telecopier; electronic messaging system; and computerized hospital information system via networking.

In an attempt to understand the complex interacting flows of an integrated delivery system or other similar system, the variables of concern may be divided functionally into three categories:

1. materials, such as food and anesthetics
2. energy, both electrical and human
3. information, such as oral messages and computer transmissions

Such a classification involves some ambiguities as one type of variable may be transformed into another. In any case, all three categories have the common feature of HMIS analysis in that their states, conditions, flows, or quantities can be represented by the concept of information flow. In other words, whatever the purpose and state of an element, its essential systems characteristic is the information brought to bear on the system's processes. The changes in the nature of the information flows determine how information contained in the variables is modified or transformed via various processes.

In short, all health services institutions, whether small community hospital wards or national health system networks, have a bewildering array of interacting variables that can be expressed as changes in information flow. The extent to which various information is to be included, transformed, and transmitted from one part of the system to another is limited only by the decision about what is important and what is not. From a business perspective, for example, information on the mineral content of a community hospital's water may be far too trivial to a facility manager deciding on the number of bed closures, whereas the global greenhouse effect may be too all-encompassing to be practically useful. Managing the content and flow of information well can be a critical, if not an essential, characteristic of an organization that excels in today's health care economy.

To be able to manage the content and flow of information in the workplace, knowledge of how to express the complex interactions among various subsystems or components in simple terms becomes an important prerequisite for health planners and administrators. Numerous tools exist in this arena to assist end users and HMIS analysts. In fact, we have already seen one of these tools—the rich picture. The rich picture is useful when documenting themes or issues for "soft," ill-defined, or fuzzy problematic situations. The objective of the rich picture is to record the problem situation in its entirety, without confining it to the agenda or biases of key actors. One advantage is that it employs the language and terminology of the environment and shows how various pieces involved are related to one another.

This chapter introduces a number of very popular tools employed in HMIS design and information architectural modeling—data flow diagrams (DFDs), flow charts, and entity-relationship (E-R) diagrams. DFDs are top-down hierarchical diagrams, which can provide successive levels of details and are particularly useful in documenting data flows and processes in a system. In contrast, flow charts emphasize the specific pathway of the procedural flow of some piece of information from a starting point to the final destination, while temporarily ignoring other simultaneous information flows. An E-R diagram is a special class of diagramming technique useful for representing data entities and relationships among these entities. This tool is used for health database modeling. Table 3–2 highlights the defining characteristics of each tool and its appropriate uses in the context of portraying an organization's information architecture.

Data Flow Diagram

One popular and frequently used technique is the data flow diagram. Alternate techniques, which are similar and often interchangeable, are referred to as information flow diagrams, node diagrams, block diagrams, data flow graphs, or even bubble charts. Like many other techniques, DFDs provide a standardized approach to systems documentation and aid in the development of future system designs. DFDs are useful for documenting the logical design of an information system by showing graphically how data flow to, from, and within an HMIS, as well as the various processes that transform the data into meaningful and useful information.

The main purpose of DFDs is to break down a system into manageable levels of detail that can be visualized, first at a very general (context) level, and then gradually in greater detail, in a process termed "leveling." For example, a walk-in clinic serving the medical needs of the community could review its overall services by sequencing the steps a patient takes to access any or all of its services. The staff's corresponding actions and flow of information can then be listed and categorized to clarify the center's operations. Thus, a large complex information process is first depicted as a context diagram. Each subprocess can also be subdivided into successive levels of "detailed" DFD with corresponding subsystem details. This ability to expand and contract levels of details as needed, depending on the particular requirements at that moment, is what makes a DFD such a valuable and flexible information flow documentation technique.

In formalizing a DFD, the basic schema of inputs, processes, and outputs becomes essential. To operationalize this relation for HMIS solutions, two different aspects, variables and processes, can be utilized. Variables here refer to

Table 3–2 A Comparison of Three Diagramming Techniques and Tools

Diagramming Methods	Key Features	Primary Uses
Entity-relationship (E-R) diagramming	Represents entities, types of relationships among entities, and sometimes attribute values of these data elements	Use for depicting data structures and database models
Data flow diagramming (DFD)	Conveys top-down data flows and processes with successive levels of details	Use for documenting data flows and processes
Flow charting	Emphasizes procedural flow of information for specific tasks	Use for portraying system linkages and procedural programming steps

the input and output data. A variable must be defined specifically before any formal analysis of the system can take place. Examples include patients who are admitted daily and drugs that are prescribed weekly. In contrast, the processes are defined by algorithmic relations or other computations and are the mechanisms for making changes to the variables over time. In essence, a DFD is a network representation of a system, which itself may exhibit varying degrees of automation.

As shown in Figure 3–4, DFDs are constructed by using four basic symbols: arrows, rounded boxes, open boxes (rectangles with three sides), and rectangular boxes.

Arrows represent the movement of data (with directions) between processes, data sources (sinks), and data stores (files). Arrows are therefore used to denote data flows. Each data flow arrow should be labeled to indicate the type of data involved, for example, "admission notification (phone)" and "chart package," as shown in Figure 3–5.

In DFDs, rounded boxes represent the operational transformation of input data to output data. Labeling of these processes typically involves verb clauses such as "Prepare patient chart package" and "Review and implement physician's orders for work requests," as shown in the example. Open boxes are used to represent data stores, that is, repositories of data used in the system. Examples of data stores are files, databases, microfiches, and binders of paper reports. In Figure 3–5, "patient charts" represent data stores.

Data sources or external entities, represented by rectangles, are the entities that lie outside the system. Patients, laboratories, wards, customers, banks, and even employees may be regarded as external entities. These data sources (or sinks) help define the boundary of the system. In our case, the emergency room, the pharmacy, and the dietetics department are examples of data sources.

To illustrate the use of DFDs, we will examine an actual application in the health service field. Figure 3–5 illustrates the flows of data involved in a surgical department at a university hospital. As noted, DFDs are used to provide both overall and detailed views of an HMIS. What takes place within a process box in one DFD can be "exploded" in greater detail by another DFD. For

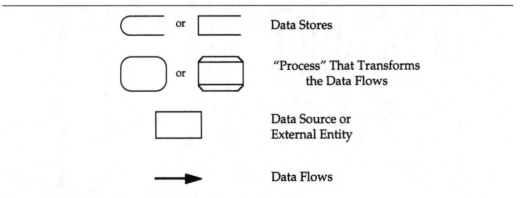

Figure 3–4 Conventional Data Flow Diagram Symbols

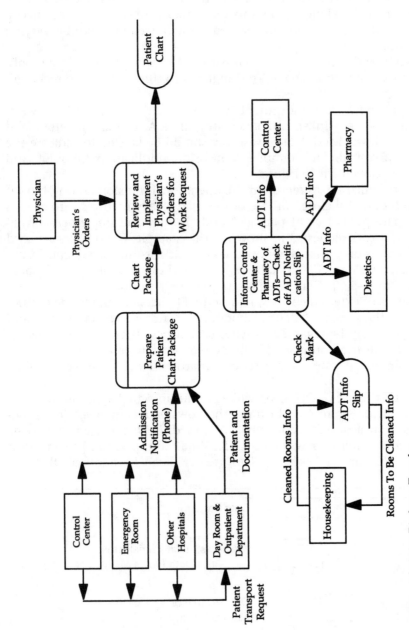

Figure 3–5 Surgical Interdepartmental Data Flows at a University Hospital

ADT = Admission Discharge Transfer

instance, the process "Review and implement physician's orders for work requests" in Figure 3–5 is expanded in the DFD shown in Figure 3–6. In other words, these two figures are "leveled" in terms of context and details. Figure 3–6 breaks down a process (from Figure 3–5) into its subprocesses.

In summary, an accurate picture of various subsystem interactions involved in a typical surgical procedure at a local hospital are given by these two figures, yet each has its own special functions. The context DFD facilitates higher-level decision-making activities like strategic planning, whereas the more detailed DFD is more suitable for aiding operational and tactical decision making.

Flow Charts

In addition to DFDs, many other analytic tools and techniques are available for use in HMIS design and development. These include paper flow charts, document flow diagrams, critical path method, GANTT charts, and Petri networks. Among the more commonly used tools in both the public and private

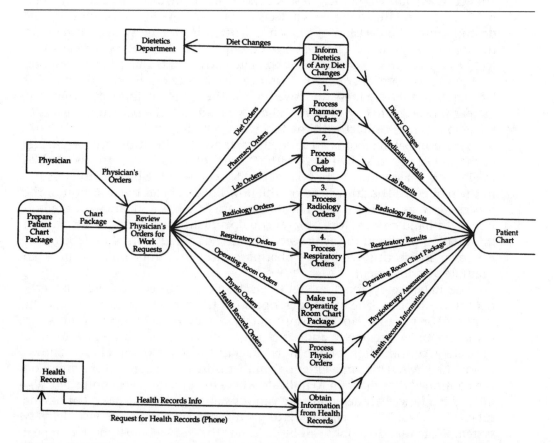

Figure 3–6 The Process of "Review and Implement Physician's Orders for Work Request" in detail

sectors of many industries are flow diagrams. Essentially, a flow diagram is a graphic representation of the steps an organization performs to produce some output. The output may be a physical product, a service, some information, or a combination of the three.

Most people associate flow diagrams with computer programming. Indeed, the computer programmers of the 1960s and 1970s popularized the use of flow charts in the business world. Similar to DFDs, flow charts show the steps in a procedure by using various symbols, with arrows indicating logical flow and diamond boxes indicating a decision process that branches in one or two ways. Many groups or individuals often adapt the symbols of a flow chart to accommodate their specified needs. Although there are dozens of specialized symbols used in flow charts, most are built from the following basic set of symbols: activity symbol (rectangle); decision symbol (diamond); terminal symbol (rounded rectangle); flow lines (arrows); document symbol (square); database symbol (cylinder); and connector symbol (circle).

The activity symbol is a rectangle that indicates a single step in a process. A brief description of the activity can be shown inside the rectangle, such as "Inject tuberculin" or "Read chest X-ray," as in Figure 3–7. The decision symbol is a diamond that designates a decision or branch point in the process. The description of the decision or branch is written inside the symbol, usually in the form of a question. The answer to the question determines the path that will be taken from the decision symbol, and each path is labeled to correspond to the appropriate answer. For instance, in our example, the diamond is labeled "Are there redness and swelling of the skin?" If there are, then the patient proceeds directly to have a chest X-ray; if not, the patient is shown to have no previous contact with the tuberculosis pathogen.

The terminal symbol is a rounded rectangle that identifies the beginning or the end of a process, by having either "Start" or "End" inside this symbol, as in Figure 3–7. Flow lines (arrows) are used to represent the progression of steps in the sequence. The arrowhead on the flow line indicates the direction of the process flow, as in Figure 3–7. The document symbol is a square with the bottom right-hand corner "torn" away. The document symbol represents written information pertinent to the process. The title or description of the document is shown inside this symbol. A pharmaceutical inventory order form is an example of a document.

The database symbol represents electronically stored information pertinent to the process. The title or description of the database is shown inside the symbol. For instance, an inventory database may be accessed to process an inventory order accurately and efficiently. The connector is a circle used to indicate a continuation of the flow diagram. A letter or number is shown inside the circle. This same letter or number is used in a connector symbol on the continued flow diagram to indicate where the processes are connected. Figure 3–7 is a flow chart depicting the various steps a patient suspected of having tuberculosis would normally have to go through in a health service delivery system. Note that diamonds can be decisions that lead a branch back to repeat an earlier step, thus creating a looping sequence.

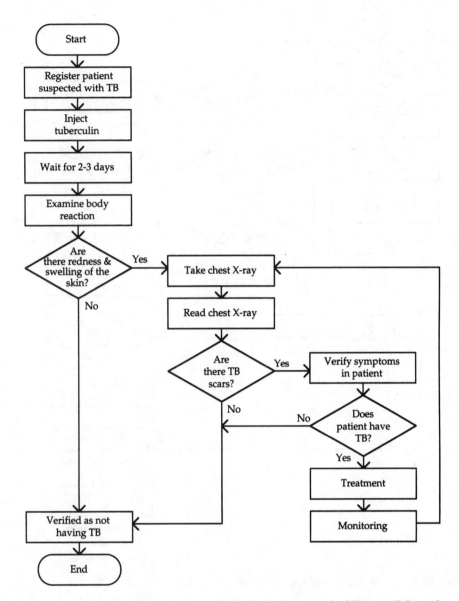

Figure 3–7 A Flow Chart of Procedures for Individuals Suspected of Having Tuberculosis (TB)

Figure 3–8 uses a flow chart format to show how a flow diagram can be developed from scratch. Usually, flow charts are constructed so that the general direction is from left to right or top to bottom; otherwise, a snakelike layout will make the flow of the process difficult to follow. The criteria for the decisions indicated by the diamond-shaped symbol need to be shown in all instances, even by referring to supporting documents where the detailed crite-

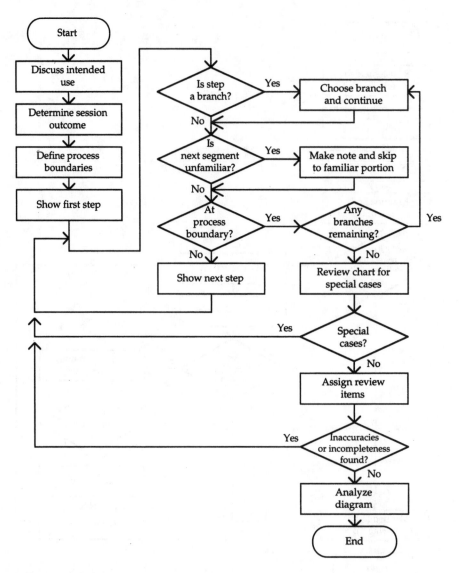

Figure 3–8 Flow Diagram Construction Steps

ria are spelled out. For instance, "Approved" decisions may refer to the criteria by which each instance is judged acceptable or unacceptable as set out in a separate but detailed reference document.

As in DFDs, flow chart "leveling" can be developed to aid in building a common understanding of the process. Here, the "high-level" flow is often called a "system" flow chart. Detailed flow charts can be constructed from each of the rectangles established in the system flow chart. Through this hierarchy of flow charting, a health organization can build a complete, accurate pictorial description of the process inherent in its HMIS design. In formatting a flow diagram within a health service organization, it is important to elicit the support of the staff to generate the diagram. This is especially true if an outside consultant has drawn the diagram. Outside consultants are not always well informed about all aspects of the organizational operations. Verification of the accuracy of the flow diagram should be made at all managerial, departmental, and staff levels.

Entity-Relationship Diagrams

Apart from DFDs and flow charts, E-R models are among the most widely used graphical aids for depicting information architecture of data-intensive organizations, such as the health care industry. Instead of focusing on the various processes and information flows in the system as with DFDs and flow charts, E-R models concentrate on showing the data structure underlying these processes and flows. In this regard, E-R diagrams are particularly useful for modeling and designing health databases. E-R models are typically used to show entities and relationships among entities, especially when there is a complex network of entities within a system. Key elements of the E-R model are entities, relationships, and attributes.

An entity is something that a user can identify in his or her workplace; for example, patients and physicians are commonly defined entities for health services organizations. Moreover, an entity of a given type may be grouped into entity classes; for example, the "Volunteer" entity class is the collection of all volunteers. In other words, each entity class can have many entity instances, for example, John and Peter may be instances of the "Patient" entity, whereas Dr. Nolan and Professor Chen may be instances of the "Physician" entity.

A relationship is an association between entities. There are generally three types of relationships in the E-R model: one-to-one (1:1) relationship, one-to-many (1:N) relationship, and many-to-many (N:M) relationship. A 1:1 relationship is a relationship between a single-entity instance of one type to another single-entity instance of another type. For example, Dr. Nolan "treats" John. Here, the relationship is a "treatment" type relationship and the association is between a single patient with a single physician. If, however, Dr. Nolan also "treats" Peter, then the relationship will now become a 1:N relationship; that is, one physician, many patients. Furthermore, if John and Peter are also referred by Dr. Nolan to Professor Chen and both John and Peter are also patients of Professor Chen, then this now becomes a N:M relationship; that is, many physicians, many patients. A physician can have more than one patient, and a patient can have more than one physician. The determination of these relationships will largely depend on the user's perspective.

Attributes are the properties of an entity class and are descriptions of the entity's characteristics. In other words, entities are conceptualized in the E-R models as having various attributes, one or a combination of which will be its unique identifier or "key" to distinguish among the entity instances. For example, attributes of the patient instance, John, may be John's personal health number, his name, age, and gender. The unique identifier in this case will be the personal health number, because no two patient instances will have the same number.

Focusing on "things" about which data must be recorded (entities), the relationships among the entities, and their attributes, E-R diagrams can provide a high-level architectural view of any health database. Moreover, these diagrams will assist in the identification of various ways to divide the database into subject databases for use in distributed systems. If there are problems or if changes are to be made in the database, E-R diagrams can offer great assistance in finding the problems and making the changes. E-R diagrams are therefore great tools for logical modeling of HMIS problem-solutions.

To illustrate the use of E-R diagrams, we will now return to the multi-community health promotion project (MCHPP) presented in the beginning of Chapter 2. Here, some of the key identifiable entities include "Supervisor," "Participant," "Health Promotion Program," and "Event." Figure 3–9 shows a simple E-R diagram describing these key entities and relationships to be captured as information in a database for use by MCHPP. For example, John Smith or other individuals wanting to get involved will be instances of the "Participant" entity. As can be seen, boxes are used in E-R diagrams to show data items or entities, and lines are used to show relationships between entities. One-to-one, one-to-many, many-to-one, or many-to-many relationships can be indicated by using different conventions; one of the more commonly employed "claws" was used. It is interesting to note that less conventional forms of E-R

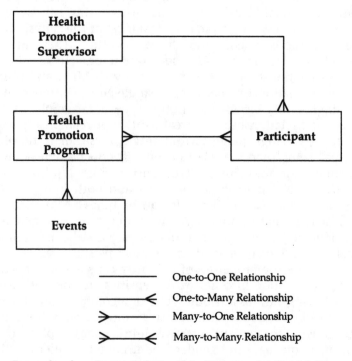

Figure 3–9 An Example of an Entity-Relationship Diagram for the Multicommunity Health Promotion Project

diagrams also allow depiction of either-or and other optional relationships. In some E-R diagrams, the attributes are also depicted. These attributes are not shown to avoid cluttering the diagram.

It is crucial that the DFDs, the flow diagrams, and the E-R diagrams reflect the actual process in place in the work environment from the user's point of view. Realistic consideration must be given to the fact that not all managers (users) may wish to disclose every process or structure actually in place because of fear of added responsibility and accountability. To this end, use of any or all of these tools may limit the analyst's ability to obtain optimal results. To counter this barrier, the atmosphere in which users are encouraged to help construct information architecture must be conducive to honest and open responses. The overall goal of the exercise needs to take precedence over personal fears or departmental biases if integrated HMIS applications are to be achieved.

Knowledge of systems thinking, health care data and database concepts, and methods for designing information architecture allows us to envision various facets of data requirements for a typical IDS. This is discussed in the next section.

DATA REQUIREMENTS OF AN INTEGRATED DELIVERY SYSTEM

Because of the increasingly complex environment in which IDS function, there is a growing trend toward networked and distributed systems. This points to the need for:

- the ability to combine a variety of data sources into an integrated data warehouse with distributed databases
- the ability to interrelate applications with linkages through various organizational databases
- the ability to share and transfer data among affiliated providers and organizations
- the ability to accommodate different providers' actions with a range of medical data required for the various phases of a patient treatment
- the option to shift data and communicate effectively among provider organizations as the need arises

Incidentally, some suggested solutions have been offered by health computing vendors for creating an integrated IDS data system as a replacement or a link bridging existing individual stand-alone organization data systems. Our focus here is on the various facets of information requirements for a typical IDS.

The SAP Healthcare Solution advocates the application of a highly integrated suite of client/server software based on the R/3 system to streamline and integrate health care business processes. Accordingly, all health care industry processes and functions may be grouped into four major areas.

1. enterprise management and communication
2. patient care management
3. diagnostics and therapy
4. support services and business support

These functional groups may further be subdivided in real terms into various subsystems of an IDS application portfolio. In other words, there could be four modules in the IDS portfolio, each with its own data and database collection, computation, and retrieval abilities, but each also linked to the other through the enterprise management and communication module.

Each module is proposed to have under its "umbrella" a collection of applications for specific procedures or operations. For instance, the enterprise management and communication module may have its own strategic enterprise management subsystem, business intelligence and data warehousing subsystem, managerial and financial accounting subsystem, and the entire supply chain management subsystem; that is, a subsystem not only providing online, real-time intra-IDS communications, but also providing electronic data interchange capabilities and communications between the IDS and the IDS's providers, payers, patients, and suppliers.

On the administrative side, the patient care management module may include subsystem applications for patient administration, patient accounting and billing, patient scheduling, patient service management, marketing and health promotion. On the clinical side, the subsystem applications would include care planning, clinical care management, care documentation, and after-care management. In other words, the patient care management module should, at the outset, be the chief source of all information needed by the IDS about a patient, both administrative and clinical. To perform this function, this module needs to move beyond the traditional functions of the ADT systems into a modern day computerized patient record system using master patient index as a unique identifier for patients. In order to collect all the clinical information about patients, this requires that the computerized patient record be linked to all IDS care units such as laboratory, pharmacy, and radiology; nursing stations; and possibly physicians' offices.

Diagnostics and therapy applications may include diagnostic support and ancillary, clinical order management, medical and clinical documentation, treatment and operation management, and clinical research and education subsystems (e.g., research administration and continuing education). To complete the repertoire, the module should also have a monitoring subsystem to collect and analyze outputs from such monitoring devices as electrocardiograms and electroencephalograms. These systems should also be equipped with a direct link to nursing stations and the computerized patient record.

On the one hand, the support services and business support module may include support services applications such as biomedical technology, hygiene services and risk management, transportation, catering, and facilities services. On the other, it may include business support applications such as human resource management, procurement (i.e., purchasing), fixed asset management, financial asset management, and equipment maintenance.

Figure 3–10 summarizes the proposed application portfolio of an IDS using a vendor system like SAP. It is worth noting that the subsystems in each of the proposed modules may not be centrally shared, but may be distributed in design, allowing only restricted views to different users depending on authority and other security clearance. All of these subsystems should, however, be

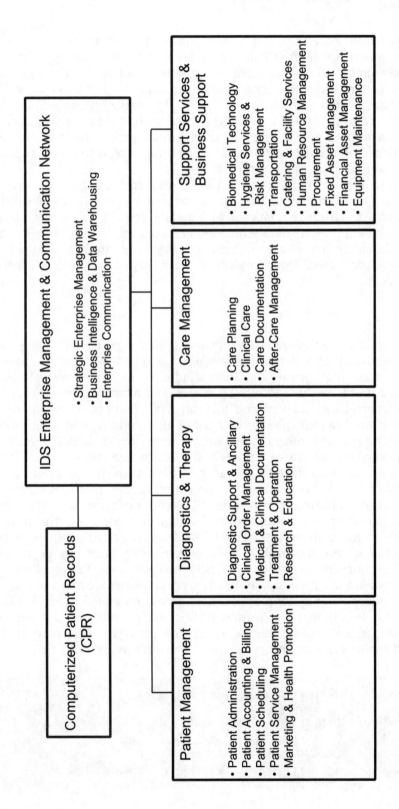

Figure 3–10 A Health Management Information System Application Portfolio for an Integrated Delivery System

directly linked to the enterprise management and communication module. For instance, the pharmacy of an affiliated provider may need to use applications from the IDS's supply chain management subsystem and at the same time be linked to the patient record (to obtain patient information). It should also be linked to the diagnostics and therapy subsystem (to receive prescription orders from physicians and to monitor the effects of medication on patients), and to the patient accounting and billing subsystem (to do patient billing). In this case, the affiliated pharmacy department will be using several connected applications under different modules of the IDS.

Finally, one needs to build into such a system a complex form of system authentication, which includes the use of layered passwords for ensuring proper data access, authorized data use and update, respect for patient rights and privacy, and appropriate data protection and security. In other words, different users should be able to access or make changes only to data captured in their respective user views depending on the authority of the users as identified by the system.

CONCLUSION

Frontiers of the medical field are advancing at an ever-increasing pace. Therefore, the amount of patient information required by health provider organizations to achieve high-quality care soars rapidly. At the same time, stringent budgetary measures have put enormous pressure on the health care industry to tighten cost control mechanisms and to form new alliances. These changes have in turn dramatically increased the need of an integrated HMIS approach in producing the relevant information with numerous desirable characteristics to reduce the need for duplicated services in the health care system.

This chapter has introduced the reader to basic concepts of health care data, elements of information and communication theory, methods of documenting information flows and structures, and various other aspects of health data sources. Now equipped with these fundamental concepts, the reader should be able to articulate an integrated HMIS design for any health organization by focusing on health data that can be effectively collected and processed to obtain the information needed by health professionals. The application portfolio proposed for a modern day IDS is an example to provide the reader with a broad overview of systems applications in an integrated health service delivery setting. It is hoped that readers will be able to integrate this knowledge with concepts discussed earlier to prepare them to cope with rapid changes and challenges encountered in today's health service industry.

CHAPTER QUESTIONS

1. Why is the distinction among data, information, and knowledge important?
2. How can one ensure data quality? What effect would there be within the organization if some of these qualities, or even one, were missing?

3. What are the elements of information theory? Provide an illustration of the theory as it applies to information transfer among patients, physicians, and providers in an IDS. What is the weakest link? The strongest?
4. Can you explain "leveling" in data flow diagrams? What is its purpose?
5. When does one use E-R diagrams as opposed to flow diagrams or DFDs?
6. How do you identify whether a health service organization is not collecting, transforming, or managing information properly? Use the example of an IDS to illustrate your answer.

NOTES

1. M.C. Yovits, Information and Data, *Encyclopedia of Computer Science and Engineering*, 2nd ed. (New York: Van Nostrand Reinhold, 1983): 715–717.

2. G.B. Davis and M.H. Olson, *Management Information Systems: Conceptual Foundations, Structure, and Development*, 2nd ed. (New York: McGraw-Hill Publishing Co., 1985).

3. H.C. Lucas, Jr., *Information Systems Concepts for Management* (New York: McGraw-Hill Publishing Co., 1978).

4. M.L. Johns, *Information Management for Health Professions* (New York: Delmar Publishers, 1997).

5. D.M. Kroenke, *Database Processing: Fundamentals, Design, and Implementation*, 6th ed. (Upper Saddle River, NJ: Prentice Hall, 1998).

6. M. Abdelhak, et al., *Health Information: Management of a Strategic Resource* (Philadelphia: W.B. Saunders Co., 1996).

7. G. Thompson and I. Handelman, *Health Data and Information Management* (London: Butterworth Publishers, 1978).

8. R.L. Ackoff, Management Misinformation Systems, *Management Science* 14, no. 4 (1967): 147–156.

9. N. Weiner, *Cybernetics of Control and Communication in the Animal and the Machine* (New York: John Wiley & Sons, 1948).

10. Ibid.

11. Y.G. Kim and G.C. Everest, Building an IS Architecture: Collective Wisdom from the Field, *Information and Management* 26 (1994): 1–11.

Chapter 4

Evolving Standards for Integrating Tomorrow's Health Care System: Toward a Service Process Model

Joseph K. H. Tan and Ashok Bhatkhande

SCENARIO

Imagine that you direct the health management information system (HMIS) infrastructure at the Brigham,[1] a teaching arm of the Harvard Medical School in Boston, Massachusetts. Over the years, you have steered your institution through a legacy of centralized, minicomputer-based support systems. Today, it has successfully migrated to a LAN-based, distributed, client-server, desktop environment with online patient information and an ever increasing number of applications. At the main campus, for example, you have no less than 3,300 Intel clients and over 120 servers connected via 70 4-Mb Novell NetWare 3.0 token rings and two 16-Mb backbones.

Specifically, this HMIS infrastructure supports major systems such as patient accounting, pathology laboratories, results retrieval, and physician order entry. Most, if not all, of these applications have been written in resource-conserving MUMPS (Massachusetts General Hospital Utility Multi-Programming System), a client/server database applications development and run-time environment.[2] The success of this sophisticated HMIS, which has proved effective in supporting telehealth services to neighboring clinics, has also positioned your institution to be chosen by a federal grant agency for piloting the next generation computerized patient record (CPR) system. This CPR is to support a distributed yet integrated health care delivery system. Clearly, your institution has the lead over most others in developing and showcasing such a CPR.

Three basic functions are envisioned for the proposed CPR: (1) it should make data easily accessible so that whenever and wherever data are entered they can be made available to the right users; (2) it should help streamline the processes encompassing care delivery; and (3) it should facilitate ordering care; that is, the CPR should allow logic to be placed above its content to guide the caregiving process. In this sense, support for decentralized data access for improving care delivery is an essential feature. As an example of guiding the caregiving process, the use of your institution's fledgling expert systems is known to support caregivers' planning and care ordering processes through automated protocol-based guidelines. Here, the CPR would contain, for example, the most recent lab results on a patient's blood or serum potassium level. As a caregiver enters an order for a drug that may have a counter-reaction in a patient with high potassium level, the system would alert the clinician and request for an order reconfirmation. Had the level been normal, the order would have been processed automatically. Such alerts at the time of entry should also be easily delivered over e-mail or the institution's paging system. Although this support feature is not fundamental to the CPR, the CPR is a prerequisite to systems such as this that must rely on patient data to aid care planning, service quality, and treatment outcome. Imagine that the CPR developed at your institution will be in Windows, but what may be sitting in your doctor's office is a mix of Macintosh and networked PCs that run on Windows. Contemplate the need for system integration and data standardization to overcome the different configurations.

It seems that putting logic above the CPR content to guide the caregiving process will be key to success. Given that every drug has several interactions, it appears that where and how you are going to match this information in the CPR is critical. G6PD deficiency may have been diagnosed once in the patient's childhood in a hospital some 2,000 miles away: Where are you going to look for your potassium values? Are you going to search the Web for the patient's name? Indeed, it may well be cheaper and easier to get a potassium reading before administering the drug, thus defeating one of the basic CPR functions that you have contemplated!

There also are other challenges. These include evolving and establishing networks to interconnect your providers and suppliers; purchasing; upgrading and managing the storage systems needed to keep track of massive patient clinical information online for tens of years; and the need to effectively monitor a patient condition over the course of multiple visits, for example, the need for "'linked data'" that would allow you to link Ms. X's visit to your institution with her visit to Massachusetts General Hospital 6 months or a year later. A key challenge here is how you can ensure the adoption of standards, that is, standards for patient identifiers, diagnoses, medical terms, informatics, and treatments. Also, think about how you are going to enforce the use of these standards across collaborating institutions and among health service providers.

INTRODUCTION

Recent mergers, consolidations, and new purchasing arrangements along with organizational efforts and pressures to contain costs are also transforming the health care industry. We are now seeing new alliances of providers being formed on a daily basis, which has created an unprecedented need to share clinical data and patient encounter information. Likewise, patients are becoming more mobile and more informed. They are demanding "best" practices and are routinely incurring billings at many institutions even for the same illness. Consequently, there is an urgent need for the integration of clinical and health management data systems.

In this chapter, the need for standardization to develop functional CPR and other integrated delivery system (IDS) applications is discussed. Apart from standards at the data coding, data schema, and data exchange levels, which will mostly support the development of an interfaced HMIS, there is a need to extend the standardization paradigm to the level of a service process model to create genuinely integrated HMISs for tomorrow's health care system. In this regard, the standardization proposed here deals with integrating service processes to overcome many of the challenges of functionality and integration faced in the next generation CPR.

Specifically, the use of a service process architecture is highlighted, and it is shown how it can contribute to achieving an integrated, not just interfaced, HMIS for an IDS. To help the reader differentiate between this philosophy and that of traditional approaches, early health record systems are reviewed. It is shown how current efforts in standardization are limited and provide insights into how the use of a service process normalization approach can be conceptualized, designed, and developed. Finally, some rules and steps for achieving integrated HMISs for an IDS are specified.

EARLY HEALTH RECORD SYSTEMS

In the precomputer era, the management of patient records in health service organizations was based largely on manual file processing systems. Over time, these practices became standardized in the form of patient registers, medical service claims, work orders, patient billing files, and books of accounts. The manual systems required health record technicians and specialists who were well trained in maintaining paper-based records, while others (e.g., physicians and nurses) delivered the services. The health manager's role was simply to enforce documentation to conform to evolving standards, such as acceptable data coding, accounting principles, and book practices.

In effect, the manual system of documentation dictated the traditional structure of the health service organization. Departments such as patient registration, finance and accounting, purchasing, and human resources have each originated from distinct documentation needs. Standardization of these documents also led to standardization of administrative, clinical, and financial procedures based on the analysis and summary of information maintained by the manual systems. There were daily drug inventory reports, statistical summaries of bed occupancy, medical accessories and equipment purchases, utilization data and performance reports, reconciliation statements, and timesheets for employees. These reports were either maintained in the registers as records or were typed and circulated among the decision makers in the organization. Analysis of the documented data might be an annual, biannual, or even quarterly exercise. The health care managers wished they could receive relevant and appropriate information well in time to change their courses of action.

With the advent of computers, automated tools were developed for electronic patient data recording. The data management systems were designed to look at the forms and data that were maintained manually (the input), to look at the flow of data (the process), and to improve the availability of summarized information (the output). Computer Stored Ambulatory Record System (COSTAR), a patient record system developed by Octo Barnett in the 1960s;

Regenstrief Medical Record System (RMRS), a summary-type patient record system implemented in 1972; and The Medical Record (TMR), an evolving medical record system developed at Duke University Medical Center around the same time as the RMRS, were among the few landmark automated health record systems that resulted from the widespread introduction of computing into health care.[3] The use of these automated systems soon indicated a considerable need for understanding data standards and how these standards can be enforced.

DATA STANDARDS

Many health professionals have realized that the lack of comprehensive data standards is key to inhibiting the sharing of medical information electronically. For example, an influential 1993 report by the U.S. General Accounting Office[4] highlighted the needs for data standards and grouped these needs into three broad categories: vocabulary standards, structure and content standards, and messaging standards. These taxonomies correspond neatly to our categories of data coding, data schema, and data exchange standards.

Data coding standards (vocabulary) aim at defining common medical terms and specifying how medical data are to be coded within the records. For example, the ICD9-CM is a standard numeric coding system adopted by many U.S. health provider organizations to ensure that similar diagnoses and procedures are similarly coded.[5] Using standard codes (i.e., the same abbreviation to represent similar conditions and treatments) will allow one to achieve not only data reliability, integrity, comparability, and consistency, but also will help one to retrieve needed data easily. New codes have continued to evolve, including ICD10 codes and numerous others (e.g., CPT, LOINC, UMLS, NDC, and NANDA).[6,7] Table 4–1 summarizes several of these codes.

Data exchange standards (messaging) ensure that electronic data can be predictably transmitted by establishing a standard interconnecting system protocol (i.e., standardizing the order and sequence of data during transmission between two points across a network or sub-network). Open systems interconnection (OSI) is an open architecture having seven layers, each demanding a different level of functionality for data exchange to materialize among different systems. More discussion of these data exchange and network architectures is given in Part III of this book. These OSI levels include physical, data link, network, transport, session, presentation, and application as described in Table 4–2. Other standards for system networking include IBM's SNA (system network architecture), DEC's DNA (DEC network architecture), TCP/IP (transmission control protocol/Internet protocol), and MUMPS. Table 4–2, extracted from Bourke, provides brief summaries of these layers and accompanying functions and a comparison of various standards that can be used in the respective layers.[8]

Data schema standards (structure and content) involve defining essential data elements in the database, such as a minimum data set (MDS), and specifying the structure, domains, rules, and relationships among these data elements to be maintained within the records to facilitate data retrieval. In the manual system, the data entry was serial and not random at the functional level. Computerization allows the data representation to become functionally complex.

Table 4–1 A Summary of Coding Systems Representing Health Care Concepts

Standard	Description
Read codes	A detailed set of codes used to explain patient care and treatment information
LOINC	Standard codes and classification for identifying laboratory and clinical terms
ICD10 codes	New diagnostic codes developed by World Health Organization (WHO), not yet used in North America
CPT4 codes	Procedure codes developed by the American Medical Association (AMA) for professional billing
National drug codes (NDC)	A comprehensive system of codes developed by the Federal Drug Administration to identify drug products and their packaging
NANDA	North American Nursing Diagnosis Association code set of nursing diagnoses
National Library of Medicine (NLM) Unified Medical Language System (UMLS)	A cross-referenced collection of codes and related information sources
APA DSM-IV	Diagnostic codes organized by the American Psychiatric Association (APA)
ECRI	Codes used to identify medical equipment
Others	Diagnosis-related group (DRG) databases, SNOMED, IUPAC Codes, Arden Syntax, etc.

Table 4–2 Layers of Open Systems Interconnection (OSI) and Other Standard Protocols

OSI Layers	Description	IBM	DEC	TCP/IP
Physical	Immediate network characteristics	Twinax (AS 400)	Twisted pair/MMJ	Twisted pair coaxial
Data link	Node to node transfer of data via access to immediate subnet	Bisync SDLC	DDCMP	Arcnet Starian Asynch
Network	Routing across subnets to deliver data packets	SNA	DNA/LAT	TCP/IP and others
Transport	Data integrity, packaging data for transmission	SNA	DNA/LAT	TCP/IP and others; NetBios
Session	Dialogue management between two end systems	SNA	DNA	TCP/IP and others; NetBios
Presentation	Data encoding	SNA	DNA	NetBios
Application	User interface, e-mail, remote database access, file transfer, document exchange, transaction	Various IBM standards	Various DEC standards	Windows SMTP (TCP) FTP; others

Source: Adapted with permission from M.K. Bourke, *Strategy and Architecture of Health Care Information Systems,* © 1994, Springer-Verlag.

Here, the data comes with different type, categorization, and transaction identities assigned at each functional level. This led to the development of widely used data schema, such as hierarchical, network, and relational data models. Complex data object models have also evolved, which allow users to view data at a high conceptual level.

DATA MODELS

In the previous chapter, it was discussed that the database is structured in a fixed format. Each record type defines a fixed number of fields (attributes), and each field has fixed length. Physical models are used to describe data at the lowest level, whereas record-based logical models are used to describe data at the logical and view levels. In contrast to logical data models, physical models are often hidden from and of little concern to end users. Therefore, our discussion focuses exclusively on record-based logical models. Of these, the hierarchical, network, and relational data models are among the most widely used. For the designer, the use of these models depends chiefly on the user's perspective and interpretation of their organizational structure and processes.

Hierarchical data models are those in which the structures are organized in a top-down or inverted tree-like structure. Health data are stored as nodes in a tree structure, with each node having one "parent" node and perhaps multiple "child" nodes, which may or may not contain health data. For instance, health data about a community health promotion project (CHPP) run by certain staff members from a community hospital may follow this hierarchical model, as shown in Figure 4–1.

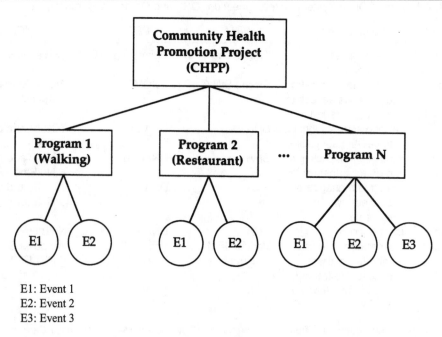

E1: Event 1
E2: Event 2
E3: Event 3

Figure 4–1 An Example of the Hierarchical Model

At the top of the tree of hierarchy is the root segment of an element of the tree that corresponds to the main record type, which in this case is the CHPP. Below the root element is a subordinate level of health data elements, possibly including the walking and restaurant programs, each linked directly to the root. Health data elements at each subsequent (subordinate) level are linked to only one element above, but they may be linked to more than one element below; in our example, the various events of Programs 1 through N. Accordingly, E1 and E2 may refer to the Walkathon event and the Walk-for-Life event of the Walking Program (Program 1).[9] The hierarchical organizational structure is best suited to situations in which the logical relationship between data can be properly represented with the one-to-many approach, that is, where subordinate levels of health data can sufficiently define all relevant attributes of the superior data element. In our case, the CHPP has several programs, which in turn are filled with numerous events. In a hierarchical health database, data are accessed logically (navigated) by going through the appropriate levels of data elements to get to the desired data element. There is usually only one access path to any particular data element.

Network data models are logical extensions of the hierarchical models. Instead of having various levels of one-to-many relationships, the network structure represents a network of "many-to-many" relationships, as shown in Figure 4–2.

Here, the CHPP and the University Health Outreach (UHO) project, for example, may require work from two or more programs: walking, restaurant, smoking cessation, and so on. Although all three of the programs mentioned here are involved in the CHPP project, only the latter two are part of the UHO project. These relationships are indicated by lines joining the responsible programs with the respective projects. In a network health database, there is often more than one navigational path through which a particular health data element can be accessed.

Unfortunately, health databases structured according to either the hierarchical or the network data model suffer from the same deficiency. Once these relationships are established between data elements, it is difficult to modify them (modification/update anomalies) by adding new relationships (addition anomalies) or by removing old ones (deletion anomalies). For these reasons, a third structure for health databases, the relational structure, has gained popularity among database designers and users over the last several years.

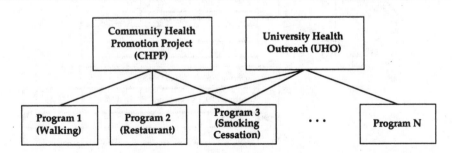

Figure 4–2 An Example of the Network Model

Relational data models are those in which all health data elements are placed in two-dimensional tables that are the logical equivalent of files. The purpose of the relational structure is to describe health data by using a standard tabular format. As long as the tables share at least one common health data element, any health data elements in these tables can be linked and the desired data elements generated in a usable fashion. The health data in the relational model, in most cases, can be linked according to the actual relationship of the various health data elements (i.e., one-to-one, one-to-many or many-to-one, and many-to-many). In the relational tables, each row, called a "tuple," normally represents a record or collection of related facts. The attributes are represented by the columns of these tables, with each attribute able to take on only certain values. The allowable values for these attributes or columns constitute the domain. The domain for a particular attribute indicates what values can be placed in each of the columns of the relationship role. The concept is analogous to a series of vectors.

Figure 4–3 provides an example of how a relational health database may be organized and accessed for the evaluation of the CHPP case. A health program evaluator may, for instance, want to find out the performance of the leader of a particular program (say, the walking program) under the CHPP mentioned previously and the number of events that have been held to date for that program by this supervisor. The evaluator would make an inquiry to the health database, usually through a query facility linked to a database management system (DBMS). A DBMS is essentially a set of programs for accessing and processing the database and its applications. The query facility provides end users with a

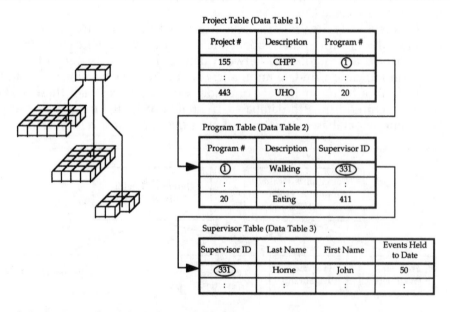

Figure 4–3 An Example of the Relational Model

structured tool for searching and making changes to the database. In this case, the query would start with the project description and search the Project Table (Data Table 1) to find out the appropriate program number, then use the number to search Program Table (Data Table 2) for the project leader's employee identification number. In turn, this identification number would be used to search Supervisor Table (Data Table 3) for the name and other attributes of this supervisor. From here, the evaluator can easily tell that there were 50 events held to date by this supervisor as a response to the inquiry.

NORMALIZATION

Standardization for relations has been achieved through a process known as normalization. A relation, as defined, is a table where all of its cells are single valued with no repeating groups and all entries in any column (attribute) are of the same kind. Data Tables 1, 2, and 3 in Figure 4–3 are all relations. Essentially, normalization converts problematic relations or tables into desirable and well-structured ones: These highly normalized relations are designed to avoid addition, deletion, and update anomalies. This means that the structure of normalized relations is designed to support data integrity, consistency, comparability, and reliability apart from achieving physical and logical data independence; that is, data can be manipulated freely in the database without the need to revise linked application programs.

Although a discussion of the various normal forms is beyond the scope of this chapter, Table 4–3 summarizes five important normal forms and the famous domain/key normal form (DK/NF). Fagin argued that a DK/NF relation has no modification anomalies, and that conversely, any relation having no modification anomalies is a DK/NF relation.[10] In other words, the highest normal form that a relation needs to achieve is DK/NF, and this is a desirable standard data schema for most database designs with very few exceptions.[11]

Despite promises in the standardization of relations and automation of database design, many end users continue to find concepts of normal forms and normalization difficult to grasp. Readers who are interested in further details on data normalization should consult Silberschatz et al.[12] or any other recently published text on database management.

INTERFACED VERSUS INTEGRATED HEALTH MANAGEMENT INFORMATION SYSTEMS

Database normalization supports data schema standards and allows data to be integrated at both the logical and view levels. Theoretically, it appears possible and highly desirable to have a single normalized database that would contain all of the enterprise's data elements to be shared among users of any health provider system. The practical problems, of course, are the need to satisfy prevailing business rules, to ensure flexibility and ease of access, and to overcome the traditional structure dictated by the complex but differing organizational and departmental business processes that have evolved or have been accumulated and established over the years.

Table 4–3 Normal Forms

Normal Forms	Description
1NF	Any relation where all cells of the table are single-valued with no repeating groups and all entries in any column (attribute) are of the same kind
	Data tables 1, 2, and 3 are in 1NF
2NF	Any relation where all nonkey attributes are dependent on all of the keys
	In data table 1 (DT1), if [Project #, Description] → Program #, then key → nonkey attributes
	DT1 is in 2NF
3NF	Any relation in 2NF with no transitive dependencies
	In DT2, if Program # → Supervisor ID and Supervisor ID → Description, then there is transitive dependencies
	To achieve 3NF, either break up DT2 into two separate tables or move "Description" to DT3, thereby reducing DT2 to 3NF
Boyce-Codd Normal Form (BCNF)	Every determinant is a candidate key In DT2, if Supervisor ID → Description, then Supervisor ID is a determinant but *not* a candidate key
	By breaking DT2 into two tables or moving "Description" to DT3, BCNF is achieved, either with Supervisor ID as a candidate key or a nondeterminant
4NF	Any relation in BCNF and no multivalued dependencies
	Multivalued dependencies are only possible when we expand DT2 to the form Program # →→ Description, Activity Events, such as Program #1 →→ Walking, Event; #1 Walking, Event #2
Domain/Key Normal Form (DK/NF)	Every constraint on the relation is a logical outcome of keys and domains In DT3, if Key (Supervisor ID, Last Name, First Name) → Events held and Events held to date are not negative, then it is in DK/NF

To address these challenges, complex semantic object models and "standard" business applications software such as enterprise resource planning (ERP), supply chain management (SCM), or customer relationship management (CRM) systems have been developed in recent years to support the semantic processing of these increasingly complex rules and established procedures of traditional organization work structure (i.e., business processes).

Complex semantic object models use a collection of semantic objects, including composite objects, compound objects, hybrid objects, association objects, parent/subtype objects, and archetype/version objects to structure the databases.[13] Briefly, an object contains values stored in instance variables within the objects. It also contains bodies of codes, called methods or messages, that operate on the object. The only way one object can access the data of another object is by invoking a method or message of that other object. Taylor identifies three mechanisms that are key to understanding object technology, as summarized in Table 4–4.[14] Software can be assembled out of basic objects, which com-

Table 4–4 Three Key Mechanisms in Object-Oriented Analysis and Design

Mechanisms	Major Concepts
1. Object	Objects corresponded to real-world objects; they may be tangible things, roles played by an individual, incidents, interactions, or specifications.
2. Message	The vehicles through which objects communicate with each other in order to carry out real-world operations.
3. Class	Objects share common characteristics and responses; classes may have multiple levels arranged in a hierarchical fashion; embodied in the definition of "class" is the concept of "inheritance."

bine related data and processes. As noted, these objects correspond to real-world objects, but they may be tangible things (bed, computer); roles played by an individual (patients, nurses); incidents (recovery, heart attack); interactions, such as object relations (membership, assignment); and specifications (patient type, physician specialty). Messages are the vehicles through which objects communicate in order to carry out real-world operations. Objects, depending on their function, are of many different types, but they share common characteristics and responses, called classes. One class, for example, might be outpatient records. All outpatient objects, such as admission and discharge records and test results, would constitute the outpatient record class. Classes may consist of multiple levels in a hierarchical fashion or in a network schema. Embodied in the definition of "class" is the concept of "inheritance." For example, if a new object is introduced into a given hierarchy, it automatically inherits all the attributes of its predecessors and may in fact generate new characteristics for the objects that come after it in the hierarchy.

Two types of tools are commonly used in representing object-oriented design.

1. the information structure diagram (ISD)
2. the state transition diagram (STD)

The ISD outlines how the objects within a class are related to each other. In the ISD, a block represents an object with attributes, and a line with arrows shows the relationship between objects and the inheritance properties. Figure 4–4 illustrates the use of an ISD to show patient–physician interactions in a hospital setting.

Whereas the ISD describes the object in relation to other objects, the STD describes the possible states that a single object can take. In the STD, a block represents one state of the object, with each block indicating actions that the object can perform, and arrows show the transition events triggered by an action. Figure 4–5 provides an example of an STD.

Object-oriented applications are developed in layers.[15] Usually, the bottom layer consists of standard classes that are the standard, reusable components. The middle layer comprises the working, reusable models of the organization that can be utilized by numerous applications. These business models may include inventory control, billing, and admission/discharge records. The

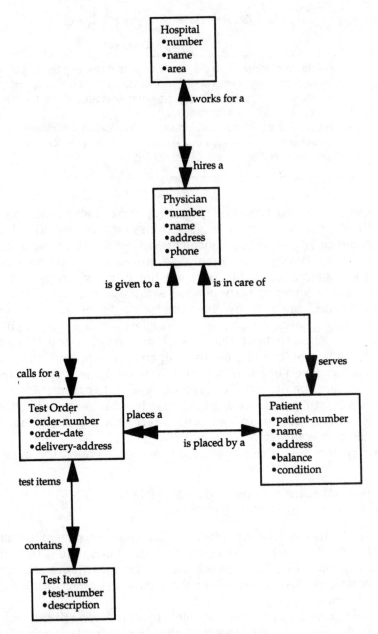

Figure 4–4 An Example of an Information Structure Diagram

advantage to having this intermediate layer is that many different applications can be built using the same basic design. This layered approach also offers increased stability because if change is necessary in one area, it can be carried out with a single "model." The whole system does not have to be re-designed, as the whole system is not tightly coupled. The top and final layer is made up

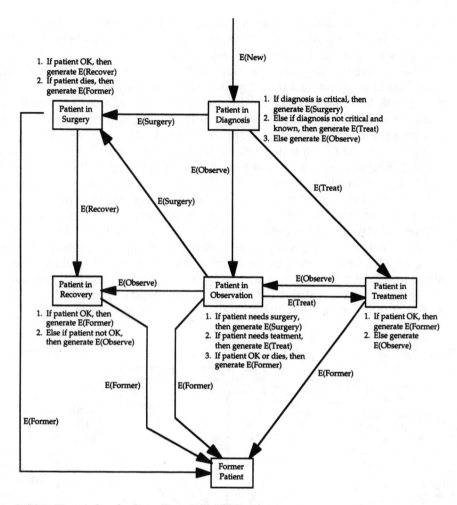

Figure 4–5 An Example of a State Transition Diagram

of workable applications that solve real problems. Thus, object applications can simply be generated by using existing working models. The overall advantage of object-orientation is the relatively fast assembly of new applications.

In general, the transformation of defined semantic objects into relations depends largely on the type of object to be represented; for instance, some objects require at least two or more relations for their representation. As the definitions of these complex objects usually separate semantic themes into group attributes, DK/NF normalization is more or less achieved automatically. In this sense, object-orientation increases productivity and reduces cost in a number of ways, including the apparent advantages of reusability, flexibility, and reliability of objects. Furthermore, because objects possess the characteristics of inheritance, maintenance requirements are also reduced. Changes that need to be made in the entire system are only carried out once, because inheritance affects the total system. These advantages make complex object data models a very attractive choice for integrated HMIS design and development. It is highly advantageous to use these models for representing the IDS work processes in fulfilling its enterprise data requirements.

Alternatively, ERP software can be used to integrate existing business processes in an organization to facilitate data integration. ERP implementation for an IDS essentially connects the different pieces of existing HMIS applications to fit into the ERP centerpiece software. Operational practices within health care organizations and subcomponents are diverse and sometimes unique. Software development has to be done on a project-by-project basis, as the service processes are not standardized. Developing software or even customizing and implementing some off-the-shelf packages is thus a lengthy and difficult venture. In this sense, the information architecture that can be achieved through integrating core business processes and requirements will be limited, complex, and expensive. Figure 4–6 shows how the ERP replaces the existing islands of HMISs for an IDS with a resulting centerpiece ERP application, which allows sharing of core administrative data. This architecture is classified simply as one of interfaced HMISs. This is because the ERP approach does not generate a centralized CPR or focus on standardizing service processes. Much of the specialized clinical data sets are still maintained separately by the

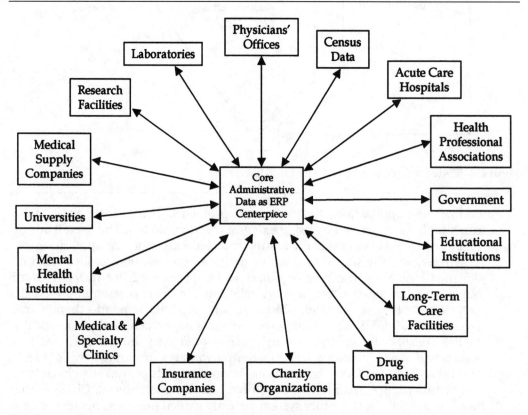

Figure 4–6 The Enterprise Resource Planning Approach

isolated clinical-based HMISs and searching for the patient potassium level will still be a problem in the Brigham example.

Currently, ERP systems are marketed as profoundly complex software requiring large investments of money, time, and expertise to be successful. If the entire organization is not sold on the philosophy of change accompanied by the use of ERP applications, unintended and highly disruptive consequences may result. Supply chain management (SCM) and customer relationship management (CRM) are applications that are only implemented after successful ERP core implementation because these are meant to enhance the electronic networking of the IDS with its entire supply chain and customer relations. Existing ERP packages include SAP, R/3, Baan, Peoplesoft, and Oracle.[16]

Past and current efforts on data coding, data schema, and data exchange standards are critical for an IDS to achieve meaningful and integrated data capture, storage, processing, and distribution. These efforts, coupled with the best database design methods (e.g., semantic object models) or the best software practices (e.g., ERP agents), can result primarily in the development of interfaced HMISs, not integrated HMISs. Unless we can also achieve normalization and standardization in the way we conduct our health care business, it would be difficult, if not impossible, to develop an integrated HMIS for an IDS. Such an integrated architecture could, in fact, be implemented in different ways, including a single, centralized client-server data warehouse[17]; a distributed, partitioned data marts maintained by affiliated organizations within the IDS[18]; or even a distributed, partitioned, partially replicated alternative with concurrency use and synchronous update control.[19] Figure 4–7 provides visual representations of these integrated HMIS alternatives.

For the rest of this chapter, the service process model as an alternative to managing the explosion of health care data and information efficiently and effectively for an IDS is discussed. The standardization of the service process across and among IDS entities will produce the integrated HMIS. With globalization, the pressure for standardizing information and normalizing health services processes across multi-providers in different countries and organizations with operational differences will be a real HMIS breakthrough, despite its many challenges.

THE SERVICE PROCESS MODEL

The service process model proposes building HMISs core applications as service process components, not as business process components. All business processes can be derivatives of a service process. Service processes of some industries have been standardized more than the others, for example, banking, airlines, and cargo operations. In addition, many industries have been massively computerized, and health provider organizations can learn from the experiences gained in computerizing these industries.

All organizations, including health care organizations, provide services. The service process is a common link between organizations, subsets of organizations, and various people who work for these organizations. To aid our understanding, the hierarchical structure is used to describe service objects. At

(a) Single centralized client-server data warehouse (DW) architecture

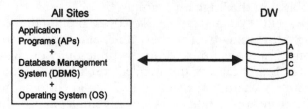

(b) Distributed, partitioned, non-replicated data marts (DMs)

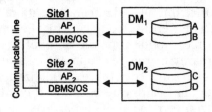

(c) Distributed, partitioned, partially replicated databases (DBs)

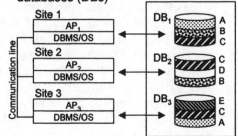

Figure 4–7 Various Data Warehouse (DW), Data Mart (DM), and Database (DB) Configurations

the root of this hierarchy is, for example, an IDS having affiliated organizations, departments, divisions, and individuals or variations of this structure. Personal identity (PID) is used to refer to an individual uniquely. When an individual becomes part of a unit (organization, department, division, and so on), he or she acquires the unit identity (logical identity—LID). Every individual in a unit must therefore have only one unique LID pertaining to that unit. A PID may be associated with several LIDs; in other words, an individual can be a part of (or acts on behalf of) several units. Unit transaction must be done by LID, not PID. A joint LID (set), representing a group of LIDs (subsets), will have its own name. A simple analogy here may be associating the joint LID to a high-level "folder" (set), LID to subset "folders," and PID to "files" in a directory structure.

All service processes have three common basic elements: a customer, a service that is provided, and a provider. Information pertaining to these elements is maintained in the master tables. Customer and provider masters are records of PID, LID, or both. A LID or a PID can be a provider or a customer depending on the service level that is executed. Because of space limitation, generic structures of these service masters are posted onto a Web site.[20]

Level and Type of Services

Service processes are simple and very consistent; in general, services can be classified into three levels, each having six major types. Uniformity in service processes cuts short the customization and implementation time for integrated HMIS applications.

Service transactions occur at three levels within a unit:

1. external services (level 1)
2. internal services (level 2)
3. procured services (level 3)

External services are services provided by the units or persons to external units or persons. Internal services are services provided within the unit by one LID to another LID. Note that at this level, there can be PID transaction. Procured services are services procured by units or persons from external units or persons.

Within each of these three service levels, service processes of (or for) units or individuals can be classified as consultative, procedural, material (consumable), facility (use of hard or soft asset), monetary, or information (maintenance). In our model, consultative services involve logical interactions between customers and providers; for example, services provided by doctors, management consultants, and clinical specialists. Procedural services involve physical interactions between customers and providers. This type of service may also involve the use of equipment, for example, a hard or soft instrument. Material services transfer the ownership of hardware or software from providers to customers. These services will result in debits or credits to material accounts of providers and customers. Facility services involve blocking and releasing of assets used. In this case, the service providers typically limit the use of their hardware or software to the customers. Examples are use of hospital beds (hard assets) or Internet services (soft assets) via an Internet service provider. Monetary services are either independent or reciprocal to other types of services. For example, money is transferred from customers to providers by various negotiable instruments, resulting in debits and credits to monetary accounts of customers and providers respectively. Information services involve mere master updating transactions. The customer, provider, and service masters are results of such service transactions and the structure of these service masters will depend on the type of the service provided. IDSs can easily customize the layout of these service masters depending on their needs and information requirements.

Common Service Processes

Services of all types within each level are processed with multiple steps. At least four of these steps are common to most service processes: request for service, acknowledgment of request, service delivery, and confirmation of service delivery. Figure 4–8 shows how these steps can be sequenced and analyzed along a value-added chain resulting in a service outcome. Services can sometimes be processed with a single step (vending), or multiple steps can be merged into a single step. It is also possible for these steps to take place all at the same time.

First, a service process is initiated through a request for service. Numerous forms have been used in the manual process for making requests (e.g., drug

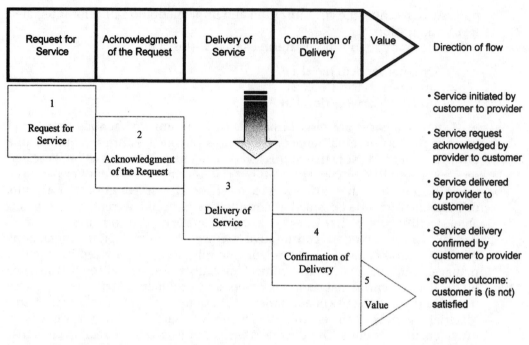

Figure 4–8 Service Steps along a Value-Chain

prescriptions and test orders). Apart from other attributes, these service request forms commonly identify the customer, the service to be provided, and the provider; that is, the basic elements of the service process. The manual forms necessitated a docket number (header) and a detailed type of reference system, which are not necessary in our standardized model. Abolishing this concept of header and details will require a change of the old mindset for many health professionals. This also means abolishing the names used for identifying all the different request forms. In the integrated, computerized model, each record will consist only of one customer, one deliverable item of service, and one provider.

In general, a request may be generated one at a time. Group requests could be made for several services grouped together. In the model, request for a higher group generates requests for the lowest details of the lowest group. Moreover, requests could be scheduled with a start time, end time, and follow-up periods. Request for a particular service may also be automatically generated at a predefined step in the service process of another. A request may serve a group of customers and may include a group of providers at the same time. Such request generation may be activated through a built-in logic to be triggered by a change in certain fields. For example, a purchase request for an item can be generated automatically when the reorder level is reached. In an integrated environment, this type of request is unnecessary, as the provider who is sharing the data will supply the item with an automated built-in request. What has a reorder level would now become a supply level. As shown in Figure 4–9,

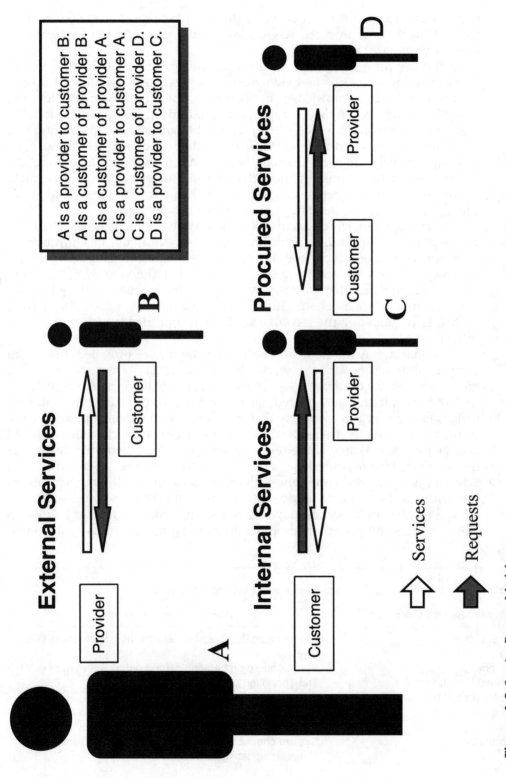

Figure 4-9 Service Process Model

requests and services flow in opposite direction between the various request levels. External and procured services are usually accompanied by reciprocal monetary transactions.

Following the service request, the acknowledgment screen of the service provider is updated with the new request. The next step, therefore, is for the service provider to acknowledge the request by some preliminary action. For example, in the case of a laboratory test request arising within a hospital, the phlebotomist will have to collect the required blood sample. In the case of a machinery breakdown, the request is made to the service engineer to carry out preliminary inspection of the equipment. As shown in Table 4–5, the "acknowledgment actions" of the different requests are noted on the system by the provider. The system also notes the user identity of the person acknowledging the request and the date and time of acknowledgment.

In the third step, which occurs after the acknowledgment is registered, the person actually responsible for delivering the service is notified through an automatic update of this person's list of pending actions. In all types of service processes, the services are delivered manually, but the records of "delivery actions" are updated electronically by the providers or subsequently by individuals acting on their behalf. This is shown in Table 4–6. Again, the identity of the person updating the records and the date and time is picked up by the system.

The final step is the need for confirming the service provided, that is, an acceptance or approval of the service by the customer. As noted, all services have outcomes; for example, a service may or may not be completed satisfactorily. The consultative and procedural services may have outcome values for various parameters as recorded by their providers. An outcome may also be the identity of another service request. As well, a service may be cancelled or rolled back at any stage. Hence, if the service is accepted, the system merely updates the acknowledgment; otherwise, a feedback occurs and the "chain" of service activities is repeated accordingly. Following the service delivery, the transaction data is archived into a service data archival table or the service database.

It is possible that services may be grouped and ordered together by a group name. A hierarchy pattern of multiple levels of groups will thus enable rapid

---

Table 4–5 Types of Service Processes and Acknowledgment Actions

Type of Service Processes	Acknowledgment Actions
Consultative	Confirmation that the provider and the customer are both ready
Procedural	Preprocedure preparation carried out by the system
Material (consumable)	Transportation of material
Facility (use of hard or soft asset)	Reservation/allotment of facility
Monetary	System checks to ensure that the service is deliverable and instruments are acceptable
Information	System checks to ensure that all information required for master updating is available

Table 4–6 Types of Service Processes and Delivery Actions

Type of Service Processes	Delivery Actions
Consultative	Recording the outcome parameters
Procedural	Recording the procedure outcomes
Material (consumable)	Transfer of ownership of material to the customer; stock records update
Facility (use of hard or soft asset)	Physical occupation of the facility
Monetary	Transfer of money to the customer; financial records update
Information	Master update

ordering of related services. For instance, the standard protocols of patient examination and treatment of related illness, or the steps of such procedures, can be considered as a group consisting of a number of services, which have outcomes. An in-built algorithm may further guide the expansion of groups into individual services. Moreover, when any service is requested at the higher level, transaction records can be automatically generated for the lowest measurable or identifiable component or parameter level. It is also possible to program a built-in logic to check if subset transactions are not occurring as part of the higher set to which these belong. Take the example of a patient consultation service. A physician consultation service would consist of medical history, physical examination, and advice consisting of investigations followed by treatment. When the service is being delivered, data entry screens for recording parameters can be made available to the consulting physician to record these observations, as shown in Table 4–7.

CONCLUSION

Only the general key features of the service process model have been presented, and discussions on service process tables, various associated service masters, the service database, various transaction updates, and queries (master queries, service process queries, and database queries) have been deferred because of space limitation. The reader should, however, already have a sense of the benefits of standardizing beyond data codes, data schema, and data exchange formats to a service process level. Standardization of all these levels, if pursued appropriately and relentlessly, holds great potential for reduced costs and complexity, greater security control, and better data management within an integrated HMIS environment for an IDS.

Table 4–7 Profiles of a Physician Consultative Service

Package	Profile	Test	Parameter	Value	Unit
Physical examination	General physical	Height		140	cm
		Weight		50	kg
		Blood pressure	Systolic	120	mmHg
		Blood pressure	Diastolic	80	mmHg

In closing, some pointers toward achieving HMIS integration in an IDS context are provided. The first significant move, as has been emphasized, is the adoption of relevant data standards. These standards play a key role in allowing organizations to integrate data: Data coding standards support meaningful sharing and exchange of data; data exchange standards allow packages of data to be predictably and securely transported across networks; and data schema standards evolve normalized database designs, thereby ensuring data integrity, consistency, and comparability while eliminating addition, deletion, and modification anomalies.

For such inter-organization linkages to succeed, Sprague and McNurlin note that all linked programs and processes should be expandable to other links in the future whether these are at community, regional, state, national, or international levels.[21] This can only be possible if data standards are upheld and stakeholders and users are educated about the significance of the standardization process. In an IDS context, the more technological advanced partners will have to pull the others along through education or some other means. Standardization requires the cooperating organizations to be involved in the ongoing development of standards. Government agencies, regulators, and third parties are often also involved. Standards task forces can be formed to operate as electronic intermediaries to facilitate the flow of information. In hammering out consensus among stakeholders involved in a standardization process, a change in one of the cooperating systems often must be coordinated with all others.[22]

The next most significant move must go beyond focusing on data standards and shift focus to a "service process" view of the way we do health care business. For an IDS, this essentially means that the service processes of the IDS have to guide the design of the core HMIS applications. Accordingly, Gates observes that:

> A business has the equivalent of autonomic processes. . . . One [such] autonomic process in business is the function that defines the company's reason for its being—its manufacturing process, for example. This function has to be as efficient and reliable as the beating of a heart. A second kind of autonomic process in business is administrative—the process of receiving payments and paying bills and paychecks, for instance. The administrative processes are as essential to a business as breathing.[23]

For IDSs, the caring (manufacturing) process is the core service process. Each person or medical equipment along the continuum of care (assembly line) acts as a customer or a provider. The administrative processes are the business processes, which can be the "value detractors" for health service providers. Imagine the number of forms and the amount of paperwork that has to be completed for a patient for a 2-day stay at a hospital. For every provider in the service process, there are many others standing behind the lines managing business processes. Hiebeler et al. note that, although businesses adopt different practices to deliver customer services, the service processes are essentially the same.[24] One company may be designing, building, and evaluating prototypes, while another may be focused on refining existing merchandise. However, both of these companies are addressing the same service process; that is, the design of products and services. The service process view cuts across internal functional boundaries and allows managers to view their companies as a whole, without the impediments of divisions and job titles or particular products. It enables them to map each process, examining each step along the way and targeting precisely where improvements can be made. In this way, each functional manager becomes accountable for the steps of the service process under his or her control rather than being accountable for forms and documentation (i.e., business processes).

Another significant consideration is to avoid posting data separately, thereby eliminating the proliferation of islands of HMISs. Posting is the essence of manual operations. In an integrated environment, all that is needed is a "view." For instance, a patient's bill and reimbursement filing forms are just different views of the same order data. In this regard, Duncan et al. observe that the integration of intra-organizational processes can significantly affect strategic management.[25] For example, linked inventory control can be updated at any time a drug, special diet, medical device, or other item is ordered, and the cost of the item added electronically to the patient's bill and reimbursement filing forms, thereby improving efficiency and reducing costs. Extending this linkage externally, the process of reordering items from designated suppliers to keep sufficient safety stock on hand can also be automated. Indeed, suppliers can be linked to customers to process orders electronically, third-party payers can be linked to health providers for billing and reimbursement procedures, government regulators can be linked to providers for documentation, and researchers can be linked to all of the various stakeholders for the purpose of conducting studies. Related to separate data posting is that of reducing, or possibly eliminating, all paper-based forms for which health care services are especially vulnerable. If all transactions between customers and providers can be captured online and directly as is the chief purpose of taking a service process approach, then all the troubles of manual follow up that may be needed would be avoided.

Finally, there is the need to provide appropriate information to the user at each step of the service process. The integrated HMIS must provide adequate information pertaining to the service. In an integrated environment, the providers will expect to have rapid access to the information requested by the customers. For most health organizations, when customers need answers to important service or product questions, their front offices typically have to scramble behind the scenes to get answers. Yamanouchi Pharmaceuticals, with sales at $3.9 billion, is the third largest pharmaceutical company in Japan. It has made information systems the key component in improving the timeliness and quality of answers to customer's tough questions. Product support personnel at Yamanouchi can immediately answer half the questions that come in from the doctors or pharmacists. To find answers to more difficult questions, they have access to Yamanouchi's Web-based Product Information Center Supporting System (PRINCESS). In contrast, no person in local hospitals is often able to answer many of the questions pertaining to the services provided.

Administrators of health care organizations can only serve with a smile if their employees and subordinates also have answers to frequently asked questions. When a doctor is ordering a drug for a patient, drug information must be displayed. Database tables in our service process model are shareable in a secured way. Moreover, databases of different functional departments or even different organizations can be merged and queried instantly if designed according to the service process model, thereby providing the information that is needed at the point of request.

The goal for single data entry points for enterprise data modeling is becoming more realizable with greater standardization efforts. When standardization goes beyond the basic data levels to a service process level, invoices and paper-based orders can be eliminated, and payments or services made without the need of a paper trail. Often, the major issues are not technical, but process reconceptualization and educational issues. Overcoming these issues is key to making intra- and inter-organizational systems work.

CHAPTER QUESTIONS

1. What are data standards? Discuss the usefulness of these standards to implementing the service process model discussed in the chapter. (Think, for example, what the purpose of a unique customer identity [PID] would be and who should share this information.)
2. How should one go about standardizing service nomenclature, for example, the service names and outcomes in the service process model?
3. The Complete Reference observes: "The economic justification for codes vanished years ago. Computers are now fast enough and cheap enough to accommodate the humans, and work in human languages with words that humans understand. It is high time that they did so. Yet, without really thinking through the justifications, developers and designers continue to use codes willy-nilly, as if it were still 1969. . . . There is an immediate additional benefit: key entry errors drop to zero because the users get immediate feedback, in English, of the business information they are entering. Digits aren't transposed, codes aren't remembered, and in financial applications, money rarely is lost in suspense accounts due to entry errors, with very significant savings." Comment on the above.
4. How can the service process model be extended to include mergers or acquisitions of organizations in terms of the amalgamation of various tables and masters?
5. Discuss the application of the service process model to the development of next generation CPR.

NOTES

1. S. Wallace, "Computerized Patient Record" Byte, May 1994 (http://www.byte.com/art/9405/sec6/art4.htm).

2. MUMPS was originally developed in the late 1960s and early 1970s for minicomputer systems at Massachusetts General Hospital, and it still has a strong presence in health care, as well as engineering and scientific markets.

3. Kunitz and Associates, Inc., Interim Report on Data Sources for Ambulatory Care Effectiveness Research: Descriptions of Selected Automated Ambulatory Medical Records Systems, February 5, 1992.

4. GAO Report, Standards for Automated Medical Records. (GAO/IMTEC-93–17, April 30, 1993).

5. The ICD9-CM is a standardized system of codes describing diagnoses developed and maintained by the World Health Organization (WHO).

6. Physicians' Current Procedural Terminology (CPT) is a coding system established in 1966 by the American Medical Association to provide a uniform language to accurately describe medical, surgical, and diagnostic services. Each procedure or service is identified with a 5-digit code. For details on other codes, refer to Table 4–1.

7. Detailed descriptions of ICD10 codes and many other coding schemes can be found in various Web sites or from links to the Duke University Medical Center site (www.mcis.duke.edu).

8. M.K. Bourke, *Strategy and Architecture of Health Care Information Systems* (New York, NY: Springer-Verlag, 1994).

9. The MCHPP project is used here to illustrate the various data models and to provide a conceptual link to related discussions in previous chapters.

10. R. Fagin, A Normal Form for Relational Databases That Is Based on Domains and Keys. *ACM Transactions on Database Systems* (September 1981): 387–415.

11. D.M. Kroenke, *Database Processing: Fundamentals, Design and Implementation*. 6th ed. (Upper Saddle River, NJ: Prentice-Hall, 1998).

12. A. Silberschatz, et al., *Database System Concepts*. 3rd ed. (New York: McGraw Hill, 1997).

13. D.M. Kroenke, *Database Processing*.

14. D. Taylor, *Object-Oriented Information Systems: Planning and Implementation* (New York: John Wiley & Sons, 1992).

15. Ibid.

16. G. Koch and K. Loney, *Oracle: The Complete Reference* (New York: McGraw Hill, 1996), 26–27.

17. V. Poe, Building a Data Warehouse for Decision Support (Upper Saddle River, NJ: Prentice-Hall, 1996).

18. E. Turban and J.E. Aronson, *Decision Support Systems and Intelligent Systems*. 5th ed. (Upper Saddle River, NJ: Prentice-Hall, 1998).

19. D.M. Kroenke, *Database Processing*.

20. Web site posting of service masters: http://education.vsnl.com/service_process/tables.

21. R. Sprague, Jr. and B.C. McNurlin, *Information Systems in Practice,* 3rd ed. (Englewood Cliffs, NJ: Prentice-Hall, 1993), 94–96.

22. One of the authors of this chapter is a member of the British Columbia Information Standards Council and has observed the difficulty and slow process to reach consensus among stakeholders involved in a standardization proposal.

23. W. Gates, *Business at the Speed of Thought* (London, UK: Penguin, 1999), 281.

24. R. Hiebeler, et al., *Best Practices* (London, UK: Simon & Schuster Business Books UK Ltd., 1998).

25. W.J. Duncan, et al., *Strategic Management of Health Care Organizations* (Oxford, UK: Blackwell Business Publications, 1996).

Chapter 5

Systems Development Methodologies: Building Information Architecture for Integrated Delivery Systems

Joseph K. H. Tan

SCENARIO

The federal government, through the Science Council of Canada, recently funded a number of sites to develop community health programs for neighborhood residents. Each site was equipped first with a Macintosh computer and a small office run by a full-time program coordinator. The council requires that the site coordinators report to the community supervisor and the medical health officer (MHO) of the region for which the community was funded. Residents of these communities interact with their program coordinators as volunteers and as participants in community health awareness programs. The council also funds a team of evaluators, who are affiliated with certain university research groups, to provide technical assistance to the various community sites and to conduct independent reviews of the various community health demonstration programs.

Imagine that you are the site coordinator for one of these communities. Apart from setting up various community health programs and managing the daily chores of tracking levels of community participation in various programs, you must also try to mobilize community support and delegate responsibilities to task forces for the different programs. Through the collaborative efforts of the community supervisor, the MHO, and, most importantly, the task forces, whose memberships mainly comprise volunteers drawn from various stakeholder groups in your community, you are able to initiate a number of healthy lifestyle programs. You are expected to report the latest developments on each of these programs during scheduled meetings and to perform your daily office routine efficiently and effectively.

Realizing the power of automation in achieving greater efficiency and effectiveness, you decide to get help from the evaluation team by asking for the design and implementation of Macintosh-based software that would track, on a real-time basis, the various pieces of information from each of the three programs currently being suggested: (1) the walking program, (2) the restaurant program, and (3) the worksite program. Because these are new programs and you are still uncertain about the response of the community at large to these planned activities, you find it difficult to give an accurate description of the process. To make matters worse, you would like to design the system yourself even though you have only taken one introductory health information system course during your training as a health administrator. You therefore realize that you would need a great deal of technical assistance from the analyst, but it is your strong belief that if you do not champion the system design and software development efforts, you may not be using the resulting system after all. In this case, you may have to rely heavily on your current manual filing system, which is proving to be inadequate in helping you carry out your various responsibilities.

In your first interaction with the analyst from the evaluation team, who is assigned to assist you with the technical details involved in designing and developing the community information system (CIS) product you want, both of you arrive at a rich picture following a general analysis of the situation for which the CIS is to be used. This rich picture is the same one as that shown in Figure 2–1 (see Chapter 2). You and the analyst then proceed to design the main menu and the organization of several possible screen layouts. Figure 5–1 shows the structure of the main menu with its interface to the various subsystem menus for your community site, which is designated as Site A by the evaluation team.

While helping you to think about how you could specify your information requirements and how these requirements might be translated into a well-structured data model, your analyst comes up with a rough entity-relationship (E-R) model. This E-R model is the same one as in Figure 3–9 (see Chapter 3). You then proceed with the analyst to design the user interface for the "main and new event" screen as well as the "new participant" screen for your community. The resulting screen displays are shown in Figures 5–2 and 5–3.

In designing these interfaces, you feel that the earlier step of trying to list the information you wanted has helped you and your analyst greatly in determining what data elements should be appearing in the respective data entry screens (views). The process has also helped to clarify the data elements to be captured in the CIS. You now realize that it is possible to generate reports by

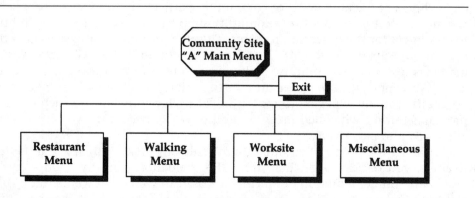

Figure 5–1 Main Menu Subsystem for Multi-Community Health Promotion Project: Community Site "A"

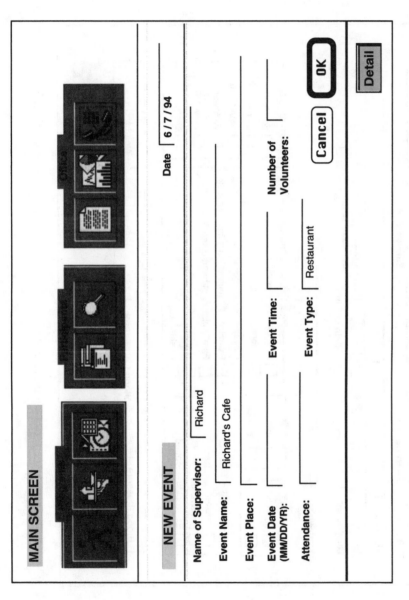

Figure 5–2 The Main and New Event Screens for Community Site "A." Courtesy of Microsoft Corporation, Redmond, Washington.

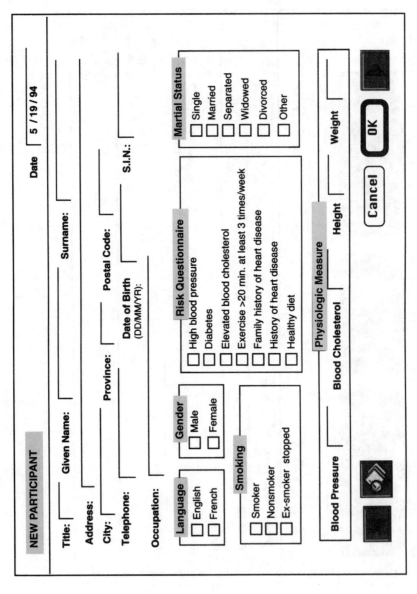

Figure 5–3 The New Participant Screen for Community Site "A." Courtesy of Microsoft Corporation, Redmond, Washington.

combining and statistically manipulating the different data elements that are entered into the CIS. Think about the kind of aggregate information you may want from the data that will be captured in the CIS to help you structure your reports on the latest developments of the different programs.

At this point, you are informed by members of one of the task forces that two of the participating volunteers would be able to spare some time to help you with computer work if you are able and willing to train them. Essentially, this would mean that the CIS must be developed to be used by these volunteers, who may have even less knowledge of computerized systems than you. Your analyst also informs you that you have the choice of customizing an off-the-shelf application to fit your needs or pursue a self-developed CIS. Contemplate how you would go about making an informed choice about this and what additional information you might want in order to manage the process of this CIS development and implementation. Remember also that you only have a very limited budget and timeline to complete the CIS project.

INTRODUCTION

In this chapter, we discuss various methodologies designed to minimize the problems of uncoordinated HMIS developmental efforts. Each methodology is based on a philosophical view, which can range from a complete focus on the humanistic side to the technical aspects of HMIS development. Some traditional methodologies emphasized systems analysis (SA), whereas others focused on systems design (SD) phases of the systems developmental life cycle (SDLC). Briefly, SA involves activities related to reviewing current information architecture and the organizational environment, whereas SD encompasses activities related to specifying new information architecture and systems requirements. More recently, contemporary models, including computer-aided software engineering (CASE) tools and Multiview, attempt to take a contingency approach, thereby providing a framework for managing SA and SD phases contingent on changes in the organizational environment.

Beyond SA and SD phases is systems implementation. Systems implementation involves the selection and inauguration of new system architecture and applications, which is the subject of an entire chapter of its own (see Chapter 11). A key phenomena in the evolution of systems development methodologies (SDMs), however, is end-user computing (EUC), which focuses on the significance of the "end user aspects" of the system development process. This chapter closes with some thoughts and recommendations on EUC.

SYSTEMS DEVELOPMENT METHODOLOGIES

Early computer applications were typically designed without adequate planning. As HMIS evolved, the need for a "methodology" became increasingly necessary. Consequently, numerous SDMs have emerged.

An SDM is a systematic approach to HMIS planning, analysis, and design.[1] A methodology is a collection of procedures, techniques, tools, and documen-

tation aids to help HMIS developers in their efforts to implement a new information architecture and system. It therefore provides a framework (consisting
of phases and subphases) that guides the developers in their choice of appropriate techniques at each stage of a project. A technique is a way of performing
a particular activity in the system development process. Widely used techniques include rich pictures, E-R modeling, normalization, data flow diagrams
(DFDs), decision trees, decision tables, structured English, action diagrams, and
the entity life cycle, several of which have already been discussed in earlier
chapters. Each technique may involve using one or more tools.[2] Examples of
tools include database management systems, query facility, data dictionaries,
fourth generation languages (4GL), methodology workbenches, project management tools, and expert systems. The phases and subphases of an SDM also
help the developers to plan, manage, control, and evaluate their HMIS projects. As an example to illustrate these concepts, imagine running a general
business election meeting. To do this, one can follow an agenda (methodology) to guide the progress of the meeting. One technique used in making decisions during the meeting may be "voting," which might entail the use of a certain "tool," such as the use of a ballot card for each member to ensure
equitable representation based on the principle of "one member one vote."

Making use of a methodology will lessen the risk of wasting resources during the course of systems development. Holloway notes that SDMs increase the
productivity of the development staff by providing a standard framework (to
avoid reinventing the wheel for each HMIS project), the right tools (to assist
successful completion of each stage of development task), effective review procedures (to identify errors and inconsistencies early), and a productivity aid (to
reduce the amount of development documentation).[3] A good SDM not only
allows health management to review the progress of an HMIS project, but also
permits the developer to identify accurately the user needs. Effective SDMs
make HMIS project planning easier by allowing both designers and users to
plan, correct, and replan the project as it progresses.

More generally, the benefits of employing a well-tested SDM include user
satisfaction, the meeting of management needs, timely development, the
avoidance of systems implementation deficiencies, and the appropriate provision of maintenance and support activities. The methodologies described in
this chapter can be evaluated on these criteria or standards.

SYSTEMS DEVELOPMENT LIFE CYCLE–BASED METHODOLOGIES

During the late 1970s, the Waterfall model was proposed as a formal
approach to systems development. It was a first generation SDM, embodying
the SDLC concept. The SDLC concept was highly regarded among health systems analysts as a way to provide much more control over SA and SD processes
than was previously possible. This model consists of six steps.

1. feasibility study
2. systems investigation
3. SA

4. SD
5. systems implementation
6. systems maintenance and review

Essentially, the life cycle concept dictates that whenever a systems review indicates that the current system is no longer adequate, a new feasibility study is then initiated for the new system, as shown in Figure 5–4.

The Waterfall model was a landmark achievement and included all the attributes expected of a methodology—a philosophy (systemic approach will lead to reduced costs and gains in productivity), a series of steps (from the feasibility study to system maintenance), a series of techniques (e.g., ways to evaluate the costs and benefits solutions), and a series of tools. Although this conventional methodology was a definite improvement, it was frequently criticized; for example, it failed to meet the needs and expectations of end users because they were not involved in the development process. Incomplete systems and large application backlogs resulted from the lack of emphasis on front-end planning. Ignoring the SA process gave rise to inflexible and overly ambitious SDs. Revisions were also not easily accommodated during the SD process. This traditional methodology involved heavy maintenance workload and was laden with problems of documentation.

The next generation SDMs integrated basic techniques and tools to create more complete specifications for the systems designer. Table 5–1 summarizes three of these SDMs: accurately defined systems (ADSs), business information analysis and integration technique (BIAIT), and business systems plan (BSP).

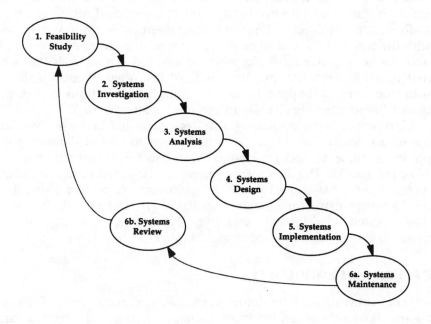

Figure 5–4 The Waterfall Model

Table 5–1 Traditional Methodologies Based on System Development Life Cycle (Second Generation Development Models)

Methods	Major Concepts
Accurately defined systems (ADSs)	Represents system inputs, outputs, processes, procedures, and files; also includes cross-referencing structures to ensure consistency.
Business information analysis and integration technique (BIAIT)	Creates a grid based on seven closed-ended binary questions to aid analysts in systems planning and future analysis.
Business systems planning (BSP)	Similar to SDLC model except that it has a two-level design stage theme and a new emphasis on strategic planning.

Many of these early methodologies, which are classified as SDLC-based methodologies, focus on the planning involved in developing HMISs that will meet the objectives of the health organization.

An ADS comprises an integrated systems representation of systems inputs, outputs, processes, procedures, and files.[4] The analysis package also includes cross-referencing structures, which ensure consistency across the sets of documents produced. Some aspects of ADSs may now be automated to assist in the development process. BIAIT addresses top management requirements by using a set of seven close-ended binary questions to generate a model that aids the analyst in determining an organization's information requirements.[5] The resulting profile is a grid (matrix) of possible responses classifying existing "order-supplier" relations and identifying the data owners and users. This matrix is then used for effective systems planning and future analysis. A BSP addresses the requirements of top management by aligning systems planning with the organization's strategic plan. Three principles are observed in BSP: the need for an organization-wide perspective, top-down analysis but bottom-up design and implementation, and the need for independence of the business plan from computer applications (i.e., changes in the business plan may take place without effecting changes in the application systems).

Except for greater emphasis on strategic planning in the analysis stage and the subdivision of the design stage into general and detailed design phases, the phases in these second generation SDMs are fundamentally similar to the Waterfall model. The lack of attention to data structuring in SDLC-based methodologies has slowed progress in software design and given rise to the need for greater structural detailing in SDMs. This brings a whole new perspective to systems development and gives rise to structured programming techniques and structured methodologies, third generation SDMs.

STRUCTURED METHODOLOGIES

The structured methodologies represent a new level of SA and SD approaches that address multiple structural issues.[6] Among the structured SDMs that have earned wide acceptance and popularity are system analysis and design technique (SADT), structured analysis and structured designs (SA/SD), and structured system analysis and design methodology (SSADM). Table 5–2 summarizes these models.

SADT was proprietary, but a public version has been released.[7,8] In addition to depicting data flows between functions, SADT diagrams portray the control under which each function operates and the mechanisms responsible for the function implementation. This is not unlike the information structural diagrams (ISD) that have been discussed in the previous chapter. Moreover, the SADT diagramming technique is supported by function descriptions and a complete data dictionary package. A data dictionary is a catalog of data types that includes their names, structure, and usage. A function that reports on cross-references between the components of a data or business model is provided. SADT therefore combines basic elements of traditional approaches with structured methods. Olle et al. describe SADT as both a data-oriented and a process-oriented methodology,[9] while Colter claims that it provides analytical detail at both high and low levels and is reasonably usable for nontechnical personnel.[10] However, SADT has been criticized as focusing primarily on the SA stage; other competing methodologies have since been developed to provide more comprehensive support for the different SDLC stages.

Unlike SADT, the SA/SD methodology clearly supports both the SA and SD stages.[11] To make the transition from SA to SD, two techniques are used—transformational analysis and transactional analysis. Essentially, these are design strategies for deriving modular structures from different parts of the DFD introduced in Chapter 3. It is claimed that continuous applications of these strategies will ultimately result in the generation of hierarchical structure charts[12] for defining the various functions to be performed by the separate modules (another variant of the data structure diagram [DSD] technique discussed in Chapter 4). SA/SD is also closely related to certain other structured methodologies such as structured analysis, design, and implementation of information systems (STRADIS), structured analysis and system specification (SASS), and Yourdon.[13] Olle et al. summarize the various perspectives of these methodologies as one of process-oriented, data-oriented, or behavior-oriented.[14]

Table 5–2 Structured Methodologies (Third Generation Systems Development Models)

Methods	*Major Concepts*
System analysis and design technique (SADT)	Both data- and process-oriented; provides analytical detail at all levels and is easy for nontechnical personnel to use.
Structured analysis/structured design (SA/SD)	Supports analysis and design stages; uses transformational and transactional analysis; generates hierarchical structure charts for defining the various functions.
Structured system analysis and design methodology (SSADM)	Supports both analysis and design stages; used by the British government.

SSADM is a powerful methodology sponsored by the United Kingdom government and has been successfully promoted as a standard in all central government computer projects in Great Britain since 1983.[15] SSADM extends soft system methodology (SSM), which used rich pictures. Like SA/SD, SSADM strongly supports the SA and SD stages of the SDLC model. As noted in Tan, the major stages in SSADM include analysis of the current system, specification of the required system, user selection of service levels, detailed data design, detailed procedure design, and physical design control.[16]

Despite their popularity, both SDLC-based and structured methodologies require the user to know precisely what information will be required in the system weeks, months, or even years in advance. Yet users often find it difficult to specify what they want, and even if they can, their wants often may not match their real needs. This is evidenced by the number of revisions that systems go through after implementation before users get to tell all the information they really need. Prototyping, a fourth generation SDM, deals with this problem.

PROTOTYPING

Over the past few years, much controversy has been generated around prototyping. This debate concerns how prototyping may best be applied to achieve the productivity gains in software development claimed by vendors. Table 5–3 presents two opposing views of prototyping emerging from this debate, the evolutionary versus the revolutionary approach.[17]

Advocates of "revolutionary" prototyping argue that the only way productivity gains in software development can be realized is by applying them in new and innovative ways. Here, the rationale is that the traditional methodological mindset (for example, the emphasis on precise specifications of application systems before they are built, the abstraction of a static set of user requirements, and the concern about code details and exactness) prevents the effective use and application of prototyping tools and techniques. Rather, these tools and techniques are meant for people who can adapt to an environment supportive of a creative trial-and-error process; for example, nontraditional programmers who will use 4GL to support interactive editing and updating until the "right" system is developed. The framework of the applications is of major concern and details should be ignored until later. Earlier methodologies address the problem of analyzing and designing a system "right"; however, there is also the problem of designing the "right system." The revolutionary approach addresses this problem.

Table 5–3 Prototyping (Fourth Generation System Development Models)

Methods	Major Concepts
Revolutionary approach	Applies programming tools and techniques in a new and revolutionary way; argues against traditional methodological mindsets.
Evolutionary approach	Merges prototyping techniques and produces an evolution of traditional and structured programming.

Advocates of the "evolutionary" approach want to see prototype techniques incorporated into the "proven" SDLC and structured methodologies, which in essence will produce a merging of traditional (structured) and new (4GL) programming approaches. They argue that prototyping using 4GL does not encourage a structured approach, which may result in considerable difficulties in interfacing newly developed applications with existing SDLC-based applications. They also argue that prototyping using 4GL provides only marginal benefits because this new approach primarily affects the coding phase of application development. Thus, it appears reasonable to incorporate prototyping using 4GL into classical SDLC and structured models in order to achieve fine-tuning of the development process in the same way that structured methodologies were incorporated to fine-tune earlier SDLC-based approaches. McNurlin and Sprague believe that many developers will likely prefer this "safer" approach when adopting new methods of 4GL programming.[18]

CONTEMPORARY MODELS

The proliferation of SDMs over the years has caused some confusion as to which methodology is best. Many argue that no one approach is superior, but each methodology has its strengths and weaknesses. Tools and techniques that are appropriate for one set of circumstances may not be appropriate for others. Choosing an appropriate methodology will therefore depend on the context, the organization, the users, and the analysts who are developing the HMIS. The best compromise is therefore to choose an approach in which the choice of techniques and tools can be made within a loose methodological framework. This gave rise to contemporary models emphasizing a flexible systems approach. These present generation SDMs synthesize many earlier approaches and include the automation of techniques and tools. The CASE method, which automates different parts of software or systems development, is one such option. Multiview is another. Both of these approaches support flexibility in SA and SD processes.

Computer-Assisted Software Engineering Tools

CASE tools can assist with any or all aspects of the SA and SD processes. The CASE tool customer usually wants a tool that will help organize, structure, and simplify the development process. The goal is to develop better software more quickly. It has been shown that close to 80 percent of the problems in a given application system stem from SA and SD stages.[19] Hence, automating the SA and SD functions, rather than only those of physical development, should make development effort more efficient and productive.

The CASE concept includes tools for building systems, platforms for integrating tools, methods for developing applications, and techniques for managing the SA and SD processes. CASE encourages an environment for interactive development and automation of core and repetitive HMIS developmental tasks. It has been called "a philosophy of application development which embraces a systems approach,"[20] in which better connections between end users (health professionals) and HMIS developers are supported. Traditional approaches focus on technical aspects of applications and the best way to solve a given problem; the CASE approach looks at the broader health organizational context and searches to identify the right problems to solve, as well as how to solve those problems.

In the past, CASE tools have provided some functions to automate different aspects of systems development, but not all of them as one truly integrated tool set covers the entire SDLC process. In this sense, an individual CASE tool automates one small, specific part of the development process. There are several categories of tools. For example, diagramming tools pictorially depict systems specifications. Screen and report painters create systems specifications and may be used for basic prototyping. Dictionaries are information management tools that facilitate storing, reporting, and querying of technical and project-management information. Specification tools detect incomplete, syntactically incorrect, and inconsistent system specifications. Code generators can generate executable codes from the pictorial system specifications. Lastly, documentation generators can produce technical and user documentation that is necessary in using structured approaches. As summarized in Table 5–4, Brathwaite describes three types of CASE tools, including SDM tools, systems development support (SDS) tools, and programmer/project productivity (PP) tools.[21]

SDM tools combine to minimize effort and maximize coordination. These tools give support for an SDM at any (or all) of the stages of the SDLC process. They can include any of the tools appropriate to the methodology being used, while enforcing methodological rules and providing expertise to the users. SDS tools provide support for SA and SD techniques used at any stages of the SDLC process, but they do not necessarily enforce a methodology. PP tools provide support for programmers/designers of software mostly at the back end of the development life cycle. Examples include project management and documentation tools. Project management will be discussed later.

Alternatively, CASE tools may also be classified according to a different taxonomy: CASE toolkits, workbenches, frameworks, and methodology companions. CASE toolkits are integrated tools that automate only one part of the SDLC process. CASE workbenches provide integrated tools to automate the entire SDLC. CASE tools that are integrated and linked with non-CASE systems developmental tools are known as CASE frameworks. IBM's application devel-

Table 5–4 Three Types of CASE Tools

Tools	Concepts
Systems development methodology tools	Combine to minimize effort and maximize coordination; enforce methodology rules and provide expertise to users.
Systems development support tools	Support systems development tools and techniques at any stage in the life cycle; do not necessarily enforce a methodology.
Programmer/project productivity tools	Provide support for software programmers and designers at the back end of the development life cycle.

opment/cycle (AD/Cycle) is one proprietary example of an open platform or CASE framework within which any CASE tool can participate. AD/Cycle can support HMIS application developers with everything CASE has to offer to date, as well as the ability to adapt and incorporate future technologies. CASE methodology companions sustain a specific methodology by automating the entire SDLC process.

It can be difficult to decide which of the many CASE tools available is most appropriate for a given situation or environment. Brathwaite[22] proposes using a series of simple questions such as:

- What are the future direction and functionality of the tools?
- Does the tool's manufacturer have a philosophy of "open architecture"?
- Does the tool interface with other CASE tools being considered?
- Does the tool provide a detailed means of prototyping?
- Does the CASE design provide analysis support for design documentation?
- Does the tool enhance project management?

Although CASE has been in existence for many years, it is still poorly interfaced with users (humans). For many years, technical aspects of SDM predominated over human aspects. Only recently has there been a shift to a more humanistic perspective. This shift has resulted in the emergence of SDMs, such as Multiview, which is discussed next.

Multiview

Multiview is a comprehensive methodology and is described in considerable detail by Wood-Harper et al.[23] The authors saw it as a blending of the previous methodological approaches but especially emphasized the influence of SSM and effective technical and human implementation of computer-based systems (ETHICS),[24] both of which strive to incorporate the human aspects of systems development. Indeed, Multiview is based on the systems paradigm (Chapter 2) and emphasizes the relationship between the organization and its environment. In this aspect, the ultimate objective of Multiview is to amalgamate the human and technical subsystems for the enhancement of HMIS development as a whole.

Multiview is a nonprescriptive methodology that strives to be flexible. As a result, it continues to evolve as an SDM. Multiview is continually refined by using "action research," whereby knowledge gained from real applications in the field is incorporated into the methodology. Multiview was originally designed to aid development of information systems for small business and small-scale HMIS projects, but it is no longer limited to this scope.[25] The methodology contains five major steps:

1. analysis of human activity
2. analysis of information (information modeling)
3. analysis and design of socio-technical aspects
4. design of human-computer interface
5. design of technical aspects

Figure 5–5 illustrates the Multiview framework and the relationships among the five stages, whereas Table 5–5 summarizes activities entailed within each of the five components of the Multiview framework.

Stage 1: Analysis of Human Activity

The objective of Stage 1 is to identify the purpose and problem related to HMISs within the context of the organization. This stage attempts to answer the question of how the HMIS is supposed to further the aims of the organization. Rich pictures (Chapter 2) are frequently used to accomplish this stage for connecting the analysts to the users' view of the problem situation. Its ultimate objective is to identify problems and avenues to relieve these problems via HMIS design and development.

The first stage of Multiview provides the information necessary to conceptualize the human activities within the health service organization and helps to understand what HMISs can do for the organization. It also provides the inputs for the subsequent stages.

Stage 2: Analysis of Information

The objective of Stage 2 is to analyze the information on data flow and data relationships collected in Stage 1. This stage attempts to answer the question of what information processing functions the HMIS is to perform. There are two primary steps: (1) the development of a functional model and (2) the

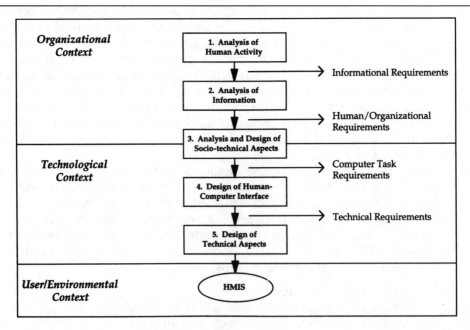

Figure 5–5 A Layered Multiview Framework for Health Management Information System (HMIS) Design and Development

Table 5–5 The Stages of the Multiview Framework

Stage	Major Concept
1. Analysis of human activity	Identifies problem within an organization and suggests HMIS solutions to solve problems.
2. Analysis of information	Uses information modeling techniques to analyze the problems of Stage 1.
3. Analysis and design of socio-technical aspects	Balances the social objectives with the technical objectives and ranks and chooses among these alternatives.
4. Design of human-computer interface	Gathers user input to create the technical design of the HMIS.
5. Design of technical aspects	Formulates the technical spefications of the HMIS.

development of an entity model. The functional model begins by identifying the main functions of the system. This model is then progressively broken down into subsystems until they can no longer be subdivided (usually four to five levels). This may be accomplished by using a DFD.

The development of an entity model serves a slightly different function. The entity model defines all entities within the system. An entity is anything that is relevant to records keeping; for example, in a bed allocation system, care providers, patients, and hospital beds are entities perceived to be useful for generating information about the system. It is also important to describe the relationship between entities and any other relevant attributes for designing an effective HMIS database.

Stage 3: Analysis and Design of the Socio-Technical Aspects

The objective of Stage 3 is to produce a design that incorporates the needs of individual users, as identified in the preceding stages, while balancing them with the technical objectives of the system. The socio-technical analysis follows a logical sequence of events that begins with the identification of separate objectives for both the social and technical aspects and then goes on to develop alternatives that blend the objectives. Alternatives are ranked according to their ability to meet both sets of objectives, and a final selection is made of the best socio-technical option. Unlike other stages, this stage addresses the question of how the HMIS can be incorporated into the working lives of the people in the organization.

Stage 4: Design of Human-Computer Interface

The objective of Stage 4 is to define the technical aspects of the system, including, for example, whether it will be command driven, have a main menu and submenus, or use a point-and-click (mouse) interface. The users are major contributors to these decisions, but this stage relies heavily on the systems analyst to guide the process and detail the final technical requirements. Equally important is the ability to incorporate the multiplicity of hardware and software already in existence within the overall HMIS design. Users should express their concerns to the analyst, who must in turn find the most appropriate human-computer interface to address these concerns. This stage attempts to answer the question of how individuals (i.e., users) can best relate to the HMIS in terms of operating and using the system.

Stage 5: Design of the Technical Components

The objective of Stage 5 is to formulate the technical requirements of the system. At this point in the development, the human needs should already be integrated into the HMIS design. Therefore, this stage is only technical because the analyst concentrates on detailing the full specifications of the HMIS design for efficient operations. This stage attempts to answer the question of what technical specifications are required for the HMIS to satisfy the needs identified in the four preceding stages.

Altogether, the Multiview methodology is characterized by several underlying assumptions. First, it provides a framework for resolving a problem. Multiview is not intended as a development prescription; but rather, it offers guidelines within which to assemble a set of tools and techniques for developing an HMIS. More importantly, it is situation dependent, and the people who employ Multiview must be knowledgeable about the methodology as well as the problem situation, the users, and the organization. The practical approach produces knowledge for subsequent applications within similar contexts (i.e., action research). Finally, it strives to integrate the human and technical subsystems, whereas past practices tended to focus on just one domain while ignoring the other.

Unlike CASE and other earlier SDMs, Multiview has great potential to aid end users in planning, designing, and developing their own applications because of its emphasis in integrating the technical and human aspects and its recognition for a more humanistic perspective. This shift has now resulted in the emergence of a whole new field of SDMs that extend to EUC, which is the final topic discussed in this chapter.

END-USER COMPUTING

The need to balance the human and technical aspects in the evolution of SDMs was fueled by the predominance of the technical components and the subsequent user dissatisfaction. The shift to a more humanistic perspective and the infiltration of the microcomputer at the worksite have led to the emergence of EUC.[26] The microcomputer explosion, along with increased knowledge of its potential, resulted in more requests for HMIS projects. EUC emerged to meet the growing demand for numerous end-user applications (EUAs) that need not rely on traditional programmers or information systems processing centers.[27]

EUC is not personal computing; personal computing is a subcategory of EUC. An end user is anyone who uses information generated by a computer. Hence EUC is any direct use of the computer by an individual whose primary interest is something other than just that use.[28] Stated simply, EUC is the capability of users to have direct control of their own computing needs. For example, a student (the end user) who is primarily interested in writing a dissertation may access a database at a university library, submit a set of requests to the computer to conduct a literature search, and use that information for the purposes of conducting his research. The student may also learn to use spreadsheets or basic statistical software for analyzing data that are collected during the various study stages and apply graphics software such as PowerPoint to generate presentation diagrams to illustrate concepts to be discussed in the dissertation. Similarly, knowledge workers as well as health managers may use computing facilities on their own to generate their own applications to aid information processing required in their work without relying on systems professionals and experts. Within the context of systems development, this phenomenon is termed EUC.

End-User Applications

EUAs encompass a wide spectrum of activities, including personal computing, communications, data retrieval/analysis, activity management, office automation, decision support, and expert system applications. These applications are the result of very high-level computer languages (i.e., fourth or fifth generation languages) that have been incorporated into end-user tools. There are two types of EUA: prewritten software packages and flexible software.[29]

Popular prewritten software packages in use today, including those rapidly emerging ones, are operating systems software such as Windows, Mac OS10, and, in the near future, the LINUX operating system; word processing software such as Microsoft Word 2000 and WordPerfect 2000; spreadsheet software such as Lotus and Excel; database software such as DB2, SALSA, and FoxPro; presentation graphics software, such as PowerPoint and ClarisWorks; online electronic communications and data interchange software, such as Eudora, First-Class and American OnLine (AOL); and Web browsers and search engines, such as Internet Explorer, Netscape, YAHOO, Excite, and Lycos.

Word processing software provide an electronic notepad for the creation of business or personal documents (i.e., memos, letters, drafts, and final reports). These programs also provide formatting, spell check, and storage options. A spreadsheet is an electronic table of rows and columns that provides a quick method for performing mathematical calculations and tabulations. Database software creates an electronic card index for secondary storage of information. Its purpose is to make the organization, storage, and retrieval of information easier and more accurate. Graphics software can provide the user with a number of options, ranging from the selection of predesigned graphics to insert within a text to the creation of presentation graphics, including tables, charts, and graphs. Communication software programs electronically link one computer to other computers, thereby providing an avenue to communicate information without the need for direct physical contact. Web browsers and engines are software that will aid the end users to surf and search for information posted on Web sites. Many of these software packages also assist in uploading or downloading texts, graphics, videos, and images. Its purpose is to create a virtual online community, much the same as a neighborhood community.

Among the flexible software are 4GL and application generators. These very high level languages, as end-user tools, allow health professionals who have only limited knowledge of computers to develop their own HMIS applications. In this sense, end-user technology can be employed in conjunction with any of the SDMs discussed earlier. For example, hospital administrators who decide to develop a rough budget forecast for the coming year may use an end-user tool such as a spreadsheet and the prototyping method; that is, they begin by designing a rough spreadsheet resembling a budget and continue to upgrade the spreadsheet until all the relevant variables for their budgets have been included.

Because of the sophistication of some tools available in the health computing marketplace (e.g., object-oriented and CASE tools), end users are now able to develop some of the more elaborate HMIS applications on their own. The range of options for HMIS development has expanded substantially over the years, and the trend is likely to accelerate with the release of more powerful and inexpensive software.

Advantages and Disadvantages

The evolution from a centralized control mechanism to individual user control has both advantages and disadvantages. There are five main advantages to EUC:

1. Users retain control.
2. Users are more committed to change.
3. Users are more knowledgeable and therefore better trained.
4. Users derive a better solution of information systems problems.
5. Users reduce their dependence on the information service department.[30]

Generally, these advantages translate into cheaper and faster HMIS application development and greater user acceptability of the products.

There are, however, several disadvantages as well:

1. the loss of the analyst in the development process, which may result in the loss of expertise, completeness, and an organizational viewpoint in the system's development
2. the ability of users to identify systems requirements correctly
3. the neglect of quality assurance procedures, including documentation
4. the difficulties in training new personnel and ensuring communications among subsystems when private information systems are predominant in an organization
5. the saturation of computer time and resources by multiple indiscriminate end-user applications

There is, of course, also increased concern regarding the organizational data sharing and data consistency. The evolution of computer capabilities has resolved some of these disadvantages, especially regarding the integrity of the data and the concerns about efficiency. However, to reap the majority of the advantages while minimizing the disadvantages, EUC must be coordinated within an organization.

Planning for Success

The emergence of the personal computers has provided for more freedom and flexibility but has also added to the complexity of designing HMISs. As health organizations become increasingly dependent on computerized systems, the ability of end users to use the systems effectively becomes critical. The personal computer revolution has placed EUC on the top-ten list of concerns for management, and EUC ranks second as a concern of overall information systems planning.

When EUC began, most projects were simple applications. Today, EUC spans the whole organization and has significant effect on the functioning of the entire information system. Studies have shown that EUC may account for 25 to 40 percent of an organization's information system. It is therefore imperative that management recognize the need to coordinate the efforts of multifaceted EUAs. It is far more advantageous to coordinate EUC than to impede its development or let it proceed fragmented.

The literature on EUC agrees on two primary guidelines for the successful inclusion of EUC within the organizational HMIS planning process:

1. *Policies and procedures for the use of system quality control.* To maximize the benefits of EUC, an organization should have strategies for promoting, managing, and controlling the evolution of EUC.[31] At a minimum, management should request the documentation of individual user applications. Organizations should also limit the set of hardware, software, and vendor options available to end users. Having a variety of microcomputers and applications can result in training difficulties and inefficiencies, maintenance difficulties, and system incompatibilities.
2. *Support services.* The development of EUAs does not obviate the need for guidance and assistance with difficult problems. The development of an information support center is encouraged by information systems experts to ensure the effectiveness and efficiency of EUA. Such centers can provide hardware, software, training, consulting, and problem-solving resources.

CONCLUSION

To a health service administrator in today's environment, it is crucial to incorporate SDMs as a key instrument in the effective and efficient development of an HMIS. To this end, administrators should be informed HMIS consumers. They must have a broad perspective of HMIS concepts (Chapter 1) and know the practical applications of tools and techniques for the development of an HMIS as discussed in this chapter. Successful HMIS development is a building block process that begins with an understanding of general systems theory (Chapter 2). Knowledge of individual system components and subsystems leads to a better understanding of how the various elements of data, information, and knowledge can be combined to create an integrated system (Chapter 3). It is also important to have a general understanding of effective data man-

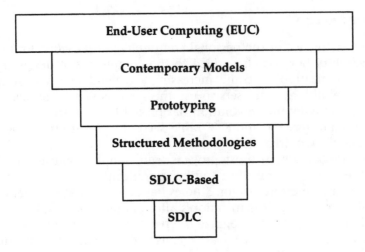

Figure 5–6 The Evolution of Systems Development Methodologies

agement and the available database technology that can maximize the potential of increasingly complex data retrieval needs and capabilities (Chapter 4).

SDMs have evolved from rigid step-by-step formulas for success to contemporary models, such as CASE and Multiview, which offer guidelines for high-quality HMIS development. Figure 5–6 is a summary of the SDM evolution. The diagram shows how each methodology has built on its predecessor to produce greater effectiveness. The advent of EUC has created awareness and consideration of end-user needs in the development of information systems.

In the end, the problem of choosing among alternative SDMs is one of recognizing the broader environmental, organizational, and technological contexts in which the need for health information SDs and development is embedded. Part II, which ends with this chapter, has provided a solid introductory foundation of the first context (i.e., the environment). Part III (Chapters 6 through 8) will continue this discussion with an in-depth analysis of the technological context of HMIS design and development, whereas Part IV (Chapters 9 through 11) will focus on the organizational context.

CHAPTER QUESTIONS

1. Define the following and describe a health-related example that incorporates these terms: (a) methodology, (b) technique, (c) tool, (d) phases and subphases.
2. Discuss the SDLC and explain why this concept is critical for understanding HMIS development.
3. Provide a list of the second, third, and fourth generation methodologies as well as the flexible and integrated methodologies (i.e., contemporary models) discussed in the chapter, and devise a taxon-

omy to contrast and compare the main features, advantages, and disadvantages of these alternative SDMs.

4. What are CASE tools intended to address? Discuss how CASE supports various aspects of systems development and devise a taxonomy to classify CASE tools.
5. List at least three tools or techniques that can be used within the Multiview framework to aid in the development of an information system. Identify at what stage each tool/technique is most appropriate, which inputs are required, and the intended outputs.
6. Define EUC and distinguish it from personal computing. Describe an example of an EUA in the health care industry.

NOTES

1. J. Rowley, *The Basics of Systems Analysis and Design for Information Managers* (London: Clive Bingley, 1990).
2. D. Avison and G. Fitzgerald, *Information Systems Development—Methodology, Techniques and Tools* (Boston: Blackwell Scientific Publications, 1988).
3. S. Holloway, *Methodology Handbook for Information Managers* (Aldershot, England: Gower Technical, 1989).
4. J. Cougar, et al., eds., *Advanced System Development/Feasibility Techniques* (New York: John Wiley & Sons, 1982).
5. D. Burnstine, *BIAIT: An Emerging Management Discipline* (New York: BIAIT International, 1980). Read this reference for a detailed discussion of the seven questions used in the BIAIT method.
6. M. Colter, A Comparative Examination of Systems Analysis Techniques, *MIS Quarterly* 8, no. 1 (1984): 51–66.
7. D. Ross and K. Schoman, Structured Analysis for Requirements Definition, *IEEE Transactions on Software Engineering* SE-3, no. 1 (1977): 6–15.
8. D. Ross, Structured Analysis (SA): A Language for Communicating Ideas, *IEEE Transactions on Software Engineering* SE-3, no. 1 (1977): 16–34.
9. T. Olle, et al., *Information Systems Methodologies: A Framework for Understanding* (Reading, MA: Addison-Wesley Publishing Co., 1988).
10. M. Colter, A Comparative Examination of Systems Analysis Techniques.
11. T. DeMarco, *Structured Analysis and System Specification* (Englewood Cliffs, NJ: Prentice Hall, 1979).
12. C. Floyd, *Information Systems Design Methodologies: Improving the Practice* (Amsterdam: North-Holland, 1986).
13. E. Yourdon and L. Constantine, *Structured Design* (Englewood Cliffs, NJ: Prentice Hall, 1979).
14. T. W. Olle, et al., eds., *Information System Design Methodologies: A Comparative Review* (Amsterdam: North-Holland, 1982).
15. E. Downs, et al., *Structured Systems Analysis and Design Method: Application and Context* (Englewood Cliffs, NJ: Prentice Hall, 1988).
16. J.K.H. Tan, Health Care Information Systems: An Organized Delivery System Perspective. In L.F. Wolper, ed., *Health Care Administration: Planning, Implementing, and Managing Organized Delivery Systems*. 3rd ed. (Gaithersburg, MD: Aspen Publishers, 1995).
17. J.K.H. Tan and J. Hanna, Integrating Health Care: Knitting Patient Care with Technology through Networking, *Health Care Management Review* 19, no. 2 (1994): 72–80.

18. B. McNurlin and R. Sprague, *Information Systems Management in Practice,* 2nd ed. (Englewood Cliffs, NJ: Prentice Hall, 1989).

19. L. Towner, *CASE Concepts and Implementation* (New York: McGraw-Hill, 1989): 2. This is a technical book that is part of an IBM series.

20. S. Montgomery, *AD/Cycle: IBM's Framework for Application Development and CASE* (New York: IBM, 1991): 9.

21. K. Brathwaite, *Applications Development Using CASE Tools* (New York: Academic Press, 1990): 108.

22. Ibid.

23. A. Wood-Harper, et al., *Information Systems Definition: The Multiview Approach* (Oxford: Blackwell Scientific Publications, 1985).

24. E. Mumford and M. Weir, *Computer Systems in Work Design: The ETHICS Method* (London: Associated Business Press, 1979).

25. D. Avison and A. Wood-Harper, Information Systems Development Research: An Exploration of Ideas in Practice, *Computer Journal* 34, no. 2 (1991): 98–112.

26. R. Panko, *End User Computing: Management, Applications and Technology* (New York: John Wiley & Sons, 1988).

27. J. Day, et al., *Microcomputers and Applications* (Glenview, IL: Scott, Foresman & Co., 1988).

28. G. Weinberger and A. Tenebaum, End-User Computing, *Computers in Healthcare* (July 1986): 39–41.

29. E. Turban, Decision Support Systems in Hospitals, *Health Care Management Review* 7, no. 3 (1982): 35.

30. H. Lucas, *The Analysis, Design and Implementation of Information Systems* (New York: McGraw-Hill, 1992).

31. G.B. Davis and M.H. Olson, *Management Information Systems: Conceptual Foundations, Structure and Development,* 2nd ed. (New York: McGraw-Hill, 1985).

Part III

Integrating Technology Architecture of Health Management Information Systems

Surveying Health Management Information System Technology Architecture: A State-of-the-Art Review for the Health Service Delivery Industry

Joseph K. H. Tan and Wullianallur Raghupathi

SCENARIO

The town of Inuvik is located on the east channel of the Mackenzie River Delta about 20 miles south of the Beaufort Sea in the Northwest Territories. The Inuvik region covers a vast geographic area of approximately 118,000 square miles. Eleven health centers located in the various communities of the Inuvik region and a regional hospital situated in Inuvik form the region's total health organization.[1]

The region's health organization serves a diverse population comprising Dene, Metis, Inuit, and nonnative peoples, totaling about 8,000 people. Access to the communities, with the exception of two that can be reached by roads, is possible only by air. During the winter months when temperatures plummet and the Mackenzie River freezes, an ice road is constructed to give road access to two other communities. The communities in the Inuvik Region range in size from Colville Lake, with a population of 50 people, to Inuvik, which is home to about 2,800 people.

The Inuvik Regional Hospital (IRH) serves as a general hospital for acute and chronic care patients for the town of Inuvik and as a referral center for the entire Inuvik Region. The hospital has an approved complement of 72 beds, with 52 beds currently staffed and in operation. Major services include general medicine, general surgery, obstetrics and maternity care, pediatrics, long-term care, radiology, laboratory, pharmacy, physiotherapy, occupational therapy, and community health promotion services. All services are provided on an inpatient, outpatient, or emergency basis. Additional specialized services and procedures are undertaken by visiting specialists or referred to an appropriate center. The total staff complement includes approximately 200 people working at the hospital and another 30 working in the health center.

In the mid-1990s, with technology advancing and resources shrinking, the senior management of IRH felt a strong need to streamline operations. Large amounts of paper flowing through the hospital and the constant scrambling of managers to assemble reports were indicative of an inability to collect and organize information in a manner necessary for staff to carry out their responsibilities effectively. The duplication of procedures in various departments lowered the level of efficiency and needed to be addressed. Health management information systems (HMISs) could provide the solution by enabling staff members and physicians to gather, manipulate, and extract data in a more timely and efficient manner, and either reduce or eliminate duplication of procedures, thereby improving effectiveness of administrative and clinical decisions. Sixteen stand-alone (not linked) personal computer workstations using mainly Word-Perfect and Lotus were addressing some of the office automation needs but were not a solution for the major issues at hand.

Imagine that you are a consultant who is familiar with current trends in HMIS technology architecture. You are asked to oversee the development of a completely integrated HMIS architecture for the Inuvik region, and your job is to see that the health organization is able to achieve its goal of an integrated HMIS. Financing will not be a major problem, as the Health and Welfare Canada and the Federal Ministry of Indians Affairs in Canada have partnered to grant full funding of up to $15 million to the Inuvik Regional Health Organization for the development of this integrated HMIS. Think about how you would go about devising an initial technology architectural plan for IRH. Contemplate some of the problems in communications in remote places of the Inuvik region and how you would ensure that the integrated HMIS is designed to overcome these problems.

INTRODUCTION

In earlier chapters, the growing importance and acceptance of an integrated technology architecture for health service management was described. An integrated technology architecture improves administrative, financial, and clinical decision making and is playing an increasingly important role in organizational control, clinical decision support, and strategic planning. There are three primary reasons for applying an integrated technology architecture. First, it will improve operational efficiency so that gaps and inadequacies in the operation of administrative systems (e.g., medical record processing, patient administration, and financial accounting management) can be bridged and linked. Second, it will promote organizational innovations by allowing new ways of doing old things. Finally, it will build strategic resources that will give broad access to timely and relevant information for effective decision making. The application of an integrated technology architecture is a growing trend in HMIS development.

Because HMISs are developed by blending informational, technological, and human resources, the focus in this chapter will be on the technological resources. However, emphasis will be place on emerging HMIS technological solutions because of the rapid advances in health care computing. To understand the role and capabilities of technology architecture in the health care environment, it is necessary to have a working knowledge of the various hardware, software, interface, and communications technology architecture available in the HMIS marketplace.

First, hardware, software, and interface architectural components are briefly reviewed. It is assumed that most readers will have a basic understanding of these technologies in this age of information explosion. Communications and network architecture are more complex and are more fully discussed in a separate chapter. Later in this chapter, emerging HMIS technology architecture is reviewed and ample examples are given to show how the different architecture, when applied strategically, is beginning to affect and reshape the future of the health service industry.

HARDWARE ARCHITECTURAL COMPONENTS

Hardware includes all physical devices (machines, storage devices, and input/output devices) that constitute a computer system. A computer system is a subsystem of an organization's overall information system and is an integrated assembly of physical devices centered around at least one processing mechanism, the central processing unit (CPU).

Figure 6–1 provides an overview of how various parts of a computer system, including the CPU, the primary and secondary storage, and the input/output devices, are related operationally.

Central Processing Unit

Often referred to as the "brain" or "heart" of the computer, the CPU is the primary core of a computer system. The CPU consists of three associated elements: the control unit (CU), the arithmetic/logic unit (ALU), and the registers.

The CU accesses program instructions, decodes and interprets these instructions, and then issues to other parts of the computer system the necessary orders to carry out the functions. The CU coordinates the flow of data in and out of the ALU, registers, primary storage, secondary storage, and various input and output devices. The ALU receives instructions from the CU and then performs the necessary mathematical calculations and logical comparisons. The registers, also called temporary storages, are used in the CU or the ALU.

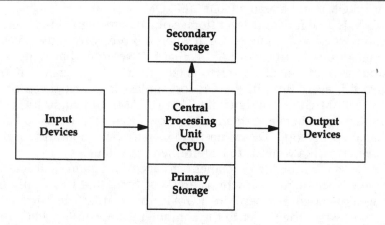

Figure 6–1 A Schematic Representation of Major Components of a Computer System

Registers are high-speed temporary storage areas used to hold small units of program instructions and data temporarily, immediately before, during, and after execution by the CPU. The CPU is designed so that data can be placed into or removed from a register faster than from a location in the main storage.

The CPU has the ability to process raw data into information and execute directions and instructions in a program. The execution of an instruction is known as a machine cycle. The machine cycles of modern computers are measured in nanoseconds (one-billionth of a second) and picoseconds (one-trillionth of a second), which determine the speed of the computer processing. Data are transferred from the CPU to other system components by way of bus lines, which are the physical wires connecting the various computer system components. The number of bits that a bus line can transfer at any one moment is known as the bus line width. Bus line width should be matched with CPU word length. Word length is the number of bits a CPU can process at any one time.

Multiprogramming involves executing more than one program at a time. The memory is divided into segments known as partitions, each of which holds a program. Virtual storage is an extension of multiprogramming, in which, instead of storing a complete program in memory, the computer will store in memory only a small part of the program at a time while the rest is stored on disk. Thus, the entire program is not needed because the computer is executing only a few instructions at a time. The CPU is therefore less likely to be waiting for programs to be transferred from disk to memory. This reduces idle CPU time and increases the number of jobs that can be done within a given time span.

Primary and Secondary Storage

Primary storage, also called main memory, is closely associated with the CPU. Primary storage holds program instructions and data immediately before or after the registers and provides the CPU with a working storage area for program instructions and data. All programs and data must be transferred to primary storage by way of an input device or secondary storage before programs can be executed or data can be processed. Types of primary storage include random access memory (RAM), read only memory (ROM), programmable ROM (PROM), and erasable PROM (EPROM).

RAM is used for short-term storage of data or program instructions. It is the memory where a program is stored when it is presently active in the computer. One major disadvantage of RAM is that it is volatile; that is, it requires a continuous application of power to retain data and programs. If the power is turned off, everything in RAM is lost, unless it is first saved or stored. Two types of RAM chips are dynamic RAM (DRAM) and static RAM (SRAM). The main difference between them lies in how often each needs to be refreshed or recharged per second. DRAM needs to be refreshed thousands of times per second, whereas SRAM needs to be refreshed less often.

ROM is used for the permanent storage of program instruction. All of the computer's standard instructions are kept here. ROM can only be read, not changed or erased. Furthermore, ROM is nonvolatile. The information it stores is not lost when the power to the computer is interrupted. PROM is a memory device in which the memory chips can be programmed only once and are used to store instructions entered by the purchaser. Once a program is written into PROM, it is permanent. EPROM is a device whose memory chips can be erased and reprogrammed with new instructions.[2]

Secondary storage, also known as external storage, supplements main memory by holding data and instruction in machine-readable form outside the computer. Secondary storage offers the advantages of nonvolatility, greater economy, and greater capacity than primary storage. Common forms of secondary storage are floppy disks, magnetic tape and disks, optical disks, optical or laser cards, and smart cards.

Small areas or spots of magnetized particles are used to represent bits on magnetic tapes or disks. Two types of access to the information stored on the magnetic media are available. Direct access allows the computer to go directly to any desired piece of data, regardless of its location on the magnetic medium, such as a floppy disk, which is a flexible disk inside a plastic sleeve. Sequential access, on the other hand, can only read and write data in sequence, one data item after another (i.e., a cassette tape).[3]

Operating like a compact disk player, an optical disk device uses laser beams to store and retrieve data. One advantage of optical disk storage is its ability to withstand wear, fingerprints, and dust. Two of the most common optical disk storage systems are compact disk–read only memory (CD-ROM) and digital versatile disks (DVDs). Data are stored onto these disks by burning small crevices into their coatings. This allows another laser device to read the disk by measuring the difference in the reflected light caused by the crevices on the disk. Each crevice represents the binary digit 0, and the smooth surface area represents the binary digit 1. Storage capacity in DVDs can be several times that of a typical CD-ROM.

Typically, each side of a compact disk is capable of storing 800 or more megabytes of information, which may include text, sound, and pictures. A DVD has the ability to hold a massive amount of information (e.g., an encyclopedia or even a series of movies). Write once, read many (WORM) format allows users to record data only once on a customized basis and then access it whenever needed. WORM disks are non-erasable and are often used to store original versions of valuable documents or data (e.g., archives).

Finally, optical or laser cards and smart cards are the emerging, secured secondary storage medium for many commercial applications. Resembling plastic credit cards, the only difference between these cards has to do with their storage (and processing) capacity. Smart cards, as the name suggests, have the added capability of "intelligent" processing.

As the use of these cards proliferates in commercial and health care applications, the cost of manufacturing and supporting their applications will become very attractive.

Input/Output Devices

A number of devices can be used to input or enter data into a system. For larger computer systems, key-to-tape and key-to-disk devices have been used, which allow data to be keyed directly onto a secondary storage device. Personal computers are often used for initial entry, editing, or correction of data before the data are downloaded to a larger system for processing.

Keyboards are inexpensive and easy-to-use devices that enter alphanumeric data. Some keyboards allow special character data input at the same time. Online data entry and data input devices are connected directly to the computer system by phone lines or cables. The mouse, a pointing device, is another example of input device. Light pens and track balls, both of which evolved from the mouse concept, are becoming popular for use with portables and hand-held devices. Voice recognition systems are also beginning to be used to capture and respond to human speech. Scanning devices, such as direct magnetic ink character recognition (MICR) systems, allow data printed in a special magnetic ink to be read by both humans and computers; the bottom part of a check is an example.

Optical scanners have also emerged. Optical data readers can read characters directly from a page without using special ink. Optical character recognition (OCR) equipment can read alphabetic, numeric, and special characters (i.e., bar codes). Image processing systems use scanners (much like miniature photocopiers) to input an image into memory. Scanned images can then be manipulated by using graphic software and reprinted as desired. Other input devices include handwriting recognition devices, data tables, and touch screens. Like voice recognition systems, these technologies are still to be perfected before they can gain wider user acceptance.

There are many forms of computer output media. The most common types are printers. Printers are classified as impact or nonimpact printers. Impact printers strike the paper during the process and include dot-matrix and daisy-wheel types. By striking the paper several times while printing, near-letter quality output can often be achieved. Nonimpact printers include ink-jet and laser printers. Other output devices are video display terminals (VDTs), plotters that draw graphics on paper, computer output microfilm (COM) devices that can place data directly from the computer onto microfilm for future use, and voice output devices that range from audio-response units to speech synthesizer microprocessors.

As we move into the future, there will be an increasing reduction in hardware size, resulting in increased processing capabilities and reduced costs.[4] Hardware will be able to perform a greater number of functions at an increasing speed. This will generate faster and more accurate information for the user.[5] Furthermore, the miniaturization trend of hardware will reduce the size of peripheral equipment, CPUs, storage, and other computer components. In addition, such hardware will simultaneously give users increased access to a greater amount of data.[6]

SOFTWARE AND USER INTERFACE ARCHITECTURAL COMPONENTS

Over the last few decades, software and user interface technologies have constituted a larger share of total system costs.[7] Advances in hardware have dramatically reduced costs; however, prices in software and user interface have increased to offset these reductions. Currently, software encompasses 75 percent or more of the cost of an organization's computer system.[8] Increasingly complex software requires more time, memories, and money to develop, and, in turn, increases the demand for the product and the salaries of developers. Two basic types of computer software include systems management software (machine executable programs designed to supervise and support the overall functioning of the computer system) and applications software (programs written to solve specific domain problems).

Systems Management Software

Systems management software is independent of any specific application area. This software manages computer resources, such as the CPU, printers, terminals, communication links, and peripheral equipment. Three main types of systems software used to manage instructions for computer hardware include operating systems (OSs), language translations programs (LTPs), and utility programs (UPs).

OS software runs or controls the computer hardware and interface with applications software. OSs are written for specific computers, and are usually stored on disk and transferred to memory when a computer is "booted" (i.e., turned on). Examples include Mac/OS10 (Macintosh) and Windows 2000. LTPs convert statements from high-level programming languages into machine code. The high-level program code is referred to as the source code, and the machine language code as the object code. In order to perform such a conversion, a compiler is used. An interpreter executes each machine language statement, discards it, and then continues to translate the next statement. UPs perform specialized functions directly related to the actual computer operation. They are considered part of systems software and are used to prepare documents, merge and sort files, keep track of computer jobs being run, manage printers and disk drives, recover lost programs, and lock confidential files.

A mainframe is a large computer that has access to extremely large amounts of data and is capable of processing these data very quickly. Mainframes use one of two types of processing approaches: batch or online processing. Batch processing is one of the oldest ways of running programs: a batch of programs is collected and run on the computer system one at a time. Online processing involves the running of a program whenever data are collected and entered into the computer system. Online processing is possible because terminals and other devices are directly connected (online) to the main computer; as a result, data files are kept as current as possible.

Applications Software

Applications software cannot be used without the system software. Application software is designed to handle the processing for particular tasks. These translate the user's instructions for the systems software, which, in turn, forward the instructions to the hardware. A company can either develop applications software itself (in-house) or use existing (off-the-shelf) software. Popular applications software include packages such as Microsoft Office 2000 and Adobe PageMaker.

A programming language is a set of symbols and rules used to write program code. Programming languages, like computers, have evolved over time. There have been five different "generations" of programming languages, as depicted in Figure 6–2.

First generation or machine language (1GL) is the most basic level of computer operation. This machine-level language uses binary coding and addresses to execute instructions. 1GL is difficult to write because of its binary representation of information as 1's and 0's corresponding to "on" and "off" electrical states of the computer. Second generation or assembly language (2GL) is a low-level symbolic language, unique to a specific computer. 2GLs replace binary digits with understandable symbols to ease programming; for example, one assembly language instruction equals one machine language instruction. Third generation or procedure-oriented language (3GL) is a high-level language that uses English-like statements in the coding of program instructions. Each instruction is thus equivalent to multiple machine-level instructions. Some common 3GLs are Cobol, Fortran, Pascal, and C.

Fourth generation language (4GL) or very high-level language is nonprocedural and more English-like than any previous generation languages. Its distinctive features include high-level queries for direct database access; interactive dialogs; simple-to-learn, helpful error messages; and use of defaults and relational database management systems. However, these application generators, as 4GLs are sometimes called, are often less efficient in terms of computer running time than 3GLs. Examples include Excel, Mantis, Ramis II, and Oracle.[9] Fifth generation language (5GL), or artificial intelligence, includes expert systems and natural language interfaces. Research in 5GLs has also advanced the knowledge of user-computer interface.

User-Computer Interface

When the concept of interface began to emerge, it was commonly understood as "the hardware and software through which a human and computer

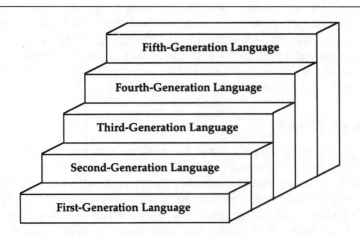

Figure 6–2 Levels of Programming Languages

could communicate."[10] As it evolved, the concept has widened to include "the cognitive and emotional aspects of the user's experience as well."[11] From a user's perspective, an interface is a discrete and tangible thing that can map, draw, design, implement, and attach items to an existing bundle of functions. Interfacing allows users to interact with the computer to perform various interactive functions.

There are two main types of user-computer interfaces: action and presentation language.[12] In action language, the user instructs the computer to take a series of actions; it is the way in which the user's intentions are translated into syntax that the machine understands. A simple example is the use of a touch screen or an icon. Presentation language is the way in which the computer communicates with the user, for example, by the use of color and graphics.[13] Four main designs for user-computer interface are graphical interfaces, iconic interfaces, direct manipulation, and group interfaces.

On the one hand, a graphical interface is associated with presentation languages; on the other, an iconic interface relates to action language. Graphical interfacing allows tables and numbers to be converted and represented spatially. Common examples include line and bar graphs, and scatter plots. These interface architectures enable visual representations of trends, taxonomies, statistical summaries, forecasting patterns, and performance reports, generally giving the user an increased understanding of data patterns and trends.[14] Iconic interfacing uses pictures or images to represent commands and objects that can be invoked by users.[15] It allows for improved performance and learning and helps to eliminate unnecessary errors. Icons allow for easy recognition and categorization and are usually faster to absorb than words. A key disadvantage of iconic interfaces is that it is often difficult to convey the desired meaning to the user without sometimes invoking other undesirable properties and connotations. Three different classes of icons are representational icons (or metaphor graphics), abstract icons, and arbitrary icons.

Representational icons or metaphor graphics[16] are prototypical images of a specific class of physical objects. These types of icons correspond to "real-world" objects, thereby enabling the user to recognize the icons and make some inferences based on them. Examples of representational icons are file folds, trash cans, and document images. Abstracts icons convey a specific concept using a visual image. Examples of abstract icons are warning labels on household products. Arbitrary icons have a meaning assigned to them; however, they are often difficult to interpret. In order for these types of icons to be meaningful and useful, there needs to be some standard definition.

Another design of user-computer interface is direct manipulation, which involves communication between a system and a user through the physical manipulation of object representations using a device, such as a mouse. The general characteristics of direct manipulation interfaces are a continuous representation of the object of interest, physical actions instead of complex syntax, and rapid incremental reversible operations whose impact on the object of interest is immediately visible.[17] In general, direct manipulation incorporates the concept of an analogy between the system and a problem domain. Through direct manipulation, the users will feel as if they are working on the actual problem of interest rather than interacting with an abstract, computer-based model.

Finally, the complexity of the user interface increases as HMISs become more complex and there is a need for communication and collaboration between several individuals. Malone defines a "group" interface as an organization interface, that is, the parts of a computer system that connect human users to each other and to the computing capabilities provided by systems.[18] A group interface provides a flexible interface that allows different individuals to communicate with one another efficiently and effectively. This has to do with the topic of telecommunications and network architectures, which will be reviewed briefly in several of the examples included in the discussion of next section. Because of the importance of this topic, however, it will be further elaborated in Chapter 8. At this point, the focus is on how the different pieces of technological architecture can be combined for health care applications.

EMERGING FORMS OF HEALTH MANAGEMENT INFORMATION SYSTEM TECHNOLOGY ARCHITECTURE FOR INTEGRATED DELIVERY SYSTEMS

Advancing computing technologies and new forms of technology architecture have contributed significantly to all industries, including the health service industry. Although the health service sector has been a little slow in adopting some of the newer architecture in its delivery systems, there is a general awareness among health service professionals that these emerging HMIS technology architectures can and will have an increasingly significant impact on the future of health services.

In this section, key emerging HMIS technology architecture that is strategically affecting the current and future health service delivery system is surveyed. Figure 6–3, adapted from Raghupathi and Tan,[19] depicts many of these architectural alternatives, including virtual patient records (VPRs), document management (DM), data warehousing (DW), networking and asynchronous transfer mode (ATM) networks, medical informatics and telematics, the Internet, intranets, and extranets.

VIRTUAL PATIENT RECORDS

VPRs may be defined as a technology architecture for housing health information from various distributed sources about one individual, which can be uniquely identified by an identifier.[20] VPR architecture is designed to convert data into a common format for electronic viewing, but the entire data set may originally have been configured differently at different places.[21] The architecture is "virtual" because users of these records need only a "view" of the required data on demand.

TeleMed is a collaborative VPR prototype project designed to support real-time interactive uses of media-rich graphical patient records between multiple users (e.g., physicians) at multiple sites.[22] Since launching the prototype with collaborating physicians from the National Jewish Medical and Research Center in Denver, researchers at the Los Alamos National Laboratory have been working hard to organize a series of workshops for achieving consensus on an international standard for a master patient index (MPI) interface.

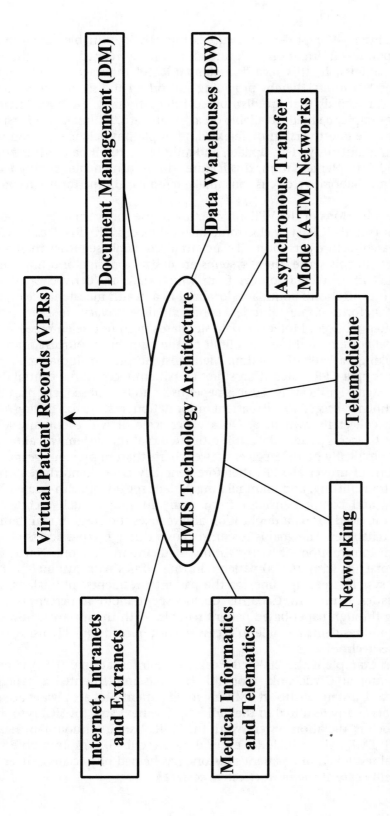

Figure 6–3 Emerging Forms of Health Management Information System (HMIS) Technology Architecture. *Source:* Adapted from J.K. Tan and W. Raghupathi, Strategic Uses of Health Information Technology, *Topics in Health Information Management,* Vol. 20, No. 1, © 1999, Aspen Publishers, Inc.

Essentially, a MPI represents a secured, uniquely identifiable patient directory with pointer information to locate all medically related information on respective patients. In this regard, a standard MPI interface would support access to these pointers, thereby providing authorized and secure access to disparate patient records that are distributed internationally. Such an interface could, for example, be made available on a "smart card." Kilman and Forslund note that in the latest version of TeleMed, multiple physicians from multiple sites can simultaneously view, update, and annotate patient data.[23] It is hoped that in real-life implementation, this feature will in turn encourage physicians to engage in collaborative discussions, make referrals, and perform teleconsultations.

Popular variations of the VPR architecture in use today include computerized patient records (CPRs) or electronic medical records (EMRs). Unlike VPRs, the earlier architecture acts more like a centralized database rather than a distributed one. In this sense, these systems are easier to design and implement because the different data sources from which data are derived often stay within the organization's boundary (localized to a health maintenance organization [HMO], for example), and data confidentiality, privacy, or security concerns are often reduced. Moreover, data standards need not be enforced across international borders, and there is a limit on the number of sources for acquiring and linking patient information. Methodist Hospital in Indianapolis, for example, sets up a CPR system that stores all patient records in a central database. The system significantly reduces paper use, and the subsequent plan is to give departments access to all patient information instead of having each department collect its own data. On a wider scale, it will eventually allow remote sites to access patient data. It is estimated that the system will allow the hospital to physically hold 25 percent fewer charts than in previous years.

Variations of universal VPRs therefore generally entail capturing, storing, retrieving, transmitting, and manipulating patient specific, health-related data both singly and comprehensively from many locations. Such architecture eliminates the need for data duplication and reduces the costs of maintaining duplicated databases. The goal is to control costs through rapid access of relevant patient information. Cabarrus Family Medicine in Concord, North Carolina, is a practice with 26,000 patients in four clinics with intranet-enabled CPRs. The system frees up time for the patients, residents, physicians, and their secretaries. Until now, Cabarrus' doctors spent about 40 percent of their time sifting through paper-based patient records. With the intranet, however, physicians and residents are able to access medical records quickly using standard browser technologies.

Another example is the 260-bed Health Care International (HCI) Limited Medical Center at Clydebank, Scotland. HCI has implemented a paperless medical record, a state-of-the-art EMR in which patient files are always accessible to doctors at any terminal in the building. The next step for HCI is to integrate the doctors' dictation systems with the EMR. Also, Intermountain Health Care's (IHC) EMR, which includes every drug prescribed, symptom observed, and medical test given in a patient's history, has helped physicians deliver the highest quality care at the most effective cost.

Finally, the adoption of VPR architecture has been slow because of practical issues, such as lack of data standards, confidentiality, privacy, and security, and other ethical issues. One proposal that is receiving much attention is the use of "smart cards" and "electronic signatories" to enhance security features of VPRs. The implementation of these combined technologies would then ensure rapid access to highly secured online information from home or at remote locations. For West Palm Beach Veteran's Affairs Medical Center, all medical records and associated paperwork have been distilled down to about 200 clinical and 1,000 administrative electronic forms that can be accessed from computers in each screening room and nursing station. These forms let doctors point-and-click to enter results of any type of examination or issue a prescription. To ensure secured transactions, all entries require an electronic signature. Although employees did require training, the paperless system was estimated to result in a physical storage cost savings of close to $500,000.

DOCUMENT MANAGEMENT

As managed care pressures hospitals and pharmaceutical companies to operate on a tighter budget, health care is turning more to technology architectures, such as DM, to put clinical and financial data online.[24] DM includes document imaging, workflow, electronic forms processing, mass storage, and computer output to laser disk.

Many hospitals need DM to handle the paper-intensive process of collecting and filing patient information. For instance, the sheer volume of patient care documentation convinced the information services department at Florida Hospital to choose a combination of document imaging and optical storage technology to image-enable more than 2,000 business processes encountered routinely in admissions, laboratory tests, insurance claims, general ledger, and accounting. These data are to be logged into a central repository. The overall purpose of the project was to provide better customer service and augment existing HMISs. Thus, in addition to character-based data, the upgraded HMISs will be able to capture, store, and manipulate documents and other data types, such as video clippings and photos. Each individual record would then contain the patient's clinical and financial information and a historical account of each patient's encounters at the hospital.

The San Jose Medical Center in California faces a similar challenge, that is, how it can access medical records speedily and make record management more efficient. The solution was to apply DM software, a relational database architecture, and a linked imaging equipment on a local area network (LAN). This resulted in the reduction of overall staffing needs and the hospital was able to collect additional revenues by handling external record requests.

Finally, the field nurses at St. Mary's Medical Center, a home health care provider in Long Beach, California, no longer spends hours at company headquarters managing large numbers of patient records. The project goal was to cut down the overwhelming paper load. The use of notebook computers and customized software has freed these nurses from attending routine administrative chores to visiting more patients. Further, the use of DM architecture has also increased revenues by streamlining the health care provider's documentation process. By employing notebooks and customizable form templates in DocPlus application, these nurses can update all patient and insurance information electronically, thereby eliminating the need to hand-write several new forms with each visit. This eventually led to faster filing of insurance documents, which in turn translated into quicker payments. Nurses were thus able to visit about 600 additional patients per month, and revenues have also increased.

DATA WAREHOUSING

Data warehousing refers to amassing enterprise-related data for strategic decision-support analysis and for knowledge discovery. Hospital chief executive officers now realize that the only way to survive and grow in a managed care market is to gain significant expertise in managing information, knowledge, and documentation. Thus, many workers in the medical field are searching for quick and affordable ways to tap into available information banks of detailed patient records. The DW concept is becoming crucial as the industry moves from a revenue-based business model to one focused on cost-outcomes information management.

Many hospitals need DW architecture to handle the tedious process of analyzing and comparing massive patient treatment outcome information. Johnson Medical Center in Johnson City, Tennessee, needed a DW for studying historical records of patient treatments and spotting trends or anomalies. Its aim was to help create report cards about physicians, thereby measuring the cost of each doctor's services at the hospital in terms of the types of treatments used, time spent with patients, and other factors. Also, the data gathered could be used to analyze cost of each treatment vis-à-vis the amount of money paid for by insurers. This architecture, then, permits comparison of information among the various departments to show profitability of each operation.

Aetna/U.S. Healthcare is building a DW architecture that is expected to collect data, such as medical claims, laboratory test results, hospital discharge data, and demographic information from three of Aetna's insurance lines. As noted previously, managed care is about managing data and information well to determine what works in improving health outcomes without correspondingly increasing the cost of health care. In this sense, analysts can use the DW to extract information to study trends related to cost and use of medical services. Moreover, the DW architecture could be used to build a medical history of enrollees by linking records of medical claims across insurance products. In fact, users can look at standard reports or build their own. Another DW project supported by Aetna identifies members who have any of 65 chronic diseases and assigns them to a risk category based on the severity of their illness. Based on this information, Aetna can encourage the patients to obtain ongoing and appropriate health care to keep their illnesses in check.

More recently, HIC, the Australian federal agency that processes all medical claims, uses data mining software to sift through seemingly unrelated data to discover subtle patterns that can be used to make strategic business decisions. Given the breadth of its transactions, HIC is a classic example of an organization that could benefit from the DW technology architecture. The staff traditionally relied on paper reports to ensure medical services were appropriately prescribed and billed. However, with HIC conducting more than 300 million transactions and paying out $8 billion annually to physicians and hospitals, the ability to monitor everything was almost impossible. By using various data mining tools, HIC's staff can now track areas never before possible. For instance, the different ordering habits of physicians in similar clinical situations can be analyzed in order to establish best practices for various treatments. Often, the key challenge is knowing what information to tap and making sure that the information tapped is reliable and valid.

Finally, the U.S. Department of Defense plans to deploy what officials say is the largest known medical DW. Since 1995, it had began converting its fixed-cost health care system to a managed care model to lower costs and increase patient care for the active military personnel, retirees, and their dependents. The managed care model is currently supported by a $450 million medical DW project called Computerized Executive Information System. The project has eliminated 14 redundant systems at an annual estimated savings of $50 million.

NETWORKING AND ASYNCHRONOUS TRANSFER MODE NETWORKS

The effect of the technology architecture reviewed here can be enhanced through electronic and digital networking, which is the logical next step for delivery of future health services. Understanding networking and ATM architecture will therefore be critical especially from the perspective of managed care as multiprovider organizations vie to provide integrated delivery of quality health services along the entire continuum of care.

Virtual health care is the formation of networks of coordinating partners where each provider does what it does best. As the information needs are often similar in many cases, providers are investing heavily in distributed, client server networks and object-oriented architecture to deliver the necessary links. In response to an industry that has become cost and marketing conscious, Orlando Regional Healthcare System has began to build an integrated delivery network to form one-stop shopping for all types of health care.

Along a community-based perspective, a few independent health organizations have grouped together to build a Community Health Information Network (CHIN). In Dayton, Ohio, for example, the greater Dayton Area Hospital Association is building links to all 20 hospitals and approximately 2,400 independent physicians within a nine-county region covering a population of about 1.4 million. Anthem, the southwest Ohio Blue Cross plan, the dominant insurer will also be connected to the CHIN. A demonstration project involving a patient encounter record system shared among seven competing hospitals was positively supported. Eventually, the system will be expanded to track encounters, imaging services, and patient status by physician. It will also have full capabilities to link to pharmacies and long-term care facilities. In this sense, the network will resemble an intranet in that it will use a common Web browser front end to access a MPI.

ATM technology architecture offers a vision of the ultimate integrated services network. Potentially, the architecture is characterized by the provision of unlimited bandwidth on demand (currently up to 2.5 Gbit/s); the integration of data, voice, and video over one cost-effective infrastructure; and the seamless interconnectivity of data systems between the local area and the wide area. Increasingly, ATM is being deployed in networks supporting bandwidth-intensive applications with well-defined quality of service such as integrated telemedicine because it supports fast transmission speeds and it is able to integrate multiple traffic streams. Radiology and teleradiology are among the applications that can benefit greatly from ATM technology. Chicago's Rush-Presbyterian/St. Luke's Medical Center, for example, is developing an ATM backbone network for its radiology department. St. Paul's Hospital, a teaching hospital at the University of British Columbia, Vancouver, is also using an ATM backbone network to connect its pulmonary research laboratory with doctors outside the hospital. The network allows the two groups to compare test results and diagnose patients quicker. For example, its application speeds up the process of diagnosing patients suffering from lung disease. In the future, it is envisaged that researchers in the pulmonary research laboratory and doctors will view slides and X-rays, trade data, and compare findings online.

Currently, physicians at Duke University Medical Center can sit down in front of their computers and call up 10MB X-ray images in 1.5 seconds. Pennsylvania's Hershey Medical Center has developed a medical conferencing application that integrates physician-to-physician videoconferencing, patient charts, laboratory results, and radiology images on a single computer screen. For Pro Medica Health Systems, an ATM network is expected to help the Toledo hospital integrate voice, data, and imaging traffic over clinical workstations. Also, this network supports a repository storing more than 700,000 patient records, giving 2,200 physicians, nurses, and other staff access to patient data.

An equally important emerging technology architecture is the Gigabit Ethernet. Its benefits can be tied to its Ethernet legacy. Gigabit Ethernet's high bandwidth capabilities will alleviate traffic congestion on large, fast Ethernet networks as well as enable ultrahigh-speed data transfers. Lowell General Hospital's move to Gigabit Ethernet could mark a trend in the way the health care industry views advanced LAN technologies. Although there still is a lot of the old technology architecture being used in hospitals, the push for newer and more strategic network architecture is inevitable as these institutions deploy some of the health care industry's most bandwidth intensive applications (e.g., medical imaging, teleradiology, and desktop video). Indeed, for hospitals to extend computing capabilities to the bedside effectively, a robust network architecture must be in place. Lowell General's Web site includes interactive heart tests, e-mail links to doctors for medical queries, and SurgeryCam, an application providing a surgeon's eye view of a surgical procedure.

MEDICAL INFORMATICS AND TELEMATICS

Medical informatics (including telematics) is concerned with "the cognitive, information processing, and communication tasks of medical practice, education, and research, including the information science and technology to support those tasks."[25] In broad terms, its emphasis is on clinical and biomedical applications of the different technology architecture surveyed, with the added possibility of integrating these clinical components either among themselves or to more administrative type HMISs. In this regard, the field of health/medical informatics and telematics has evolved very broadly over the past several years.

At the clinical level, applications utilizing artificial intelligence, neural network, and fuzzy logic techniques are being developed to provide clinical decision support to physicians. The primary objective of these applications is to assist physicians and other medical experts in diagnosis and treatment. Tan and Sheps use the term "health decision support systems" (HDSSs; more specifically, clinical decision support systems and expert systems [CDSSs and ESs]) to characterize these applications.[26] As such, the focus here is on general HDSS, CDSS, and ES applications; the discussion on health telematics will focus chiefly on telemedicine, one of its key applications.

An example of a CDSS is an interactive videodisk system that helps enter personal health data to weigh the pros and cons of surgery. It is believed that such software will promote shared decision making and holds the promise of improved quality of care without increasing costs. Richard Foster, medical director of a 40,000 member HMO operated by South Carolina Blue Cross/Blue Shield, has recommended the use of the equipment.[27] Patients and doctors who tried it found that it enhanced the physician–patient relationship. Others trying similar programs include Massachusetts General Hospital in Boston; Dartmouth Hitchcock Medical Center in Hanover, New Hampshire; Veterans Affairs; and several regional Kaiser Permanente HMOs.

The Lahey Clinic in Burlington, Massachusetts, faced several problems. Hospital statistics were maintained as hard copies, and it was difficult to disseminate this information to department heads and managed care organizations. Therefore, managed care organizations were reluctant to refer their patients and physicians to Lahey because of its lack of current information on cost and clinical performance. The clinic also risked losing patients to larger hospitals. To overcome these problems, Lahey installed HealthShare One, an HDSS. Not only did the HDSS help Lahey improve online access to key operational data while cutting costs, but also it enabled Lahey to tell potential patients how well it was performing on certain medical procedures compared with its competitors. The DW embedded in the HDSS further permitted management to do queries and perform complex comparative cost analysis. In the end, the HDSS was able to cut costs, attract new business, and help improve Lahey's quality of service.

In the area of ES applications, the development of a computerized system for more accurate monitoring of the fetal heart rate during the human birthing process was reported.[28] The data would be fed into a rule-based ES and a neural network to classify the situation as normal, stressed, indeterminate, or ominous. In another ES example, a computerized voice response system provides medical advice for 100 common ailments. The advice, available via telephone 24 hours per day, is based on a caller's self-reported symptoms, consultation history, and the latest medical research. The system also tracks the improvement or deterioration of the patient's condition during follow-up calls. In St.

Paul, Minnesota, an ES that spots irregularities in doctors' bills is saving Fort's Benefits Insurance Company/Woodbury an estimated $540,000 a year. In the case of LDS Hospital at Salt Lake City, an automated patient information system is used to detect adverse drug events, such as allergies, unpredicted drug interactions, and dosage problems. The ES alerts staff to such possible occurrences and is purported to identify adverse drug events 60 times better than practitioners.

Patient care management and patient education is increasing the demand for integrated HMIS, HDSS, and ES applications among hospitals, HMOs, and other agencies. A new strategy against escalating health care costs is disease management. The Henry Ford Health System in Detroit, and Sentara Health system in Norfolk, Virginia, keep patients with chronic illnesses, such as asthma or diabetes, out of the hospital and the emergency department by teaching them how to prevent these attacks. Both health systems are developing real-time, client-server ESs to prompt caregivers to follow standard guidelines as they enter orders for care, such as prescriptions or lab tests, into a clinical system. The prompts will be based on standard practice guidelines that are developed through ongoing analysis of medical outcome and cost data. Health care providers need online advice about the best treatment; hospitals need to track and analyze the results of each course of treatment to come up with these guidelines.

Telemedicine is a key area of health telematics that connects geographically dispersed health care facilities via video and telecommunication. More simply, telemedicine is the use of digital networks to perform long distance diagnoses of diseases and disorders. The telemedicine system at Pathway Health Network in Massachusetts uses videoconferencing systems for urban medicine. This has enabled linking the network of hospitals. In the short term, this has helped build strong physician-to-physician relationships across the hospitals. In the longer term, it is anticipated that the network system will improve patient care delivery. The system is used primarily for consultations among physicians. In another example, the Texas Department of Information Resources expects to save 50 percent annually by running a two-way, statewide video network to deliver medical help and educational programming to all corners of the state. One purpose of the video network, called Vidnet, is to eliminate the high cost of transporting prison inmates hundreds of miles to state health centers for medical care. Vidnet allows physician assistants at prisons to transmit images to, and confer with, doctors at the University of Texas medical branch, thereby speeding postoperation follow-up. Through easy and inexpensive remote access capabilities, Vidnet is believed to have extended telemedicine to a large population.

Finally, Indian River Memorial Hospital in Vero, Florida, needed high bandwidth capacity for telemedicine applications. It opted for an ATM backbone with switched Ethernet. ATM packages voice, video, and data traffic into 53-byte cells switchable at very high speeds. It also enables diverse traffic to travel over the same network architecture, so that it provides Indian River the high-volume heterogeneous networks needed to support telemedicine activities. The scalability also makes ATM an attractive technology for hospitals expecting mixed high-bandwidth traffic and requiring meshed connectivity.

These features would be typical of hospital-wide area networks carrying large medical records files, telemedicine video, and radiological image traffic. Indian River's clinicians and administrative staff can now access a surgical scheduling system, physician billing software, and the Internet.

THE INTERNET, INTRANETS, AND EXTRANETS

The Internet may generally be conceived of as a complex web of networks.[29] Briefly, Internet services include electronic mailing (e-mail), newsgroups, file transfer protocols (FTPs), and other information transfer and exchange services, such as Telnet and the World Wide Web (WWW) access using browser software (e.g., Mosaic, Netscape Navigator, and Microsoft Internet Explorer). Presently, this technology architecture has become an important interactive research and communication tool for aiding both medical professionals and health consumers in search of health-related information and knowledge.

Conceivably, there are many examples of Internet use to provide relevant health information and services. A notable strategy here is to provide users such as patients, physicians, hospitals, and others with access to online insurance service data. The benefits of electronic filing of insurance benefits and claims include cutting costs for the company and its network of hospitals, physicians, and corporate clients as well as improving access and usability for members. This may also cut agency and other labor costs while providing insights to health care trends and medical practices.

For example, Blue Cross/Blue Shield of Massachusetts facilitates access to online insurance services via WWW server and onsite multimedia kiosks equipped with modem connections to the insurance carriers' customer service operations. The Internet services provide users with access to information about particular Blue Cross services and health care and medical data. The Web site also provides a front end for medical information available at other points on the Internet, such as OncoNet, a repository for data on treatment for cancer patients. These kiosks allow users to search and print physician and hospital database information and to peruse information about drugs, treatment alternatives, and Blue Cross services. The kiosks also provide telephony links to customer service representatives and member services. Corporate customers have claimed that being able to provide services and information to users directly over the Internet and via kiosks can significantly reduce the cost of in-house insurance support and education.

Fundamentally, the intranets and extranets are extensions of the Internet concept because these use the same hardware and software to build, manage, and view Web sites. Unlike the Internet, however, these virtual private networks are protected by security software known as "firewalls" to keep unauthorized users from gaining access. In essence, an intranet is a private computer network built for the purpose of providing Internet-based services only to inside organizational members. Similar to the intranet concept, the extranet extends network access privileges to certain partners, giving them access to selected areas inside the virtual private network, thereby creating a secure customer or vendor network.

To date, intranet and extranet architectures have been tapped by a growing number of hospitals for in-house and external sharing and distribution of medical information. For example, Aetna/U.S. Healthcare of Hartford, Connecticut, uses an Internet-based service that lets members change their primary care providers online. The EZenroll application handles the critical process of adding, dropping, or changing health plans. Members gain access, often through their intranet, with a user name and password supplied by their employer, who also approves the transactions online. Implementation of computerized patient records via this technology has been shown to be generally reliable and secure. Moreover, Web-based transactions provide the potential to reduce some of the inherent inefficiencies of paper forms and provide the needed integration and interoperability among different vendors' biomedical and HMISs. Kaiser Permanente, northwest region, developed an intranet site to communicate with its geographically dispersed customer base. This intranet includes clinical practice guidelines for physicians, scheduling, and important links to medical sites.

Group Health (GHNW), another northwest HMO, decided to Web-enable the company's patient accounts data so that users at outlying physician offices would be able to query the data. GHNW has been among the first to recognize the potential of intranet technology to aid in sharing information in a cost-effective, user-friendly manner. The systems were based on a client server architecture where clients accessed data from a database. Previously, the information had been disseminated in paper form. The new intranet was not expected to improve patient health in any way but it provided a better solution than a costly closed network (i.e., in favor of Web technology).

Geisinger Health Care System of Danville, Pennsylvania, the largest U.S. rural HMO, is believed to be rapidly emerging as an industry leader by leveraging on network architecture to reinvent health care. Its system concept includes the extension of intranets for use by patients. In this regard, the organization replaced disparate legacy systems with a universal workstation concept that resulted in an Ethernet backbone. The network allows Geisinger to offer innovative services such as Tel-a-Nurse, a system that permits users to call in with medical questions that are answered by nurses who have access to relevant information and expert knowledge through the intranet. A clinical management system was also installed in the network. Geisinger's physicians can then use digital cameras to take pictures of patient injuries, making these pictures accessible via the intranet. Geisinger's intranet is also being used to support patient education. For example, the radiology department, which performs diagnostic procedures such as X-rays, mammograms, and magnetic resonance images, has a kiosk placed in its waiting room where patients can click onto the radiology home page and get a list of the various departmental procedures.

CONCLUSION

The health care industry is finally viewing technology architecture as a strategic resource in housing health-related information services and cost-effective decision support on demand. Instead of relying on handwritten notes buried in poorly organized paper files, physicians, nurses, and other health providers are now turning to different forms of advanced technology architecture. VPRs, DM, DW, virtual public and private networks, and telematics are only some of the architectural configurations available to enhance rapid access to current and useful information needed for quality patient care. In the next two chapters, some of these will be elaborated upon, and other forms of architectural configurations will be discussed.

The next HMIS breakthroughs are expected to be in the areas of integrated systems, intelligent networks, and robotics. Indeed, the ability to integrate clinical and administrative information about patients means that physicians can provide better care at lower costs. For example, an integrated HMIS can provide health professionals in a distributed clinical setting with an online, real-time history of patients included in a standard MPI interface linked to a DW. This architecture will typically combine DW, electronic data entry, messaging, and graphical user interface tools to permit physicians and hospital management to track and analyze patient care history, test results, and cost information. Brigham and Women's, an integrated HMIS pioneer, implemented the Eclipsys Sunrise application, a Web-based suite of rules-oriented applications. The hospital estimated saving between $5 to $10 million annually. In another example, Beth Israel Medical Center, to succeed in the highly competitive deregulated health care industry, networked intelligently its radiology system by building an ATM-based medical imaging system and connecting it to a laboratory in which robots process tests. The ATM-based network let the hospital extend its services to St. Luke's–Roosevelt Hospital Center. The network was key to the merger, especially in speeding bandwidth-intensive processes, such as the new radiology system.

Although technology architecture can facilitate easy and rapid access to critical health information and knowledge for providers and consumers alike to support all kinds of administrative, financial, and clinical decisions, it also opens up vulnerabilities. The overall prospect of storing health information in electronic form, for example, raises concerns about standards, ethics, patient privacy, data confidentiality, and security. Unless proper controls, procedures, and policies are in place, emerging technology architecture will also invite the acquisition of data by unauthorized intruders and even the misuse of information by authorized users. In fact, if the concerns are not sufficiently addressed, these can discourage the health care industry from exploiting technology architecture and make health care consumers hesitate to share information.

Just as with information architecture, applications and use of technology architecture must be done in the midst of maintaining confidentiality, privacy, and security. As noted in previous chapters, medical information standards for the nomenclature, coding, and structure also must be developed. These must be universally accepted to accomplish uniformity of definition and meaning of terminology. Standards for electronic signatures, especially for the validation of physician prescriptions, in the era of the Internet must be discussed. These are exciting times for the health care industry and information technology industry. The strategic integration of the two will revolutionize health care delivery in the decades ahead while opening up new areas for applications and research.

CHAPTER QUESTIONS

1. Describe what is meant by technology architecture. How does the concept differ from that of information architecture? Use examples to illustrate your answer.
2. What are the four fundamental components of a computer system? Discuss the difference between a personal desktop computer versus a hand-held palmtop computer in terms of these components.
3. Health care managers have much knowledge and experience about the decision environment, but lack knowledge and experience about advancing technology architecture. Discuss strategies to help educate health care managers to keep abreast of the knowledge in this area. How would knowledge in this area aid health care managers in their decisional roles?
4. Many examples have been cited on how health care organizations have been able to save money by adopting appropriate technology architecture for organizational task performance. What are the barriers and impediments to these ventures? Illustrate your response with examples from your own work experience or from some of the case examples provided in the chapter.
5. Following the case examples provided in the chapter, search the Web and other sources for other similar case examples in the different areas of hardware, software, communications, and user interface technological applications and attempt to organize your results into major taxonomies.
6. Justify your groupings given in your response to question 5, and provide an organizing framework as an alternative format to categorize the case examples provided in this chapter.

NOTES

1. Condensed from *Healthcare Computing & Communications* 6, no. 3 (April 1992): 30–35.
2. K.C. Laudon and J.P. Laudon, *Business Information Systems: A Problem-Solving Approach* (Hinsdale, IL: Dryden Press, 1991).
3. J. O'Brien, *Introduction to Information Systems in Business Management*, 6th ed. (Homewood, IL: Richard D. Irwin, 1991).
4. T.K. Zinn, HIS Technology Trends, *Computers in Healthcare* (February 1991): 46–50.
5. C. Dunbar, It Comes Down to Managing Minutes, *Computers in Healthcare* (March 1992): 6.
6. S.L. Mandell, *Dr. Mandell's Ultimate Personal Computer Desk Reference* (Toledo, OH: Rawhide Press, 1993).
7. P.J. Hills, *Information Management Systems: Implications for the Human-Computer Interface* (Toronto: Ellis Horwood, 1990).
8. J. Burn and E. Caldwell, *Management of Information Systems Technology* (Orchard, Oxfordshire: Alfred Waller, 1990).
9. J.K.H. Tan, An Introduction to Health Decision Support Systems: Definition, Evolution and Framework, in *Health Decision Support Systems*, ed. J.K.H. Tan with S. Sheps (Gaithersburg, MD: Aspen Publishers, 1998), 25–32.

10. I. Benbasat, et al., *The User-Computer Interface in Systems Design* (British Columbia: Faculty of Commerce and Business Administration, University of British Columbia, 1993).

11. B. Laurel, ed., *The Art of Human-Computer Interface* (Reading, MA: Addison-Wesley Publishing Co., 1992).

12. I. Benbasat, et al., *The User-Computer Interface in Systems Design*.

13. J.K.H. Tan, Graphics: Theories and Experiments, *Computer Graphics Forum* 11, no. 4 (1992): 261.

14. J.K.H. Tan and I. Benbasat, Processing of Graphical Information: A Decomposition Taxonomy To Match Data Extraction Tasks and Graphical Representations, *Information Systems Research* 1, no. 4 (December 1990): 416–439.

15. D. Gittens, Icon-Based Human-Computer Interaction, *International Journal of Man-Machine Studies* 24 (1989): 519–543.

16. W. Cole, *Metaphor Graphics and Visual Analogy for Medical Data,* Section on Medical Information Science (San Francisco: University of California at San Francisco, 1988).

17. I. Benbasat, et al., *The User-Computer Interface in Systems Design*.

18. T. Malone, Designing Organizational Interfaces, *Proceedings of CHI'85* (1985): 66–71.

19. W. Raghupathi and J.K.H. Tan, Strategic Uses of Information Technology in Health Care: A State-of-the-Art Survey, *Topics in Health Information Management* 20, no. 1 (1990): 1–15.

20. J. Mullich, Intranet Gives HMO a Shot in the Arm, *PC Week* (February 3, 1997): 27–34.

21. D.G. Kilman and D.W. Forslund, An International Collaboratory Based on Virtual Patient Records, *Communications of the ACM* 40, no. 8 (1997): 111–117.

22. Readers interested in the TeleMed project may want to consult http://www.acl.lanl.gov/TeleMed.

23. D.G. Kilman and D.W. Forslund, An International Collaboratory Based on Virtual Patient Records.

24. T. Hoffman, Document Management Helps Medicine Go Down, *Computerworld* (June 10, 1996): 24.

25. R. Greenes and E. Shortliffe, Medical Informatics—An Emerging Academic Discipline and Institutional Priority, *Journal of the American Medical Association* 263, no.8 (1990): 1114.

26. J.K.H. Tan with S. Sheps, eds., *Health Decision Support Systems* (Gaithersburg, MD: Aspen Publishers, 1998).

27. M. Freudenheim, Software Helps Patients Make Crucial Choices, *The New York Times* (October 14, 1992): C8.

28. Patent Watch, *Computerworld* (February 24, 1997): 110.

29. A.T. Stull, *On the Internet: A Student's Guide* (Upper Saddle River, NJ: Prentice-Hall, 1997).

Chapter 7

Data Warehousing, Data Mining, and Integrated Health Decision Support Systems: A Comprehensive Cancer Surveillance System Architecture

Guisseppi A. Forgionne, Aryya Gangopadhyay, Monica Adya, and Joseph K. H. Tan

SCENARIO

Based in Washington, DC, OYN Health Plan[1] is a large nonprofit, managed care organization comprising hospitals, primary care centers, and ambulatory care centers. OYN also acts as an insurance company, contracting with many health care providers. As of January 2000, OYN served over 600,000 enrollees.

With an average of over a million claims each month, OYN faces an especially challenging task in claims processing. Currently, OYN's legacy systems comprise many isolated (some nonrelational) databases and antiquated online transactional processing (OLTP) systems, each of which supports a range of overlapping tasks. Claims processing is slow because of backlogs, and errors are made because duplicated databases have conflicting information. To deal with this, OYN has been attempting to integrate various databases to provide middle management with better information for routine decisions. Most distressing to OYN management, however, is the fact that none of these efforts has resulted in providing top management with answers to strategic questions on accessibility, quality, and costs of medical services from its providers.

Imagine that you are a health management information system (HMIS) consultant hired to lead OYN into using electronic commerce (e-commerce). To help ease this massive claims processing load, you recommend that OYN implement Healthcare Electronic Commerce Decision Technology System (HEDTS), a comprehensive, integrated decision support system to link OYN's claim information systems directly to its providers' other information systems. HEDTS' essential features include the capability to perform complex claim analyses and evaluations and to generate periodic claim and other e-commerce status reports, claim forecasts, simulation results and recommendations for claims, and other e-commerce actions. Beyond this, you further suggest that OYN purchase the full capabilities embedded in HEDTS, which can additionally support clinical and administrative end user decision making through embedded applications software, including a decision support system (DSS) generator, an executive information system (EIS) product, and an expert system (ES) shell. As many OYN executives are not familiar with database concepts or the need for integrated DSSs, think about how you may want to structure a 1-hour presentation and how to portray HEDTS diagrammatically to help OYN management understand the need for a system such as HEDTS.

Despite the huge amount of capital required to implement HEDTS, you strongly believe that within two years of operating HEDTS, OYN will have sustained enough cost savings to recover and benefit from this investment. Hence, to justify your recommendation and to further illustrate how HEDTS will help OYN, you provide management with the following case scenario.

When Ms. Patient (who is one of OYN's enrollees) pays an initial visit to Dr. Jones (a physician contracted by OYN), for example, HEDTS permits the receptionist to access a status report on Ms. Patient's medical history. This history details her insurance information, including covered benefits, deductibles, and required copayments. Once inside the treatment room, Ms. Patient will find Dr. Jones viewing her medical records on the doctor's own terminal. After examining Ms. Patient, Dr. Jones can access HEDTS' medical advice module (an embedded ES) by keying in detected symptoms on a diagnostic screen. He can then receive a suggested diagnosis and treatment plan. To refine this plan, Dr. Jones can further perform sensitivity analyses (with the embedded DSS). This will result in a plan recommending the best alternative in terms of procedure code, deductible, and required copayment. When Dr. Jones accepts the recommended plan, HEDTS can immediately trigger an electronic claim request to OYN. Ms. Patient may, however, not have the deductible and copayment on hand, so the receptionist can flag the system. Immediately, HEDTS can generate a bill that can be handed to Ms. Patient before she leaves the treatment center. In the meantime, OYN's claims center can process the claim sent in electronically by Dr. Jones and send a check through HEDTS for the exact reimbursement.

Over time, HEDTS can also provide OYN with Dr. Jones' billing history. Similar transactions with other OYN providers can begin to generate the billing history segment of a data warehouse. By selecting HEDTS' problem/opportunity screen through the embedded EIS, OYN can further display utilization patterns for medical services across regions, providers, particular clinicians, or service categories. OYN can then use these patterns to assess any potential over-utilization of medical services, cost distributions, regional variations, and other pertinent problems or opportunities. Moreover, OYN can also detect fraud, target marketing efforts, and help design the most cost-effective health plans by performing additional analyses on these utilization patterns through the embedded DSS. For instance, because OYN is a managed care organization, management will be interested in integrating outcomes measurement with appropriateness, accessibility, and practice guidelines for measuring quality improvement. By accessing HEDTS' outcome management module through the embedded EIS, OYN management will be able to compare expected and actual patient outcomes. A report of these comparisons can further help OYN management identify patient problems, required health care interventions, time required for implementation of health care services, as well as accessibility, quality, and costs of health care services. Contemplate what other potential or possible benefits can result once HEDTS is in place at OYN. Think also about how OYN should go about evaluating HEDTS to ensure that the system does provide added values to the company.

Generally speaking, OYN's need for newer and better computing capabilities reveals how HMIS functions have progressed over the years. Note that the emphasis during the early periods of data-focused transactions is on doing isolated but highly structured tasks better, faster, and cheaper. In terms of OYN, the scope and type of automated activities that fall into this realm are the legacy systems, which mostly focused on improving operational efficiency in the processing and management of large volumes of data to support administration of patient care management and financing operations. The next shift in HMIS applications at OYN was mainly to direct attention toward data integration and report generation to achieve functional effectiveness. During this next stage of automation, OYN's emphasis is on creating better data structures and data retrieval capabilities to provide middle management with readily available answers to important queries. In this regard, it is no longer a matter of whether lots of data have been collected and processed but whether relevant and useful information can be made available out of the massive data that are being collected to support critical routine decisions. Although OYN management is clearly concerned about the need for this shift to evolve from focusing on data to information management, top management at OYN still feels frustrated about the lack of information to provide clear strategic directions. This is precisely why you have been consulted, and this is the point where OYN must again make the next major shift in health computing.

Indeed, the recent diffusion of advanced computerized support and improved technology architecture has the potential to lead many health organizations such as OYN to new levels of automated assistance. These advances, which have to do primarily with knowledge management, include data warehousing, geographical information system (GIS), EIS, ES, and health decision support system (HDSS) methods such as data mining, neural networks, and model-base management. This latest era of rapid progress in integrated health computing is seen as the empowering of end-users to apply integrated decision support and expert methods in clinical and strategic health management problem solving. Emerging HMIS technology architecture, including virtual patient records; document management; data warehousing; networking and ATM networks; medical informatics and telematics; as well as the Internet, intranets, and extranets that are reviewed in the previous chapter fit into this last era of health computing. Figure 7–1 depicts the evolution of these major eras of health computing leading to integrated health decision support technology architecture.

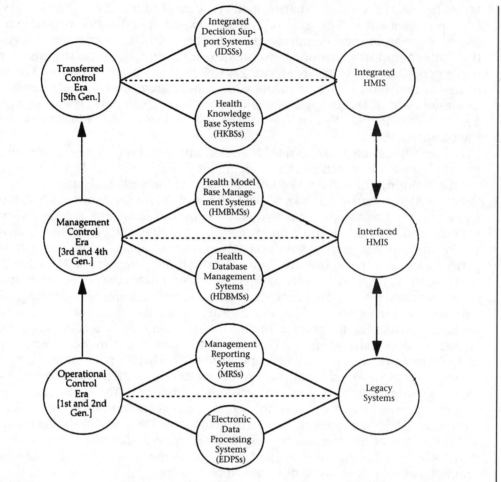

Figure 7–1 The Evolution of Legacy Systems to Interfaced and Integrated Health Management Information Systems (HMIS)

INTRODUCTION

In this chapter, our focus is on major advancing information and knowledge management technology architectures and how the different architectures can be combined to support health service delivery at regional and national levels. Accordingly, we first focus on underlying concepts of differing technology architectures and methods, including data warehousing, data mining, online analytical processing (OLAP), multidimensional databases (MDDBs), GISs, EISs, DSSs, and ESs. We then shift focus to show how these various concepts can be combined as an integrated architecture for a comprehensive cancer surveillance system (CSS). In addition, issues relating to the evaluation of such a system and its applications in public health service management will be highlighted.

DATA WAREHOUSING

The concept of a data warehouse is that of an integrated source of data organized and formatted, and even sometimes stratified, for management decision support and strategic planning. It differs from conventional database concepts in that rather than focusing on daily operations, a data warehouse uses relational data to support forecasting of trends and discovering of data patterns. In other words, it is a data depository to make operational data available for use in DSS, EIS, and other applications (e.g., ES) to support strategic thinking and knowledge discovery.

Moreover, a data warehouse provides a solution to the data access challenge faced in many DSS and EIS applications development because it contains data that are not only decision relevant, but they are already aggregated and filtered from legacy systems (i.e., the OLTP systems) and from various external sources. Consolidating such critical and decision relevant information into a data warehouse further provides an opportunity for the organization to restructure its DSS strategy. For example, the data warehouse can be used to identify competitors' strategies and provide insights to unfilled market niches.

Typically, the architecture of a data warehouse includes a large physical database, a logical data warehouse, several data marts, and associated DSS, EIS, and other applications. The physical database, which contains the data, can be centralized to maximize its processing power, or it can be distributed among departmental functions (i.e., a federate architecture) to ease maintenance. Alternatively, the physical database can have a tiered architecture, where different servers are used to manage different data sets ranging from highly summarized data to more detailed summaries.[2] The logical data warehouse contains the metadata (the "rules"), processing logic to separate, aggregate, and repackage the data, and information on navigating the data warehouse. In this sense, the data warehouse serves not only as a database, but also as a knowledge base. The data marts are subsets of the data warehouse that have been built over time, for example, departmental or functional data marts. Finally, DSS, EIS, and ES are typical applications that can use the data warehouse.

DECISION SUPPORT SYSTEMS

A DSS is an interactive, user-controlled system designed specifically to facilitate the decision maker in utilizing data and models for solving semi-structured (i.e., non-routine and non-repetitive) problems.[3] Therefore, the key distinguishing feature of a DSS from an OLTP application is its focus on enhancing decision-making effectiveness and not operational efficiency. In this sense, DSSs move toward automating cognitive (effectiveness) rather than physical (efficiency) aspects of health managerial and clinical task performance. Figure 7–2 shows a schematic representation of a DSS structure with its various subsystems, including the computer, the data, the model, the communications, and the user subsystems.

The computer subsystem consists of hardware and software. The data subsystem manages the stored data (database) through a database management system (DBMS), which is capable of several functions:

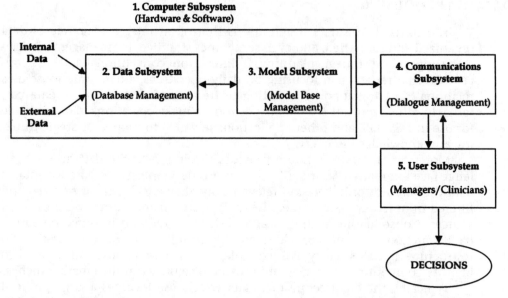

Figure 7–2 Structural Components of a Health Decision Support System (HDSS). *Source:* Adapted from J.K.H. Tan and S. Sheps, Health Decision Support Systems and Executive Information Systems: Basic Characteristics, Structure and Operation, *Health Decision Support Systems,* p. 36, © 1998, Aspen Publishers, Inc.

- combining data from external and internal sources
- adding, deleting, and updating its own database
- structuring data to allow for different "logical" views of the data for different users (managers, physicians, nurses, etc.)
- consolidating large and complex data files in a standardized manner for efficient and effective processing

One unique characteristic of data built into a DSS, which differs from feeding the data into OLTP predecessors, is the potential to capture not only quantitative ("hard"), but also qualitative ("soft") data, for example, the user's ideas, insights, logic, and experiences as expressed in the form of estimates or professional judgments. A DSS is able to do this because the types of decisions to be supported by the system are semi-structured (i.e., it is programmable only to a limited extent) as opposed to the routine and structured solutions characteristics of OLTP applications.

The model subsystem constructs, manages, and links models needed by the model builder through the model base management system (MBMS). The MBMS is capable of interrelating models with appropriate linkages throughout the database. According to Turban and Aronson,[4] the model base of a DSS may be subdivided into prewritten catalogued routines (or packages) and flexible software. Types of routines that are included in the prewritten category are structured report generators, built-in computational functions (e.g., mathematical and trigonometric functions), computer simulation, standardized financial functions (e.g., net present valuation), statistical routines (e.g., regression analysis), and sensitivity analysis ("what-if" analysis). Flexible software includes subroutines useful for constructing additional ad hoc routines and reports.

The user-system dialogue interface or the DSS communications subsystem may be viewed as comprising two-way communications—from the user to the DSS and from the DSS back to the user. DSS developers attempt to facilitate interaction between the computer and the user by integrating both the technical and behavioral aspects of computing. Computers have a great capacity for processing large amounts of information simultaneously according to a predetermined logic and have virtually unlimited storage capacity. On the contrary, humans have limited information processing and memory capacities, but possess knowledge, experience, and intuition.

The last element is the user subsystem. The health manager or clinician plays a significant role in the specification, design, and implementation of the DSS for decision modeling and analysis. Because it is the user who will ultimately determine the success or failure of a DSS, the user must provide specifications for the design of the DSS. Indeed, several studies have found that user involvement in the DSS development process contributes positively to decision performance as measured by higher user satisfaction and higher quality decisions. Finally, note that there are many categories of user levels, including individuals, groups, and community organizations, which should be considered in any DSS development and implementation.

EXECUTIVE INFORMATION SYSTEMS

An EIS may generally be distinguished from a DSS in two broad aspects.

1. It is a less technically oriented, but more strategically information friendly system.
2. It is designed especially for top management.

Keegan and Baldwin define an EIS as a "workstation based information system that integrates information from the important parts of a health care organization to give executives a high level perspective on key performance indicators and trends affecting their institutions."[5(p.58)] Once the executive has correctly defined the critical pieces of needed information, the EIS is programmed to access quickly and review this information at any level of the organization. In this sense, the function of an EIS is similar to that of a television. The EIS offers a convenient way of looking at the world and a medium for distributing information visually.

In addition to the sophisticated information retrieval and analysis capabilities, some EISs allow executives to communicate directly with outside organizational stakeholders via electronic mail, voice mail, computer conferencing, and bulletin boards. To provide these functions, an EIS must consolidate data from various sources within and outside the organization and reorganize these data. Internal sources include existing legacy systems that are both manual and automated. From a combination of this information, a comprehensive picture of the organization's performance and progress in various functional areas will be captured and relayed by the EIS. One special feature of EISs, often over-looked by the user in EIS design, for example, is the capability of these systems to allow for drill down analysis (i.e., the capability of these systems to work down to increasingly greater levels of details) to be performed on the data.

EXPERT SYSTEMS

The ES concept is that of a computer-based consultation program that uses both knowledge-based and inference-ruled procedures to simulate the deci-sion-making process of an expert. In this context, an expert is a highly skilled individual who has advanced training, knowledge, and experience in a particu-lar field (e.g., physician specialists or management consultants). Experts sup-port their colleagues in solving difficult problems requiring specific areas of knowledge. Experts have the ability to interact positively, the technical skills to perform their roles, the aptitudes to acquire and use knowledge, the compe-tence to organize and synthesize information, and the abilities to judge and make sound decisions in the absence of complete information. In this sense, an ES is an automated "expert." Figure 7–3 shows the architecture of an ES consisting of four basic parts: the knowledge base, the knowledge acquisition process, the ES shell, and the user interface.

The knowledge base contains the knowledge (specific facts and relevant data) about the expert domain. The knowledge acquisition process enables rel-evant portions of the knowledge base to be built and updated. The ES shell provides computational facilities for applying the knowledge base to user deci-sions, and the user interface allows interactions between the users and the sys-tem. Each of these ES components will now be briefly discussed.

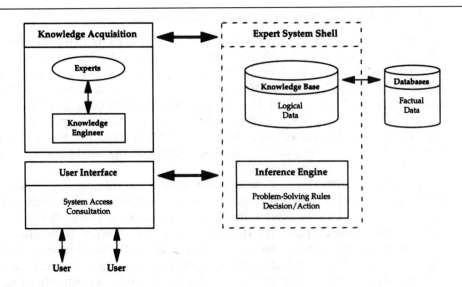

Figure 7–3 Architecture of Expert Systems

The distinction between a database and a knowledge base is often empha-sized for ESs. Computer databases are collections of individual observations or data points that are organized only for providing information, and not for cre-ating new knowledge. A database, for example, might record an observation such as, "Mr. John Doe had a blood pressure of 180/110 millimeters of mercury 24 hours ago, and a heart attack today." A knowledge base makes both the pre-vious observation and a new observation, derived from analyzing the initial observation: "Hypertension is associated with increased risk of myocardial infarction." Thus, the knowledge base incorporates both "facts" and "rules" for manipulating assimilated data, in order to create new knowledge, whereas databases contain only facts.

ESs acquire knowledge through a process that can be defined as activities or methods involved in the extraction of data, information, and experience. This acquired knowledge serves as an operational template to problem solve and is built on a foundation of formal study and heuristics (rules of thumb). Knowledge acquisition is a time-consuming process typically undertaken by a knowledge engineer whose task is to mine the necessary information ("rules") from the expert to construct a knowledge base.

The ES shell is the programming environment of the ES. ESs can be pro-grammed by using either artificial intelligence languages such as LISP and PROLOG or advanced software tools, known as ES shells. ES shells or building tools are user friendly, providing the advantage of a rapid development envi-ronment capable of quickly generating user-interface screens, capturing knowledge bases, and managing strategies for searching the rule base. Thus, the ES shells provide not only a substantial amount of the computer codes that would otherwise need to be written, tested, debugged, and maintained, but the tools and specific techniques for handling knowledge representation, reason-ing, and explanation. One well-known example of an ES shell is EMYCIN (which stands for Empty MYCIN), derived from MYCIN,[6] an ES designed to assist with the diagnosis and therapy of bacteremia and meningitis.

The inference engine is one component of the ES shell, standing between the knowledge base and the user, and controls the use of the knowledge base in solving problems. Analogous to the human problem-solving process, the inference engine performs three functions:

1. identification of applicable rules
2. conflict resolution or selection of the best rule for next step processing (and, where necessary, addition of new facts to the knowledge base)
3. rule execution and solution updating

To determine which rule to apply next, these functions are continuously iterated by a rule-chaining mechanism, which is part of the inference engine. Essentially, the inference engine classifies the outcome and recommends a line of action along with explanations for the suggested solution. These explana-tions may include rankings and specific probabilities of the alternatives, together with the probability of the recommended solution. The rules used to arrive at the given solution are normally made available through the ES user interface, either automatically or at the user's request.

The user interface allows effective communications between users and the ES. It is through the user interface component that the interviewer and inference engine communicate their questions, solutions, and explanations.

ADDITIONAL TECHNOLOGY ARCHITECTURE AND METHODS

In this section, we briefly discuss concepts of data mining and data mining tools, OLAP, multidimensional database (MDDB), and GISs, all of which may be used as front-end, back-end, or even as embedded tools in relation to DSS, EIS, and ES applications using the data warehouse.

Data mining (or sometimes referred to as data dipping) is simply the exploration of data for hidden knowledge and patterns. Advanced multidimensional visualization tools and other sophisticated tools are often used to assist end-users to data "mine," to ask ad hoc questions, and to discover unexpected results from a creative thinking approach. Examples of data mining tools include artificial neural networks, case-based (analogical) reasoning, statistical methods, genetic algorithms, and explanation-based learning.[7] Artificial neural networks parallel certain multi-attribute, multi-criteria information processing capabilities of human brain cells. Its architecture is based on that of a biological neural network, comprising processing elements, that allows for the easy implementation of fuzzy logic; that is, the transformation of simultaneous ambiguous input information to somewhat recognized patterns of activities. Case-based reasoning is a methodology in which inferences are formed and knowledge derived from historical cases. Statistical methods are becomingly increasingly complex, and many statistical methodologies are in fact embedded in various data mining techniques. Genetic (evolutionary) algorithms are essentially iterative procedures for generating new populations of evolving structures through reproduction, crossover, and mutation operators so as to effect "best" candidate solutions (chromosomes) to specific domain problems. Explanation-based learning assumes that a theoretical rationale exists to justify why an instance may (not) be considered a prototypical member of a class. Even so, many of these newer tools can often be combined with conventional software, such as spreadsheets, multidimensional color graphics, and even animated simulation.

OLAP refers to end-user computing in DSS and EIS environments, using data from the data warehouse. In contrast to OLTP, which is typically done by systems professionals, OLAP are activities such as queries, ad hoc report generation, statistical analysis, and multimedia applications development, which are completed by nonprofessionals. Typical tools used to support OLAP include structured query language, spreadsheets, data mining tools, and data visualization tools.

MDDB refers to a database in which the data are organized and accessible in several dimensions such as by region, by service type, by provider identity, and by time (four dimensions), as with data placed in a data warehouse. MDDB requires multidimensional modeling methods for analysis and display of its multidimensional data. Multidimensional data can also be manipulated and displayed using multidimensional spreadsheet and graphics software.

Finally, a GIS uses spatial data such as digitized maps and is capable of representing a combination of text, graphics, icons, and symbols on maps. Figure 7–4 is an example of a screen design showing the various regions for locating community health units in British Columbia, Canada, that can be generated from a GIS.[8]

At this point, it is important to ask how these differing technology architecture concepts and methods that we have reviewed may in fact be combined

Figure 7–4 Screen Design of Local Community Health Units in British Columbia, Canada. *Source:* Adapted with permission from HPB, Health Economics and Planning Branch, Ministry of Health and Ministry Responsible for Seniors, Victoria, British Columbia.

into a functional, integrated architecture solution to support public health service delivery at regional and national levels. In this regard, our focus here will be on a comprehensive CSS architecture.

A COMPREHENSIVE CANCER SURVEILLANCE SYSTEM ARCHITECTURE

Commenting on future directions for comprehensive public health surveillance and health information system development, Thacker and Stroup[9] note that the current approach in the United States to public health surveillance is "fragmented" and argue that the reasons for the inability of current surveillance systems to detect epidemics of health problems are because of the following:

- nonexistence of surveillance for the specific problem
- untimely (and poor quality) data maintained by existing surveillance systems
- uncoordinated surveillance practices
- inadequate funding
- weak societal and public commitments

In responding to these comments, they further note the need for evolving a comprehensive network of compatible health information systems linked electronically and readily accessible to public health practitioners on a timely basis. In this section, we will attempt to show specifically how such a comprehensive, integrated architecture may indeed be conceptualized for a CSS.

A long-term public objective is to reduce the incidence, morbidity, mortality, and costs associated with the national cancer burden on the oral complications of cancer therapies, especially as it relates to oral and pharyngeal cancers.[10] For this purpose, it is necessary to monitor populations; collect relevant cancer screening, incidence, treatment, and outcomes data; identify pertinent cancer patterns; explain these patterns; and translate the explanations into effective diagnoses and treatment programs. In other words, it is not enough just to collect the relevant data; rather, the data must be converted into meaningful variables for potential analyses. For example, in order to identify patterns in the data and to build explanatory models for these patterns, the data must be converted into the variables relevant to the explanatory models. Moreover, these models must also be tested and validated against the previously collected and processed cancer surveillance data. Hence, throughout this lengthy and complex cancer surveillance process, a need exists for ongoing manipulation and transformation of the data sets until meaningful and useful information, knowledge, and wisdom can be derived for use by the public health practitioners.

A key problem, however, is that the available data for assessing the diverse aspects of cancer surveillance are currently being captured in diverse formats and scattered throughout many organizations. Moreover, the varied formats and locations for housing these data have created burdensome tasks for clinicians, administrators, policy makers, researchers, analysts, and other stakeholders who seek to assess the national cancer burden from the available data. Because there is limited sharing of data across interested groups because of the heterogeneity of these data sources, a comprehensive CSS must therefore be able to apply available methodologies and technologies to collect, reformat, cleanse, filter, and even link data from many sources, including population-based systems (e.g., cancer registries and vital records), provider-based systems (e.g., private managed care encounter reports, fee-for-service insurance billings, and discharge summaries), payer systems (e.g., multiple payer databases, Medicare, and Medicaid), and other administrative systems (e.g., records on environmental and occupational hazards).

Because the success of data acquisition is highly dependent on the abilities, skills, and domain knowledge of the interested parties and stakeholders, who must identify the data pertinent to their analyses and evaluations, a greater awareness of available analytical tools and applicable decision aiding technologies is needed among stakeholders and interested parties. Otherwise, it is possible that even the most talented and skilled parties will have incomplete knowledge and wisdom about what is being studied. Simply stated, cancer data collection, processing, and analysis are time-consuming and costly processes. In this regard, the use of an intelligent agent architecture, which is also computer-based, will ease the timely selection, categorization, and storage of the surveillance information. In this way, much useful information, knowledge, and wisdom await to be uncovered in the joint effort to simplify, and perhaps even shorten, the complex cancer surveillance process.

The Cancer Surveillance Process

As we have seen, a number of technology architecture and analytical approaches may be applied to assist interested parties in collecting, processing, and analyzing cancer data. For example, methods to view the secondary data sources, extract the relevant data components, capture the key data elements, and warehouse the captured data have been discussed by Kimball[11] and others.[12] In addition, Fayaad et al.[13] and others[14] have proposed using data mining techniques to access the data warehouse and to detect care, outcome, and therapy patterns. Still, other researchers have advanced sophisticated statistical methodologies to develop explanatory models for the detected patterns.[15,16]

Finally, an integrated DSS technology architecture, which combines DSS, EIS, and ES architecture, can also be used to deliver the methods, techniques, methodologies, and developed models to the interested parties. To examine how a sampling of appropriate data mining techniques and how embedding them within an integrated DSS/ES/EIS architecture can significantly enhance future cancer surveillance, we will take a closer look at the sequence of activities involved in the cancer surveillance process, as depicted in Figure 7–5.

As shown, the first step is to acquire, extract, and warehouse pertinent cancer data. The second step is to apply statistical and artificial intelligence data mining techniques to detect cancer patterns hidden in the data warehouse. In the third step, additional statistical methodologies are used to identify variables correlating with the patterns, formulate hypotheses of variables that cause cancer, and test the hypotheses. To some extent, these evaluations will be guided by, and rely on, the judgment, insights, and experience of the researcher or analyst. Finally, an integrated system architecture is envisioned to deliver and provide all of the needed functions of a comprehensive CSS.

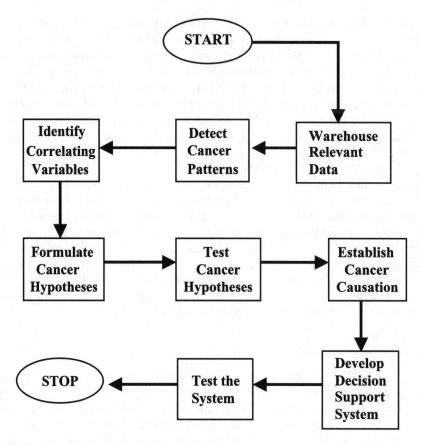

Figure 7–5 The Cancer Surveillance Process

More specifically, the components of the CSS architecture will comprise a data warehouse, a GIS, an EIS, and a DSS/ES component, as shown in Figure 7–6. We now explain each of these components briefly and illustrate their functions in the CSS architecture.

Data Warehouse

The CSS data warehouse will have three components: a database, a model base, and a knowledge base. The database, as we have noted, will capture and store geographic, demographic, environmental, health outcome, and health care data. An example of a major source for data extraction into the CSS database is the Maryland Medicaid claims data. These data, which include medical, dental, rehabilitative, and other health care services claims by children, minorities, women, and others (e.g., the underserved), are currently managed for the state by the University of Maryland Baltimore County's Center for Health Program Development and Management (CHPDM). Nine years of these data, including various profiles categorized in the CHPDM data warehouses,

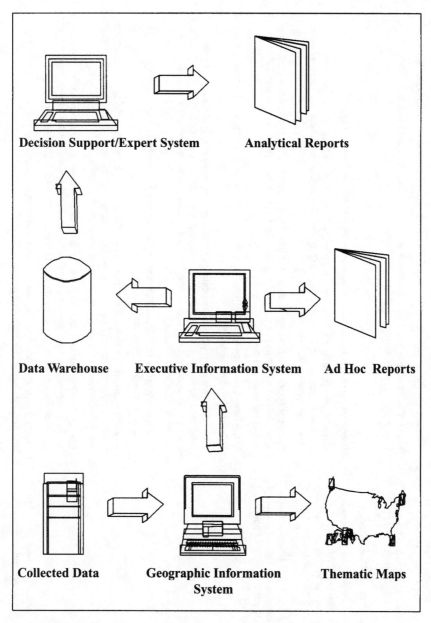

Figure 7–6 Components of Cancer Surveillance System Architecture

are available. Table 7–1 provides an overview of the CHPDM files, and Table 7–2 profiles one summary view of the relevant data captured in these files.

The model base (i.e., an organized repository of models and algorithms) will capture and store GIS, health, and statistical models required and desired by interested parties. These models will permit CSS users to compute and predict cancer-relevant variables, describe and explain the spatial, temporal, and

Table 7–1 Center for Health Program Development and Management (CHPDM) Data Files Structure

Category	Nature of Files	Contents
Eligibility	Demographic and other information used to determine Medicaid eligibility. Each file has one unique record for each Maryland Medicaid recipient number or head of household	**Yearly Eligibility (ellg)**—provides person-level data including Medicaid recipient number, sex, race, age, birth date, and monthly eligibility status
Claims	Utilization and cost information for dental, home health, inpatient, long-term care, outpatient, pharmacy, physician, and special services. Each claims file contains information on a full fiscal year based on date of service, obtained through filtering and summarizing programs developed by the state of Maryland Department of Health and Mental Hygiene (DHMH) and the CHPDM.	**Dental (dent)**—provides utilization and expenditure information for dental care
		Home Health (hhlth)—provides home health–related services, such as skilled nursing visits, physical therapy, and speech therapy; also provides claims data on medical day care, personal care, and some medical supplies
		Inpatient (inpt)—provides claims data for the facility component of inpatient care, including care at acute hospitals, state chronic hospitals, state and private psychiatric centers, and state residential treatment centers
		Long-Term Care (ltc)—provides nursing home, mental retardation facility, and medical or surgical intermediate care facility claims data
		Outpatient (opt)—provides claims data for the facility component of outpatient services, such as clinic visits, emergency department visits, radiology and laboratory services, supplies, psychiatric day care, and physical and occupational therapies (similar services provided to inpatients are recorded in the inpatient file)
		Pharmacy (pharm)—provides claims data on all pharmaceutical services provided to Medicaid recipients for a filled prescription
		Physician (phys)—provides claims data on services provided by clinical providers in all settings. Clinical providers include physicians, registered nurses, dentists, optometrists, nurse practitioners, registered physician assistants, MSW social worker, and dietitians
		Special Services (spec)—provides claims data on transportation and ambulance fees, oxygen therapy, medical laboratory services, physical therapy, school health, durable medical equipment and supplies, and other miscellaneous services not contained in the above files
Summary	Eligibility status, annual payment, and other person-based information developed by the CHPDM staff from eligibility and claims data.	**Yearly Summary Files**—provide person-based summaries of annual eligibility, demographics, service utilization, and expenditure data
		Monthly Summary Files—provides monthly summaries of expenditures for the eight types of services: dental, home health, inpatient, long-term care, outpatient, pharmacy, physician, and special services. Another file provides monthly expenditures across all types of services

Table 7–2 Summary Profiles in Center for Health Program Development and Management Data

	American Indian or Alaskan Native	*Asian or Pacific Islander*	*Black, Not of Hispanic Origin*	*Hispanic*	*White, Not of Hispanic Origin*	*Other or Unknown*	*Total*
Female	709	7,968	207,364	11,663	130,651	7,796	366,151
Male	382	4,722	125,599	6,428	79,458	4,289	224,178
Unknown						24	24
Total	1,091	12,690	335,963	18,391	210,109	12,109	590,353

space-time relationships between the identified variables and cancer development, and make use of these relationships to simulate overall and oral cancer incidence and mortality in general and special populations.

The knowledge base will contain the knowledge (facts and rules) necessary for understanding, formulating, and solving problems relating to cancer incidence and prevalence. It will capture and store spatial and temporal profiles linked to cancer incidence, development, and mortality patterns. This knowledge base will also be readily accessible to the integrated DSS applications component, namely, the DSS, EIS, and ES applications embedded in the CSS.

Geographical Information System

The embedded GIS will serve as a front-end application to the processing of the profile data. As previously indicated, besides extracting data and creating thematic maps, the GIS can provide inputs for the EIS. These inputs consist of the geographic, health outcome, environmental and natural resource, demographic, and health care variables associated with the desired geographic area.

The GIS can use data mining to extract patterns of cancer occurrence and incidence. For instance, data mining techniques can identify certain regional characteristics that appear to have an impact on higher incidence of cancer in the area. The GIS links these findings and data to spatial dimensions and transfers the linked data to the embedded EIS.

EXECUTIVE INFORMATION SYSTEM

Two processors embedded in the EIS—a DBMS and an intelligent DSS processor—provide most of the data processing, management, and distribution functions.

The DBMS extracts geographic area conditions from the GIS, takes ad hoc queries by the user in an interactive manner, displays the query results in attractive reports, and stores the information in the data warehouse. The intelligent DSS processor captures the DBMS-generated data, updates the DSS's spatial and temporal statistical models, performs DSS analyses and evaluations, and generates detailed reports of the results automatically without human (manual) intervention. In this way, the EIS helps the building of the data warehouse and then does the access and reporting from the data warehouse.

For ease of use, the EIS will provide an open and scalable OLAP solution using the World Wide Web with the thin-client architecture, as shown in Figure 7–7.

In this architecture, reports and graphs of multidimensional data stored in the MDDB server can be easily generated and viewed by the clients. Here, it is important to note that the multidimensional data contained in the MDDB would have been previously transformed and derived from the raw data contained in the database of the data warehouse via the database server. Users can run queries and generate reports using any HTML-based browser without having an application session being run on the client. This architecture also reduces the cost of client-server management by centralizing the data and applications on the server, and the architecture makes it simple to distribute and upgrade applications and add new OLAP users.

Data Mining

Complex data mining techniques,[17] such as neural networks, genetic algorithms, and statistical methodologies will also be available to extract cancer patterns in the data. This mining can facilitate information analysis using

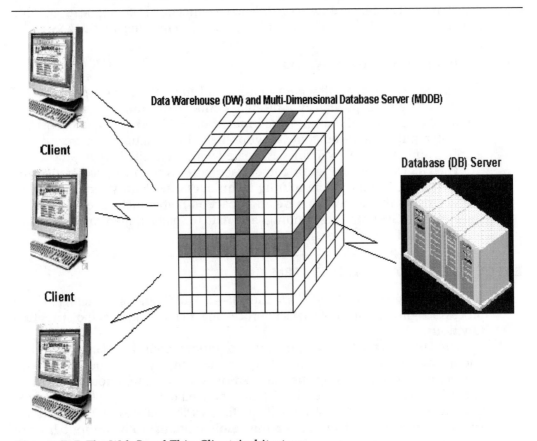

Figure 7–7 The Web-Based Thin-Client Architecture

either predictive or descriptive modeling.[18] Descriptive modeling is exploratory in nature and contributes to the discovery of previously unknown patterns, trends, and associations in the data. Predictive modeling allows the examination of data in a more traditional way by testing specific hypotheses. For instance, health care providers may anticipate an increased incidence of cancer in areas that have radioactive waste disposal units. By relying on historical data, data mining techniques can test for this hypothesis in areas where such waste disposal is prevalent.

The use of data mining is expected to reveal important patterns in several areas, for example, key factors impacting cancer care, recurrence, and prevention. These patterns are expected to be revealed at the population, subpopulation, and individual levels. Explanatory and other statistical models can then be used to refine patterns that emerge from the use of these techniques. Further, such validated findings will eventually allow users to develop rules that can be encoded into the CSS knowledge base.

Decision Support System/Expert System

The integration of EIS, DSS, and ES can be done in several ways. In our case, the information generated by the EIS is used as an input to the DSS. That is, the EIS will provide the focused data required for the DSS analyses and evaluations.

The DSS/ES (an intelligent DSS) will then guide the investigator through the intelligent modeling and the management of the database, model base, and knowledge base in the data warehouse. The ES component also enables the reasoning (explanations and supporting knowledge) to be provided for GIS, EIS, and DSS analyses and evaluations.

The integration of these components results in a comprehensive CSS architecture, which is discussed next.

The Comprehensive Cancer Surveillance System Architecture

Figure 7–8 depicts the comprehensive CSS architecture. As the figure illustrates, interested parties can utilize the various CSS components both interactively and in an integrated fashion to process inputs into desired outputs.

Inputs

As noted, the CSS has a data warehouse that continually captures and stores the relevant cancer surveillance information from a variety of sources, has the models and algorithms for making sense out of the stored information, and has the rules, historical management actions, and policy issues that are accumulated over time from active user interactions with the system.

In processing the cancer surveillance information, for example, multiple equation statistical models can be used to establish independent and joint causation between the cancer patterns and their determinants. This model would then predict why the spatial patterns are occurring for specific demographic, spatial, and other profiles. The model would also determine if there are devia-

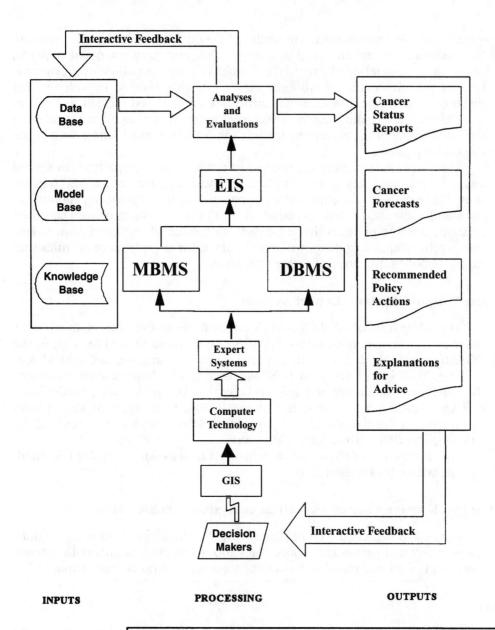

Figure 7–8 The Comprehensive Cancer Survellance System Architecture

tions from the profile, and therefore, if there is an epidemic at hand, and identify the specific causes of the epidemic.

In addition, the CSS learns from these processing sessions and builds the knowledge base with matching profiles, which are linked to different patterns so that future similar patterns and causes indicative of an epidemic will be easy to detect.

Processing

The EIS component can call on intelligent agents to filter profile data, focus the filtered information, and communicate problems (e.g., deviations from expected cancer development patterns) and opportunities among interested and affected parties. For example, based on profile data made available from public and private sources, stakeholders and interested parties can use the EIS and DSS/ES interactively to perform analyses and evaluations.

In general, major data warehouse processing for cancer surveillance include:

- organizing data into parameters needed for the spatial, temporal, and space-time cancer analyses
- structuring models that represent and simulate overall and oral cancer development patterns in an integrated and complete manner
- simulating overall and oral cancer incidence and mortality under specified health care, health outcome, demographic, and environmental profiles

Additional processing will also involve the following:

- masking individual identities from publicly released health data
- disease surveillance
- identification of stabilized rates
- exposure assessment
- genetic activity profiling
- interactive spatial data analysis
- kriging
- drill downs on outlying statistics
- disease rate analyses
- small area variation analyses
- space-time clustering
- standard mortality rate analyses

Outputs

By controlling processing tasks in a desired fashion, it is possible for the user to produce visually attractive tabular and graphical claims status reports that describe the provider's clinical and administrative environment, track meaningful trends, and display important patterns. Claims condition forecasts, provider policies, payer program simulation results, and recommended claims actions can also be generated as outputs. The CSS can also depict the reasoning that leads to the suggested actions. These explanations and supporting knowledge may even be portrayed visually. For example, by making desired CSS selections, the user will be able to simulate expected overall and oral cancer incidences and mortalities in general and in special populations, compare actual results with the expected occurrences, and obtain a brief explanation for the deviations.

Feedback Loops

Feedback from the processing provides additional data, knowledge, and enhanced decision models that may be useful for future cancer surveillance activities and tasks. Feedback from the output (often in the form of sensitivity analyses) is used to extend or modify the original analyses and evaluations.

As an example of a complete interactive session, imagine a user, Mr. X, entering the CSS. Using the GIS, he may decide to display a map depicting what is occurring in a particular area and begin querying what would be expected to occur in the absence of an epidemic using the OLAP facility in the embedded EIS. Next, he may then drill down to a very concentrated area to determine if the deviations are focused in one area or general to the entire region. At this point, he has a choice to use clustering models provided in the MBMS or use artificial intelligence–based data mining techniques to try to identify the pattern. Following this, he could call on the ES component to request an explanation for the detected pattern. Such an explanation would in turn call up the multiple equation statistical model provided in the DSS/ES component, which would analyze whether the incident is caused by a specific factor or a series of interrelated factors specific to the region. With this information in hand, he could further perform sensitivity analyses to find out what would happen if certain conditions change or if policies were changed. All results could be displayed on the maps with or without supporting tables, thereby justifying the analyses and evaluations.

CANCER SURVEILLANCE SYSTEM EVALUATION

Conceptually, the CSS architecture just described appears promising as it provides a seamless approach to ease the complex cancer surveillance process. This promise, however, must still be evaluated. In this sense, measures must be developed to assess the effectiveness of the proposed system in reducing the national cancer burden and a research design and methodology implemented to test CSS effectiveness against these measures. This section presents a general CSS evaluation plan.

Cancer Surveillance System Effectiveness

CSS effectiveness is difficult to measure and includes many dimensions. For example, effectiveness of decisions resulting from the use of CSS can be measured at the input level (e.g., relevance of data extraction and pattern detection), at the processing level (e.g., tests of goodness-of-fit of the models and the pertinence of variables used in the models), and at the output level (e.g., the quality and cost of diagnostic and treatment outcomes). Moreover, a termination point for these analyses and evaluations would also need to be determined.

The CSS must support the process of, as well as outcomes from, cancer surveillance decision making. As indicated, this surveillance involves a multi-criteria assessment of effectiveness. Further, one general measure (i.e., process) is, at least partially, intangible in nature. Under these circumstances, Forgionne and Kohli argue that the evaluation of system effectiveness should be on the basis of the multi-criteria model shown in Figure 7–9.[19,20]

As shown, the overall criterion or composite decision value is determined by the process of, and the outcome from, using the CSS. Outcome, in turn, is set by cancer surveillance performance and decision-maker maturity (increase in decision-making ability, skills, and domain knowledge), and process is prescribed by phase and step proficiency, personal efficiency, and personal produc-

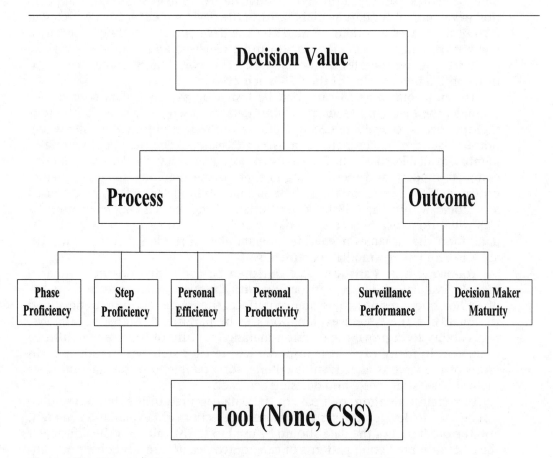

Figure 7–9 System Effectiveness Multiple-Criteria Evaluation Model

tivity. Several measures may fall within these general categories. The two most obvious alternatives (choices) will be using or not using the list of CSS support tools provided (i.e., CSS support not used versus CSS support tool used).

Equal or different weights can be assigned to each of these assessment variables. Variables not included in the analysis can be given zero weighting. Similarly, each support tool can receive an equal or disparate weight in the overall evaluation. In a completely impartial scheme, each variable would receive an equal weight, and each tool would have the same weight. By aggregating the estimated weights through the hierarchy, the evaluator will obtain an overall rating for each provided support tool. The overall criterion ratings then provide a basis for identifying decision value from the supporting aids; that is, highly effective tools will receive the largest decision values.

Research Design and Methodology

For the purpose of research evaluation, a prototype of the CSS can be initially developed through a proven adaptive design strategy using rapid application development toolkits available within the development software. Detailed technical changes can then be made by the developers over time (typically a few weeks), and the system changes can be reviewed and evaluated by some other stakeholders besides the developers. This evolutionary process can continue until a final version of the CSS is achieved.

The implemented CSS can then be tested on available data sources, for example, the Maryland Medicaid claims data we discussed earlier. In the testing, the idea is to evaluate CSS operations and results objectively. First, warehoused data can be compared against actual values. The next step will be to identify available spatial and spatial-temporal variables, model components, complete models, and methodologies that, as the literature suggests, predict cancer incidence and mortality. These simulation models can then be captured and stored within the CSS to "operationalize" the models. In this sense, the CSS will automatically access the data warehouse, extract literature pertinent data, form the variables needed for the simulation models, and use the variables to estimate the model's parameters.

Following this, statistical tests can then be conducted on the estimated models. Evaluations of user satisfaction with the speed, relevance, and quality of ad hoc query results; the system interface; the model appropriateness; and the quality of the system explanation can be performed. Moreover, the system's ability to improve the decision-making maturity of the user can also be evaluated. In many cases, it is important to test for statistical significance in terms of the various effectiveness criteria, for example, user satisfaction, user maturity, decision speed, and decision accuracy.

In system validation, one part of the data captured in the data warehouse can be used to develop the system's pattern detection and explanatory models, and the other part of the data should be used to statistically test the efficacy of the system in predicting patterns of care, outcomes of care, and effects of cancer therapies (Figure 7–10).

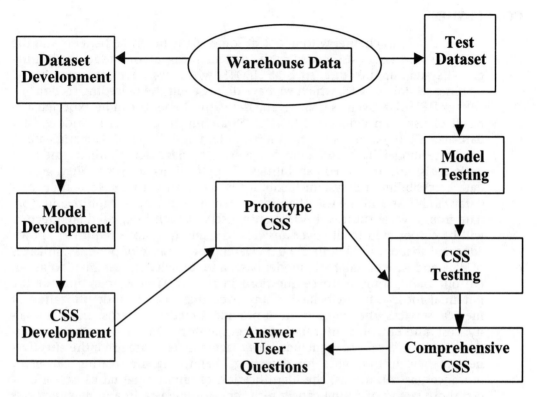

Figure 7–10 Research Design for the Cancer Surveillance System (CSS) Evaluation

A priori hypotheses are important to guide the research process. In the case of testing the CSS effectiveness, examples of specific hypotheses may include:

- The CSS can detect important patterns in the health claims data, such as practice patterns at various treatment stages, end-of-life care patterns, long-term complication patterns for survivors, and diagnostic test use patterns.
- The CSS can explain the underlying causes of the detected patterns, such as the factors influencing care received at end-of-life, the effect of carve-out contracts for cancer treatment on treatment patterns and outcomes, and environmental, biological, and hereditary causes of cancers.
- The CSS can use predictive modeling to identify subpopulations that can potentially have higher incidence of cancer and who can consequently affect the cost structures of cancer care.
- The CSS can improve the clinical and administrative practice of cancer surveillance.

In short, the CSS evaluation plan can assess whether or not the proposed system architecture can aid in reducing the national cancer burden.

CONCLUSION

We close this chapter with a look at some of the potential benefits and the problems and issues associated with implementing a comprehensively integrated system architecture, such as HEDTS, which we have presented in the opening section, or CSS, which we have discussed in the preceding section.

For HEDTS, as well as CSS, several derivative benefits can be expected as a result of using an embedded EIS/DSS/ES architecture. These include greater data accessibility and system flexibility, potential linkages of data and ease of database, model base and knowledge base management, enhancement of basic tools, and increased capabilities of applications software. First, greater data accessibility and system flexibility is achieved with the formation of a data warehouse and the use of an integrated architecture to capture and store data from diverse sources. In this sense, users of such integrated architecture will be empowered to discover answers to many questions requiring knowledge and wisdom hidden in the data warehouse because of potential linkages of data and ease of database, model base, and knowledge base manipulation. On one hand, some of these questions in the HEDTS case may include the potential for fraudulent behavior; any overutilization or underutilization of medical services; the comparison of provider practice patterns; and the quality, cost, and outcome information of competitors. On the other hand, questions in the CSS case may include how diagnostic tests are used; the effectiveness of new technologies for detecting, diagnosing, or treating cancer or precancerous conditions; the identification of environmental causes of cancer; those factors affecting cancer recurrence or metastasis; and new methods for the prevention and treatment of oral complications of radiation or chemotherapy.

Enhancement of basic tools and increased capabilities of applications software ultimately imply that such an integrated architecture can be applied efficiently, effectively, and intelligently. Interested parties, armed with pertinent knowledge and wisdom derived from the use of HEDTS or the CSS, for example, will be in a better position to effectively evaluate the efficacy of specific treatments and interventions. Even so, the use of integrated architectures has its share of problems and limitations. For example, it is harder to justify funding for the systems because of the complexity of doing a cost-benefit, cost-effectiveness, or feasibility analysis. There are also too many alternatives in performing the integration, and many developers or builders often lack the expertise or experience to undertake these systems integration projects. Moreover, changes in established practices, existing organizational culture, and learning may have to take place to accommodate new technological and management processes.

Finally, integrated systems, such as HEDTS and CSS, will require rigorous evaluations before their values can be established. If found effective, however, these integrated architecture prototypes can serve also as templates to guide similar future health care analyses and solutions. Based on results from previous, related research, the potential cost savings can be expected to reach several billion dollars.[21]

CHAPTER QUESTIONS

1. How does data warehousing facilitate health care management, in general, and cancer surveillance, in particular? Be specific about the technical capabilities provided, the personnel and organizational requirements met, and management objectives achieved.

2. Health care managers have much knowledge and experience about the decision environment. Yet data mining can contribute significantly to the manager's understanding and wisdom. Illustrate this contribution with an example from your personal experience and from the cancer surveillance application.

3. Decision support, executive information, and expert systems along with artificial intelligence each help users better manage health care. What additional support, over and above the support offered by each stand-alone system, can be achieved using an integrated decision technology system such as HEDTS or CSS? Illustrate the additional support with an example from your personal experience and from the cancer surveillance application.

4. The health care managers typically must rely on a variety of technical experts to help construct information systems that support decision making. There may be a need for operations researchers, statisticians, database specialists, and so on. How can an integrated decision technology system such as CSS facilitate this process? Illustrate the support with an example from your personal experience or from the cancer surveillance application.

5. Health care organizations are often geographically dispersed. This dispersion creates coordination problems for the manager of the organization. How can an integrated decision technology system such as CSS facilitate such coordination of effort? Illustrate the concept with an example from your personal experience or from the cancer surveillance application.

6. The chapter notes that systems like HEDTS and CSS can save health care organizations and society billions of dollars. Give some examples of the potential savings from the use of the CSS.

NOTES

1. G.A. Forgionne, A. Gangopadhyay, J.A. Klein, and R. Eckhardt, A Decision Technology System for Health Care Electronic Commerce, *Topics in Health Information Management* 20, no. 1 (1990): 31–41.

2. Y.S. Wang, D.C. Yen, and D.C. Chou, An Analysis of Data Warehouse Development, in *ACME Transactions 1998, Proceedings of 1998 International Conference of Pacific Rim Management*, eds. L. Tsui, Q. Zhu, and C.H. Chang (Dearborn, MI: University of Michigan-Dearborn, 1998), 178–183.

3. J.K.H. Tan, Health Decision Support Systems and Executive Information Systems: Basic Characteristics, Structure, and Operation, in *Health Decision Support Systems*, ed. J.K.H. Tan with S. Sheps, (Gaithersburg, MD: Aspen Publishers, 1998).

4. E. Turban and J.E. Aronson, *Decision Support Systems and Intelligent Systems*. 5th ed. (Upper Saddle River, NJ: Prentice-Hall, 1998).

5. A.J. Keegan and B. Baldwin, EIS: A Better Way To View Hospital Trends, *Healthcare Financial Management* 46, no. 11 (1992): 58.

6. E.H. Shortliffe, *Computer-Based Medical Consultations: MYCIN* (New York: Elsevier Science Publishing Co., 1976).

7. E. Turban and J.E. Aronson, *Decision Support Systems and Intelligent Systems*.

8. J.K.H. Tan with S. Sheps, eds. *Health Decision Support Systems* (Gaithersburg, MD: Aspen Publishers, 1998).

9. S.B. Thacker and D.F. Stroup, Future Directions for Comprehensive Public Health Surveillance and Health Information Systems in the United States, *American Journal of Epidemiology* 140, no. 5 (September 1994): 383–397.

10. National Institute for Health, *Cancer Surveillance Using Health Claims-Based Data System* (Washington, DC: National Cancer Institute, 1998, PA-99–015).

11. R. Kimball, *The Data Warehouse Toolkit* (New York: John Wiley and Sons, 1996).

12. R. Barquin and H. Edelstein, *Planning and Designing the Data Warehouse* (Upper Saddle River, NJ: Prentice-Hall, 1997).

13. U. Fayaad, G. Piatetsky-Shapiro, and P. Smyth, The KDD Process for Extracting Useful Knowledge from Volumes of Data, *Communications of the ACM* 39, no. 11 (1996): 27–34.

14. A. Agrawal and R. Srikant, Mining Sequential Patterns, in *Proceedings of the IEEE International Conference on Data Engineering* (Los Alamitos, CA: IEEE Computer Society, 1995).

15. D.J. Berndt and J. Clifford, Finding Patterns in Time Series: A Dynamic Programming Approach, in *Advances in Knowledge Discovery and Data Mining* (Cambridge, MA: AAAI Press/MIT Press, 1996): 229–248.

16. J.H. Friedman, Multivariate Adaptive Regression Splines, *Annals of Statistics* 19 (1989): 1–141.

17. L.S. Borok, Data Mining: Sophisticated Forms of Managed Care Modeling through Artificial Intelligence: Review, *Journal of Health Care Finance* 23, no. 3 (1997): 20–36.

18. P.R. Limb and G.J. Meggs, Data Mining—Tools and Techniques, *British Telecom Technology Journal* 12, no. 4 (1995): 32–41.

19. G.A. Forgionne and R. Kohli, HMSS: A Management Support System for Concurrent Hospital Decision Making, *Decision Support Systems* 16 (1996): 209–229.

20. G.A. Forgionne and R. Kohli, A Model To Measure DSS Effectiveness: Theory and Empirical Analysis, *Journal of Decision Systems* 7, no. 2 (1998): 105–122.

21. G.A. Forgionne, HADTS: A Decision Technology System To Support Army Housing Management. European, *Journal of Operational Research* 97 (1997): 363–379.

Chapter 8

Communications System Architecture: Networking Health Provider Organizations and Building Virtual Communities

J. Michael Tarn, H. Joseph Wen, and Joseph K. H. Tan

SCENARIO

Imagine that you have been asked by the Regional Health Board of Green Atlantis Community to oversee the design of a community health information network (CHIN), which would provide general health information and knowledge support to residents of Green Atlantis and link them electronically to available health provider networks and other key community services, such as police, fire, and ambulance. The deadline for implementing this project is January 1, 2005.

For a start, you have been provided with the following vision. The year is 2005 and homes, hospitals, and other health providers of Green Atlantis are all linked on a high-speed CHIN. This architecture will allow every Green Atlantis household, for a small fee, to have access to unlimited interactive health information. Homes will be installed with interactive and digital television sets that function as Web-based computers linked to the Internet communications system. These interactive machines will be as easy to use as the telephone. Various menus will be easily accessible, as will the health menu that will link any of the community residents to the GREAT*net, the CHIN to be implemented for Green Atlantis. The patient file server, health provider information server, and medical information server will all be found on GREAT*net. These servers will comprise massively paralleled supercomputers. When Ms. Resident of Green Atlantis needs advice for a complaint about her health, about any given disease, or about what to do when an inheritable disease is identified in her family, she can make use of the medical information server to ask questions about her own health concerns, whether hereditary, habit related, or environmentally influenced. She can even learn of options for treating her illness. In every case, the medical information server is kept updated with new procedures, treatments, symptoms, literature, and diagnosis.

The home system will be entirely voice driven and remote controlled. This will make it enjoyable and easy to use. It will allow users to "drill down" to a level that is helpful to both the professional and the layperson. The ease-of-use factor will minimize apprehension, while allowing the user to delve deeper into GREAT*net. Information will be presented in terminology that can be augmented with images. With population demographic information, it is anticipated that GREAT*net will also be programmed to provide a multiple language option.

Within GREAT*net, the home system can be linked via satellite to employers, payers, hospitals, doctor's offices, other health provider networks (e.g., pharmacies, laboratories, and diagnostic centers), and the 911 fire, police, and ambulance network. GREAT*net will be a comprehensive, integrated health network, and the emergency network connected to GREAT*net will allow automatic calls to the police, ambulance, or firefighters. The medical information service will contain extensive health sciences databases, which will be constructed specifically for the purpose of general public use. Different databases can be called upon, depending on the user's needs, so that the responses are uniquely tailored to each inquiry. The medical information server also will be able to deliver customized information based on the user's personal characteristics such as age, sex, race, and occupation. GREAT*net will offer many features that are valuable to the public, one component of which may be health and lifestyle.

Based on results of a recent survey, you were told that the health and lifestyle assessment module will be the most valuable to the Green Atlantis residents. It will be able to identify behavioral, genetic, and environmental forces that may be causing an adverse effect on an individual lifestyle. Upon identifying the prioritized risks, the module will be able to provide the user with more in-depth information through specialized loops or algorithms before returning to complete the general assessment. As needed, further algorithms that explore other potentially problematic areas can be utilized as the inquirer indicates their possible importance. Through this interactive means, the inquirer can "converse" with the software as if talking to a real doctor. At the end of each session, the program will provide an audio and a visual list of steps that the user can follow to alleviate an aliment, such as changing diet, breaking smoking habits, and reducing alcohol intake, along with an explanation as to why it is worth making these changes. The user will also be able to get a personalized copy of the session both printed on paper and electronically stored on a smart card, optical disk, or some other medium. Such flexible storage and updating will be feasibly done in the comfort of one's home or anywhere the same system can be made available. The health and lifestyle assessment mode will also be able to assess the inquirer's complaint in order to determine how critical the person's condition may be. For example, it will be able to advise the user to seek help immediately or later. If a condition appears truly urgent, the user will be enabled to seek immediate care, and the program will give the user the opportunity to call 911 automatically.

At the conclusion of the interaction, the software will make several suggestions to the inquirer. For example, it may suggest that all is well and refer the inquirer to the health maintenance module, which indicates the key risk factors that are present and suggests what these implications may be. If further information is requested, the user may be linked to a specialized database that will provide more specialized information. For any problem, the health and lifestyle assessment module can offer a full description of the relevant resources and also will allow the user to access other modules, such as neighborhood centers and support groups' databases, to see what is available (e.g., smoking control workshops, dietary advice, general counseling services) or what is relevant to the condition.

The general health treatment adviser and referral module is another mode that inquirers will be able to access. This is where the user can link to the health provider network. Here, the user can access all connected managed care groups, specialized treatment centers, hospitals, physician clinics, and a variety of community resources run jointly or independently within the community. A booking for a facility in which the user is permitted to access can be made using a smart card, and the confirmation of such a booking can be supplied instantly after each interaction. The module also will be able to supply general information on these facilities and allow detailed questions or messages to be forwarded to the respective offices. Imagine you have been told that part of the project funding will be coming from the different sponsoring health provider organizations in return for being able to offer their services online with GREAT*net. Think about the communications requirements and standards and the different network architecture and configuration that may have to be in place to make GREAT*net a success.

INTRODUCTION

In Parts I and II, it was demonstrated that standards and appropriate information architecture are necessary, although insufficient, conditions for evolving integrated delivery systems (IDSs). In Part III, which includes this and the previous two chapters, the focus shifts to technology architecture, which is critical for building integrated health networks (IHNs). As noted in Chapter 6, the topic of communications and information networking warrants a chapter of its own because of its increasing significance. Essentially, the concentration here is on the communications system requirements and networking aspects of technology architecture not only for integrating health provider organizations, but also for building and connecting virtual communities.

INTEGRATING HEALTH PROVIDER ORGANIZATIONS

To date, empirical evidence has shown that most of the health care organizational transformations have been done under one of two major expansion modes: consolidation or complementation.[1,2] By applying a top-down reasoning, the modal properties eventually suggest the technological requirements of the health care organization. In this section, this approach is used to examine the two prevalent modes of expansion and their modal properties. The examination of these modal properties will in turn assist the reader in understanding the different organizational structural characteristics, economic rationales, and managerial requirements. In the next section, the corresponding communication requirements are identified, more specifically, those key communication configurations and system architecture for supporting and achieving these expansion modes.

Consolidation

Consolidation occurs when two or more health provider organizations, which are alike in terms of interests and capabilities, combine via merger or acquisition. It usually occurs when a health organization attempts to remove or take control of a rival in a region to gain market dominance. The economic rationales for consolidation are enhancement or preservation of market power and consolidative economies.

Consolidation may sometimes be seen as a "market sheltering activity" intended to reduce price competition.[3] The result of this counter-competitive activity is the formation of a local quasi-monopoly or market dominant health provider organization. The most significant objective is to preserve or enhance market power. Market power exists when a firm is able to sell its products or services above the existing competitive price level or decrease the costs of its primary activities below the competitive level, or both.[4] Although cost-cutting is one of the major consolidation motives in the health service area, market power is the major dynamic. A good example is the rise of managed care organizations in which the biggest players, such as health maintenance organizations (HMOs), decide where the money goes. However, health provider organizations are also consolidating both within and across specialties to try to expand market power. For example, Columbia/HCA's aggressive expansion exemplifies a typical path of health organizational consolidation toward a dominant market power.

Apart from increased market power, an exceptional advantage of consolidated arrangement is consolidative economies. Consolidative economies are the realization of aggregate economies and operational efficiencies through resource sharing and elimination of redundant operations. Figure 8–1 exemplifies this arrangement.

Consolidation often occurs in a market where a health care enterprise consolidates a local company that has an established regional network. The rationale here is that a fast and less costly way to enter a new local or regional market is to acquire well-established distributors that already have experienced sales representatives and strong customer relations rather than build such a position under fierce competition. The consolidation may follow an initial merger or acquisition. The market-based approach gives the provider a local focus but creates opportunity for synergy, enhanced revenue, and efficiency.[5] For example, Columbia's South Florida Division (CSFD) benefited not only from national purchasing initiatives that lowered supply costs, but CSFD also gained local leverage in pooling physicians' credentialing activities, which allowed physicians to gain privileges on multiple medical sites and in purchasing products from a single vendor.

The core administrative requirement for consolidation is the development and enforcement of a common managerial system (CMS). Consolidative econ-

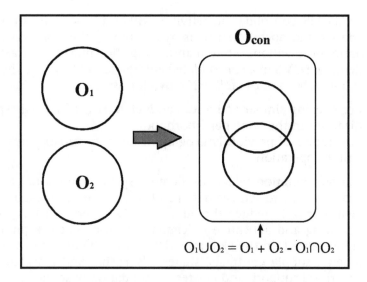

$$O_1 \cup O_2 = O_1 + O_2 - O_1 \cap O_2$$

O_{con} = consolidated health care organization = $O_1 \cup O_2 \ldots O_n$
where $O_1 \equiv O_2 \ldots \equiv O_n$
     and: $O_1 \cup O_2 \ldots O_n < O_1 + O_2 + \ldots O_n$
        (because of elimination of redundancies, etc.)
F_{con} = consolidated functions = $F_1 \cup F_2 \cup \ldots F_n$
where $\forall O_j \leftarrow F_j$
     and: $F_{red} = (F_1 + F_2 + \ldots F_n) - (F_1 \cup F_2 \ldots F_n) > 0$
        = functional and resource-related redundancies
G_j = operating area/geographic market of O_j = {$G_1, G_2 \ldots G_n$}
$G_{con} = G_1 \cup G_2 \cup \ldots G_n$

Figure 8–1 Consolidation Mapping. *Source:* Adapted with permission from Tarn (1998), Exploring the Impact of Geographic Dispersion on Information System Requirements, Dissertation, Virginia Commonwealth University, Richmond, Virginia.

omies and the preservation of market power depend on the level of organizational consistency maintained. To achieve a high level of organizational consistency, organizations expanding via consolidation are mainly concerned with the degree to which headquarters can regulate the interdependence between corporate constituents.[6] Traditionally, a CMS can be initiated through a formal managerial process, for example, the establishment of management ground rules or the building of commitment to the strategic objectives of consolidation.[7] As a result, the single CMS can furnish a common language, a common set of performance measures and operating methods, and a common vertical and horizontal distribution of power.[8] A CMS is developed and enforced through consolidated procedures, systems, performance standards, and evaluation criteria. For instance, Columbia/HCA expanded by acquiring local hospitals.[9,10] By matching the specialties of neighboring units in close proximity, Columbia/HCA integrated the local units into corporate delivery networks, which resulted in a common system for all of the area hospitals.[11]

Under a CMS, consolidation activities will lead to a significant reduction in administrative and operational costs by combining the common functions of the separate organizations while maintaining the same level of activity in the new system. The CMS in a consolidated enterprise will facilitate the implementation of one or both of the following two forms:

1. normalizing similar activities conducted by the original separate organizations in the same neighborhood
2. integrating all previously geographically nonoverlapping activities into a single operation

The implementation will consolidate dispersed functional and resource-related redundancies to achieve net operational efficiencies. Even so, the entire process will not only reduce the administrative overhead, but also facilitate resource sharing and allocative efficiencies. Consolidative economies, therefore, can be realized. In the Columbia/HCA case, the new network eventually acquires better supply contracts, shares advertising and marketing expenses, reduces overhead support, and creates consolidation of services.

Complementation

Complementation is the selective conjunction of two or more health care organizations with disparate but potentially complementary capabilities, interests, and core competencies. The key economic rationale for complementation is the pursuit of symbiotic effects or transactional economies. In biology, symbiosis is the living together of two dissimilar organisms based on a mutually beneficial relationship in which each is dependent upon and receives reinforcement from the other. Organizations in this category also carry similar characteristics. The symbiotic effects may take the form of transactional economies. The transaction cost theory emphasizes the importance of the structures that govern the exchange of goods and services between persons or across boundaries.[12,13] Transactional economies are the reduction in costs associated with the internalizing of these exchanges to reduce uncertainties or establishing symbiotic interdependence. Scott writes that "symbiotic interdependence can occur when two or more organizations that are differentiated from one another exchange resources."[14(p.198)] Because of achieving transactional economies, the union of two complementary health provider organizations can expand their previous geographic boundaries, or increase operating density in an area for each other without significantly increasing their internal investment in specialty equipment, facilities, and human resources.

From the aspect of value chain or vertical complementarity, the relationship between complementary companies is similar to manufacturer-retailer dependence. Manufacturers supply products for retailers, whereas retailers provide retail or distribution outlets for manufacturers. A descriptive example is the merger of Vencor and Hillhaven, the nation's second-largest nursing home chain. Before their merger, Vencor was a Kentucky-based chain of specialty hospitals, and Hillhaven was a Washington-based nursing home operator. Osterland reports, "Vencor treats chronically ill patients, particularly those with respiratory problems, through a network of 36 hospitals, while Hillhaven provides nursing home care and rehabilitation service. . . . Therefore, if Hillhaven patients get sick, they can be placed in Vencor hospitals. If Vencor patients improve, they can be referred to less intensive Hillhaven facilities."[15(p.20)] Vencor and Hillhaven are trying to position themselves to handle patients from residential care to all of their health care needs prior to an acute-care hospital setting.

The Vancor-Hillhaven case also clarifies the major distinction between complementation and consolidation. On the one hand, health care organizations consolidating are usually competitors that are alike and normally operate in the same business market but in different locations; therefore, the purview of the combined organization is often close to the sum of their previous geographic spreads. On the other hand, complementation requires the union of health care organizations with complementary capability, interests, or core competencies in production/service in order to increase the density of corporate operational activities in a location or to increase the area of service.

The core administrative requirement of complementation is the development of bridge provisions and cooperative processing systems to manage the intersect-centered activities. Figure 8–2 exemplifies this arrangement.

Because each entity (Oi), after union, basically continues to operate as a quasi-autonomous unit (Ui), the organizational integration of complementation mainly focuses on the intersection between entities. Therefore, the structural arrangement of complementation is toward a more lateral orientation. In this sense, the correlation between corporate entities reduces the need for a control-oriented managerial apparatus because control can be accomplished through the interchange of delivering and receiving services in intersecting activities.[16] Hence, headquarters exhibits less formal control but calls for the bridge protocols to link inter-unit planning, control, and problem-solving activities. From the aspect of administrative apparatus, liaison units or collaborative relations can be established for the mutual inter-unit relationships and processes.[17] Setting procedures, priorities, and constraints to regulate crossing activities can develop bridge protocols; for instance, Vencor-Hillhaven's cross-referral system as a bridge system (B) efficiently serves and coordinates both Vencor (U1) and Hillhaven (U2) patients and facilities.

There are two systems perspectives to bridge provisions: cooperative processing systems and quick response arrangement. The objectives of these bridge provisions are to access systems of both units and to search for the best solution for the united whole. According to Figure 8–2, the system integration in complementation only focuses on the intersected activities. This is because the information/transaction processing tasks to support all the intersecting activities between units have a critical influence on the efficiency and effectiveness of the linkages. Because complementation represents a combination of both quasi-autonomy units and their intersection, the integration of information and transaction processing may be conducted through centralizing certain critical systems or building bridges across originally independent systems.[18] For information and transaction processing, this intersection requires cooperative processing systems that promote the interoperability of key appli-

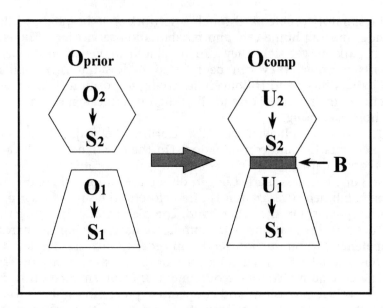

O_{prior} = health care organizations prior to combination = $\{O_1, O_2\}$
S_{comp} = complementary capabilities, interests, or core competencies in health care service
　　　= $\{S_1, S_2\}$
where　$O_1 \rightarrow S_1$ and $O_2 \rightarrow S_2$
　　　$S_1 \neq S_2$ and $S_1 = \sim S_2$ (or If $S_{comp} = 1 \rightarrow S_1 + S_2 = 1$)
O_{comp} = combined organization = $\{Hq, U_1, U_2\} = O_1 \cup O_2 = U_1 \cup U_2 + B$
where　Hq = headquarters
　　　U = corporate unit
　　　B = bridge or intersecting managerial system
　　　$Hq \rightarrow B$, $O_1 \rightarrow U_1$, $O_2 \rightarrow U_2$
$G_{comb} = G_1 \cup G_2 = (G_1 + G_2) - (G_1 \cap G_2)$　and $0 \leq (G_1 \cap G_2) \leq (G_1 \cup G_2)$

Figure 8–2 Complementation Mapping. *Source:* Adapted with permission from Tarn (1998), Exploring the Impact of Geographic Dispersion on Information System Requirements, Dissertation, Virginia Commonwealth University, Richmond, Virginia.

cation programs, that facilitate information sharing, and that manage intersecting-centered transactional activities. To exemplify these cooperative processing systems, contemporary client-server based information technologies can bridge heterogeneous systems and manage the distribution of transaction-oriented functionality.[19,20]

KEY HEALTH CARE COMMUNICATION CONFIGURATION AND SYSTEM ARCHITECTURE

Table 8–1 summarizes the modal properties of consolidation and complementation for health organizational expansion. As noted, each mode can be expected to require a set of communicational facilities to support its modal properties. The rationales for the two popular modes now provide the basis for

Table 8–1 Summary of Modal Properties

Mode	Configurational Characteristics	Economic Rationales	Core Administrative Requirements	Empirical Referent
Consolidation	Combination of two or more health care organizations that are alike in terms of interests and capabilities	Enhancement/preservation of market power or regional market dominance; realization of aggregative economies via resource sharing and elimination of redundancies	A common managerial system to normalize similar activities and collapse all previously nonoverlapping activities into a single operating framework	Columbia/HCA
Complementation	Selective conjunction of two or more health care organizations with complementary capabilities, interests, or core competencies	Pursuit of symbiotic effects or transactional economies	Development of bridging provisions or cooperative processing systems, etc., to manage intersect-centered activities	Vencor and Hillhaven Hospitals

Source: Adapted with permission from Tarn (1998), Exploring the Impact of Geographic Dispersion on Information System Requirements, Dissertation, Virginia Commonwealth University, Richmond, Virginia.

suggesting the types of communication configuration and system architecture most appropriate to each mode.

Communication systems and networks support both inter- and intra-organizational information exchange and provide the communication links among interfaced health management information system (HMIS) components at different locations. Communication networks significantly reduce geographic limitations, compress time, and reorganize inter- and intra-organizational relationships.[21] The focus of the communication requirements for the expanding health provider organizations is not only the establishment of effective and efficient telecommunications linkages, but also includes the enforcement of organizational integration requirements. These concerns become critical if a health organization's units are widely dispersed because of technical limits to the capabilities of these communication systems to support the organization. Conversely, within the capabilities of current communication systems and networks, a health care enterprise is able to continue extending its reach to new locations while having accessibility to the central headquarters.

Table 8–2 illustrates five essential categories of health communication configuration and system architecture relative to their applications for consolidation and complementation, including the hub-and-wheel (H&W) communication configuration; open systems (Internet, electronic data interchange [EDI], and extranet); intranets; groupware and group communication support systems (GCSSs); and executive information systems (EISs).

Table 8–2 Key Communication Configuration and Systems

Communication Systems	System Functions	Consolidation	Complementation
Hub-and-wheel (H&W) communication configuration	To promote positive interaction between units and/or provide "clearing-house" capabilities	Essential	Essential
Open systems (Internet, electronic data interchange and extranet)	To provide two-way access for exogenous agencies, provide for the exchange of standard-formatted transactions, and support electronic ordering and invoicing, etc.	Supportive	Supportive
Intranets	Unmediated reticular linkages; support for intelligence exchange between headquarters and local units	Supportive	Essential
GCSS (Group Community Support Systems); Groupware	Pertinent for contexts emphasizing cooperative/ collaborative relationships (intra-unit or interorganizational)		Essential
Executive information system (EIS)	To enable organizational oversight and provide for data tracking and reporting	Essential	

Source: Adapted with permission from Tarn (1998), Exploring the Impact of Geographic Dispersion on Information System Requirements, Dissertation, Virginia Commonwealth University, Richmond, Virginia.

Hub-and-Wheel Communication Configuration

As shown in Figure 8–3, H&W communication configuration consists of two parts: the hub and the wheel. The hub configuration involves systems that enable the health care headquarters to mediate or monitor inter-unit exchange, providing clearinghouse capabilities. The wheel configuration, however, includes systems that increase local responsiveness to support the functional linkages between units.[22] Technology architecture supported by the H&W communication configuration includes end-user and client-server computing. First, client-server computing supports the hub configuration. It is a processing architecture in which a single application is partitioned among multiple processors (clients) that cooperate the process in a single, unified task (server).[23] Because this architecture maintains a many-to-many system linkage, a local area network (LAN) and wide area network (WAN) are used to bond together the geographically dispersed clients and servers. This establishes the fundamental configuration of a hub network system. In contrast, end-user computing supports the wheel configuration. End-user computing features

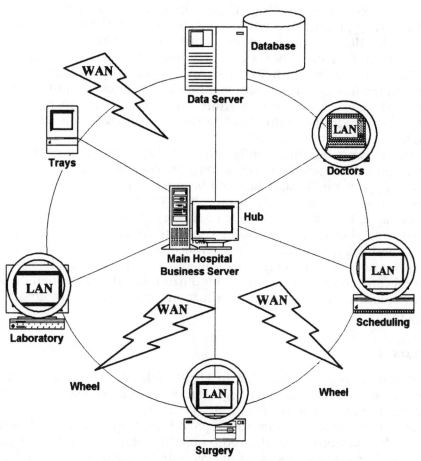

Figure 8–3 Hub-and-Wheel Communication Configuration

applications developed and/or maintained by local unit[24] and may often involve LAN-based connections.

Accordingly, the H&W network topology normally exhibits a two-tier network configuration. For one layer, a client-server-based distributed networking system is commonly installed between headquarters and the remote units as a control and coordination channel. This type of system, forming a hub configuration, supports health organizations expanding via consolidation. In many cases, this transformation demands a common managerial system to consolidate all activities into a single operating framework via resource sharing and elimination of redundancies. Not only does this communication configuration provide clearinghouse capability that enables the headquarters to coordinate all consolidated activities, but also it supports the development of a common health delivery network. In this sense, an IHN can provide integration of clinical, financial, and operational data that align and support institutional business plans.[25]

The other layer is usually configured by a number of LANs. The inter-unit linkages are typically achieved via a private access-protected WAN. An alternative to the H&W communication connections is to construct a proprietary organization-wide network via a satellite-based WAN that can effectively link far-flung LANs. Notably, the popular WAN applications include various satellite communications (e.g., geosynchronous satellites, point-to-point fixed radio link satellites, very small aperture terminals [VSAT] supporting the Internet, direct broadcast satellites, mobile and personal communication satellites, and low-earth-orbit [LEO] satellites).[26]

H&W communication configuration is also an essential requirement for health provider organizations expanding via complementation. This configuration supports the linkages between heterogeneous systems, which are common to those specialty health organizations. The H&W network configuration, for example, is usually the vehicle of choice for the units to access the LAN-based bulletin board systems or the corporate common databases with know-how information via central computer-mediated communication systems.[27-29] As such, the configuration not only empowers health care headquarters as the central core resource controller or coordinator, but allows the remote units to be more efficient and responsive to situations where unit-level connections are required.

Open Systems

Open systems, as illustrated in Figure 8–4, provide a strong supportive capacity to a health provider organization expanding via consolidation or complementation. The key functions of open systems are to provide two-way access for exogenous agencies and to provide for the exchange of standard-formatted transactions (e.g., electronic ordering, billing, and invoicing). Open systems do not simply focus on the versatility of data exchange and the support of a wide range of digital applications and services. The architecture also provides an organization with broad access to regional competencies and opportunities and a method for scanning worldwide health care markets. Among the most important open-system networks are the Internet and the enhanced wide-area access services, electronic data interchange (EDI), and extranet. These architectural configurations provide open-system interconnections for a health provider organization to gather contextual and business-related intelligence and to gain access to worldwide information sources and external online databases.[30-32]

First, as Internet usage expands worldwide, the need for faster data transmission has become a vital and immediate issue. An example is the need to download medical-related data quickly from various Web sites as health providers and individuals are relying more on the Internet to acquire information. Moreover, as Web sites increase in size, the method of accessing the Internet and the equipment used at the user's end will need to be adapted to handle the increased bandwidth needed to load the videos, graphics, and other multimedia-based materials that have proliferated on the Internet and the Web. Today, many HMISs are linked to the Internet; these systems typically combine

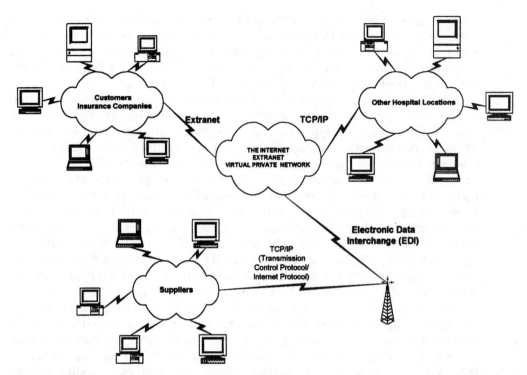

Figure 8–4 Open Systems, Including the Internet, Electronic Data Interchange, and Extranet Configuration

Internet protocol (IP) networking with databases, Web browsers, and servers. Thus, the most critical issue at present is to create a fast Internet connection. In this regard, integrated services digital network (ISDN) and asymmetric digital subscriber line (ADSL) have important technological contributions to the Internet access and inter-organizational communications.

ISDN uses a digital phone line and is one of the first digital subscriber lines. A digital subscriber line is a modem or a modem pair and not a telephone line that transmits duplex data (i.e., data travels in both directions simultaneously). The speed of the data is 128 Kbps over copper lines up to 18,000 feet. ISDN or DSL modems use twisted pair bandwidth and a technology called pair gain applications in which digital subscriber line modems convert a single POTS (plain old telephone service) line into two POTS lines. With this method, the telephone company installs the analog/digital voice functions at the customer's premises for both lines.

An initial advantage of using ISDN is that both voice and data communications can occur simultaneously on one line. The speed of data transmission is also a major advantage. An ISDN line transmission speed is much faster than any regular telephone modem. When ISDN was first introduced to the market, it was thought to be the solution for fast Internet access and, when available, it was the technology of choice for connecting doctors' offices or clinics and telecommuters and, to a much smaller extent, the consumer market.[33,34] However, the installation of the terminal adapter and ISDN modem is difficult and expensive apart from the conflicting standards used and the distance limitations imposed by various telephone companies. This has lessened ISDN's growth as newer technology gets introduced.

The ADSL, an emerging Internet access technology, uses power and switching to stuff megabits of data into twisted copper wires designed for 4 Hz voice.[35] These regular copper telephone wires are attached to a modem-like device, which is needed for each end of the copper wire. Similar to ISDN, ADSL does not require a second phone line; therefore, telephone calls and Internet access coexist on the same circuit.[36] There are many potential advantages to using ADSL technology. The ADSL modem will alleviate Internet congestion by providing a separate data channel that circumvents the telephone companies' switches.[37] Also, when comparing ADSL to cable modems, most physicians and patients already have phone lines installed in their homes, offices, or clinics with the telephone companies having a billing system capable of handling such service[38] in the form of point-to-point ADSL, which further implies that the user does not have to share the bandwidth with anyone else.[39]

Second, EDI systems are also open systems used to transmit intra- or inter-organizational standardized electronic transactions and documents.[40–43] Transactions occur between computer applications, eliminating the need for mailed or faxed transactions, thereby decreasing human intervention. Typical health-related documents include test orders, claims, and invoices. In addition, many health care organizations are now exchanging production and material requirements planning schedules, services, and quality information. In general, data and information flow from an EDI system to a value-added network (VAN). The VAN has the benefit of added security because the data is accepted on behalf of one health organization from another based on a preestablished relationship. The VAN also verifies these transactions for valid EDI transactions.

EDI advances traditional batch-oriented operations to real-time, online transaction processing. It provides for the exchange of standard-formatted documents, such as requests for quotes, purchase orders, and billing and invoice statements.[44] For example, Catholic Healthcare West uses EDI to support business office processes and consolidate multiple disparate systems into a single solution, a consolidated data repository of claim data available online to all authorized staff.[45] Furthermore, EDI systems are also an important medium for inter-organizational activities and a proficient bridge between two autonomous corporate units. EDI-based systems have become the backbones of several regional health delivery networks because these can integrate the marketing, logistics, and distribution functions of the master organization and its suppliers. For instance, a managed care organization can use data from its suppliers' operations to monitor performance or exchange information electronically with its trading partners.[46,47]

Extranet is an Internet version of EDI. An extranet facilitates the exchange and processing of high volumes of health data from one computer to another. Flanagan notes that extranets have been used by companies to communicate with customers, suppliers, trading partners, and numerous other audiences who contribute to the operating efficiency or other performance measures.[48] The application of extranet involves the conversion of written documents into structured, machine-readable formats that facilitates the transfer of data by computer from one company to another. In essence, an extranet represents the bridge between the public Internet and the private corporate intranets. McCarthy states that although the Internet belongs to everyone, intranets belong to individual organizations who build private, ideally secure networks using Internet protocols.[49] Extranets are a slice of an intranet that provides a public window into company services or collected data. Nonetheless, these networks are an important part of the business strategy, product delivery system, and customer support apparatus of health organizations. Basically, extranets may be considered an open computer processing environment that links the business with its suppliers and customers. The implementation of an extranet will and should have ramifications on how health care organizations conduct their businesses and will drastically change the cost structure of the different activities in the value chain.

Finally, as open systems also allow other external agencies to access the organization, these have also been developed as newly emerging networks for electronic commerce, such as the Internet-based Commerce Net for interchanging the industry-standard EDI-based transactions or documents, including electronic ordering and invoicing.[50,51] These Web-based open system networks have gradually become the mainstream of emerging technologies.

Intranets

An intranet is a corporate network that uses the Internet protocols and structure on internal LANs or WANs but cannot be accessed through the general Internet.[52] This network starts with a high-power server, a central filing cabinet that lets users share files and applications and exchange e-mail with each other. Although a server can connect users inside a company to the outside world of the Internet, it can carry special software to set up a firewall to prevent outside Internet users from tapping into unauthorized areas of the company's system. Indeed, intranet has been gaining strategic attention among health provider organizations. Large and small organizations use intranets to publish documents for inter-organizational distribution. For organizations with thousands of employees spread out over hundreds of sites, this can be a great cost saving and effective inter-organization communication strategy. With globalization, an intranet offers a timely solution to these dilemmas. Figure 8–5 illustrates a typical intranet communication configuration.

An intranet is used to establish proprietary unmediated reticular communication linkages between headquarters and corporate units to exchange information. This particular function promotes additional communications support for health provider organizational expansion, specifically for operations transforming via complementation. This mode of expansion demands a more efficient informal channel for coordination and collaboration of integral activities. These activities require inputs from both formal and informal sources, especially when intersecting activities require inter-unit relational linkages or

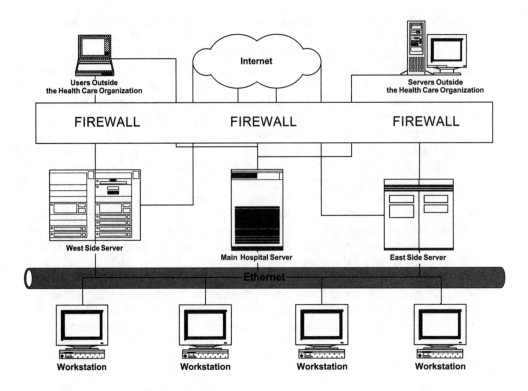

Figure 8–5 Intranet Communication Configuration

involve quasi-autonomous units, such as between two specialized hospitals. Technologically, intranets also complement the previously introduced H&W communication configuration for more effective local responsiveness in sharing research and development and know-how information. It is also an important supportive communication system to health organizations expanding via consolidation because it can facilitate the development of a common operating framework for the consolidated functions or services. For example, Koala (Columbia's corporate intranet) provides a common intra-communication network as Columbia/HCA continues building comprehensive networks of health care services in local markets and consolidates various services to deliver patient care.[53]

As well, intranets provide the tool for capturing and sharing corporate knowledge. This knowledge sharing capability makes it possible for a health provider organization to market new and better services faster than its competitors and to meet or exceed the expectation of the customers. Health organizations have used their intranets for distributing information and computing applications; for everyday communications, such as online medical newsletters; and even as virtual meeting places for work groups. Health executives who travel can use the corporate intranet as a means of keeping in touch with headquarters and staying abreast of late-breaking vital or critical information. In summary, intranets support free access to internal online databases, the communications of corporate grapevines, and the information inter-changes among the dispersed units.[54]

Groupware and Group Communication Support Systems

The key integrative transformation-related function of groupware and GCSSs, as depicted in Figure 8–6, is for emphasizing cooperative or collaborative relationships. With a lateral orientation, these facilities fill in a communications requirement for complementation. This is because those health provider organizations expanding via complementation require the establishment of cooperation-oriented processes to support the intersecting activities between their quasi-autonomous corporate units.

Collaboration means working together and sharing information with each other. The value of collaboration and its potential contributions include increasing productivity, reducing costs, growing profits, and improving service or product quality. The collaborative process involves the collective wisdom, knowledge, and even subconscious minds of the collaborators. This powerful phenomenon is becoming a requirement to effectively compete in today's

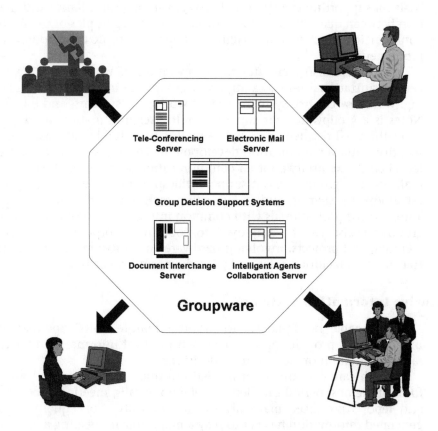

Figure 8–6 Group Communication Support Systems and Groupware

health care marketplace. Technological support for collaborative group work is usually referred to as groupware. Groupware affects the way people communicate with each other. Affecting interpersonal communications results in affecting the way people work, and eventually, the reporting and power structure of the organization.

A significant amount of research has been conducted on the use of computer-based systems to support collaborative group work. To date, there is empirical evidence to suggest that GCSSs can improve the quality of decision making, enhance user satisfaction, and increase the efficiency of group meetings. The technical rationale is that GCSSs are specific in their ability to establish real-time communication among distant locations via public or proprietary WANs and to provide a common and shared interface with representational capability. In other words, a GCSS can facilitate cooperative work and group collaboration with information control, support communication processes among group members, and reduce communication barriers such as distance, cultural, and linguistic differences in groups.[55] GCSSs ultimately offer the opportunity for interaction among remote units and are specifically capable of collecting and exchanging different inputs or decision predicates from widespread sources. From this perspective, GCSSs establish the communication basis for supporting the relational linkages among subsidiaries and the interaction between quasi-autonomous corporate units. Examples of GCSSs are videoconferencing, electronic messaging systems, electronic boardrooms, and local group networks.[56-62]

Groupware also facilitates the cooperation of work groups across health care organizational units. Examples of groupware include electronic calendaring, workflow control systems, shared workspace systems, and e-mail.[63] Lotus Notes is a groupware that supports multi-user information sharing and provides threaded discussion groups, e-mail, customizable databases, scheduling, security, and even application development. The access-limited electronic bulletin boards exemplify another communication support. As the extension of e-mail systems, groupware can support widespread remote units or special interest groups by sharing and broadcasting technical and business information among those professionals with common interests and problems. Additionally, groupware also can be employed to coordinate corporate shared resources, facilities, and projects, involving hardware and software, communication and transmission facilities, rules and procedures, and expertise.

Executive Information Systems

EISs enable headquarters to monitor remote units' operational performance and to provide top managers with critical information that can facilitate coordination on key strategic decisions.

Health care executives get needed information from many sources in the form of memos, periodicals, letters, telephone calls, meetings, social activities, and reports produced manually or electronically. Consequently, computer-generated information has yet to play a major role in meeting a lot of the executives' information needs as much of the information for health executives comes from noncomputer sources. Therefore, for EISs to meet these needs, these systems must be concerned with data and ways of interacting with the data.

By definition, EISs collect, filter, and extract a broad range of current and historical information from multiple applications and multiple data sources, both internal and external to an organization, to provide executives and other decision makers with the necessary information to identify problems and opportunities. EIS functions are therefore essential for health provider organizations expanding via consolidation because the concept involves the extension of organizational communications system to widespread health care units or networks. The principal application of EISs contribute to those health provider organizations that demand process consistency and coordination.

Finally, the EIS architecture is complementary to the H&W communication configuration. This is because EIS can assist top management in extracting, filtering, compressing, and tracking critical data from dispersed corporate units, while providing online access, trend analysis, exception reporting, and drill-down capabilities.[64,65] Drill-down is an exceptional capability of EISs because it allows central headquarters to access or track the detailed operational status and performance indicators of a remote unit by conducting a reverse exploration of a critical point of data. Likewise, EISs, by monitoring the indicators preset by the executives at the headquarters, can quickly and automatically identify the unit that has not met corporate operations or performance requirements.

BUILDING VIRTUAL COMMUNITIES

Up until now, we have concentrated mostly on IHNs. More recently, the communications system architecture and network topologies that we have discussed have been expanded to build CHINs in several metropolitan areas across the United States, Canada, Europe, and particularly in the United Kingdom. A preview of CHINs was given in the form of a case presented at the beginning of the chapter, therefore, it is appropriate at this point to briefly introduce the CHIN concept and then contrast the difference between IHNs and CHINs.

Basically, a CHIN may be conceived as a network that links health care stakeholders throughout a community. More specifically, it is an integrated collection of telecommunication and networking capabilities that facilitate communications of patient, clinical, and financial information among multiple providers, payers, employers, pharmacies, and related health care entities within a targeted geographical area. Ideally, it represents the full promise of community networks in several ways.

1. It has the ability to transmit clinical, administrative, and financial data with seamless connectivity in a standardized electronic format.
2. It has the ability to securely house data for controlled public access.
3. It has the open, nonexclusive participation of providers, payers, purchasers, physicians, and other key stakeholders within a community of care.

4. It has the formation of a separate enterprise for which governance and management would include a viable implementation and financial plan.

Central to the success of CHINs is therefore the concept and feasible implementation of a computerized patient record system at the community level.

As summarized in Exhibit 8–1, IHNs serve owned and affiliated entities, whereas CHINs serve entire communities, including health care providers, payers, employers, and even competitors. In this sense, the organizational structure of CHINs may be similar to one of an extended complementation network. Thus, in contrast to the governance structure for IHNs, which is essentially owned and financed by a single health enterprise, ownership of and governance for CHINs would be likely through a coalition with community and sponsoring vendor members represented on the governing board. Indeed, ownerships of some U.S. CHINs are in the hands of vendors with usage and access fees imposed on providers and users.

More importantly, IHNs basically focus on facilitating patient care, whereas CHINs focus on general and market-oriented information sharing. Accordingly, information sharing provided via CHINs will be somewhat more restricted to promotional and marketing materials as CHIN participants are fearful of giving away sensitive trade information that would be leveraged by their competitors. Conversely, participants in IHNs need to share critical and sometimes sensitive information to improve patient care delivery. Finally,

Exhibit 8–1 Integrated Health Networks versus Community Health Information Networks

Integrated Health Networks (IHNs)	**Community Health Information Networks (CHINs)**
• Serves owned and affiliated entities • Governance structure may be owned, financed, and managed by the enterprise, and supported by internal information services staff • Facilitates patient care and cost/quality utilization measurement for patients of the enterprise • Provides the groundwork for the CHINs • Closed system	• Serves entire community including health care providers, payers, employers (as well as competitors); organizational structure likened to one of an extended complementation network • Governance structure is typically via a coalition with community and sponsoring vendor members represented on the governing board and is supported and maintained by CHIN representative members • Focus on general and market-oriented information sharing • Connects the participants in the IHNs to other unaffiliated community members and resources • Open system

IHNs provide the groundwork for CHINs, whereas CHINs connect the participants in the IHNs to other unaffiliated community members and resources.

Based on these contrasting features between IHNs and CHINs, it may be purported that communication systems, such as H&W configuration, open system architecture, intranets, and groupware used in supporting and creating IHNs, may need to be combined appropriately and extended to support and develop CHINs. Currently, the concept of the CHIN is evolving and many pre-developments of CHINs are just beginning to appear throughout various countries, notably in the United States and the United Kingdom. Two prime examples of CHINs that have received considerable attention in the literature include the Wisconsin Health Information Network (WHIN) and the London and Regional Global Network (LARG*net).

Figure 8–7 shows the various participants involved in WHIN, including hospitals, physicians, payers, IHNs, laboratories and imaging centers, pharmacies, medical information services, the government, and others (e.g., home health care, ambulance services, employers, etc.). In terms of systems architecture, WHIN is an open system design intranet with three independent components working together to make the flow of information possible:

1. WHIN connect software to give users access to the network
2. WHIN processor interface software to connect providers of health information
3. WHIN switch to route requests for information and corresponding responses between users and providers, besides managing the network security

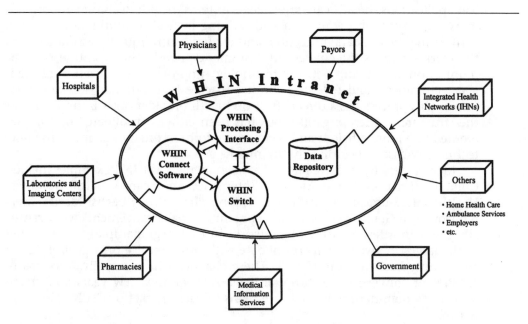

Figure 8–7 Participants of Wisconsin Health Information Network (WHIN). *Source:* © Joseph K.H. Tan

Another key piece of the WHIN architecture is the shared, or common, data depository.

LARG*net, as the name suggests, is aimed at growing and supporting metropolitan and regional connectivity in and around London and surrounding areas to allow sharing of information and related services and to facilitate the growth of cooperative network applications among members. It is envisioned to be a nonprofit organization with memberships extended to any sector organization whether public or private (health care, education, industry, government, and so on). Governance of LARG*net will be through a board of directors comprising up to 10 sponsoring members, 2 community representatives and 2 regular member representatives. The primary role of LARG*net will be to work with various service providers to develop a communications network, which will interconnect member organizations. In essence a regional intranet, LARG*net is not intended to be an Internet provider but aims to promote the development of a CHIN, one in which member organizations can interact at much higher bandwidth and by more direct communication paths. More information on LARG*net can be found at www.johns.largnet.uwo.ca.

CONCLUSION

Communication and network systems provide a direct support for health care business operations (services and products) and bridge HMIS applications. Such applications include medical records coding, information retrieval systems, integrated telematic health care systems, telemedicine, multimedia medical applications, health care knowledge systems, health decision support systems, expert systems, education and training in health informatics, security, confidentiality and data protection, and quality control/quality assurance.[66] As the market mirrors the changes in customer demands, the evolution of communication system and network technology improves the utilization of medical technologies and redefines the health care hardware and software platforms. This process has a direct effect on health provider organizations in that the structure of these organizations has been either consolidated or complemented to a more efficient and competitive form in order to adapt to the new technology-based operating environment.

More generally, we have referred to such mergers as IHNs. Examples include Columbia/HCA, National Medical Enterprises–American Medical Holdings, HealthSouth-Surgical Care Affiliates, Upjohn-Pharmacia, Hoechst-Marion Merrell Dow, and Glaxo-Wellcome. Such organizational arrangements will eventually result in a few health care networks in each regional market, and some of the largest networks will consolidate with other service organizations on a community basis to form CHINs. These changes will eventually force many closures or conversions of hospital beds over the next few years and create only a few dominant managed care plans in each market or CHIN-associated networks.

CHAPTER QUESTIONS

1. Describe the two health care organizational expansion modes. What are their economic rationales and administrative requirements?
2. What strategic competitive benefits do you see in the health care consolidation expansion and complementation expansion?
3. What are the business benefits of H&W communication configuration to the health care organizational expansion via consolidation and complementation modes?
4. How can open systems support health care organizational expansion?
5. What is the business value of the Intranet?
6. How does groupware support health care organizational expansion? Describe its capabilities for collaborative work.
7. How important are EISs to senior executives? What are the benefits of using EISs for organizational expansion?

NOTES

1. A. Monroe, Healthcare Deals Multiply, *Investment Dealers Digest* 61, no. 49 (December 4, 1995): 14–18.
2. R.C. Coile, Health Care Outlook 1997–2005: Transitions, Transactions, and Transformations, *Journal of Lending & Credit Risk Management* 79, no. 8 (April 1997): 18–22.
3. H. Leibenstein, X-inefficiencies Xists—Reply to an Xorcist, *American Economic Review* 68 (1978): 203–211.
4. W.G. Shepherd, On the Core Concepts of Industrial Economies, in *Mainstreams in Industrial Organization*, eds. J.W. DeJong and W.G. Shepherd (Boston: Kluwer Publications, 1986).
5. J. Hopping, The Layered Look, *Health Systems Review* 30, no. 3 (May/June 1997): 24–25
6. P.C. Haspeslagh and D.B. Jemmison, *Managing Acquisitions* (New York: The Free Press, 1991).
7. B.R Robinson and W. Peterson, *Strategic Acquisitions: A Guide To Growing and Enhancing the Value of Your Business* (Burr Ridge, IL: Irwin, 1995).
8. P. McKiernan and Y. Merali, Integrating Information Systems after a Merger, *Long Range Planning* 28, no. 4 (August 1995): 54–62.
9. J. Morrissey, Columbia Wraps up Mass. Venture, *Modern Healthcare* (May 6, 1996): 26.
10. S. Lutz, Columbia Completes Deals in N.C., Texas, *Modern Healthcare* (May 6, 1996): 26.
11. University Hospital Blurs Richmond, Va., Battle Lines, *Modern Healthcare* (April 22, 1996): 40–41.
12. O.E. Williamson, *Markets and Hierarchies: Analysis and Antitrust Implication* (New York: The Free Press, 1975).
13. O.E. Williamson, *The Economic Institutions of Capitalism: Firms, Markets, Relational Contracting* (New York: The Free Press, 1985).
14. W.R. Scott, *Organizations: Rational, Natural, and Open Systems* (Englewood Cliffs, NJ: Prentice Hall, 1992).
15. A. Osterland, Acquire, then Digest: Vencor—Specialty Hospital Chain Acquires Nursing Home Operator Hillhaven, *Financial World* 164, no. 14 (June 20, 1995): 20.

16. S. Zuboff, *In the Age of the Smart Machine* (New York: Basic Books, 1988).

17. F. Ostroff and D. Smith, The Horizontal Organization, *McKinsey Quarterly* 1 (1992): 148–167.

18. P. McKiernan and Y. Merali, Integrating Information Systems after a Merger, *Long Range Planning* 28, no. 4 (August 1995): 54–62.

19. J. Gantz, Are You Ready for Cooperative Processing? *Networking Management* 8, no. 4 (April 1990): 54–55.

20. J. Smith, There's More Than One Road to Client-Server, *Computing Canada* 18, no. 16 (August 4, 1992): 40.

21. M. Hammer and Y. Mangurian, The Changing Value of Communications Technology, *Sloan Management Review* 28, no. 2 (1987): 65–71.

22. J.H.M. Tarn, *Exploring the Impact of Geographic Dispersion on Information System Requirements* (Richmond, VA: Virginia Commonwealth University, 1998). Dissertation.

23. B.H. Boar, *Implementing Client/Server Computing* (New York: McGraw-Hill, 1993).

24. E.A. Regan and B.N. O'Connor, *End-User Information Systems: Perspectives for Managers and Information Systems Professionals* (New York: Macmillan, 1994).

25. S. Noble, D. Farley, and B. Kleaveland, Zero Tolerance for Billing Errors, *Health Management Technology* 20, no. 4 (May 1999): 16–20.

26. A.S. Pombortsis, Communication Technologies in Health Care Environments, *International Journal of Medical Information* 52 (1998): 61–70.

27. L.F. Graham and S. Raatz, Collaborative Computing, *CPA Journal* 63, no. 11 (November 1993): 32–36.

28. J. Diamond, Modem Sharing and Collaborative Computing, *Network World* 12, no. 19 (May 8, 1995): 35.

29. J.R. Howells, Going Global: The Use of ICT Networks in Research and Development, *Research Policy* 24, no. 2 (1994): 169–184.

30. J.A. Carroll, Online Intelligence, *CA Magazine* (August 1992): 27–31.

31. T. Grantham, Businesses Warming to Lure of ISDN, *Computing Canada* (June 20, 1996): 29–31.

32. J. Fritz, Optimizing WANs with ISDN, *InfoWorld* 18, no. 35 (August 26, 1996): 69–72.

33. I. Brodsky, Cable Modems to the Rescue? *Telephony* 232, no. 25 (June 23, 1997): 20–26.

34. J.W. Ellis IV, Hot Again . . . But for How Long? *Telephony* 232, no. 5 (August 4, 1997): 28–32.

35. G. Gilder, Piping Hot, *Forbes* (February 23, 1998, ASAP Supplement): 110–120.

36. A. Kupfer, Telcos Fight Back, *Fortune* 135, no. 5 (March 16, 1998): 144–146.

37. G. Wheelwright, Keeping the Faith, *Communications International, London* 24, no. 1 (January 1997): 53–54.

38. T.B. Fowler, Internet Access and Pricing: Sorting Out the Options, *Telecommunications (Americas Edition)* 31, no. 2 (February 1997): 41–44.

39. A. Littwin, ADSL: Ready for Prime Time? *Telecommunications (Americas Edition)* 30, no. 12 (December 1996): 35–44.

40. J.F George, J.F. Nunamaker, and J.S. Valacich, ODSS: Information Technology for Organizational Change, *Decision Support Systems* 8, no. 4 (August 1992): 307–315.

41. P.K. Sokol, *From EDI to Electronic Commerce—A Business Initiative* (New York: McGraw-Hill, 1991).

42. I.K. Allison, Executive Information Systems: An Evaluation of Current UK Practice, *International Journal of Information Management* 16, no. 1 (1996): 27–38.

43. K.A. Walstromm and R.L. Wilson, An Examination of Executive Information System (EIS) Users, *Information & Management* 32 (1997): 75–83.

44. E.A. Raether, Issues in EDI Implementation, *Production & Inventory Management Review & APICS News* 10, no. 9 (1990): 47–54.

45. G. Wallin, A New Look at EDI, *Health Management Technology* 20, no. 5 (June 1999): 22–23.

46. A. Hald and B.R. Konsynski, Seven Technologies To Watch in Globalization, in *Globalization, Technology, and Competition: The Fusion of Computers and Telecommunications in the 1990s*, eds. S.P. Bradley, J.A. Hausman, and R.L. Nolan (Boston: Harvard Business School Press, 1993).

47. G. Reed, Transforming EDI from a Communications Link to a Knowledge Solution, *Healthcare Financial Management* 53, no. 6 (June 1993): 86.

48. P. Flanagan, The 10 Hottest Technologies in Telecom, *Telecommunications* (May 1997): 25–32.

49. S.P. McCarthy, Welcome to the Extranet, *Logistics Management* (May 1997): 66–72.

50. J.A. Senn, Capitalizing on Electronic Commerce: The Role of the Internet in Electronic Markets, *Information Systems Management* 13, no. 3 (1996): 15–24.

51. M.J. Tucker, EDI and the Net: A Profitable Partnering, *Datamation* 43, no. 4 (1997): 62–69.

52. T. Fetherling, Columbia: Siting an Online Opportunity, *Marketing Health Services* 17, no. 2 (Summer 1997): 40–44.

53. Intranet Lexicon, *Business Communications Review* 26, no. 6 (1996): 8.

54. L. Fried, Advanced Information Technology Use: A Survey of Multinational Corporations, *Information Systems Management* 10, no. 2 (Spring 1993): 7–14.

55. A. Pinsonneault and K.L. Kraemer, The Effects of Electronic Meetings on Group Processes and Outcomes: An Assessment of the Empirical Research, *European Journal of Operational Research* 46, no. 2 (May 25, 1990): 143–161.

56. W. Zachary, A Cognitively Based Functional Taxonomy of Decision Support Techniques, *Human-Computer Interaction* 2 (1986): 25–63.

57. K.L. Kraemer and J. King, Computer-Based Systems for Cooperative Work and Group Decision Making, *Computing Survey* 20 (1988): 115–146.

58. J. Morrison and O.R.L. Sheng, Communication Technologies and Collaboration Systems: Common Domains, Problems and Solutions, *Information & Management* 23, no. 2 (August 1992): 93–112.

59. B. Langham, Mediated Meetings, *Successful Meetings* 44, no. 1 (January 1995): 75–76.

60. J.A. Sprey, Videoconferencing as a Communication Tool, *IEEE Transactions on Professional Communication* 40, no. 1 (March 1997): 41–47.

61. H. Row, Real-Time Collaboration Tools, *CIO* 10, no. 12 (April 1, 1997): 90–99.

62. D. Sykes, M. Symonds, and D. Van Doren, Collaboration in the Information Age, *Business Communications Review*, Multimedia Collaboration and Messaging Supplement (May 1997): 3–5.

63. N.F. Kock and R.J. McQueen, Using Groupware in Quality Management Programs, *Information Systems Management* (Spring 1997): 56–62.

64. H.J. Waston, R.K. Rainer, and C.E. Koh, Executive Information Systems: A Framework for Development and a Survey of Current Practices, *MIS Quarterly* (March 1991): 13–30.

65. P. Palvia, A. Kumar, N. Kumar, and R. Hendon, Information Requirements of a Global EIS, *Decision Support Systems* 16, no. 2 (February 1996): 169–179.

66. A.S. Pombortsis, Communication Technologies in Health Care Environments.

Managing Domain and Control Architecture of Health Management Information Systems

Health Management Information System Strategic Planning and Managerial Accountability: Specifying Domain and Control Architecture

Joseph K. H. Tan

SCENARIO

Following a series of strategic planning meetings, corporate management at the New World Medical Center (NWMC) has decided to take a lead role in the application of health information technologies for managerial decision support and patient services. Imagine yourself to be the chief information officer (CIO) of NWMC. The president and chief executive officer (CEO), Mr. Little, a graduate of the Stanford Business School, has been very supportive of your attempt to implement two innovative systems: Thinktank and Commute.

Thinktank is an experimental management group decision support system that runs on an AT&T 3B2–4000 minicomputer under the UNIX operating system. Several private terminals are networked into the system together with a separate public terminal attached to a special projector for transmitting all messages appearing on the public terminal onto a large public screen. The main use of Thinktank, as you have envisioned at this time, is for internal electronic communications among the senior management team and to support virtual group meetings that follow a weekly agenda. Group participants have the option to interact with the system at any time during the week to input their decisions into the system. The outcomes of these decisions are collated and summarized automatically by the system at the end of each week on the basis of majority votes and other statistical rules built into the system. These results are then revealed to all company staff by displaying them on the public screen. The president and CEO then acts accordingly.

Thinktank is also useful for several group tasks, for example, in one experimental meeting agenda, the exercise may be to identify a set of five critical success factors (CSFs) for the center that could be used to direct corporate strategies in the next few years. In this regard, Thinktank will use anonymity to mask the status differentials of the participants and thus will lessen the fear of retaliation. Thinktank can be used to perform other more structured tasks as well; for example, it can be used to select general physicians (GPs) and specialists from among those who have applied to practice at the center based on a list of weighted criteria provided by participating decision makers.

In contrast, Commute is primarily an electronic data interchange (EDI) and networking system that connects NWMC with those GPs and specialists contracted by the center for its ambulatory services. These GPs and specialists also have attending and practicing privileges at the center. The main uses of Commute at this time are external communications and business-to-business networking. Physicians who are contracted by NWMC are automatically provided with terminals linked to the Commute system. Commute has the capabilities of exchanging and receiving real-time information on patient referrals. NWMC customers requiring only ambulatory care attend at the offices of the referring physicians. At the end of such visits, the referring physicians are required to complete profiles of the patient services rendered and perform electronic billings, which are instantly dispatched to the center. Commute then summarizes the information from the physicians and uses a case-mix classification scheme to generate utilization and billing reports comparing all NWMC referrals for each quarter. These quarterly reports can then be used by management to assess issues regarding whether to extend or terminate contractual relationships of NWMC with affiliated physicians on the basis of comparative practice patterns.

In preparation for the next stage of the strategic planning meeting, Mr. Little has asked that you brief the other managers of NWMC and the physicians affiliated with the center on the benefits to be realized from the implementation of Thinktank and Commute. Think about the benefits and competitive advantages that may be gained by NWMC use of these systems and what challenges may be faced in relying on these systems to steer future directions. Contemplate especially how you may address some of the questions raised by the audience, including how management decisions would have been made differently without Thinktank, how referral patterns of NWMC and physician practice patterns may differ with or without Commute, and what long-term effects these systems may have on corporate culture and the public image of NWMC.

INTRODUCTION

As we enter a period of change, essentially from the hierarchically controlled organization to the information-based organization,[1] the need to understand strategic planning and managerial accountability in health management information systems (HMISs) is a key challenge for health executives and senior management. The goal of this chapter is to review the essence of health management functions and roles and to relate critical aspects of HMIS strategic planning and strategic management to health managerial performance. Drawing briefly from the discussions of previous chapters on systems thinking, information process design, and technology architecture management, this chapter concentrates on the roles and responsibilities of health managers and discusses how the concepts of strategic planning and management can be applied to harness various information, technology, domain, and control architecture components of an integrated HMIS to achieve the goals and objectives of the information technology (IT) service department and, more generally, the higher-order mandates and visions of the health service corporation.

MANAGEMENT: WHAT AND HOW?

The science of management, unlike the physical sciences, is relatively poorly structured because of the unpredictable nature of managerial roles and decision making. In addition, many variables are involved in the interactions between management and staff workers (or human resources) and between management and other parts and resources of health organizations, such as financial resources, health facilities and equipment, health technologies, health information resources, and health programs, services, and task activities. Therefore, apart from overall management functions and decision making, health managers are also responsible and accountable for many administrative duties inside and outside the organization. Resolving conflicts among different groups of people advocating different viewpoints; taking charge of emergencies when these arise (e.g., a disruption of work arising from a worker strike); dealing with changes in the external environments so as to adapt to new governmental regulations and policies; and charting the future of the organization or agency by bringing about innovative and creative changes are among the duties managers must perform in today's rapidly changing health service industry.

From an organizational behavior standpoint, Longest defined "management" as "a process with both interpersonal and technical aspects, through which the objectives of the health service organization are specified and accomplished by utilizing human and physical resources and technology."[2] This view fits the previous discussion on systems theory and the dynamics of systems behavior when applied in a health care organizational context. Using the language of systems theory, the traditional process of health management may be conceived as the art of planning, organizing, directing, and controlling resources, such as people, plant and equipment, money, materials, technology, and information to accomplish some predetermined objectives.[3-5] For health service organizations in particular, the end result of these objectives is the production of efficient, effective, and excellent (top-quality) health services.

Figure 9–1 shows a systemic view of general health managerial roles and functions as the closing of gaps between HMIS resources on the one hand and organizational goals and objectives on the other hand. The failure to achieve some or all of these organizational objectives is a failure in general management functions, and hence there may be a need to review, renew, or reengineer the management process to enhance organizational performance. It is at this point that strategic know-how and managerial accountability come into play.

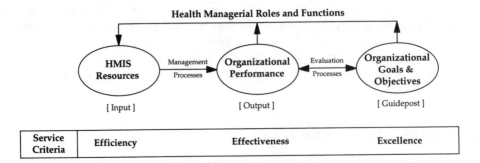

Figure 9–1 A Systemic View of the Health Management Process

For now, the focus will be on the basic functions of a health service manager. Later, the focus will be on strategic planning and managerial accountability.

THE PLANNING, ORGANIZING, DIRECTING, AND CONTROLLING MODEL

Henri Fayol is often regarded as the chief contributor to the concept of the four fundamental managerial functions commonly identified in the PODC model—planning, organizing, directing, and controlling.[6]

Figure 9–2 shows the ordering and relationships among these major functions. Several other functions, including decision making, and human resource responsibilities, such as staffing and coordinating, have since been added to this list through the works of numerous others,[7,8] such as those of

Figure 9–2 The Planning, Organizing, Directing, and Controlling (PODC) Model

Chester Barnard.[9] These various perspectives will also be incorporated in the discussion.

In general, the management of a health service organization is thought to begin with most planning activities being carried out by a senior executive team. This process entails the formulation of formal statements of vision, mission, strategic goals, and objectives of the organization by involving the CEO, board members, and others in the senior executive team. For a health corporation, these often include the chief medical officer (CMO), the chief financial officer (CFO), the CIO, and the chief operational officer (COO). The mission statement essentially defines the strategic focus of the corporate business, such as the delivery of efficient, effective, and top-quality health services to a neighborhood community.

As part of the planning process, senior health service managers also make many other strategic decisions that involve the conscious design of strategies and the development of viable alternatives, such as closing the number of beds allocated to various health programs when undergoing budget cuts. The planning function interfaces intensely with the environment and is considered a high-order function of the organization. It is distinguished from the other functions by its focus on the strategic level, that is, above and beyond the operational and tactical levels of managerial decision making in the classic three-tier organizational decision-making framework as depicted in Figure 9–3.

After planning, health managers must marshal and organize necessary and sufficient resources to accomplish the vision, mission, and predetermined goals and objectives of the corporation. This activity ranges from establishing formal structures and designing a pattern of roles and relationships among subordinates, to designing work systems, specifying procedures and flows, and structuring people-task relationships.[10] Personnel planning, or the determination of middle management positions, and the selecting, orienting, training,

Figure 9–3 The Hierarchical Nature of the Management Control Feedback Loop

and evaluating of health professionals and clinicians either directly or indirectly, as through delegated authority or representation, are also critical organizational functions for senior health managers. This is especially true because these activities are concerned with delivering health services rather than manufacturing commercial goods and services. Many people can easily place a dollar value on goods, such as a video camera, or services, such as a haircut, but would find it difficult to assess the cost of a heart transplantation operation. The value of the operative procedure depends, in large measure, on the nature and organization of professional services rendered, in particular, the quality of health provider–patient interactions.

Apart from the need to organize health service personnel and other resources efficiently and effectively, health managers must also direct (or actuate) by supervising and motivating their subordinates to fit individual goals and objectives within the planned vision, mission, goals, and objectives of the organization. This means that they must attempt to integrate the individual workers into an organized system of work. In this regard, the commitment shown by the workers to have their work completed in a professional and timely fashion is a reflection of management success. Directions in a health service organization need not come only from daily supervision, but can also arise informally from the corporate culture. The use of directives, policies, and established procedures exerts and extends the directing functions of management in different ways. In the end, the roles played by the CEO, the CMO, the CIO, the COO, and other members of the senior management team (e.g., the board members) will shape the actual directions and activities taken by various other players in the corporation.

Moreover, health managers need to control and evaluate the performance of the institution by establishing standards and ensuring the efficient and effective accomplishment of stated goals and planned activities. This is where the feedback mechanism of the system (evaluation loop) is put to work. Often, this control is hierarchical in nature and may be instituted at various levels of the organization; for example, middle management will exercise control over operational and tactical activities of subordinates, whereas senior management will focus control over the professional and managerial activities of middle and frontline managers. Behaviors not conforming to expected standards may be adjusted (changed) by means of enforcing an effective review mechanism (e.g., a written warning, retraining, or providing further professional development for a worker). Figure 9–3 shows the hierarchical nature of this quality control-feedback loop in health organization management.

The sequence underlying the PODC model, although appearing cyclical in nature, is, however, iterative in practice. These various functions are interwoven and health service managers perform them simultaneously, often in no particular order but as a part of a continuum. Today, the traditional PODC model does not need to dictate a strong formal line-staff reporting relationship nor imply a top-down organizational chain of command. The paradigm of organizational change in this classical perspective can easily be transformed from one of reacting to internal pressures, usually through intense managerial control in a more or less stable environment, to one of open, consensus-driven and proactive management style in a turbulent health care environment.

As the job of a health service manager becomes more complex because of increasing turbulence in the health care environment, there is a need to adopt new perspectives, create innovative mechanisms, and provide new tools and techniques to support managerial tasks. These new perspectives will be discussed later in the chapter; at this point, the focus is on the three managerial performance criteria that form the basis for HMIS success.

MANAGERIAL ACCOUNTABILITY AS THE BASIS FOR HEALTH MANAGEMENT INFORMATION SYSTEM SUCCESS

In this section, the concentration is on three key performance indicators that determine the success of HMIS solutions within the context of the health service delivery industry. On the basis of the understanding that the ultimate goal of all managerial functions and activities is to accomplish some purposeful and meaningful outcome, the question then becomes one of how the outcome of health service management is measured and what role HMISs should play in assisting health management in this endeavor.

In reviewing the literature, it appears that there are three basic categories of systems-related measures of health service managerial accountability when thinking about HMISs: service efficiency, effectiveness, and excellence.[11,12]

Service Efficiency

Service efficiency implies minimizing cost (effort) per service unit, that is, performing services the right way in terms of least cost or effort incurred for a specific service. For example, high service efficiency may entail the expectation that HMIS solutions will lead to faster and greater accessibility of clinical services. Service efficiency assumes that HMISs will provide for the financial viability of the organization and enhance the administrative capability of the organization to gather, update, and maintain an appropriate database that can support the delivery of health services in a cost-effective and timely manner. Examples of benefits in this category include reduced operational costs, such as unproductive labor and excessive inventories, increased revenue due to a greater number of patients that can be serviced by each health service provider, improved cash flow optimization, improved allocation and use of financial and human resources, reduced delays (i.e., waiting time), and increased work productivity and information processing capabilities in the organization. Stated simply, it is the fulfillment of the promise of automation to make information resource handling more efficient and less effortful, thereby eliminating costly administrative financial errors and unnecessary human resource problems.

Apparently, traditional HMISs in the form of basic financial accounting and transaction processing systems (TPS) have been chiefly concerned with service efficiency. Zerrenner observes that such systems are typically characterized by large centralized databases and are thus justified largely on the basis of cost savings resulting from the automation of clerical and accounting functions.[13] Admittedly, large data systems such as TPS are designed primarily to improve organizational efficiency rather than effectiveness. That is, these applications can be expected to produce cost-effective reports, but those reports may not necessarily meet management needs in achieving the corporate vision, mission, goals, and objectives. In the past, these systems have almost always been large-scale systems that are also batch processed rather than real-time processed; that is, the transactions are bundled together and processed periodically, which explains why these systems are so cost-effective. Missing transactions are detected through counting the number of transactions or using some other totals, such as financial totals. Today, real-time processing (i.e., data updates made to files as soon as the transaction takes place) even for large-scale systems is a common reality because of rapid advances in computing hardware, software, and communication technology.

One of the major criticisms that has been aimed at traditional TPS-based systems (e.g., stand-alone medical records and registry systems, pharmacy and food service inventory systems, nurse scheduling systems, and cost accounting systems) is that of data overloading; that is, these systems normally produce a full house of reports that are of virtually no "managerial" use, creating a so-called data rich, information poor organizational environment. Zerrenner notes that "What most information systems do not do is search for the relevant data and then turn them into meaningful information. Presentation of the data is equally important. It can include ratios, historical perspectives, comparisons, and other internal or external data and can be presented in meaningful form, for example, in tables, bar graphs, or scatter graphs."[14]

Thus, although TPS-based applications in hospitals and other health provider organizations produce reports in an efficient and cost-effective manner (i.e., compared to manual production), these reports may not necessarily be wanted or needed by management. These systems then fall short of accomplishing higher organizational goals and objectives such as service effectiveness and excellence.

Service Effectiveness

Service effectiveness implies maximizing the benefits that can be achieved from performing specific services, that is, performing the right services. For example, high service effectiveness may entail the expectation that HMIS solutions will lead to better-quality patient care services and the provision of more appropriate services. Indeed, one may become so engulfed with increasing service efficiency that the need for service effectiveness is overlooked. This implies that the services performed on patients should not just be "band-aid" solutions resulting in readmitting patients within a short period for the same problems. Such a system is ineffective, although it may provide efficient care. Service effectiveness, therefore, is the concern of higher administrative and clinical decision-making levels as opposed to the more operational level of service efficiency. At this level, HMIS solutions that may be of interest are those that will call attention to benefits such as better allocation or more appropriate utilization of health service resources, improved quality of patient care, and more effective clinical decision, for instance, the integration of fragmentary and isolated data sources, the elimination of data registry duplication, and the reduction of irrelevant data reporting that will ultimately contribute to higher quality patient care. Tan et al. discussed the benefits of automated utilization care plan for effective clinical and patient care data management.[15]

Unlike service efficiency, which is normally measurable by the amount of time and effort taken or cost incurred to complete a service from beginning to end, the difficulty of focusing on effectiveness in HMIS applications is embedded within the broader issue of measurement. That is, from whose standpoint is service effectiveness to be defined (i.e., the patient, the physician, or the provider)? For instance, service effectiveness from a patient's viewpoint may just be the caring attitude of the service provider and the extra effort and time taken by the clinical staff to ensure that the patient is fully comfortable about the care process. Instead, service effectiveness from a provider's viewpoint may be the determination of what is an appropriate length of stay (i.e., to reduce the chance of the patient's being readmitted for the same illness after discharge). Generally speaking, service effectiveness may be improved if health service managers empower themselves and their subordinates with decision support, executive support, and knowledge capturing, or knowledge transferring technologies[16] As these and similar technologies have been discussed in earlier chapters, they are only briefly mentioned here.

Decision and executive support technologies use automated databases and decision models to enhance health service executive, managerial, and clinical decision-making processes. Expert technology, in essence, is the automation of knowledge transfer and managerial learning processes. One of the key benefits of using advanced technologies is to allow novice and less experienced workers to have access to expert opinions without paying the high consultation fee required by the use of a human expert. Advanced technologies are intended to empower the users to make informed choices in an effective and intelligent manner. Moreover, these technologies retain expertise, skills, and knowledge among organizational workers. Also, they preserve what might have been lost through the retirement, resignation, replacement, or death of acknowledged company experts.

Because advancing HMIS technologies is now in a stage of rapid diffusion among health service organizations, it is believed that it will have dramatic and significant effects on managerial and clinical effectiveness over the next few years.

Service Excellence

Service excellence means being at the leading edge in terms of quality service delivery. In essence, this involves the strategic positioning of the organization within the industry marketplace and the achievement of customer (i.e., both internal and external "customers") satisfaction. For example, the expectation that HMIS solutions will lead to service differentiation and a recognized professional image is an instance of service excellence. The move to apply

HMIS design to transform the practice of medicine is perhaps one of the consequences of the "corporatization" of health services in the United States and more recently in Canada.[17] According to Fried et al., "Corporatization is an organizational restructuring in the direction of an organizational form typically found in industrial corporations, characterized by clearly articulated corporate objectives and a division between corporate and operational levels."[18] Corporatization in health services in North America has occurred mainly through multi-institutional arrangements such as the sudden exponential growth of managed care and multiprovider organizations. These multi-institutional arrangements, with changes in their corporate structures and their business orientations, have in turn forced many independent hospital clinics and physician-owned practices to rethink their present structures to become increasingly competitive in the new health care environment.

Service excellence implies being at the cutting edge. It involves enhancing both the internal and the external professional image and perceptions of the staff through heightened customer loyalty and satisfaction. Medical and non-medical staff, for example, can be imbued with the ability to implement high-quality programs and services successfully by supplying them with the automated support and communication infrastructure, enabling them to leave more time for patient care and services. Ultimately, designing HMISs to gain strategic and tactical advantages for the organization through quality differentiation from services offered by other organizations can enhance the image of the organization to its customers (i.e., patients, payers, and physicians) and thus position the organization at the forefront of the health service industry. Kropf notes that this can be accomplished, for example, through generating first-class, real-time, accurate, and more relevant information systems for strategic planning and decision making, marketing, and locking-in of customer (i.e., employees, associated clinicians and physicians, suppliers, and patients) loyalty.[19]

Apart from the decision support and expert technologies, another class of HMIS applications that is particularly useful to health provider organizations competing in the new economy is the integrated telecommunication systems. Integrated telecommunication systems have the capabilities to enhance current decision support and information sharing technologies, such as group decision support systems, teleconferencing systems, teleradiology, and telemarketing systems. Other examples include the use of decentralized and distributed database processing to support end-user computing and the application of local area networks (LANs), wide area networks (WANs), Internet, intranets, and extranets to facilitate the sharing of core patient data and applications among providers.

Exhibit 9–1 summarizes the various HMIS solutions that may be appropriate for service efficiency, service effectiveness, and service excellence.

Among the most perplexing challenges facing health care CEOs and senior managers in today's rapidly changing health care environment are the tasks of planning and achieving the long-term success of their health service organizations. This challenge demands that the skills and ability of health service executives be intelligently used to recognize the new environmental threats and

Exhibit 9-1 A Classification of Health Management Information Systems (HMIS) Designs for Achieving Service Efficiency, Effectiveness, and Excellence

CRITERION	KEY EMPHASIS	HMIS SOLUTIONS
Service Efficiency	Minimize Cost (Effort) per Service Unit	• Nurse Scheduling Systems • Pharmacy and Food Service Inventory Systems • Medical Record Systems • Utilization Management Reporting Systems • Cost Accounting Systems
Service Effectiveness	Maximize Benefits and Values of Service Performed	• Electronic Billing Systems • Utilization Forecasting Systems • Responsibility Reporting • Performance Tracking Systems • Integrated Database Systems • Information Center for End-User Computing (EUC)
Service Excellence	Best Practices	• Teleradiology • Nursing Expert Systems • Other Medical (e.g., Laboratory) Intelligent Agents • Real-Time Systems • Strategic HMIS Applications • Continuous Quality Improvement (CQI)

opportunities, to seize the competitive initiatives in the new health care economy, and to manage the organizational change processes needed to counterbalance these environmental changes. Today, and more so in the future, HMISs should no longer be viewed simply as tools to automate and assist an organization in achieving its efficiency and effectiveness goals and objectives, but also should be regarded more as the engine for the long-term growth and strategic survival of the organization. This brings us to strategic information system planning (SISP), which is the next topic to be discussed.

A FRAMEWORK FOR HEALTH MANAGEMENT INFORMATION SYSTEM STRATEGIC PLANNING AND ALIGNMENT

As with many aspects of the HMISs field, the concept of strategic IT planning and alignment arises chiefly from theories and experiences in the private business sector. Organizations have increasingly been turning their attention to opportunities for achieving competitive advantages through IT. This new phenomenon may be attributed to several key forces.

- changes in economic conditions, which include factors such as long-term inflationary pressures and rising interest rates
- structural changes that are caused by global competition and major shifts in global economy

- new information technology economics, for example, changing tele-communications and network cost performance

Other environmental forces, which include changes in population, demographics, privacy, security, legal, and social factors, are also important. These issues are further elaborated in other chapters.

In light of today's economic climate of fiscal restraints, SISP may be considered one of the most fundamental tasks that a CEO and HMIS executive can perform together to achieve desired strategic positioning of the organization. The challenge for SISP is to demonstrate how IT can make the greatest contributions not only to the efficient and effective conduct of a health service enterprise, but also to achieve service excellence. Although it mainly entails conceptual work that must inevitably be prospectively defined as opposed to well-structured operational activities, SISP gives the HMIS manager the opportunity to recognize broad initiatives, prioritize commitments, and identify those applications and technologies that will help the health service organization carry out its current business strategy more successfully. SISP also provides the organization with means to identify opportunities to use IT to create new business strategies and the chance to develop a vision of IT that has the highest potential to contribute to long-term organizational success. A fundamental question therefore is: What is SISP? Lederer and Gardiner define SISP as "the process of identifying a portfolio of computer-based applications that will assist an organization in executing its business plans and realizing its business goals."[20]

For health service organizations, HMIS strategic planning is therefore needed to guide the use of IT as a competitive "safeguard" for future organizational growth and survival.[21] As health service organizations have become increasingly vertically and horizontally integrated in recent years, the need to develop cutting-edge, institution-wide information systems for strategic decision making has become paramount. The rapidly changing health care climate has fostered new incentives for the development of organizational strategies that reach far beyond the traditional service efficiency mission statements still relied upon by many hospitals and other health service CEOs. Today, health CEOs are paying more attention to developing innovative programs and making strategic decisions about future directions. This then requires a general conceptualization of the target areas of the HMIS strategic planning process.

In order to achieve effective HMIS administration and management, Earl notes that a well-designed SISP should target the following four areas:

1. aligning investments in IT with corporate goals
2. exploiting various aspects of IT for service excellence
3. achieving efficient and effective management of IT resources
4. developing IT policies and procedures[22]

In this sense, CEOs and HMIS managers need to address several critical questions during the SISP process. These include how IT can be used to generate new health services in response to new market demands, how IT can be used to distinguish among services provided by the corporation from those of competitors, and what supporting HMIS applications and infrastructure are needed to make the new strategy work.

Figure 9–4 shows a top-down (hierarchical) stages planning model that can be used as a general framework to guide HMIS strategic planning, design, and development. This framework is consistent with and extends that of Bowman et al.[23] The philosophy of HMIS strategic planning underlying this framework is that the information and technology architecture in place will determine the organization's ability to support the type of business functions and processes encountered in health service delivery. In turn, the design of an organization's business functions and processes should determine the necessary information needed to support the business goals and strategies. A number of techniques can be and have been used to facilitate the HMIS strategic planning process. However, one problem that frequently occurs is knowing which specific technique to use in the wide flow of activities for developing a long-range HMIS plan.

A fundamental concept of HMIS strategic planning is that the organization's strategic plan should be the basis for the HMIS strategic plan.[24] However, the alignment of HMIS strategies with corporate strategies is often overlooked in health service organizational HMIS strategic planning. In many cases, HMIS planning occurs in isolation from the organization's strategic plan; the result is that top management lacks appropriate information for making strategic decisions and solving problems effectively.[25] In a study conducted by Dunbar and Schmidt, it was observed that only 5 to 10 percent of the majority of U.S. hospitals' current strategic plans applied to HMIS planning.[26] To ensure the sur-

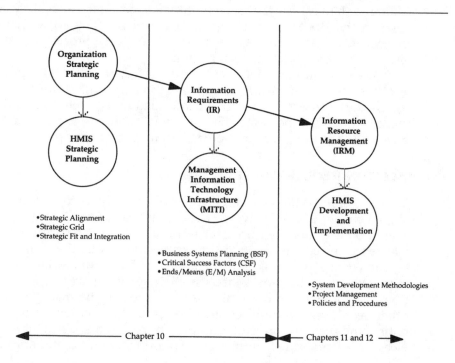

Figure 9–4 A Framework for HMIS Strategic Planning: A Top-Down Stages Planning Model

vival of health service organizations in this century, they recommend that at least 35 percent of the total strategic plan include tie-ins with information system plans.

The SISP framework presented helps to clarify the generic planning activities, the order of activities, and the alternative techniques, methodologies, and strategies that are applicable at each stage. It can be used to aid HMIS planners to recognize the nature of planning problems in a health service organization and to select the appropriate stage of planning to move the health organization forward in terms of HMIS strategic planning. In any case, it is important that strategic alignment exists between the organizational and HMIS goals and objectives and that such an alignment precedes the elicitation of information requirements, the hiring of experts, and the acquisition of software and hardware to implement HMIS.

Essentially, the strategic alignment of goals between senior management and information systems people within a health enterprise has three major implications.

1. the integration of information systems mission with core vision of the health enterprise
2. a fit between the information system and organizational culture
3. the alignment of information system management philosophy with organizational philosophy

Henderson and Thomas suggested that strategic alignment means more than linking information system strategies to organizational strategies.[27] Although they concur that such a linkage is necessary to achieve congruency between the HMIS and the organizational plans, they argue that it alone is inadequate to ensure success. Technology, structures, processes, and skills must also "be fitted to match this integration."

Once strategic alignment has been achieved, and the HMIS goals and strategy have been clearly delineated, the next step in HMIS strategic planning is to specify the necessary organizational information requirements for the development of the HMIS portfolio. The next section discusses information requirements (IR), the next stage of the HMIS strategic planning process.

INFORMATION REQUIREMENTS

Successful HMIS planning requires not only corporate-HMIS strategic alignment but also effective IT resource management.[28] Ideally, HMIS managers would want to ensure that technology and information resources are adapted to meet the needs of the organization's functions and activities. In practice, HMIS planning and management has emphasized the role of top management in the process because of the growing acceptance that information is a corporate resource and as such needs to be managed just like any other health organization resource, for example, labor and capital. The most critical and the most difficult tasks in information management for health service organizations are identifying and prioritizing information needs.

Information Needs

The problem of having data but no useful information in health service organization planning situations is usually a result of too much rather than too little information. This problem occurs because in an organization as complex as a health maintenance organization (HMO), for example, massive amounts of data are collected to serve many different purposes. In most cases, data collected for particular uses are not necessarily transferable to other uses. Consequently, it is critical that the right information needed by CEOs and managers is supplied by the HMIS; this requires that appropriate steps be taken to identify these needs.

Informational needs vary in terms of focus and volume according to the level of planning and decision making within an organization.[29] In general, the decisions that health service managers make may be classified into two broad categories: (1) strategic decisions that relate to the formation of organization policies, and (2) operational decisions that relate to the day-to-day operations and the formation of the organization procedures. It is important that the information providers recognize this distinction because the different decisions require different types of information to be provided at different times (and probably in different formats).

Strategic decisions are business positioning decisions that influence the future direction and strategy of the organization. At this level, individuals address what are essentially value and identity considerations. They seek to determine the "business" of the health service corporation and the philosophies and beliefs that underlie it, in essence, those "soft" concepts that are so difficult to translate into "hard" facts. Little quantitative or statistical information is needed at this level. However, individuals must be able to look at the corporation as a whole and express its desired contributions to society and to various stakeholder groups. For example, one HMO may decide that its long-term goal is to offer specialized geriatric care to meet the growing needs of its area. Similarly, another HMO may decide to focus on providing ambulatory care services and concentrate on establishing linkages with community agencies as part of its strategic plan. As these are one-time decisions, it is very difficult to forecast the relevant categories of information needs. However, the types of decisions to be made will be known even if the precise decisions themselves are not. Thus, it is possible to make a reasonable judgment as to what information may be required.

Operational decisions are short-term decisions that relate to the planning, coordinating, monitoring, and control of day-to-day activities of the health service organization. As these decisions involve repetitive decisions made on a regular basis, the accuracy, specificity, and volume of information required are easier to predict. For instance, the pharmacy department of a hospital will need information on the inventory of drugs, the number of prescriptions filled and repeated, the physician who prescribed the medication, and the patient who received the medication. Because this information is easy to predict, it will not be difficult to determine the data elements that would have to be included in an HMIS designed for the pharmacy manager.

Lower level management generally makes more operational decisions, whereas top management makes more strategic ones. However, this is not always true as the types of decisions made also depend largely on the type of business and the business situation. When developing an HMIS it is therefore important to consider the needs of the end user, in this case the health service manager, to ensure that information provided is accurate, timely, and relevant to the decision or problem at hand.

Sources of Information

Much of the critical information required for HMIS planning is difficult to elicit, whether directly or indirectly. Through in-depth discussions and interviews, numerous techniques have been suggested for extracting IR. Figure 9–5 shows three of the more commonly used approaches. These include business systems planning (BSP), CSFs, and ends/means (E/M) analysis.

Each of these techniques reflects a different way of thinking about IR, and their use in combination can increase the probability of obtaining a more comprehensive set of information requirements. The following three sets of questions posed to managers are reflective of each of the three respective methodologies.

1. *BSP*. What decisions or problems do you face, and what information do you need to deal with the situations?
2. *CSFs*. What factors (activities) are most critical to achieving business success for your organization, and what information do you need or must you monitor to achieve successful progress?
3. *E/M analysis*. What are the outputs (ends) from your activities, and what information (means) do you need to judge performance (efficiency and effectiveness) relative to outputs?

Health service analysts should be warned that during the interviews and fact finding, the fewest possible constraints should be imposed (i.e., asking open-ended questions and assuming that nothing that is currently in place will remain that way). Later, considerations of allocating limited resources may rule out some suggestions from the interviews, but creative solutions would not have been stifled.

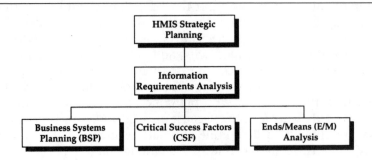

Figure 9–5 Three Approaches for Organizational Information Requirements Analysis

In addition to various interview techniques, job descriptions are a useful source of information about the organization.[30] Most organizations today have job descriptions that outline the main activities and accountabilities of management level staff. Anyhow, it is quite appropriate to inventory the current HMIS portfolio and to catalog the hardware, software, and application functions performed by each application system that is operational. This provides the basic data for analyzing the current HMIS applications portfolio and the internal IT infrastructure.

The objective of analyzing the results from fact-finding is to ensure that the most complete picture possible of the information needs of the organization can be defined with a relative priority for each. Once this has been established, the information needs can be grouped logically into an organization data model and implemented as databases. The business functions that access the information can then be assessed to identify potential application systems.

INFORMATION REQUIREMENTS METHODS

Almost all of the current IR approaches are model-based, requiring some form and combination of data, process, or object models to be produced. In other words, development of HMISs historically has been based on techniques that are independent of technology (i.e., data analysis, functional analysis, data flow analysis), as discussed in Chapter 5. The primary use of these models is to create an information road map that guides the coherent definition of the target applications and database portfolios needed to support the health organizational business in the future. These in turn are used to design the required control and domain architecture along with some form of resource management plan to put HMIS strategic planning progressively in place.

Business Systems Planning

BSP is an example of a process-based approach to determining IR.[31] BSP was originally developed by IBM and is used in many private sector businesses for information system planning. The concept underlying this approach is that business processes (groups of decisions and activities required to manage the resources of the organization) are the basis for information system support. As processes remain relatively constant over time, the requirements derived from the processes will reflect the transactional and decisional support needs of the organization. In addition, if the process is "reengineered," the information requirements and system support are already part of the planning.

Figure 9–6 shows how a top-down analysis of the business goals and objectives of a health service organization can be used to drive the bottom-up design and implementation of an organization's HMIS portfolio using the BSP philosophy. Essentially, the BSP approach relies on interviews with top management to define and plan the IR of the health service organization. In the interview process, managers are asked questions designed to specify key decisions and problems. These questions are related to their job responsibilities

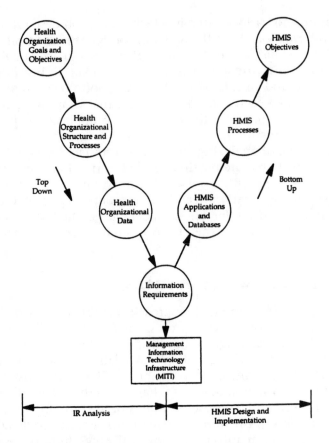

Figure 9–6 Business Systems Planning: Top-Down Information Requirements (IR) Analysis and Bottom-Up Health Management Information Systems (HMIS) Design and Implementation

and objectives, their current information needs, and their perceived projection of information needs. For example, managers may be asked the following.

- What are the major decisions you must make that affect your specific objectives?
- What type of internally generated information do you use to meet your objectives?
- Within the next 5 to 10 years, do you anticipate emerging technologies or changing business practices to affect the nature of your responsibilities and managerial objectives?
- If so, how will these changes affect your informational needs?

The BSP approach begins with a top-down analysis of IR and ends with a bottom-up HMIS design and implementation strategy. The information requirements (processes) identified are consolidated into a statement of needs that can be used to identify logically related categories of data that are cross-referenced to the business goals, objectives, structure, and processes. In turn, this information is then used to engineer the control and domain architecture of the organization, which will be used to drive or define corresponding databases and applications, HMIS processes, and HMIS goals and objectives.

Put together, this methodology allows a critical reexamination of tasks within a process that does not serve a purpose or add value to the business solutions of the health service organization.

Critical Success Factors

The CSF concept, first introduced in business administration, has recently received considerable attention in the field of health service administration and planning.[32-34] CSFs indicate the key areas of activity in which favorable performances are necessary to ensure the survival and success of an organization.[35] Therefore, CSFs refer to prime informational factors that alert health service managers and planners to the positioning of critical components and task processes within an organization. Implicit in the CSF concept is the question: What key performance indicators (information) are needed to measure the attainment of a set of goals whether they are identified at the level of the individual, group, organization, or enterprise?

CSFs have been defined by Rockart as "the limited number of areas in which results, if they are satisfactory, will ensure successful competitive performance for the organization. These are the few areas where things must go right for the business to flourish."[36] The philosophy is derived from the same thinking as the 80/20 rule: that is, 80 percent of organization business needs can be met with 20 percent of the information currently available in the HMIS.[37] The

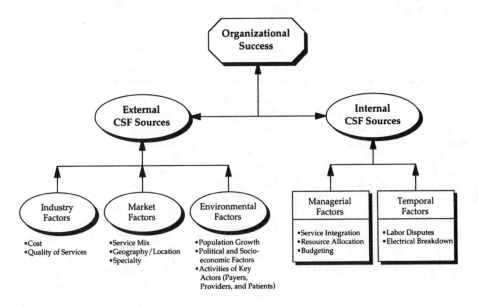

Figure 9–7 The Rockart-Bullen Five Prime Sources of Critical Success Factors (CSF)

key to CSF identification is therefore dependent on successfully eliciting the 20 percent critically needed information.

CSFs have two main functions: (1) to encourage individual employees to focus on the issues that are most important, and (2) to help them think through and sort out their information needs in these areas. CSF analysis often forces executives to make explicit the unconscious or implicit CSFs that they have been using for some time. Past experience has shown that the identification of generic CSFs is the most important step in the CSF process. Figure 9–7 illustrates the five Rockart-Bullen prime sources from which CSFs can be derived.[38] These include industry factors, market factors, environmental factors, managerial factors, and temporal factors.

The first three sources are external, whereas the last two are internal sources. Examples of these factors, relating to the health service industry and health service organization setting, are also provided in the figure.

In applying the CSF approach, the first step is to establish the objectives of the organization as a whole. From this point, the organization's business strategy should be derived. The next step is to generate the CSF required to realize the strategy and thus achieve the stated objectives. This is accomplished by eliciting the critical information set from the staff through a series of interviews or brainstorming sessions. Although there is no one standard procedure for the evolution of a CSF planning process, Figure 9–8 shows five phases and their respective benchmarks that are considered indicative of a "successful" application of the approach.[39-41]

Phase 1: Understanding All Externalities

Phase 1 involves achieving a better knowledge of, and reducing uncertainties about, potential threats, and effects of changes resulting from external forces acting on the organization: specifically, identifying the CSFs associated

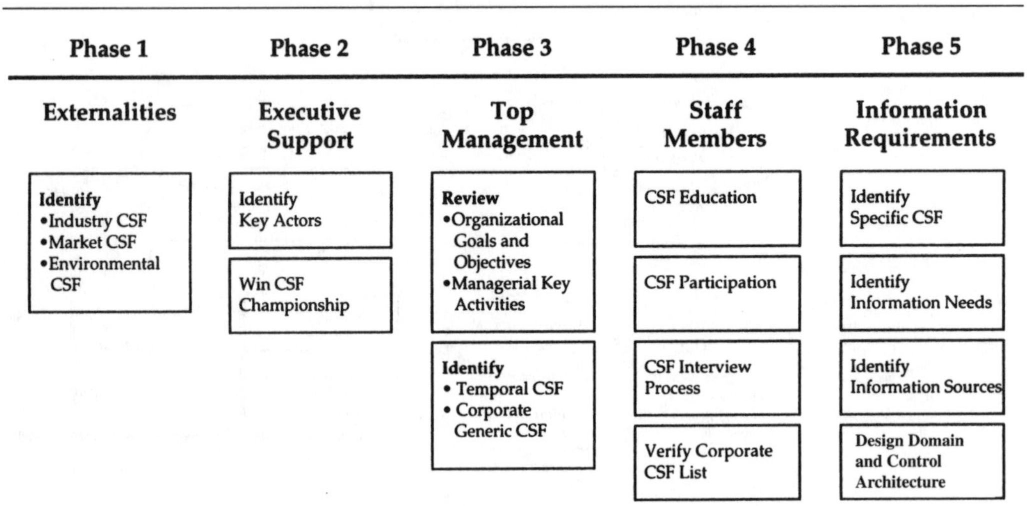

Phase 1	Phase 2	Phase 3	Phase 4	Phase 5
Externalities	**Executive Support**	**Top Management**	**Staff Members**	**Information Requirements**
Identify •Industry CSF •Market CSF •Environmental CSF	Identify Key Actors	**Review** •Organizational Goals and Objectives •Managerial Key Activities	CSF Education	Identify Specific CSF
	Win CSF Championship		CSF Participation	Identify Information Needs
		Identify • Temporal CSF • Corporate Generic CSF	CSF Interview Process	Identify Information Sources
			Verify Corporate CSF List	Design Domain and Control Architecture

Figure 9–8 The Five Phases in the Critical Success Factor (CSF) Methodology

with the three external sources discussed earlier, industry, market, and environmental factors.

Examples of CSFs relevant to health services that can be identified from three external CSF sources might include "cost" and "quality of services" (industry factors); "service mix," "geography/location," and "specialty" (market factors); and "population growth," "political and socioeconomic factors," and "activities of key actors (payers, providers, and patients)" (environmental factors).[42]

Phase 2: Winning Executive Support and Championship

Phase 2 involves identifying the key actors and decision makers within the organization and gaining the active support of a CSF champion, in particular a member of the senior management team.

The "activities of key actors" is an environmental CSF, which implies that in carrying out Phase 1 and Phase 2 the actions in both are actually mixed rather than isolated. The support of senior management will increase the motivation of their subordinates in the organization to be receptive to the adoption of the CSF methodology, an important criterion for success if the methodology is to work.

Phase 3: Revisiting Corporate Mission and Goals and Reviewing Managerial Objectives

Phase 3 involves reviewing the organizational mission statement and clarifying managerial goals and objectives in order to specify a core set of issues. These issues are then redefined in terms of key activities that would "fit" these goals and objectives. In this way, a core set of generic CSFs can first be identified and later specific activity sets can then be determined at the individual managerial level.

The identification of internal CSFs including managerial function and temporal factors also occurs at this point. Examples of CSFs for these two categories would be "service integration," "resource allocation," and "budgeting" (managerial factors), and "labor disputes" and "electrical breakdown" (temporal factors).[43]

Phase 4: Promoting Staff Education and Participation

Phase 4 involves educating organization staff members on the CSF concept and encouraging their participation in the CSF interview process. Active involvement of the unit staff members in the CSF interview process prevents the threat of potential biases in CSF identification that may result from a limited participation.

Phase 5: Translating Critical Success Factors from Generic to Specific and Linking Specific Factors to Information Requirements

The final phase involves aggregating and prioritizing generic corporate CSFs, refining them to specific level CSFs, and linking these specific level CSFs to the information needs of management groups. The resulting CSF-generated information "map" is used to guide the design of domain and control architecture for the organization.

In essence, the fifth phase of the CSF planning process can be considered the point where technological or analytical solutions are finally applied by the organization to design a functional HMIS portfolio.

Ends/Means Analysis

The information systems technique of E/M analysis is based on systems theory (Chapter 2). As such, it can be used to determine IR at the level of the organization, the department, or the individual manager. The technique separates the definition of ends (or outputs), which are goods, services, and information generated by an organizational process, from the means (or inputs) used to accomplish them. The methodology begins with the ends and works back to the means related to achieving these ends.

Figure 9–9 illustrates how the ends from one process, whether it is viewed as organizational, departmental, or individual, is the input to the same or some other process. For example, the hospital accounting process provides budget information for other organizational processes. If the hospital has a deficit, the organization may respond by laying off employees or reducing expenditures in hospital services. Similarly, the deficit information may also be used to adjust the budgeting process for the future years.

In E/M analysis, health service managers are asked to define the outputs (ends) and the inputs (means) related to all their decision-making activities. In addition, they are asked to identify performance evaluation measures at two major levels, that is, the efficiency and effectiveness of performance. Efficiency criteria can include timeliness, accuracy, productiveness, responsiveness, and capacity of the reporting system, whereas effectiveness criteria can include appropriateness, reliability, flexibility, and acceptability of the HMIS generated

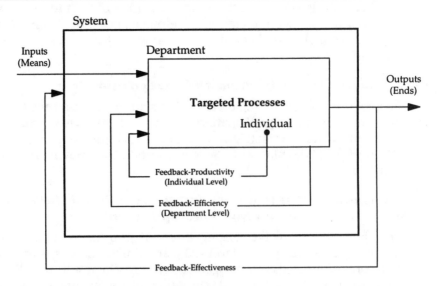

Figure 9–9 An Ends/Means (E/M) Analysis Model

reports. Another level of possible feedback is the productivity performance of individual workers. The information or feedback developed from E/M analysis is then used to determine IR for the new system. For example, the manager of a hospital pharmacy department may request information on drug inventory to evaluate the filling of an order that is requested (efficiency). Overall, the information could be used to determine if the drug inventory system in place is appropriate for the level of order-filling activities (effectiveness). Similarly, the pharmacy manager may want to compare the prescription patterns among physicians for different caseloads to evaluate the drug utilization by a particular physician (productivity). E/M analysis has been used in various industrial settings with very positive results.

A problem with many current IR methods is, however, that their applications often result in the generation of a limited set of primarily efficiency-oriented information. Most researchers now agree that it is important to use multiple IR methods to bring out the efficiency and effectiveness dimensions of IR more fully to improve the specification of the control and domain architecture needed to deliver an HMIS portfolio that supports managerial accountability in health service organizations.[44]

MANAGERIAL ACCOUNTABILITY*

Beyond the discussion of strategic planning and the process of diagnosing end-user needs using various IR methods, there is very little understanding of the design and development of a HMIS portfolio from a strategic management and managerial performance perspective. Defining managerial accountability is key to this understanding. The term "managerial accountability" refers generally to an understanding of the set of predetermined and desired criteria by which management and employees alike can be judged to be held accountable for particular decisions or actions vis-à-vis some clearly defined role/responsibilities within a health care organization.

Just as with any other organization, profit- or nonprofit-oriented, the performance of the organization may be assumed to be based on links to measurable indicators or criteria underlying managerial accountability as an essential and meaningful construct. In terms of HMIS design and development, successful managerial accountability is often conditioned on having an ideal, integrated HMIS portfolio that goes beyond the actual, piecemeal HMIS applications to support managerial decisions. In this sense, two pertinent and related questions regarding the strategic design and development of an integrated HMIS portfolio within the framework of managerial accountability just described will be explored. First, what is the ideal, integrated HMIS portfolio a health organization will need in order to achieve strategic expertise and competitive advantage? Specifically, how does this portfolio link industry performance standards with managerial performance and accountability? Second,

*Source: This section is reprinted from J. Tan and R. Modrow, Strategic Relevance and Accountability Expectations: New Perspectives for Health Care Information Technology Design. *Topics in Health Information Management*, Vol. 19, No. 4, pp. 84–97, © 1999, Aspen Publishers, Inc.

how should the limitations of past, isolated HMIS applications be reconciled with the benefits presented by the superior arrangement of the ideal, integrated HMIS portfolio in the context of changing managerial accountability?

Integrated Health Management Information System Portfolio

For HMISs to be strategically relevant, they should ideally perform the integrative function of linking management actions throughout the organizational system to performance. This linkage provides the basis for holding each manager accountable for his or her performance within the boundary of the organization's mandate and purpose. In order to provide the linkage to hold the manager accountable, a key condition is explicit and clearly defined measures of industry performance or standards for benchmarking managerial performance.

Because organizations may differ, that is, public versus private, the measures of industry standards for benchmarking and monitoring managerial performance likely will change in the context of differing kinds of organizations. For instance, within the private sector, it may be that the explicit industry standards can be defined in terms of returns on investments, market shares, or some other clearly defined markers. All management decisions transpiring in such an organization environment would then be clearly linked to performance measures so that the quality of the decision making can be judged relative to these measures. Thus, if a vice president of human resources in a health organization has the mandate to minimize unnecessary personnel costs related to absenteeism or turnover, and these overhead costs undermine profitability and productivity of the organization, then when absenteeism or turnover is high, productivity and profitability will fall. Conversely, when absenteeism or turnover is low, the organization will experience gains in profitability and productivity. On this basis, an integrated HMIS portfolio for the organization will link relevant and useful information on absenteeism or turnover to organization profitability and productivity measures. This series of linked information could be used by management to target interventions, such as work scheduling to lower absenteeism or turnover. Thus, it is the existence of these industry standards that determines the basic composition and information processing structure of the integrated HMIS portfolio.

Bridging the Performance Gaps

Unless explicit industry standards exist, both the quality of the intervention and the calibration of organizational performance cannot be accurately and reliably assessed. That is, having ambiguous industry performance measures will lead to poorly defined managerial accountability which can in turn easily cripple the organization's ability to design effective HMIS solutions.

In the absence of clearly defined industry success measures, managerial accountability will have no explicit and measurable reference, and how organizational decisions are made and their effects on performance will lack a conceptual basis necessary to validate measures. To maintain the performance of the organization relative to predetermined managerial accountability and to guide subsequent actions and interventions for closing the organizational performance gap, both analysts and managers must be able to communicate using a common language. Only when managerial performance can be benchmarked to the industry standards will we then be able to design integrated, performance-based HMISs. Further, incentive systems (e.g., merits and salary increases) should also be created to link to the appropriate performance measures.

The purpose of strategic thinking is to choose among alternatives to maximize performance relative to competitors. Strategic planning therefore becomes the specification of the process of implementing the course of action, and strategic management is the actual implementation of the course of action. Closing-the-gap analysis requires analysts and managers to focus on the identifiable (and measurable) difference between expected and observed performance. The ideal, integrated HMIS portfolio provides the links among measurable industry standards and indicators, managerial performance, and accountability measures. Based on a thorough understanding of the various links for the required information, the current HMIS portfolio can then evolve to adequately support the decisional role, responsibilities, and actions of the managers in generating the desired information, and it will not just provide massive but isolated databases that may in fact overload managers with irrelevant and unwanted data.

CONCLUSION

Today's health service managers must develop corporate values, provide strategic directions and visions, define product mix and market, determine new ventures, and ensure realization of corporate goals. The emerging role of the health service manager is therefore to champion and propagate the corporate vision and build the desired corporate culture, apart from retaining the usual planning and control functions. The key to good management, therefore, is to maintain a dynamic balance among various stakeholders and to take on different roles at different times as the situation dictates.

The potential use of information systems technology as a competitive "weapon" to achieve strategic advantage is one of the leading interests of academics and practitioners in HMISs. However, more research is needed to investigate the role of information in strategy development and organizational adaptation in the health care sector. This will require both a better understanding of the strategic planning process in general and studies of health managerial behavior and the accountability concept in health service organizations.

As HMIS development in the past has been driven largely by environmental influences, there has been a corresponding lack of coherent policy for IT applications in most organizations. This has resulted in HMISs being developed in isolation with little capability for integration across functions. The development of an effective, integrated HMIS portfolio that contributes to the long-term success of health service organizations will require more than the merger of existing administrative and clinical systems. A proactive strategy that is based on the health care organization's strategic vision and clearly defined managerial accountability will be necessary to ensure that HMISs meet both current and emerging organizational needs.

CHAPTER QUESTIONS

1. Why is "management" often considered both a science and an art?
2. Distinguish between "process efficiency" and "system efficiency" and between "process effectiveness" and "system effectiveness" and provide the rationale for the need to reengineer HMIS design, development, and management process.
3. What is meant by the "corporatization of medicine," and what are its implications for the design, development, and use of HMISs?
4. What do you perceive as the possible reasons that have led to management information system development occurring at a slower pace in the health service sector than in the business sector?
5. Compare and contrast the value of using the BSP, CSF, and E/M methodologies in the health service field. Why is the use of a combination of these techniques advisable?
6. To illustrate the relationships among strategic alignment, information requirements, and managerial accountability, draw a rich picture (refer to Chapter 2). Include the major steps and subsystems involved, and include the people and the entities that comprise these subsystems.

NOTES

1. P.F. Drucker, Coming of the New Organization, *Harvard Business Review* 66, no. 1 (1988): 40.
2. B.B. Longest, Jr., *Management Practices for the Health Professional*, 4th ed. (Norwalk, CN: Appleton & Lange, 1990), 35.
3. F.C. Munson and H. Zuckerman, The Managerial Roles, in *Health Care Management: A Text in Organizational Theory and Behavior*, ed. S.M. Shortell and A.D. Kaluzny (New York: John Wiley & Sons, 1985): 38–76.
4. J.G. Liebler, et al., *Management Principles for Health Professionals* (Gaithersburg, MD: Aspen Publishers, 1984).
5. H. Mintzberg, *The Nature of Managerial Work* (New York: Harper & Row, 1972).
6. H. Fayol, *General and Industrial Administration*, trans. C. Storrs (London: Sir Isaac Pitman and Sons, 1949).
7. L. Gulick and L.F. Urwick, eds., *Papers on the Science of Administration* (New York: Institute of Public Administration, 1937).
8. O. Tead, *Administration: Its Purpose and Performance* (New York: Harper and Brothers, 1959).
9. C. Barnard, *The Functions of the Executive* (Cambridge, MA: Harvard University Press, 1968).
10. O.J. Kralovec, Achieving Information Systems Benefits, in *Information Systems for Ambulatory Care*, ed. T.A. Matson and M.D. McDougall (Chicago: American Hospital Association, American Hospital Publishing, 1990), 79–96.
11. J.K.H. Tan with S. Sheps, eds., *Health Decision Support Systems*. (Gaithersburg, MD: Aspen Publishers, 1998).

12. R. Kropf, *Service Excellence in Health Care through the Use of Computers* (Ann Arbor, MI: Health Administration Press, 1990).

13. W.C. Zerrenner, *Improved Management through Automation,* in *Information Systems for Ambulatory Care,* ed. T.A. Matson and M.D. McDougall (Chicago: American Hospital Association, American Hospital Publishing, 1990): 45–54.

14. Ibid.

15. J.K.H. Tan, et al., Utilization Care Plan and Effective Patient Data Management, *Hospital and Health Services Administration* 38, no. 1 (1993): 81–99.

16. A.W. Kushniruk and V.L. Patel, Knowledge-Based Health Decision Support Systems: Cognitive Approaches to the Extraction of Knowledge and the Understanding of Decision Support Needs in Health Care, in *Health Decision Support Systems,* eds. J. Tan with S. Sheps (Gaithersburg, MD: Aspen Publishers, 1998).

17. D. Smitton, Corporatization of Medicine: The Use of Medical Management Information Systems To Increase the Clinical Productivity of Physicians: A Commentary, unpublished essay supervised by J.K.H. Tan, Faculty of Medicine, University of British Columbia (1991).

18. B.J. Fried, et al., Corporatization and Deprivatization of Health Services in Canada, in *The Corporate Transformation of Health Care. Issues & Directions,* ed. J.W. Salmon (Amityville, NY: Baywood Publishing Company, 1990), 167.

19. R. Kropf, *Service Excellence in Health Care through the Use of Computers.*

20. A.L. Lederer and V. Gardiner, Strategic Information Systems Planning: The Method/1 Approach, *Information Systems Management* (Summer 1992): 13–20.

21. K.K. Kim and J.E. Michelman, An Examination of Factors for the Strategic Use of Information Systems in the Healthcare Industry, *MIS Quarterly* (June 1990): 201–214.

22. M.J. Earl, Experiences in Strategic Information Systems Planning, *MIS Quarterly* (March 1993): 1–10.

23. B. Bowman, et al., Three Stage Model of MIS Planning, *Information and Management* 6, no. 1 (February 1983): 11–25.

24. P.J. Pyburn, Linking the MIS Plan with Corporate Strategy: An Exploratory Study, *MIS Quarterly* 7, no. 2 (1983): 1–14.

25. D.W. Conrath, et al., Strategic Planning for Information Systems: A Survey of Canadian Organizations, *INFOR* 30, no. 4 (1992): 364–378.

26. C. Dunbar and W.A. Schmidt, Information Systems Must Represent 35 Percent of Total Strategic Plan, *Computers in Healthcare* 12, no. 7 (1991): 22–24.

27. J.C. Henderson and J.B. Thomas, Aligning Business and Information Technology Domains: Strategic Planning in Hospitals, *Hospital and Health Service Administration* 37, no. 1 (Spring 1992): 71–87.

28. K.K. Kim and J.E. Michelman, An Examination of Factors for the Strategic Use of Information Systems in the Healthcare Industry, 201–214.

29. C. Cashmore and R. Lyall, *Business Information: Systems and Strategies* (Englewood Cliffs, NJ: Prentice Hall, 1991).

30. Ibid.

31. E.A. Van Schaik, *A Management System for the Information Business: Organizational Analysis* (Englewood Cliffs, NJ: Prentice Hall, 1985).

32. J.K.H. Tan, The Critical Success Factor (CSF) Approach to Strategic Alignment: Seeking a Trail from a Health Organization's Goals to Its Management Information Infrastructure (MII), *Health Services Management Research,* 12 (1999): 1–13.

33. C.R. Ferguson and R. Dickinson, Critical Success Factors for the Directors of the Eighties, *Business Horizons* 25, no. 3 (May/June, 1982): 14–18.

34. C.P. O'Connor, A Data Set for Hospital Planning, *Healthcare Management Review* (Fall 1979): 81–84.

35. C.V. Bullen and J.F. Rockart, A Primer on Critical Success Factors, in Working Paper No. 69 (Cambridge, MA: Center for Information Systems Research, Massachusetts Institute of Technology, 1981).

36. J.F. Rockart, Chief Executives Define Their Own Data Needs, *Harvard Business Review* 57, no. 2 (1979): 81–85.

37. W.C. Zerrenner, Improved Management through Automation, in *Information Systems for Ambulatory Care*, ed. T.A. Matson and M.D. McDougall (Chicago: American Hospital Publishing, 1990): 45–54.

38. C.V. Bullen and J.F. Rockart, A Primer on Critical Success Factors.

39. E.W. Martin, Critical Success Factors of Chief MIS/DP Executives: An Appendum, *MIS Quarterly* (December 1982): 79–81.

40. A.C. Boynton and R.W. Zmud, An Assessment of Critical Success Factors, *Sloan Management Review* (Summer 1984): 17–27.

41. M.E. Shank, et al., Critical Success Factors Analysis as a Methodology for MIS Planning, *MIS Quarterly* (June 1985): 121–129.

42. M.C. Munro and B.R. Wheeler, Planning Critical Success Factors and Management Information Requirements, *MIS Quarterly* (December 1980): 27–38.

43. G.O. Eni and J.K.H. Tan, Going North on a Northbound Trail: A Model for Achieving Health Management Goals and Objectives, *Health Services Management Research* 2, no. 2 (1989): 146–154.

44. H.J. Watson and M.N. Frolick, Determining Information Requirements for an EIS, *MIS Quarterly* 17, no. 3 (September 1993): 255–269.

Chapter 10

Health Management Information System Resource Management: Safeguarding Domain and Control Architecture

Joseph K. H. Tan

SCENARIO

On February 6, 2000, Yahoo! Inc., was completely shut down in the middle of the day for 3 hours as it struggled to get out of a planned attack on its site that mimicked the sending of hundreds of thousands of requests per minute for access to the site. The same problem occurred to Buy.com, Inc., the next day, just hours following its initial public offering. Other e-commerce sites that experienced the same sort of cyber-attacks later included eBay, Amazon.com, CNN.com, and E*Trade. Margaret Whitman, the Chief Executive Officer (CEO) of eBay, commented: "We have not seen anything of this magnitude before not only at eBay but across so many sites. This is probably the single largest denial of service that the Internet has seen."[1]

Imagine that instead of these high-priced e-commerce portals, which apparently carry secure and highly confidential data, the planned attacks were launched on a series of digital health networks that are providing real-time integrated health promotion, disease management, and telemedicine services. What would have been the consequences of these attacks? What lessons can be learned from the experiences of our e-commerce business counterparts?

Other types of equally malicious attacks that could also be consequential may include "sniffing" the packets of data being transmitted by health care e-commerce portals, the use of "applets" to modify or destroy important files sitting on the health providers' or the users' hard disks, the faking of electronic billing requests or of Web pages to deflect and redirect medical and insurance copayments fraudulently, and the stealing of valuable health information from these networks for purposes other than what it is intended. How would you go about preventing such occurrences?

Today, accurate and timely information has become vital in delivering quality patient care. With rapid advances in information technology, there is need for combining our knowledge on computer information systems and medicine in order to design, develop, and implement secure health information systems to gather, process, transmit, and disseminate information pertaining to patient demographic, financial, and clinical care data. In the case of digital health networks, the collection, transmission, and dissemination of such information are expected to cut across vast geographical boundaries. Despite the many sophisticated measures that experts in health information security have taken to ensure computer security through the use of firewalls, intrusion-detection systems, encryption, and digital signatures, the recent attacks we have experienced with e-commerce sites are no assurance that health management information systems (HMISs) will be any safer or more secure.

Imagine yourself to be the chief information officer (CIO) overseeing the functioning of one such digital health network. By capitalizing on the trend toward globalization, your vision is to expand the network currently used primarily for electronic consultation and management of a wide range of diseases in the North American market to new markets in Latin America, Europe, and Asia. Contemplate what steps you would take in evolving a tightly knitted, secure, and distributed network to link payers, providers, referral centers, and the patients. Think about the key information resource management issues in the use and administration of such an architecture for streamlining health care consultation and disease management across the various markets.

INTRODUCTION

The health service delivery industry is becoming very information intensive. Health data, whether clinical or managerial, are required as inputs in decision making at virtually all levels of a health service organization. Accordingly, the most successful health service organizations are those that can make the best possible use of their health data from the external environment and from within the organization.[2]

The management of health information resources in a health service system and the management of the health system itself are very closely related. Health information resource management (HIRM) is a concept that begins with viewing information resources including health data, health information flow, health information technology, health information personnel, and health information systems portfolio as major corporate resources that should be managed using the same basic principles applicable to managing other traditional economic assets. It is a mind-set designed to elevate the significance of effective and efficient management of health data within a health system.

HIRM is not a new concept. It has existed as long as health organizations have kept patient records. However, over the last few decades, the health service industry has been somewhat behind other businesses in computer automation.[3] The reason for this is not only cost constraints, but also the management styles, thinking, and attitudes of administrators in health service organizations. In this respect, the main purpose of this chapter is to provide a new perspective on health service management, in particular, the significance of its role in health information resource management.

More generally, the topics covered in this chapter are intended to provide managers (particularly, the CIO) of health service delivery organizations with a framework that will help them identify their health information resource needs; obtain accurate, timely, and relevant health data fundamental to effective decision making; view management of health information resources as part of managerial roles; exert controls to safeguard health data security and protect privacy; and relate to the concept of quality management and continuous improvement in HMIS design and development.

HEALTH INFORMATION RESOURCES

As we learned previously, well-managed communication channels can help reduce uncertainties in the information transmitted, and this in turn reduces uncertainties in the functioning of a health service organization. In this respect, information may be viewed as a vital resource for the survival, growth, and continuing development of a health service organization.

The significance of viewing health data as corporate resources may be justified in several ways. First, information is vital for the effective management and performance assessment of an organization. Second, effective planning, decision making, and operation of any health service facility are virtually impossible without proper access to, and the utilization of, appropriate and meaningful information. Third, the process of generating relevant and meaningful health data to assist decision making will by itself consume a significant amount of resources. Finally, as cost containment pressures grow and as new information technologies emerge, the need for information changes with time; this trend will intensify the urgency of managing the information resource in a health service organization more efficiently, effectively, and securely.

In highly successful health service organizations, the CEO, CIO, and other senior managers should be trained in the intelligent and respectful use of information and information systems. In particular, information systems in a health service delivery context are often important for supporting decision making relating to many aspects of health and health care, whether privately or publicly. These include the promotion of wellness and the prevention of illness; the monitoring, evaluating, controlling, and planning of health service resource allocation and utilization, and the curing of diseases; the formulation of health and social service procedures and policies; and the advancing of knowledge about health and health care through research and other educational channels.

Inefficient, ineffective, and insecure use of information is not only wasteful and dysfunctional to a health service organization, but severely limits the organization's ability to handle complex decision-making tasks that are necessary to thrive in a dynamically changing environment. Examples of inefficient use of information in a health service organization include collecting information that is not needed; storing information long after it is needed; disseminating information more widely than is necessary; employing poor and inadequate means for collecting, analyzing, storing, and retrieving information; duplicating collection and storage of the same basic information; and experiencing difficulty in assisting potential users to gain access to accurate, relevant, and meaningful information.[4]

Evidently, then, information systems are important corporate resources in a health service organization. Because health data are the raw materials or building blocks from which useful and meaningful health information can be generated (in all HMISs), there is a need to take a closer look at the fundamentals of health data administration.

Health Data Administration

Secure, efficient, and effective health data administration is critical for successful HIRM. Four areas of data administration that are applicable to health service delivery have been identified by Fry and Sibley.[5] These include availability of health data; quality of health data; independence of health data; and management's control of health data.

One of the primary goals of health data administration is to enhance the availability of health data. Specifically, this implies that a large part of the organization health data (i.e., databases, programs, models, and processes) should be available to be shared among a wide range of end users, for example, everyone from executives to line staff in a health service organization. Such sharing of health data reduces average cost by having the community pay for the health data and the individual users pay only for their use. Under these circumstances, however, the health data do not belong to any individual, program, or department; rather, ownership of these data belong to the community as a whole.

Accordingly, health data must achieve a certain level of standardization in order to support a high degree of data availability and data sharing. At the physical level, system compatibility embraces processor types, operating systems, databases, and applications. HMIS managers should decide on data standards and ascertain the use of uniform software throughout the health service organization. For instance, if a department that uses Windows and Microsoft Word interacts heavily with another department that uses Mac OS/8 and WordPerfect, then document transfers between the two departments may become somewhat inefficient. Therefore, if the appropriate health data are not available for consultation in an important decision situation because of hardware, software, or even interface incompatibility between various departments of a health service organization, then a wrong decision or action may be made. For example, in the case of a digital health network that is to share information across different countries, and even different continents, as discussed at the beginning of the chapter, there is need for compatible hardware and software that coordinate information updates, language translations (where necessary), and hardware and software compatibility to enhance data exchanges via a common portal.

Although the availability of health data does not ensure that the correct or relevant decisions will be made, the quality of the available health data does. In other words, high-quality health data must be maintained to ensure high-quality decisions. Very often, poor-quality health data may result when data are wrongly keyed, altered by human error during subsequent manipulations, altered by a computer program with a bug (erroneous with respect to the intended needs), altered by a mechanical error, or destroyed by a major catastrophe such as a mechanical failure of a disk.

To maintain health data quality, errors must be detected and investigated to determine how they occurred. Corrective and preventive actions should also be taken to eliminate or prevent future errors. In general, the quality and integrity of health data depend on the validity of inputs and the proper recording of periodic updates. These operations must be carefully controlled or monitored in efficient and effective health data administration, which brings us to the concepts of health data independence and management control.

Health Data Independence

There are two aspects of health data independence—physical independence and logical independence. Health data are physically independent if the program or ad hoc requests are relatively unaffected by the storage or access methods. Such systems provide a discrete number of choices for implementing the physical storage of health data. For example, physicians and nurses who are requesting data from a patient medical record database do not need to know how the data were physically stored or accessed: All that they see and interact with is the computer interface.

Logical health data independence refers to the ability to make logical changes to the health databases without significantly affecting the programs that access these databases. This form of independence has the capability to support various system or user views of the health database and to allow for modification of these views without adversely affecting the integrity of total applications. By analogy, end users (i.e., physicians and nurses) can request individual views of the patient records and make changes to the database without the need to know the software codes used to access and protect the integrity of the data.

Lastly, effective control of health data is necessary if the organization database is expected to support the proper functioning of a health service organization. The management of the health service organization must be able to control both the people who enter the health data and those who have access to the entered health data. Irresponsible use and unauthorized changes made to health databases can cripple the functioning of the health service organization. Data security can be accomplished easily by implementing controls at various levels. One level (system level) of controls seeks to protect the integrity and confidentiality of the stored health data by using, for example, passwords and antivirus programs. Another level (procedural level) of control is aimed at protecting the daily operations of the information systems, whereas physical facility controls are essential for the physical protection of the computer systems. This very important issue of privacy and security will be elaborated on later in the chapter. At this point, management of health information resources for health service organizations is discussed.

FIVE ASPECTS OF HEALTH INFORMATION RESOURCES MANAGEMENT

The recognition of health information as a corporate resource leads us to various aspects of managing this important resource; for example, the processing of health data into useful information requires both human and material resources. In particular, a health service organization will need both information technology capabilities and professional expertise to operate, maintain, upgrade, and plan for all of these health data processing activities.

Figure 10–1 shows that elements such as hardware, software, and personnel are considered basic health resources, and as such, they will need to be appropriately managed. This particular aspect of HIRM is known as the health resource management (HRM), which centers on the basic organizational components (e.g., personnel).

The health service organizations that will excel in the 21st century and beyond will likely be those that view their health information as a corporate resource and manage it well. Apart from this fundamental health resource aspect of HIRM, a taxonomy of HIRM is emphasized in four other dimensions[6]

1. health strategic management (HSM)
2. health technology management (HTM)
3. health distributed management (HDM)
4. health functional management (HFM)

All five aspects of HIRM should be carried out with the purpose of producing timely and high-quality information useful for achieving specific health organizational goals and objectives. In practice, however, HIRM is realized through an iterative process that involves planning, organizing, directing, and controlling. It requires the recognition that the involvement of top management in HMIS functions is as important as in any other organizational functions.

Figure 10–2 shows that the five aspects of HIRM have to do with the organizational environment (health strategic management); organizational task domains, products, and services (HFM); organizational communications and control infrastructure, that is, information administration and information networking (HDM); organizational technology (HTM); and organizational computing and human resources including hardware, software, and personnel (HRM).

HSM outlines the importance for HIRM to provide more than just computer services; in effect, the outcome of HIRM must be information-based products that will be useful to the strategic thinking and positioning of the health service organization in the external marketplace. Therefore, HSM dictates the overall purpose of HIRM, which is to contribute to the high-level achievement of health service organizational goals and objectives.

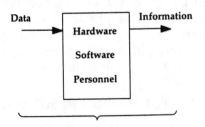

Figure 10–1 Basic Elements of Health Information Resources: The Health Management Aspect

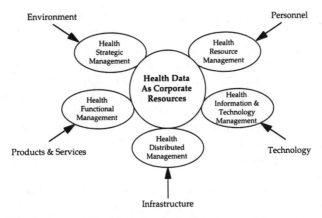

Figure 10–2 The Five Aspects of Health Information Resources Management

Figure 10–3 shows that HSM encompasses the management of corporate as well as HMIS strategies. Essentially, it is aimed at achieving organizational strategic alignment as discussed in the previous chapter (Chapter 9). HFM stresses the importance of using managerial know-how in HIRM, for example, continuous quality improvement (CQI) and total quality management (TQM) for carrying out task performance as discussed in the final section of this chapter. HMIS products and services should no longer be viewed as a special, separate case, but should be managed in the same way as any other functions of the organization. HFM domains include systems development, financial management, and personnel management.

HDM domains consist of network administration, database administration, systems integration, facilities administration, and end-user support. The responsibility of HDM should not be delegated solely to the CIO, but to all lev-

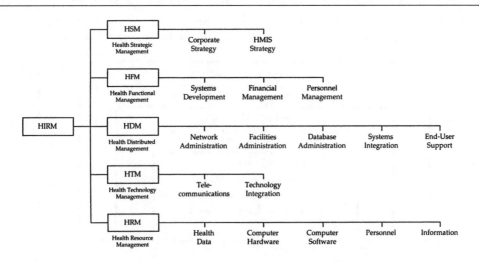

Figure 10–3 Functions and Domains of Health Information Resource Management (HIRM)

els of the organization, as it entails all functions of the organization and requires the commitments of all individuals. This is another aspect of HIRM in which concepts of CQI and TQM play a critical role.

HTM emphasizes the importance of integrating all technologies that process and deliver information, including transactional systems, telecommunications, office systems, and Web-based information processing. The planning, utilization, and operation of all the information technology of a health service organization should be coordinated for optimal effectiveness and efficiency.

Altogether, these various dimensions define HIRM and the philosophy on which it is based. As a management activity, HIRM regroups a wide range of managerial functions, which in turn summarize and regroup the tasks that are carried out by the CEO and CIO. The roles of CEO/CIO with respect to HIRM are discussed later. Now, the topic of security and safeguarding health information resources, including health data, information, computer hardware, software, and networks, is discussed. The secure and effective management of these basic resources will benefit the entire health service organization.

Safeguarding Health Information Resources

As we have noted, one of the queries arising from HIRM is the security issue, which can be overcome by the implementation of controls at various levels: systems control, procedural control, and facility control (Figure 10–4). In this section, the means of achieving procedure controls and issues relating to backup, disaster recovery planning, and security of equipment to facilitate effective HIRM are discussed. In the next section, particular attention is given to security and confidentiality of health data networks, in particular, concerns over computerized patient records (CPRs).

Procedural controls are an important aspect of systems security. These controls specify how the information services of the health service organization should be operated for maximum security and for high accuracy and integrity

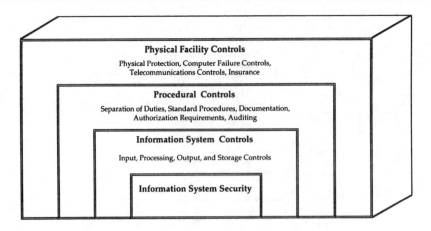

Figure 10–4 Levels of Data Security

of the HMIS functions and operations. There are three major means of achieving procedural controls.

1. separation of duties
2. standard procedures and documentation
3. authorization requirements

Systems development, computer operations, and control of health data and program files should be assigned to separate groups to prevent the possibility that a single group will gain unrestricted access to all related HIRM functions. Development of standard procedures (through manual and software help displays) promotes uniformity and minimizes errors and fraud. In addition, to enhance system uniformity and minimize potential destruction, there should be a formal review and authorization on any major system development projects, program changes, or system conversion by the CIO, departmental head, or a supervisor, all of whom are expected to reach a certain level of security clearance.

Procedures for effective health data backup include regular copying or duplication of programs, files, and databases for disaster recovery; adequate logging of transactions to reconstruct any lost data; detection of missing or incomplete records; and institution of other backup operational procedures for use during system failures, such as having an alternative manual or computerized system to be up and running in the shortest possible time. Fault-tolerant procedures, which are designed specifically for fault treatment, error detection, and recovery, provide a high degree of system stability and reliability.[7] Policies governing the process and the frequency of the procedures are also crucial in protecting the health data integrity. For instance, whereas duplicated data can be secured and stored in a separate location from the central site, procedures must exist for continuing systems operations during downtime experienced at the primary site, whether scheduled or unscheduled. In addition, highly sensitive files should be backed up on disks and the disks secured to prevent unauthorized access.

Because of the high cost of computer hardware and software, security measures to protect the investments are essential. Location of terminals, printers, and other accessories in secure areas that can be locked when not in use is advisable. Name tags, access codes, and physical cable-lock systems are examples of inexpensive ways of protecting hardware and software systems.

Viruses, which are another threat, can infect operating system files on computer hard drives or floppy disks. These programs also can intentionally try to alter or destroy data in a computerized database, such as a CPR system. For example, viruses can invade a CPR, even unintentionally, through a floppy disk or through a network. Security procedures to protect CPRs and networks from viruses include:

- checking bulletin boards and unauthorized software with an anti-virus program
- using and enforcing effective security codes and passwords for network users

- periodically running antivirus software programs on network servers, workstations, and nodes without floppy drives

Security, confidentiality, and privacy of clinical, financial, and management health data (whether computerized or not) are major concerns for health service organizations. A balance between restrictive user access and data sharing must be established through the development and enforcement of stringent HMIS policies and procedures. The management and retention of patient records and the security of health networks are particularly important.

Management and Retention of Patient Records

Accordingly, one of the high-priority areas requiring strict information management and confidentiality is patient records. Stringent legislative controls govern access to patient records, in particular, mental health records. All health record departments should have specific policies and procedures governing record access, storage, and retention both within the department and throughout the institution, because these records contain sensitive information.

All sensitive health information should be maintained in designated areas and be subjected to strict security control. Such information should only be used in areas that are considered private and inaccessible to unauthorized personnel. For example, terminals should shut down automatically when not in use, and mechanisms should be in place to disconnect terminals after a specific number of invalid attempts to access the system. Written policies should delineate who can access what information and for what purpose; for instance, researchers may access a specific population's health information for the purpose of research and education. Health records personnel must be trained experts in aspects of confidentiality, record access, and storage and should become excellent resources in policy development.

The general rule of health service facilities is that no information is released without a written consent from the patient, unless otherwise legislated (e.g., emergency or unusual situations). Thus, policies and procedures are essential to guide health professionals and health records personnel in safeguarding confidential information in both normal and emergency or unusual circumstances. Examples of unusual circumstances where access to a patient's record may be requested include: review by a coroner in preparation for an inquest, litigation against the hospital or physician, and potential for litigation because of serious misadventure or complication.

In general, access to CPRs should be restricted to health providers involved in the patient's care. Patients can legally access their own (manual) records, provided such an access is requested in writing and, if possible, endorsed by the patient's physician. Policies and procedures should be established to govern these aspects of record confidentiality. The health service facility must have clear policies delineating who has authority to grant access. Health records personnel are responsible for preventing alteration or tampering of patient records and should rely on administrative policies and procedures to support these efforts. The following guidelines may help to safeguard confidentiality and security of information.

1. establishing a formalized mechanism to alert users to an unusual circumstance
2. duplicating and safekeeping a record when an unusual circumstance is identified
3. limiting access to the copied version of this record whenever possible
4. numbering and counting of pages in the record

Facsimile machines have been a popular method to transmit hard copy health information. They present the opportunity for rapid transmission of both written and graphic information, which can greatly facilitate health service in urgent or emergency situations. However, this mode of transmission is easily opened to interception by unauthorized individuals. Therefore, transmission of patient data or record by facsimile should occur only in urgent or emergency cases and should be conducted between health records departments where there is strict control to ensure the information is received in an appropriate manner. The point is that issues related to confidentiality, security, and privacy should not impede patient care.

Retention of records is another major issue of concern in HIRM because patient records and other information may be needed for legal defense. The retention period should be at least as long as the limitation period during which the organization can be the target of a lawsuit. Retention periods may vary depending on the type of facility and the governing legislation. The courts have also extended limitation periods depending on the patients involved.

Destruction of health information is also controlled by legislation; therefore, written institutional policies must specify methods of destruction to be used, such as shredding or burning; methods of routine destruction of daily paper accumulation that contains health data; periodic destruction of inactive or outdated recorded health data with particular attention to designating personnel who will witness or attest to the destruction in writing; and erasure of health information recorded or stored by electronic means on tapes, disks, or cassettes.

Safeguarding Computerized Patient Records and Health Networks

CPRs and health networks add another layer to the confidentiality and security issue. The information on computer databases is no different from the documentation in the manual patient records. Thus, policies, procedures, and guidelines to govern access to information and to maintain confidentiality and security are just as necessary as they are for written patient records.

Attention on security and confidentiality regarding CPRs, particularly CPRs available over the Internet or on health networks, has been increasing and will continue to increase. On the one hand, although most patients typically maintain a positive attitude toward CPR use, they are nonetheless concerned about the confidentiality of the records. Ornstein and Bearden interviewed 16 patients of 8 different physicians from a medical university and found that one strategy to ease this concern is to have patients informed about records and their uses.[8] Borst noted that most patients thought computer-based medical records were unsafe because of their vulnerability to blackmail.[9] Inevitably, insurance companies and future employers can use these records to make decisions on who to insure or hire, and therefore the potential exists to discriminate against cases of mental illness, people with HIV infection, or other ill-fated problems.

On the other hand, technologies have been developed and are available to ensure the security of CPRs on networks and the Internet. These include Internet security software such as firewalls, intrusion-detection programs, digital certificates, and authentication and authorization software. For example, Andreae discussed how public key cryptography could be used to enhance authentication and authorization of data transfer reliably, thereby eliminating access to confidential information on networks.[10] Unfortunately, because as much as 60 percent of all cyber crime goes undetected or unreported, nobody really knows the extent of cyber attacks that exists today. However, the same legal requirements that apply to paper records apply also to computer-based records. Waller and Fulton argued that "insiders" (i.e., the employees who use the computers on a daily basis) pose the greatest threat to security, as they are "closest" to accessing the data.[11]

All employees and health data users also should be asked to sign a pledge of confidentiality that incorporates computerized health information within its scope. As well, reporting of breaches of security should be included in the policies along with a statement of disciplinary measures for violation of the security of computerized data. It may be important to note that the acceptance of the computer signature as a legal signature for admissibility as evidence in court is not yet clearly established.

Principles of documentation in the context of computerized health information should meet legal and professional standards. Appropriate orientation programs, ongoing educational seminars, and attendance at conferences are essential to ensure that managers, health record professionals, and other hospital staff are fully aware of the policies and procedures governing information access, security measures, and confidentiality expectations.

Finally, essential aspects of computerized health information systems security are the use of audit controls and the enforcement of original policies and procedures regarding systems and information access. For example, users should have authorized access only to data files necessary for accomplishing their work, and breaching of policies must be swiftly and professionally handled to ensure confidence in data integrity and protection of confidentiality.

In this business, it should be noted that the biggest concern is the loss of public trust and image. Imagine how patients would feel about giving away their personal information to an organization incapable of and unable to protect the privacy and security of this information.

THE ROLES OF THE CEO AND CIO IN HEALTH INFORMATION RESOURCES MANAGEMENT

The importance of health information as a corporate resource in health services can no longer be denied. Any health service organization looking to survive and grow must recognize the need to treat HMISs as a resource. CEOs, in accepting the challenge of managing health service organizations, must ensure that HMISs are implemented in an orderly fashion with a view to the future and an emphasis on integration. The CIOs must expand their role from one of technical information system managers to those who take executive responsibility and understand the need to integrate HMISs into the strategic plan of organizations in order to meet their goals, objectives, and strategies.

Role of the Chief Executive Officer

We begin with a brief review of the emerging roles of the CEO for a health service organization. First, today's health service CEO must be a visionary, particularly one who provides strategic directions and visions, understands the health care environment and its changing marketplace, and recognizes the political and socioeconomic forces that affect the delivery of health services. Second, the CEO must be a leader in the true sense of the word. In this role, the CEO plans, organizes, and defines organizational product mix and new programs and services. Apart from retaining the usual planning and control functions, the CEO must form liaisons with various stakeholders in the system to build strategic alliances and to ensure a healthy corporate image both outside and inside the organization. Finally, the CEO must be a manager in terms of both managing corporate culture and managing organizational change process. The CEO needs to establish a workplace in which all medical, clinical, and health service support staff can be motivated to provide efficient, effective, and high-quality services. In other words, the CEO must be able to earn the respect of those subordinates and line staff who report to him or her and be able to delegate authority to the right person when the need arises.

In today's turbulent health care environment, the CEO should not be personally responsible for developing and managing information. Instead, he or she must ensure the development of the appropriate infrastructure and the availability of the expertise within the organization and assist in the challenge of positioning the organization in an information system technology marketplace that is consistent with its positioning in the health care marketplace.

In a general survey conducted by Cohen, the role of the CEO in computerization was investigated through interviewing eight CEOs in various health service organizations throughout North America.[12] All of them had different approaches and insights, and this was reflected in the mix of directions their organizations were taking with respect to HIRM. Although these CEOs exhibited different reactions, all of them felt that they had played a key role in the development or management of HMISs. The following represents a cross-section of some of their comments.

- Computerization will now involve integration at every turn; information is a key resource that needs more attention from hospital administration.
- We needed a master plan that would allow us to eventually connect every department and produce excellent management information system information; the key to successful computerization is massive top management involvement.
- It's really important for hospitals that are computerizing to have a flexible master plan that can be adjusted every year.
- It's pointless to introduce an information system if it is not done in concert with looking at your organization and how it is structured.
- One of the biggest challenges is resisting pressure from the individual department to move off the master plan for finance and administration into patient care areas.
- Practice participative management that involves as many employees as possible in decisions that affect them.
- You've got to hire people with excellent skills and give them the authority to get the jobs done right.
- A successful computer system is 80 percent people-dependent and only 20 percent technology-dependent.

As one may conclude, although these CEO approaches to HIRM vary dramatically, their concerns cover all of the five dimensions of HIRM discussed previously. For example, HSM, which has to do with strategic alignment, is clearly expressed by several of these CEOs as the need to tie HMIS directions with organizational goals and objectives. Also, from a CEO's perspective, information and people are seen as key resources to successful HIRM. HTM and HDM are highlighted in combination by the need for technological integration and future connectivity, whereas HFM is also emphasized in at least one of the CEO comments, indicating the need to practice participative management techniques for effective HIRM. Although there may not be a definitive role for a CEO, in general, the pivotal roles of a CEO in HIRM should include:

1. having a member of senior management, for example, a CIO, take primary and supreme responsibility for developing and sharing of HMISs within the health service organization
2. acting as a role model (e.g., fostering an HMIS culture throughout the organization)
3. working effectively with the CIO to ensure that a state-of-the-art HMIS architecture is in place, as noted in previous chapters

Having established the significance of health data and all HMIS components, activities, and functions as corporate resources, and having acknowledged the role of the CEO in its overall management responsibility for HIRM, the discussion now turns to the role of the CIO, sometimes known as the chief technology officer (CTO), in HIRM.

Role of the Chief Information Officer

A CIO is a senior manager whose responsibility lies primarily in the management and control of HMISs and networks. In general, a CIO serves two important functions. These are: (1) assisting the executive team and governing board in effectively managing health information resources to support strategic planning and management of the health service organization; and (2) providing managerial oversight and coordinating functions in data administration, information processing, and telecommunications throughout the organization.

Today, the role of the CIO has significantly changed from that of its predecessors, the manager of management information systems, and the manager of health data processing even before that. The CIO has achieved an increasingly important role and should be positioned in the top management team of an organization. Whereas previous managers of management information systems were seen more as functional managers, CIOs are now considered executive managers who play an important role in the strategic planning and decision-making processes of an organization.

Some of the longer-term responsibilities of CIO may include

- policies, procedures, guidelines, or standards for information resources
- strategic planning for information resources, linked to business planning, to provide improved organization functions and competitive advantage
- approval/acceptance of computing technology expenditures
- coordination of information technology, functional units, and environments
- education of management, especially top management, on uses of technology
- environmental scanning

Short-term responsibilities may include consultations on present problems and day-to-day general managerial work.[13]

For many health service organizations, however, the immediate step required to advance the current state of HMISs for the organization would be a broad-based program using the shared knowledge and skills of technicians, managers, and users. More importantly, this would require the CIO to take the leadership role. The mandate would be to provide the directions toward advancement of the HMIS capacity in the health service organization. These directions will depend largely on the type of training and experiences of the CIO. In the growing complexity of the HMIS environment, there are eight major functions expected of the CIO.[14]

1. operations management
2. communications management
3. corporate-wide HMIS planning
4. information center or end-user computing (EUC) support
5. data resources management
6. project management
7. systems development and maintenance
8. quality management

These are also shown in Figure 10–5.

Operations management deals with the overall technological context of the health information system. Procedures and methods that deal with the

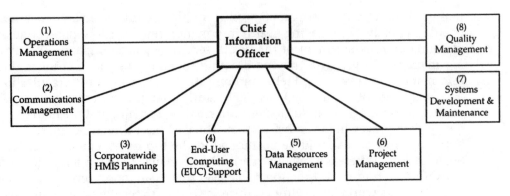

Figure 10–5 Eight Major Functions of the Chief Information Officer

scheduling of hardware and software installation and deinstallation, planning of system capacity, operations security, and recovery from disaster or equipment failure all fall under this function. Communications management involves the collection, relay, and transmission of data between sources in and around the organization, and identification of the forms of transmission data to be communicated and reproduced. Above all, the alignment of the HMIS plan to the strategic plan of the organization is an integral part of corporate-wide HMIS planning.

Data resources management involves the analysis and administration of data and the design and administration of the database. EUC support is the function of the HMIS that responds through staff specialists to the ad hoc requests for data or analyses from end users. Project management is management toward the effective implementation of a proposed information systems project. Most information systems projects, however, are never completed on time, within budget, and according to plans. Systems development and maintenance are integral roles of the CIO and involve flexible thinking and insightful and long-term overviews of the administration and effects of information systems on the organization.

Finally, quality management is achieved through a comprehensive approach that entails the structuring of review (audit) and approval procedures for applications, hardware, and software systems; establishment of an integrated HMIS supportive of TQM; and establishment of the domain of responsibility and authority of the HMIS function.

Each of these functions, require specialized training and years of experience as a CIO. As changes in the functions occur, the role and outlook of the CIO will necessarily be transformed as well. To move to a new paradigm for engaging HIRM thinking up to this point, the concepts of CQI and TQM are alluded to throughout this chapter.

A TQM/CQI PARADIGM: THE HEALTH MANAGEMENT INFORMATION SYSTEM IMPERATIVE

The TQM/CQI approach represents a total paradigm shift in health service management, and the burden of its successful implementation falls squarely on the shoulders of top management. In many organizations, health service organizations included, the application of TQM/CQI ideology begins with CEO interest and curiosity, which evolves into a "conversion process" wherein the CEO internalizes the principles and starts to refocus the organization's management philosophy. From this point, senior management is increasingly integrated into the process. A formal quality management body or council is established with the intended purpose of filtering through the various facets of the organization.

A key question to be answered for health service organizations is therefore: How should the CEO (or the CIO) visualize the quality management process, and what role can integrated HMIS play to promote successful quality management? Figure 10–6 shows a schematic view of the strategic and functional ties between the TQM/CQI and HMIS concepts.

Figure 10–6 depicts the two contexts (i.e., environmental and organizational contexts) that continually define and shape the TQM/CQI paradigm for the corporate system, but the apparatus for promoting and ensuring quality management success is no more than the integrated HMIS. In short, it is the design of an intelligent information analysis (IIA) system that will continually drive the TQM/CQI paradigm top-down through the system in achieving the goals of service excellence, effectiveness, and efficiency.

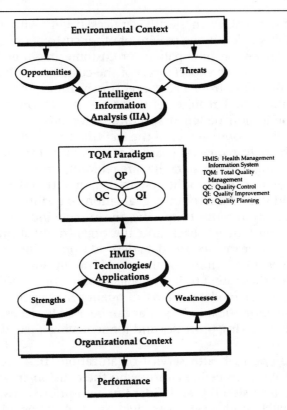

Figure 10–6 The Paradigm of Total Quality Management (TQM): A Health Management Information System Perspective

On one hand, an information analysis of opportunities and threats in the environment to shape the strategic understanding of quality management implications for the enterprise is needed. This will result in asking questions such as: What is it that we produce (outcome)? Are we producing the right products and services that meet customer (patient) needs?

On the other hand, an information analysis of particular strengths and weaknesses of the system processes within the corporate context will point to areas where the enterprise might particularly consider applying quality management. Some of the questions to be asked here are: How do we produce what we produce (process)? Are we producing these products (services) in the right way? Quality management involves asking whether a health service system is producing the most needed services in the best possible way—a concept that epitomizes the ideal of system optimization.

More specifically, IIA is an information collection, monitoring, and control system that parallels the concepts of Juran's quality trilogy of quality planning, quality control, and quality improvement. We examine each of these facets and its relation to integrated HMIS in greater detail.

Quality Planning: Defining Quality Health Management Information System Input

Defining quality in health services begins with quality planning. This involves, first, identifying patient or other customer satisfaction, which in turn depends largely on how patient or customer requirements are met. In other words, what are the expectations of the customer with respect to service quality? The responses from a customer survey, for example, can be translated into specific individual requirements for the health organization's IIA, a critical HMIS application designed specifically for promoting quality management. This is a direct consequence of the fact that the needed action can be produced only if the right request is heard. Consequently, for quality management to be operative, high-quality data that are relevant, timely, meaningful, and accurate must be used as input to the system (i.e., quality HMIS input).

In addition, data from the evaluation of quality performance (i.e., quality HMIS output) in terms of specific, measurable indicators must be available to generate constant feedback into the organizational quality management IIA system. This means that the data derived from these measures, as well as information generated from them, provide additional valuable inputs that are needed for the system to improve its product or service quality. This information processing model pertains to quality management thinking, which will eventually form the mind-set that can be used for redesigning health managerial decision-making processes and for achieving a paradigm of CQI in a health service system.

Therefore, in health service organizations that are trying to put quality first, the ability to define clearly who their customers are is an important first step. The next step is then to identify high-priority customer needs accurately and to match these needs to product (service) characteristics. In any case, quality HMIS inputs are then processed by using appropriate and available HMIS technologies to give management the information needed for job design (or, redesign) that will produce the needed quality products or services. Hence, it is also equally important for the organization to spell out the types of products and services that are acceptable to the customers, and this is where quality HMIS output comes into play.

Quality Control: Monitoring and Evaluating Quality Health Management Information System Output

The question to ask regarding what outcomes should be monitored in health services has been explained by Donabedian.[15] The CEO, CIO, and other senior managers should ask: If we are successful in the services we are carrying out, what change should we see in the customer (the outcome indicator)? For example, if our customers are patients, then changes could include changes in health state, changes in health knowledge, changes in health behavior pertinent to future health states, or more simply, changes in patient satisfaction with health services.

In conjunction with these outcomes, tasks/decisions/processes must be carried out in order to reach the outcome (e.g., test, drug, procedure, education, interaction, etc.). Various chains of events eventually produce an outcome, and this chain of events should indicate to health service professionals whether they are on the right track to reaching quality goals. This is the realm of process analysis. Sometimes, in health service delivery, it is difficult to say where a process ends and an outcome is reached. The problem is amplified when outcomes are multidimensional. Again, in the case of patients, we must ask: When did the patient become different? We then judge the answer in terms of our preset standard for "different."

In this regard, one should keep in mind that outcomes do not directly assess quality of performance. Outcomes only permit an inference regarding the quality of the process that occurred. The degree of confidence in that inference is based on the strength of the (causal) relationship between the processes and the outcome. Only when this relationship is sound can one draw conclusions regarding quality based simply on outcomes. Although the evaluation of process and performance is the entire focus of quality management, a holistic look is taken at the measurement and evaluation of final outcome from a quality HMIS perspective.

An issue that deserves mention in terms of quality control is the integrative property of outcomes (i.e., quality HMIS output), which makes it difficult to isolate with certainty the process contributions that lead to negative outcomes. Outcome measures the combined effects of all causes operating inside and outside the system. Differentiating causes of negative outcomes is therefore emphasized in quality management performance evaluation.

Quality control should focus on both systemic causes (common causes that arise from within the system) and extrasystemic causes (special causes that are external to the system). In other words, quality management effort directed to systemic causes affects the total system (i.e., it affects everyone in the system) and will thus produce a permanent change in the level of quality performance, whereas quality control that focuses on extrasystemic causes alone may produce only temporary improvement and the average of the majority remains the same.

Moreover, in order for an organization to control quality and to produce desirable outcomes, it must also explicitly state indicators and measures, both of which require the appropriate design of HMISs. Indicators are needed to determine what level of performance quality is or is not acceptable. They are set against standards, and if standards are not being met, indicators reflect where the gap in performance exists. Examples of indicators in health service delivery are length of stay and the patient mortality rate for a particular procedure. Measures specify what is collectible and chartable by line staff using available technology. Such technology is to be employed by process improvement teams to monitor daily work and should incorporate data collection and charting methods. Measures should reflect the relation between outcomes and key process variables and should show changes seen in indicator values over a period of time. The quality measuring process should be simple and carefully planned by using a flowchart.

As we can see, the organizational system described has within it a feedback mechanism that helps the organization control the gap between its desired quality outputs (preestablished) and actual outputs. For this feedback or control component of the system to function with regard to quality management, goals and objectives must already be set. The corrective action that subsequently can be taken then is a response to a discrepancy between the desired and the actual output in the system. This action is needed in order to bring actual performance in line with desired performance and to reduce inappropriate variations in the system. The main idea here is to improve the entire process continuously and not simply to meet standards. This brings the discussion to the last and perhaps most important component of Dr. Juran's quality trilogy—quality improvement.

Quality Improvement: Monitoring, Investigating, and Modifying Quality Health Management Information System Processes

One should note that within the process of quality management, the goal is continuous improvement. To this end, the standards alluded to in the preceding framework are broad standards depicting quality states for which monitoring is carried out. Finison emphasizes that the stages of the process should be a translation of professional standards into operational requirements, and not a translation of current reality into operational standards.[16]

From this framework, a chain of activities leading to a particular quality outcome can then be designed. Undertaking processes (services) that lead to quality can be expressed in the form of an information flow diagram (flowchart). At each point in the flowchart, quality criteria, indicators, and measures should be included. These steps are outlined so that quality services can be carried out effectively and efficiently, or are monitored to ensure that they are carried out in such a manner.

TQM/CQI thinking advocates the use of a scientific approach to process improvement. Sahney and Warden note that alteration of the process "based on whims and hunches amounts to tampering and destabilizes the process."[17] A popular process improvement methodology is that of the Deming-Shewhart plan, do, check, act (PDCA) cycle:[18]

- *Plan.* This is to study the process and to decide what needs to be changed to improve the system.
- *Do.* This refers to the gathering and analysis of data or inputs.
- *Check.* This refers to the checking of data and the study of the effects of the recommended changes.
- *Act.* This is to determine what parts of the improved process should be standardized.

The traditional notion that the management is in charge of planning, the health professionals are in charge of doing, the supervisors and senior health professionals are in charge of checking, and the nurses and other health professionals are in charge of acting is fast giving way to the concept that every member of a health service delivery organization must practice the entire cycle in order to make the improvement effort successful. Moreover, the PDCA cycle should be practiced in daily routines, as well as in nonroutine situations. The simple act of self-checking and reflection is expected to bring new insights into currently adopted procedures and organization. As may be seen, the PDCA methodology relies largely on intelligent information processing by every member of the health service organization.

In addition to the PDCA approach, an important principle for quality process improvement is what the Japanese call Genba, Genbutsu. Genba means to go see the place where the problem is occurring, and Genbutsu means to observe the material or product with the defects itself.[19] Too often, managers of health service delivery organizations rely too much on meetings and printed reports to understand the services provided by the organization: that is, they are remote from the action. The essence of Genba, Genbutsu is captured in the saying "seeing is believing," which is far more effective than presenting information in meetings and reports alone. Health organization managers are therefore encouraged to visit patients and health professionals in the wards and waiting rooms and to communicate directly with them. The same principle applies to the collection of firsthand information, which essentially implies a redesign of current HMISs for quality purposes.

Put together, the process improvement methodology implies, first, identifying a critical process in the system, bringing it under statistical control, and eliminating any undesirable extrasystemic causes; and, second, using the PDCA cycle and other approaches to improve the process incrementally by eliminating systemic causes one by one. The health professionals are reminded that all steps in the process must have measures associated with them. As the process occurs, data are collected and analyzed. The final outcome (the stage that is determined to be the outcome) is also measured and evaluated.

From an HMIS perspective, the IIA system acts as feedback so that corrective actions in response to variations in the system can be used to bring actual performance in line with the desired quality level, if this is not already the case. All subsystems of the system (the organization) function individually in their processes (inputs, processes, and outputs related to quality) and must eventually interact to provide the organization with its overall goals and objectives and mission (quality). The feedback that occurs within the whole system (all subsystems included) should be seen as a positive progression toward quality, and not as a negative policing of organizational processes.

Thus, the system can then see where improvements can be made and where accountability for particular processes can be assigned through the feedback/control loop. Very often, the entire system tries to achieve the best quality while also trying to conserve resources. In effect, certain criteria are to be maximized while cost is to be minimized. As Daigh explains, cost and quality are not conflicting but complementary.[20] High quality need not increase cost but instead should result in improved productivity and reduced waste in the system. The author states that poor quality is what is expensive. The kind of quality that produces an appropriate service for a patient reduces errors, rework, inefficiency, and waste. All these attributes result in reduced costs.

TQM/CQI thinking employs a very different philosophy, namely, decentralization using project teams. Multidisciplinary project teams of frontline employees collect and analyze data from clinical and administrative sources, both internal and external to the organization. The project team determines the type and scope of data to be collected, collects the data itself, and determines how it will analyze the data and how the data will be used to take corrective action. As it is common in quality management organizations to have several project teams working concurrently on different problems, there is often data sharing among the various project teams. This sharing of information eliminates redundancy of collection and analysis and is the key function of an IIA, the central functioning of a quality-focus HMIS in the organization. In other words, organizations need to take a good look at how their design of HMISs can be used to promote quality management throughout the subsystems of the total system.

Other significant roles of IIA in promoting quality management are data presentation and dissemination. With the shift from centralization of problem solving to decentralization, the organization must plan and implement strategies to manage the emerging data. Centralized information systems management alone is no longer the ideal means to aid these quality project teams. The transition to quality management necessitates the change from a centralized mainframe information system to an integrated but distributed technology, supported by IIA and other HMIS subsystems, which each project team can readily access and utilize to solve quality problems. Whereas traditional HMIS designs provided only summaries of counts and percentages that were not widely disclosed, quality management utilizes many graphical tools to demonstrate data that are widely distributed.

CONCLUSION

It should now be evident that information resources have to be considered as critical corporate resources that must be managed using the same basic principles used to manage other assets. In the future, as health care facilities increase in complexity, so will the volume of health data. Therefore, it is essential to have a secure, well-managed, and quality-focused information system. An important step toward achieving this is to evolve an integrated HMIS with an embedded IIA. Such a system is critical for managing the organization health information resources and ensuring that the organization will thrive in the future.

CHAPTER QUESTIONS

1. Define HIRM and describe its purpose.
2. What does HIRM provide to managers of health service delivery organizations?
3. What are the five aspects of HIRM?
4. Why should health data be considered corporate resources?
5. What are the uses of information systems in health service delivery organizations?
6. What are the four major aspects of data administration in health database management?
7. Please indicate whether the following statements should be included in the job description of a CEO or a CIO.
   - Be responsible for developing and managing information.
   - Ensure that a key executive/manager who has a primary and unmistakable responsibility for developing and sharing information within the organization is appointed.
   - Act as a role model (e.g., be organized and positive), as all other strata of management and staff within the organization may take their cue from him or her.
   - Responsible for managing the organization's information.
   - Work effectively with the other chief officers to ensure that the processes for managing information within the organization are effective.
   - Assist the executive team and governing board in using information effectively to support strategic planning and management.
   - Provide management oversight and coordinate information processing and telecommunication systems throughout the organization.
   - Have an in-depth understanding of the current caregiving environment.
   - Be an active leader in the development of the organization's information systems plans for the future.
   - Have a sound understanding of the information systems industry, particularly in relation to health care.
   - Ensure the development of the appropriate structure and the availability of the expertise within the facilities and assist in the challenge of obtaining the right information and interpreting it appropriately.

- Be an executive who understands and advocates that information is a corporate asset to be used and protected with the same care as any other corporate asset.
- Anticipate the appropriate time for implementing leading-edge technology.
- Create a current state-of-the-art management information technology infrastructure that supports the organization's overall plans, goals, and objectives.

NOTES

1. I. Sager, et al., Cyber Crime, *Business Week* (February 21, 2000).
2. A. Mingione, Search for Excellence within a Systems Development Project, *Journal of Systems Management* 37 (1986): 31–34.
3. R. L. Nolan, et al., Computers and Hospital Management: Prescription for Survival, *Journal of Medical Systems* 1, no. 2 (1977): 187–203.
4. Central Computer and Telecommunications Agency, *Managing Information as a Resource* (London: Her Majesty's Stationery Office, 1990), 4.
5. J. Fry and E. Sibley, Evolution of Data-Base Management Systems, *Computing Surveys* 8, no. 1 (1976): 7–42.
6. J.A. O'Brien, *Introduction to Information Systems in Business Management*, 6th ed. (Homewood, IL: Richard Irwin Publishers, 1991).
7. T. Anderson and P. Lee, *Fault Tolerance: Principles and Practice* (Englewood Cliffs, NJ: Prentice Hall, 1981).
8. S. Ornstein and A. Bearden, Patient Perspectives on Computer-Based Medical Records, *Yearbook of Medical Informatics* (1995): 247–251.
9. F. Borst, Synopsis: Computer-Based Patient Records, *Yearbook of Medical Informatics* (1995).
10. M. Andreae, Confidentiality in Medical Telecommunication, *Lancet* 347 (1996): 487–488.
11. A. Waller and D. Fulton, The Electronic Chart: Keeping It Confidential and Secure, *Journal of Health and Hospital Law* 26, no. 4 (1993): 104.
12. L. Cohen, Computerization: The Role of the CEO, *Dimensions* 66, no. 4 (1990): 28–33.
13. C.S. Stephens, et al., The Nature of the CIO's Job, *MIS Quarterly* 16, no. 4 (December 1992): 449–467.
14. J.K.H. Tan, Graduate Education in Health Information Systems: Having All Your Eggs in One Basket, *Journal of Health Administration Education* 11, no. 1 (1993): 27–55.
15. A. Donabedian, The Role of Outcomes in Quality Assessment and Assurance, *Quality Review Bulletin* (November 1992): 356–360.
16. L.J. Finison, What Are Good Health Care Measurements? *Quality Progress* 25, no. 4 (1992): 41–42.
17. V.K. Sahney and G.L. Warden, The Quest for Quality and Productivity in Health Services, *Frontiers of Health Services Management* 7, no. 4 (1991): 11.
18. B.C. James, TQM and Clinical Medicine, *Frontiers of Health Services Management* 7, no. 4 (1991): 42–46.
19. L.J. Kerr, Achieving World Class Performance Step by Step, *Long Range Planning* 25, no. 1 (1992): 46–52.
20. R.D. Daigh, Financial Implications of a Quality Improvement Process, *Topics in Health Care Financing* 17, no. 3 (1991): 42–52.

Chapter 11

Health Management Information System Implementation: Implementing Domain and Control Architecture

Joseph K. H. Tan

SCENARIO

The Fraser-Burrard Regional Council (FBRC) is planning to integrate and consolidate information technology applications for five local health service facilities in order to resolve problems in the way their information resources are organized and managed. To date, the various facilities have catered to their own specific information system needs with a mix of hardware and software capabilities supported by a variety of vendors. Apparently, there is a considerable amount of information that overlaps among the different systems. As a result of the move to regionalize the health service delivery in the Fraser-Burrard area, FBRC would like first to implement an intranet that will link existing local area networks among the five primary care facilities within the region with the vision of extending these linkages to the wider community of physicians, para-professionals, long-term care institutions, clinics, and other health care agencies and organizations in the region and elsewhere via an extranet. For example, the council wants and needs to have the capability to link directly with the government and private insurance services to share critical and sensitive data electronically. Ultimately, it would like to be able to be integrated with all the major information systems in the regional health service sector to achieve a completely integrated regional health service system.

The present health management information system (HMIS) architecture of the five facilities consists simply of separate site databases running on isolated local area networks. In this regard, each of the sites may also carry a duplicate copy of a database of another site from which data are shared. Updates to the data have not been timely because of poor coordination among the facilities. Some facilities have hired trained data administrators to oversee this task on an ongoing basis, whereas others have simply requested for the updates whenever needed. Accordingly, many problems have been encountered with the current configuration of the separate database systems, including inconsistency of data updates and increasing cost and technical complexity of maintaining duplicate databases.

The present configuration can be schematically represented by Figure 11–1.

The money budgeted for the proposed intranet and extranet architecture is quite substantial, thereby enabling the council to investigate alternatives using the very latest technology and advances in systems software. However, the council is experiencing great resistance to their plan despite the fact that much of the network and communications technology is in place or readily available to link the various subsystems within the Fraser-Burrard region. Other organizations involved, and even some arms of the government, are not prepared to permit any outside access to their individual systems for fear of security breach. Moreover, the majority of managers and systems people within these five individual facilities do not feel that they have the time nor the resources necessary to help develop an effective way of allowing their systems to be integrated. FBRC is seen as a "fat cat" that can afford all the very latest in technology innovation, and, needless to say, there is a great deal of animosity as well.

You are the newly appointed chief information officer (CIO) to undertake this implementation project on behalf of the FBRC. Your first assignment is to analyze the information systems of the various health service facilities within the FBRC mandate so that they can realize their ultimate goal of a completely integrated regional health service information system. During your preimplementation analysis, several issues were raised.

- How can you convince all parties involved that the implementation of a completely integrated regional HMIS is to everyone's advantage?
- Contemplate what some of the specific benefits of system integration might be to the different care facilities, the insurance company, and the government.
- How could the proposed intranet-extranet architecture be successfully implemented to link the different systems?
- What would happen to the current setup of FBRC's information systems following the implementation of the proposed intranet/extranet architecture?

Site 1: Database 1

(includes DB 2)

Site 2: Database 2   Site 3: Database 3

(includes DB 4)   (includes DB 5)

Site 5: Database 5   Site 4: Database 4

(includes DB 1 & 3)   (includes DB 1 & 2)

Figure 11–1 Current Configuration of Health Databases for Five Facilities in the Fraser-Burrard Region

- What are some of the postimplementation needs, in particular, the need for evaluation, maintenance, and upkeep of the new system?
- How would you, as a CIO, ensure that other members of top management and various staff members will be adequately trained to use the new system comfortably?

Think about how you and the chief executive officer (CEO) can and should work together, and consider how you would address many of these concerns, drawing from your own experience with managing information systems and what you know about HMIS resource management and implementation.

INTRODUCTION

The implementation of an HMIS in a health service organization is a process whose success is dependent on the fulfillment of a number of key activities. These include strategic planning, a thorough preliminary systems analysis, broad and detailed systems design specifications, user training and education, and hardware and software vendor selection.

Success in the implementation of HMIS technology is deeply rooted in strategic planning. It must take into consideration a comprehensive but operable organizational strategic plan, one that drives the strategic HMIS plan. Therefore, several aspects of organizational planning and management considerations must precede HMIS implementation. First, proper implementation of any HMIS applications requires a concerted effort to advance an implementation plan, to incorporate designs, and to involve skillful human interactions and liaisons. Second, successful HMIS implementation demands competent health information resource management (HIRM). Finally, successful implementation can be achieved by utilizing a variety of program management techniques that allow for ongoing monitoring of project progress.[1]

In practice, certain critical factors can influence the success of HMIS implementation. For example, two broad areas that have played key roles are (1) the application of well-tested guidelines and standard protocols and (2) the enforcement of ethical and legal concerns. Figure 11–2 shows that once HMIS planning is fine-tuned to address success factors for HMIS implementation on the one hand, and organizational planning and management considerations on the other, the actual steps including specific activities for HMIS implementation can be specified, directed, monitored, and controlled by project planning and management directives.

This chapter serves as an overview of HMIS implementation. It highlights the steps necessary to successful implementation of HMIS in a health service organizational setting. The chapter draws from previous parts of the book, in particular Chapters 9 and 10, to show how HMIS implementation is no more than an outgrowth of strategic planning and HIRM. Even so, because of the growing complexity of HMIS applications and the huge amounts of investments involved in HMIS projects, all (or most) health service organizations

Figure 11–2 The Implementation Process

today require that success be a prime criterion in any HMIS implementation effort. We therefore begin with a look at the critical success factors (CSFs) for HMIS implementation.

CRITICAL SUCCESS FACTORS FOR HEALTH MANAGEMENT INFORMATION SYSTEM IMPLEMENTATION

To date, a number of critical factors have been found to affect the success of HMIS implementation in health service organizations. Top management should focus attention on these CSFs and seriously consider them before any major HMIS implementation exercise is undertaken. In other words, management should try to position the organization to be ready for HMIS technology adoption. More particularly, management must pay special attention to those factors that are likely barriers or constraints to the implementation process. Minor issues that do not warrant top management consideration can be delegated to middle managers, who can oversee these issues or control them with inputs from top management on an ad hoc basis during the actual implementation. However, there may be times when minor issues are truly major issues in disguise, and if so, these should then be flagged for top management intervention.

In general, the CSFs for HMIS implementation fall into one of three broad categories of user characteristics, systems design characteristics, and organizational characteristics. Figure 11–3 shows specific examples of factors from each of the three categories that contribute to successful or unsuccessful HMIS implementation.

User Characteristics

Among the variety of factors believed to influence HMIS success, user characteristics (i.e., the "people problem") are by far the most extensively stud-

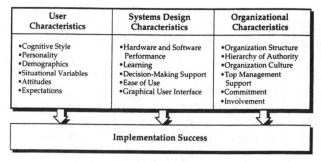

Figure 11–3 Characteristics of Implementation Success Factors

ied.[2,3] Examples of factors in this category are individual differences (e.g., cognitive style, personality, demographics, and situational variables), cognitive behavior, user attitudes, and user expectations of what the HMIS can do for them.

HMIS implementation often carries with it great expectations. It is not unusual, for instance, to find that users who are not well trained and who have little or no knowledge of system capabilities become disappointed with the final results of HMIS implementation because the end product does not match their expectations. Therefore, it is sometimes important to emphasize and promote HMISs only as a tool rather than as a solution to health service organizational problems, although the ultimate role of HMISs is to support decision-making and problem-solving activities.

The argument that HMISs are a "mirage" is familiar.[4] Clearly, the HMIS itself is not a panacea, but it will certainly help managers make better choices as well as speed up processes that were previously handled manually. Adopting an attitude that HMIS applications are the ends and not the means sets up impossible goals and expectations that can only result in unfulfilled expectations. Consequently, this is another reason to involve personnel from all departments or programs in the planning and implementation of HMISs right from the beginning. In so doing, one can generate positive attitudes and feelings among end users, with realistic expectations that can only enhance successful HMIS implementation. Further, the adoption of a comprehensive user education program can serve to increase the likelihood of meeting operational objectives sought in the initial planning of an HMIS.

Among various personal reactions to HMISs, resistance is the most destructive behavior related to HMIS implementation. Dickson and Simmons noted five factors relating to resistance.[5] First, the greater operating efficiency of HMISs often implies a change in departmental or divisional boundaries and a high potential to eliminate duplicating functions. This can create a sense of fear of job loss among operational and clerical workers. Second, HMISs can affect the informal organizational structure as much as the formal one by creating behavioral disturbances such as doing away with informal interactions. Third, whether individuals will react favorably to HMIS implementation depends on their overall personalities (e.g., younger, inexperienced workers are less likely to resist change than older, more experienced ones) and cultural background (e.g., the replacement of interpersonal contacts with human-computer interface). Fourth, the presence of peer pressure and previous experiences with HMIS implementation can also influence the organizational climate for success. Finally, the management techniques used to implement HMISs, for example, the use of project planning and scheduling methodologies, directly affect user perception of the system.

The recognition of potential dysfunctional user behaviors is a first step to successful HMIS implementation. User orientation, training, education, and participation are ways to minimize the behavioral problems that may follow the introduction of HMISs in health service organizations.

Systems Design Characteristics

Apart from user characteristics, systems design characteristics also play an important role in determining the eventual acceptability of the HMIS installed. Examples of factors in this category include hardware and software performance, the characteristics of information and decision-making support provided to the user, and systems interface characteristics, such as the availability or incorporation of easy-to-use and easy-to-learn features into the HMIS.

The essential ingredients of any computer-based HMIS are the hardware, software, and firmware. Common sense dictates that configuration of wares be applicable to the organizational performance and strategies. For an organization's information needs to be satisfied from a systems design perspective, they need to be articulated and documented during the early planning stages and acted upon by using tailored implementation techniques. Further, the reliability of hardware and software is critical to HMIS performance. It is important to acknowledge, for example, that most information needs demand a certain amount of flexibility, notwithstanding the needs for completeness, accuracy, validity, reliability, frequency, and currency (timeliness) of information to be supplied to the user.[6] Flexibility necessitates an ability to cope with growth and variability in an ever-changing health service environment.

Systems interface is a subject that could fill an entire chapter of its own. To relate this topic to HMIS implementation, examples are provided. First, HMISs should be designed in the way nurses (i.e., users) organize themselves. For example, nurses organize their thoughts about patients by using patient room numbers as a constant frame of reference.[7] Inevitably, when a dietetics system in a hospital uses the alphabet as an organizing scheme, the systems interface becomes inadequate to support the nurses in performing their routine activities. This has happened in real life, where a group of nurses and clerks who were exposed to the system complained about the time it took to enter diet orders and changes into the HMIS. They became less efficient and increasingly anxious, frustrated, and dissatisfied with the system. The result was to abandon the system unless the software was redesigned to follow through with the patient room number organizing scheme.

Second, HMIS interface design should incorporate favorable factors, such as the proper use of graphics and color.[8] One hospital information system used bright primary colors that were "hard on the eyes" and thus distracting during prolonged use. The hospital information system also produced graphics that were difficult to read and interpret. The system was almost abandoned until it was discovered that both the graphics and colors were changeable. These cases illustrate the significance of human-computer interface in HMIS implementation success.

Third, the design of HMISs should consider the users' previous knowledge. For instance, in a long-time care facility, nurses who were acquainted with the "file-drag" iconic-based operation of Macintosh systems for years have found the command-based operation on IBM-type systems extremely cumbersome and incomprehensible. In that case, the incorporation of Windows software resolved a significant part, if not all, of the problem.

Organizational Characteristics

Organizational characteristics can also influence HMIS implementation success. Examples of variables include organizational structure and power (e.g., the authority hierarchy), organizational culture, and other managerial factors, such as top management support, commitment, and involvement.

One of the key areas affecting implementation success is the influence of top management. Exercising sound project control, resolving issues in a timely manner, allocating resources accurately, and avoiding short-lived changes in critical areas are all serious management considerations.[9] The strategic alignment of corporate HMISs planning and the application of proper project planning and scheduling will together serve to prevent costly delays in HMIS implementation. Such an alignment also ensures that the organization is not forced into a reactive as opposed to a proactive role.[10] Here, a proactive strategy anticipates industry trends and instills innovative processes for competitive advantages and operational efficiencies, whereas a reactive strategy takes into account current industry trends and chooses to adopt a known process developed elsewhere.

Key strategies to achieve successful HMIS implementation include a realistic situational assessment, accurate identification of necessary resources, and development of an action plan.[11] It is therefore critical to encourage top management involvement in many areas, and there should be a CIO or another knowledgeable senior member of the management team taking charge of HMIS implementation.

Implementation of HMISs in health service organizations is no different than in business organizations. Long-term success is affected by the degree of commitment and involvement of all end users and especially the support, commitment, and involvement of top management. All users need to invest their energy in the planning and implementation of the HMIS in order to create a system that is accepted. Top managers in particular must provide support and act as role models to their subordinates. Potential heavy users, such as middle managers, physicians, nurses, and support staff, also need to be committed and involved in the process of HMIS implementation in order to improve the likelihood of its long-term success.[12,13] In short, HMIS success requires inputs that come directly from all users, not just systems professionals.

STRATEGIC PLANNING AND MANAGEMENT ISSUES

Our analysis of CSFs for HMIS implementation reveals a number of critical considerations involved in the planning and management of an HMIS. Often, careful attention to these details in the early planning stages can facilitate the creation of strategies that will enhance the success of the HMIS implementation process.

Figure 11–4 shows the various types of planning and management issues that will influence the process and the strategy chosen to optimize HMIS implementation for a health service organization. The discussion in the rest of this section will focus on staffing issues, organizational project management, end-user involvement, and vendor involvement.

Staffing Issues

Issues associated with HMIS staff can be addressed by first simply asking the question: Do we have the adequate human resources and HMIS expertise to carry out a successful implementation project? The answer to this question will normally require the use of an internal audit of the current HMIS staffing situation. There can also be a projection of future staffing needs if the project has a long-term focus.

For new organizations, HMIS development is relatively straightforward; that is, all individuals with the needed skills are simply to be recruited externally. However, once beyond that, it is a more complicated process. It becomes necessary to identify potential knowledge gaps in HMIS staff that need to be filled. The following are more specific questions that need to be answered.

- Are the current staff members already working at capacity?
- Are there any information systems staff members on payroll at this time?
- What level of knowledge does the current staff have, and how does this affect recruitment and training?

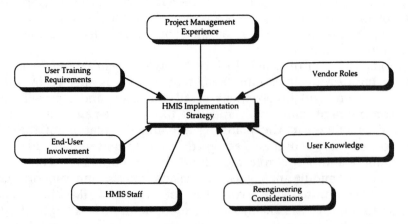

Figure 11–4 Planning and Management Issues

- How many new staff members will be needed, and when will they be needed?

The answers to these questions will enable the planning of staffing strategies to be layered into an HMIS implementation plan. It is critical that these considerations be addressed so that arrangements can be made well in advance to hire the necessary staff or to plan for the needed training. For instance, carrying through with an implementation schedule will require data on the availability of staff members with HMIS expertise for certain periods. Conversely, the training of staff members and the scheduling of recruitment will depend on the overall implementation schedule. Clearly, a lack of personnel with the necessary skills will slow the process of HMIS implementation, often leading to increased pressure and frustration among the existing staff members and possibly resulting in missed opportunities associated with on-time and "seamless" project completion.

Although the staffing issues can be resolved at the systems implementation stage, management of health service organizations must establish clear reward policies to encourage the retention of experienced staff members. Gray documented that the demand for new systems personnel of all types grows at a rate of 15 percent per year, whereas the turnover of information systems personnel averages about 20 percent per year.[14] Reducing this high turnover rate will immediately improve productivity and reduce operation costs.

To reward good technical HMIS personnel, health organizations can use a "dual career path" or a "professional stage model."[15-18] In the former, a pathway of promotions in the technical level is created to parallel the managerial path in rank and salary. For example, a technical staff member would be promoted from programmer to systems analyst, then to systems specialist, and finally to senior technical specialist. In the latter, the path for promotions can be from apprentice to colleague to mentor to project sponsor.[19] Both models provide significant incentives for the return of experienced staff members past the initial stage of HMIS implementation, thereby sowing the seed for long-term success.

After examining various staffing issues at the system level, an important issue at the individual level—user knowledge—will be discussed briefly. HMIS implementation in health organizations requires an assessment of in-house systems and expertise knowledge. This assessment should take into account future user needs. Together with staffing needs assessments, management can ascertain the educational requirements of the organization. By doing so, the organization also avoids heavily diverting its resources to educating and training users during and after the online implementation. Thus, educational planning including general training for managers, technical training for HMIS professionals, as well as specific end-user training to satisfy the needs of various user groups will help ensure a smooth and timely HMIS implementation.[20]

Numerous difficulties, both expected and unexpected, associated with the initial 3 months of online operations can be prevented through proper orientation and HMIS staffing and training. In certain cases, this responsibility can even be off-loaded to software vendors. This approach may be particularly desirable for "turnkey" systems prepackaged and serviced by a single vendor. However, the costs in the long run can be significant.

Alternatively, if the organizational structure is capable of supporting this role with an internal training department and knowledgeable personnel, it may be more cost-effective to provide the staff education in-house. If in-house training is to be conducted, the training personnel should be able to distinguish two levels of training—holistic level training and technical level training.

The holistic (or ideological) training here refers to training modules focused on the systems, and not the operational, perspective. Systems goals and benefits, systems constraints and limitations, organizational effects, and functional implications are sample topics for this level of training. In short, holistic training intends to bring the entire system into view and to analyze its relationship with its surrounding elements (the macro view). This kind of training should be directed primarily to managerial staff who need to view HMIS in its entirety and secondarily to operational staff who are more concerned with the day-to-day operations (the micro view).

The technical (or operational) training is aimed at familiarizing the appropriate personnel with the operational aspects of HMISs that pertain to their tasks. This level of training may encapsulate such topics as completing forms, report abstracting, data validation, standard data input or update procedures, and introduction of routine tasks. This kind of training is directed primarily to technical or operational staff who are concerned with the day-to-day use of the HMIS and secondarily to managerial staff who also need to know the procedures of their subordinates.

In any case, it should be recognized that the use of a team approach in-house does have the additional benefit of increasing user acceptance and reducing resistance in the long run. Regardless of how a health service organization is planning to conduct the needed training for its staff, the quality of the training should be stressed, because well-managed training for information systems operations has the potential to reduce anxiety and potential user resistance and to promote a team approach to improve the implementation of an HMIS, especially if behavioral factors are considered during the process.

Organizational Project Management

The style of project management is extremely dependent on the organizational culture and on the depth of experienced personnel who are available to manage such a process. In many instances, experienced project managers with both technical and application knowledge are difficult to find. Consequently, outside consultants are often used. However, time is needed to educate these consultants on specific situational and historical characteristics, both internally and externally, that can at times be significant enough to make outside consultation counterproductive. As for within the health organization, there is often a tradeoff. Although team or committee management of the implementation process provides the benefits of internal knowledge, user acceptance, and overall effectiveness of implementation,[21] the need for a fresh look from an unbiased outside perspective should not be overlooked.

Although it is difficult to make specific recommendations with respect to HMIS implementation, certain techniques are useful in project management. Here a brief examination is given to some of the commonly used techniques for project scheduling and program coding.

To ensure that the system implementation is completed by a certain date, a detailed and realistic schedule needs to be prepared and followed at the initial and subsequent planning stages. At the same time, the schedule should be flexible enough to accommodate some unexpected delays. Moreover, a detailed timetable for implementation is often essential to inspire management confidence in the installation plan. Here, two techniques to assist project scheduling are discussed—the critical path method (CPM) and Gantt charts.

When using the CPM, the duration of all the tasks involved and the sequence (indicated by arrows) of all tasks need to be compiled in a network representation, as shown in Figure 11–5. In the figure, the numbers in circles represent different stages of implementation, the letters represent different tasks involved, and the numbers beside the letters represent the number of days needed to complete the task.

After translating the implementation schedule into a network representation, the critical path of the network can then be determined. The critical path is the sequence of activities that will take the longest period to complete. The time needed to complete all the activities on this critical path is the minimum

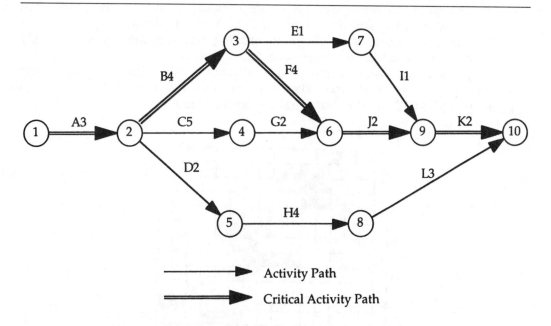

Note: Letter-number pairs represent the name of the path and the amount of time it takes to travel it. For example, "A3" indicates that path A takes 3 days.

Figure 11–5 A System Implementation Schedule in a Network Representation for the Critical Path Determination

Path	Days Required
A→B→E→I→K	11
A→B→F→J→K	⑮
A→C→G→J→K	14
A→D→H→L	12

Figure 11–6 Possible Paths through the Critical Path Network in Figure 11–5

period required to complete the entire project. Figure 11–6 lists all the possible paths (activities in sequence) and the time needed to complete each. In this example, the path through activities A-B-F-J-K is the longest, requiring 15 days for completion. This is therefore the critical path of the project. In other words, the project cannot be completed in less than 15 days unless certain tasks are started early or shortened.

Another way of representing the details in Figures 11–5 and 11–6 is to use Gantt charts, which represent projects tasks with bar charts. They are often easier to construct and understand than CPM but may capture and generate less information. Figure 11–7 shows a Gantt chart for the same project described. It is worth mentioning that the exact start and end dates of certain noncritical tasks can be moved without causing delay to the overall schedule. For instance, if every other task on Figure 11–6 commences and finishes on time, task L can be postponed for a day without delaying the final completion date.

Program coding, or, simply, programming, refers to the process of writing instructions that the computer system can execute directly. This is usually a very labor-intensive task, and as a result coordination among programmers will need to be emphasized. Here two useful coordination techniques—data dictionaries (DDs) and walkthroughs—are introduced.

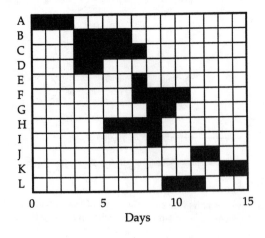

Figure 11–7 A Gantt Chart Representation of the System Implementation Schedule in Figure 11–5

A DD can be computerized or manually compiled and contains definitions and proper uses of entities that are in alphabetical order. A DD should also have the identities of database programs used; the names of all the data fields found in the database, along with the names of the programmers that use them; and descriptions of the data and the personnel responsible for the data. It therefore resembles a regular dictionary. DDs are useful in program coding coordination, as they allow the names of data elements to be cross-referenced, help programmers to locate blocks of codes that are reusable in new applications rapidly, and ensure that all codes are consistent with the overall application.

Another very useful tool in program coding is conducting a walkthrough (or review). A walkthrough can take place at various stages of program design and development. It is essentially peer evaluation and testing of a programmer's work, with the primary objective of soliciting constructive feedback. In other words, walkthroughs act as control points in programming, making sure that what is programmed is in line with specific goals and objectives and other operational constraints. It is not in any way directed personally at the programmer.

Reengineering Considerations

Often when new HMIS applications are implemented, work flows and processes change drastically because of the inherent differences of daily operations with the computerization. Even without the changes because of computerization, users will still find changes to daily operations as their tasks at work gradually change from time to time. Whereas adequate training initially helps better prepare end users for some of these changes, end-user involvement in the reengineering process can greatly enhance satisfaction with computerization. This again relates to the importance of the "people aspect" in HMISs.

In order to gain maximum benefit from an HMIS, all operations must be redesigned periodically to accommodate environmental changes and maximize operational benefits, while still maintaining the necessary controls in the process. If the delivery systems are not reengineered to meet new organizational needs, the increase in efficiency brought about by the HMIS may be offset by the unmet demands in the environment.

Often, it is inefficient simply to automate old systems processes, as computerization lends itself to a new work flow, thus demanding extra personnel and resources. A good example of this is the attempt to automate patient charts to mimic paper-based systems currently in place. This document is primarily a legal document on paper, but once in an HMIS, it can become a much more versatile tool. Very often, health organizations are reluctant to rely totally on the computerized system and therefore opt to keep the paper copy for backup. Therefore, health professionals are required to continue filling these forms manually, which essentially is a duplication of effort and creates unnecessary workload.

To decide how the operation of the HMIS (or part of this operation) is to be reengineered, it is useful to solicit inputs from the staff already acquainted with the existing procedures. Team or committee forums on system-supported group decision settings are excellent means to decide what should or should not be modified. This leads us to the topic of end-user involvement.

End-User Involvement

In health service organizations, the planning and development of HMISs are recognized to be slow compared to their pace in the business world. However, lessons learned in the business sector have been found especially useful; one such lesson is the empowerment of end users through their involvement in systems planning and design.

HMIS planning and development require active (not passive) end-user involvement throughout the entire process in order for implementation to be truly successful. It has been recognized that unless HMIS staff, physicians, and nurses are involved in systems planning and ongoing evaluation, HMIS success will be short-lived.[22] In fact, in the health service system, which consists of a much broader group of individuals representing many technical and professional groups, it seems wise to extend this to users of all the different modules or areas of HMISs. For this to materialize, adequate time and resources need to be allotted, and critical committees and internal and external liaisons have to be established such that all aspects of HMISs can be optimized while generating organization-wide user acceptance.

Specific considerations with respect to acceptance of end users include the effect of the change on the need satisfaction of the affected personnel, the position of those affected, and the leadership style of those managing the change. Furthermore, direct involvement of application program vendors, which is the next topic of discussion, is often of critical importance.

Vendor Involvement

The traditional view that vendors specialize only in sales of equipment or computer software is fast giving way to the realities of the vendors of today. Although the primary function of computer systems vendors is and will continue to be the actual equipment sale, there is rapidly increasing emphasis on the sale of "services" beyond the realm of equipment maintenance. In other words, vendors can be and in fact very often are involved in some degree of systems development and implementation, including HMIS implementation. IBM is a prime example of such a vendor.

The options with respect to the roles of vendors vary between two extremes. Here the term "vendor" usually refers only to software vendors, as they dictate much of the implementation. However, the hardware vendor is important when considering outsourcing HMIS services. On the one hand, there can be complete turnkey implementation by the software vendor (turnkey systems are prepackaged, ready-to-go application programs that are often products supplied by a single vendor). On the other hand, there is the option of exercising complete in-house organizational control. Between these extremes lies the most used option, a blend of vendor and organizational responsibilities, with each performing in areas of specialty to tailor the process to the needs of the HMIS implementation.

Depending on the strengths of the organization and the vendor, areas of responsibility that can be shared include analyst support, project management, user training, hardware and facilities planning, software modification, interface development, conversion assistance, procedure development, and implementation audits. The means through which vendors can be involved vary from one organization to another. In some cases, a single vendor acts as the sole handling agent for all technical problems and even some user training; in others, several vendors may have to cooperate to deal with systems problems.

Nevertheless, there are generally six steps through which a health organization can solicit and apply useful inputs from vendors.

1. initial conceptualization
2. strategic planning
3. feasibility study
4. request for proposals
5. proposal evaluation and selection
6. physical implementation

These, as well as postimplementation upkeep issues, will be outlined later in this chapter.

Additional Considerations

A few other considerations that are not often described in the literature can help to ensure smooth HMIS implementation. The first of these is related to the concept of quality. Several methodologies can be adapted to address quality in health service delivery. The methodology continuum consists of quality control, quality assurance, continuous quality improvement, total quality management, and reengineering (see Chapter 10). Depending on the organization's information status, implementation may be facilitated by the inclusion of any one of these principles.

Another consideration that needs to be taken into account pertains to the manner in which health service organizations have been changing the way they measure performance. Many organizations are progressing from an efficiency and throughput approach to an effectiveness and outcome measurement approach. Experiencing the economic pressure perceived by many businesses, health organizations are also increasingly being pressured to link the utilization of various health resources to their level of outcome and demand, and, in many cases, to justify the utilization with the outcome produced.

Although almost all organizations are run differently with respect to performance measurements, management styles can directly affect HMIS implementation. For example, the structure of management within organizations, such as departmental organization, program management, matrix design, hierarchical design, and circular design, can influence HMIS implementation. In keeping with the changing priorities in the health service delivery system, there has been a demonstrated need for more highly integrated HMIS.[23] Thus, it is critical to keep these considerations in mind when making decisions regarding any HMIS implementation project.

It is also crucial to keep in mind that leadership roles exhibited by the CEO and the CIO can affect the success of HMIS implementation. Information technology, therefore, needs to be integrated from the cultural perspective of an organization. In order for this to occur, the CEO and CIO must leverage HMISs in achieving goals and objectives of the organization and communicate this effectively within the organization.

In particular, Austin has called attention to several areas that should be addressed when monitoring and evaluating HMIS implementation: productivity, user utility, value chain, competitive performance, business alignment, investment targeting, and management vision.[24] Although it is recognized that these criteria suit profit-oriented organizations, several seem equally applicable to nonprofit health service organizations.

SYSTEMS IMPLEMENTATION

Regardless of the strategies utilized in the implementation of an HMIS, there are several steps most health organizations should take in order to optimize internal and external processes in a manner that ensures an efficient and effective outcome. In general, these steps fall into two broad stages, preimplementation preparation and postimplementation upkeep, each of which will be discussed in greater detail.

Preimplementation Preparation

The stage of preimplementation preparation begins with the initial conceptualization of HMISs and ends with the initial online operation of the system. The major steps included in this stage are initial conceptualization, strategic planning, feasibility study, request for proposal, proposal evaluation and selection, and physical implementation.

Initial conceptualization can be considered the first step to developing an HMIS. This can take place in a variety of ways. For instance, the CEO of a long-term care facility may be impressed by an HMIS in another health organization in the same community; the board of directors of a health facility may have discussed HMIS in their 10-year plan; staff members of a health maintenance organization may complain about their aging islands of technological applications. In short, the initial conceptualization represents a genuine wish to consolidate and improve the information flows and storage in a health organization.

As stated previously, incorporating organizational strategic planning into HMIS strategic plans is a desirable milestone in any HMIS implementation. HMIS development must be based on a strategic information plan that is aligned with the organization's mission, vision, goals, and objectives. Adopting a strategic approach will help focus measurable goals and objectives for information technology implementation that best suits internal and external information needs. Only in this way can the necessary factors and considerations, such as outcome measurement, future technological change, networking, and process reengineering, be included.

Once strategic information planning is completed, a feasibility study can be carried out. In general, this study aims to determine the extent to which the implementation and the upkeep of an HMIS are feasible. It includes results from various meetings with the board, middle management, and even staff members who are likely to be affected (user involvement) to solicit their inputs. It also incorporates financial (how much is available) and physical (whether the facility is too crowded for extra equipment) feasibility research. Moreover, the feasibility study also can make recommendations on the schedule of implementation, its speed, and other issues of concern. In many health service organizations, the reports for the feasibility study need to be approved or endorsed by the board of trustees. In these cases, the feasibility study report also will be acting as project proposals subject to extensive inquiries. The study reports always should be produced professionally and should be subjected to peer review.

Following the feasibility study, the detailed goals and objectives of an HMIS can be outlined on the basis of an internal and external needs assessment. Needs assessment makes it possible to formulate a request for proposal (RFP) for the various hardware and software vendors to submit bids. The RFP can include details on the organization, its information needs, and the specifics of the organization's goals and objectives that the system is expected to fulfill. When vendor replies are received, it is then possible to correlate proposals on the basis of such internal objectives as budget and infrastructure compatibility issues in terms of existing hardware and software.

This leads to the next stage of proposal evaluation and selection, which is followed by physical implementation. A section of discussion is dedicated to each of these important steps.

Proposal Evaluation and Selection

As soon as all the proposals have been submitted, it is time to evaluate them to make a selection. In the evaluation process, two methods commonly used are benchmark tests and the vendor rating system. In a benchmark test, the health service organization provides the vendors with a set of mock data. This set of data then acts as inputs in a prototype of the proposed system. The prototype system is then asked to perform a list of computations expected to be performed by the real system. The actual performance of these prototype systems is then compared with the prespecified standards for evaluation.

Benchmark testing attempts to create an environment that is as close to the real clinical setting as possible. Because it is the prototype systems being tested, it is not uncommon to find that the real, constructed system may perform at a lower level because of the heavy load of information to be processed in real life. Nevertheless, benchmark testing gives the organization a "concrete" feel for what the system would look like and how it would function (to some extent) in the clinical setting.

In comparison, the vendor rating system is simply a system in which the vendors are quantitatively scored as to how well their proposed systems perform against a list of weighted criteria. Commonly used criteria include user friendliness, data management, graphical and reporting capabilities, forecasting and statistical analysis capabilities, modeling, hardware and operating system considerations, vendor support, and cost factors.

The importance of the "people" aspect to the success of HMIS implementation cannot be overemphasized. As a direct consequence, user friendliness should be a prime concern when evaluating system proposals from vendors. User friendliness can be manifested in a variety of ways. The consistency of language command, the use of natural language and touch screen, automatic grammar checker and spelling correction, the availability of the "Help" and "Undo" commands are examples of features of user-friendly hardware and software. Moreover, menus and prompts, novice and expert modes, spreadsheet display of data and results, as well as what-you-see-is-what-you-get features also contribute to the user friendliness of the system.

HMISs are designed to be advanced "data-processing" facilities. They should have adequate data management tools to handle the massive volumes of data to be processed in the day-to-day operation of a health service organization. Such features as common database manager, data security measures (log-in password, etc.), simultaneous access (without significant trade-off in performance), data selection, DD, and data validation should be included in the HMIS.

The primary function for an HMIS is to produce timely and accurate information for health decision making. Accordingly, an ideal HMIS should have the capability to generate standard and custom reports and to report variables and computations. In terms of graphical reports, HMISs have the ability to generate basic plots and 3-dimensional charts, multiple graphs per page, and a preview of graphical outputs. Moreover, multicolor support, integration of graphical and text files, and compatibility with existing graphics devices should be additional assets of an HMIS.

For strategic and tactical planning purposes, the ideal HMIS should be able to support appropriate forecasting and statistical applications. Linear regression, multiple regression, curve fitting, seasonal adjustments in time series, and multivariate statistics are examples of common forecasting and statistical functions required by health service organizations in higher-level planning. In particular, the HMIS should be able to treat time as a special dimension.

"Modeling" refers to the ability of the system to comprehend procedural logic (within definitions), to detect and solve simultaneous equations and to compute mathematical and financial functions and user-defined functions. Functions like these are probably not used in the day-to-day operation of the system but would come in handy in systems reengineering and reprogramming, probably because of periodic evaluation.

Another theme emphasized throughout this book is systems integration. The selection of HMIS should consider this. In practice, this can be viewed in terms of hardware and operating system considerations. Compatibility with various operating systems (icon-based versus command-based), microcomputer support, compatibility with workstation requirements, printer and plotter support, as well as server and network compatibility should also be considered when selecting an HMIS.

As discussed in an earlier section, vendor involvement positively influences HMIS implementation. In selecting an HMIS, the amount of vendor support can definitely be a valid selection criterion. Vendor support can be provided in a variety of ways: consultation, training, active research and development, maintenance of local branch offices, technical support personnel, and continuing enhancements. Also, the financial stability and credibility of the vendor should be confirmed before reaching a final decision.

Probably the most important factor for all health organizations is the cost. In evaluating HMIS proposals, it would be very helpful to bear in mind how the costs are calculated and what items are or are not included. A modular pricing approach combined with some form of "packaged offer" is one of the more common approaches. In this case, the management should pay particular attention to the initial license fees, license renewal fees, maintenance arrangements, documentation, and resource utilization, as well as hidden conversion costs. Certainly, the cost of training and staffing has to be estimated by the management itself.

Exhibit 11–1 presents a sample evaluation sheet used in a vendor rating system. Note that although these criteria are generally applicable to all health service organizations, specific criteria are more important to each organization by virtue of its unique environment. These should be specified separately and weighted accordingly.

Physical Implementation

Once the vendors are chosen, a contract is signed, thereby beginning the physical implementation stage—the stage when the most "action" takes place. The stage of physical implementation actually consists of several steps, including recruitment of personnel, training of staff, acquisition of equipment, installation of equipment, uploading of initial data, system testing, documentation, and online implementation.

All of these steps are performed in a logical progression (some carried out simultaneously) depending on the needs of the organization and how these are reflected in decisions based on the described factors and considerations. The keys to a smooth implementation process are effective planning and project management. Some variations may be necessary, depending on the differences in each organization, but some common steps (including some earlier steps) in initial HMIS implementation are shown in Figure 11–8.

Among these steps, the recruitment of HMIS personnel and training of existing staff members have already been discussed. The modes of acquisition and installation of the equipment are highly dependent on the characteristics of each health organization, as well as on the contract between the vendor and the management. In addition, whether the equipment is acquired over some period or at the same time ultimately depends on the payment scheme agreed upon by the vendors and the management.

The uploading of initial data and systems testing are sometimes conducted simultaneously. The initial sets of data are used to test whether the system is functioning at the desired level. If there are any significant discrepancies

Exhibit 11–1 A Sample Evaluation Sheet for Health Management Information System Proposals

VENDOR RATING							
Vendor:				Proposed System:			
Criteria	Weight	Score	Weighted Score	**Criteria**	Weight	Score	Weighted Score
User Friendliness •Language Command •Help Command •Undo Function •Others: _____				**Data Management** •Common Database Manager •Security •Simultaneous Access •Others: _____			
Reports & Graphs •Report Format •Basic Graphs •Graph Previews •Others: _____				**Forecasts & Statistics** •Linear Regression •Multiple Regression •Curve Fitting •Others: _____			
Modeling •Mathematical Functions •User-Defined Functions •Procedural Logic •Others: _____				**Hardware & Operating System** •Hardware Compatibility •Operating System Compatibility •Workstation Compatibility •Others: _____			
Vendor Support •Consultation •Training •Technical Support •Others: _____				**Cost Factors** •Total Budget •Leveraged Payment •Maintenance Cost •Others: _____			
Total Score:							
Additional Comments:							
Evaluated By:_____ Signed: _____ Date:_____							

between the predesignated level of performance and the actual level, the system may have to be modified. Accordingly, there should be ample time allotted to these two steps.

Very often, documentation can proceed simultaneously with systems testing, because the structural layout of the system is already fixed. Any additional modifications along the way can then be documented as updates or memos. Ideally, there should be at least one copy of the master documentation with details on how to operate the system at the technical level and on how to manage the system at the tactical and strategic levels. Periodically, the distributing copies as well as the master copy should be updated, incorporating the ad hoc updates or memos.

Online implementation involves four common approaches:

1. parallel approach
2. phased approach
3. pilot approach
4. cutover approach

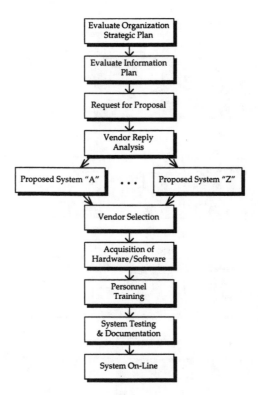

Figure 11–8 Common Steps of Initial Implementation of a Health Management Information System

In the parallel approach, systems activities are duplicated, as the old system and the new system are both operated simultaneously for a time so that their results can be compared. In the phased implementation approach, different functional parts of the new system become operative one after another. This approach is relatively safe and less expensive than the parallel approach because the systems are not duplicated. The pilot approach requires the installation of the new system in sites that are representative of the complete system (e.g., in a small geographical area). This means that certain locations or departments are to serve as "alpha" pilot test sites first, followed by other "beta" pilot sites or departments until all sites operate under the new system. The cutover approach is also called the "cold turkey" or "burned bridges" approach. Essentially, this approach requires the organization to "flip the switch" to the new system all at once. If the results are not satisfactory, the system can be revised and activated again.

Figure 11–9 gives a diagrammatic representation of the four common approaches to online implementation. As to which approach is most suitable, it depends directly on the specific environment of each health service organization. For instance, the general level of HMIS knowledge in the staff, the availability of resources for systems implementation, and the amount of data handled per day will and should all affect the choice of online implementation approach.

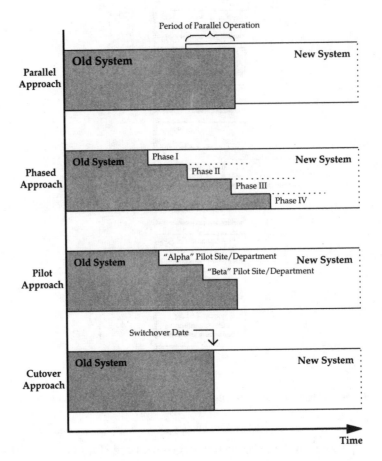

Figure 11-9 Common Approaches to Online Implementation

Postimplementation Upkeep

Although full online implementation of an HMIS is a prominent milestone, it is definitely not the end of the story. Once the new HMIS has been fully implemented, the system operates as an information production and processing facility. Ongoing maintenance is essential to achieve implementation success in the long run.

In general, ongoing upkeep is required because of problems within the system and changes in the environment. Problems within the system may be errors that have not been discovered by previous tests or may develop primarily because of unexpectedly heavy workload. Changes in the environment include those in related systems (e.g., inventory order systems) and those in the organization of human resources. In many cases, simply because of the long time it takes to develop an HMIS, there are some deviations between the initial planning and the final product (i.e., the HMIS installed). These deviations also contribute to the need for close postimplementation monitoring.

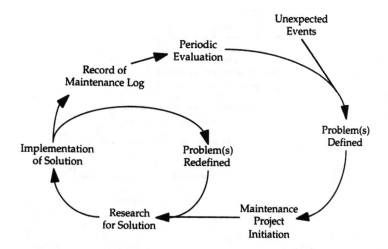

Figure 11–10 A Sample Maintenance Cycle for Health Management Information Systems

Regardless of why the system needs to be maintained and modified, the maintenance cycle depicted in Figure 11–10 captures the major steps involved. Problems are usually discovered in either unexpected events or periodic systems evaluations. Postaudits (or postevaluations) are intended to evaluate the operational characteristics of the system, thereby acting as control points throughout the operation of the system. Once the problem is defined, a maintenance project can be initiated. Very often, because of creativity and the uncertainty involved, this type of project is relatively unstructured, characterized by numerous attempts to search for the ultimate "ideal" solution. Here, tools in systems modeling and systems thinking (Chapter 2) will be very useful.

After a feasible solution is found, it is then implemented and tested. If the problem is still not completely solved, it may need to be redefined. Attempts to search for the ideal solution are then resumed. If the problem is solved, the project can be completed by recording on maintenance logs and by producing the appropriate documentation for circulation.

It is also worth noting that documentation does not just take place at the end of the maintenance cycle. Rather, it occurs throughout the entire cycle in the form of documentation of problems, written requests for change, and memos on possible sources of problems and solutions. The documentation at the end of the cycle therefore emphasizes the incorporation of all these forms and memos into a mini-report that can be used for future reference or incorporation into the system manual.

Figure 11–11 recaptures the main steps of the overall schema of HMIS implementation. Throughout the entire implementation process (both preimplementation preparation and postimplementation upkeep), active involvement of both the users and the managers cannot be overemphasized, for reasons described earlier.

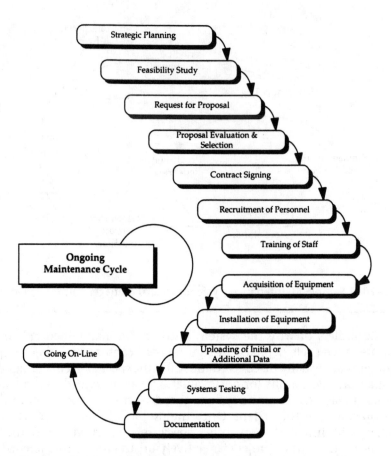

Figure 11–11 The Overall Schema of a Health Management Information System Implementation

STANDARDS AND LEGAL ISSUES

After examining the various steps of HMIS implementation, we now turn to HMIS standards and legal issues. At present, a growing number of governmental bodies and standard councils have been formed to assist in the establishment of practical standards and guidelines for the development and implementation of HMISs in various health service delivery areas and across various jurisdictions. Although these standards and guidelines may serve as useful educational and implementation protocols, it is important that they be optimized to meet specific organizational and systems needs.

Health Management Information System Standards and Guidelines

In general, the standards and guidelines outlined here have been developed or adopted for recommendation by the British Columbia (BC) Health Information Standards Council, of which this book's author serves as a council member. More generally, the council owns and manages the health information standardization process in BC, Canada; directs the consensus process; establishes priorities and the standards agenda; and provides coordination between related standards and guidelines based activities. Stakeholders provide inputs to the council and participate in working and review committees to help develop or endorse standards. Ultimately, it is the Ministry of Health that approves the recommended standards and guidelines.

Standards may pertain to many types, for example, data standards, applications standards, and technology standards. The standardization of these various elements is essential to facilitate secure information sharing within the health system. The key difference between health information management standards and guidelines is that the former is more or less suggestive of a mandatory compliance whereas the latter suggests voluntary compliance. The council has a mandate to provide management information standards and guidelines for implementation of HMISs in BC health service organizations to allow the efficient and effective sharing and comparing of health service resource utilization among stakeholders. It is important, however, to note that these standards, while applicable to BC, may in fact also be generally considered as potential standards for adoption consideration by any other jurisdiction, should a need exist for that jurisdiction to set a standard in the study area. In the same vein, health information management standards adopted elsewhere would be used as a starting point for consideration by the BC Standards Council prior to generating their own standards.

To date, key among the standards projects that have been tabled and studied intensively by the BC Standards Council include a proposed provider data standard to uniquely identify licensed individual providers and the types of goods and services associated with these providers, a lab test standard for the electronic exchange of lab test data, facility data standards, place data standards, a minimum patient data set for electronic clinical records, a mental health minimum data set, a continuing care minimum data set, rehabilitation data reporting standards, Canadian Classification of Interventions, security standards of health information holdings, electronic health claims data standards, and many others (e.g., health registries and PharmaNet).

Some guidelines have also been developed and delineated from a functional center framework, with applications and limited reporting aspects. Additional features of the guidelines worthy of mention include workload measurement systems, cost accounting (i.e., direct, indirect, variable), and service volumes. In general, these guidelines, however many there are, form a good framework for addressing efficiency using HMISs. Yet they lack the wider appeal and endorsement of the health data standards. Like the standards, these guidelines are unfortunately limited in their scope of applicability; for example, they are meant to be developed for Canadian hospitals, just as the Joint Commission on Accreditation of Healthcare Organizations has guidelines that are mainly applicable to U.S. hospitals.

Standards and guidelines are needed for both United States and Canadian health care facilities to support HMIS applications under way; to set consistency of applications between one application and another; to improve health of clients; to improve utilization of administrative and clinical resources; to support the effective management of health information; to facilitate and enhance data sharing, analysis, and comparability across functional, jurisdictional, or geographical boundaries; and to support the integration of data, application, and technology. It is hoped that more standards and guidelines will be developed in the near future to synergize HMIS development and implementation efforts.

Legal Issues for Health Management Information Systems

To complete the discussion of HMIS implementation, the focus shifts to some legal aspects of HMIS development. Medical, legal, and ethical issues are an increasing consideration when developing and implementing an HMIS. Generally, these issues are treated in the same way as paper-based systems, but it is important to bear in mind that specific legislation with respect to HMISs is in a state of constant flux.

In Canada, patient access to personal health care information is clearly defined by the supreme court ruling of McIrney versus MacDonald, and is further backed by the Freedom of Information Act at the provincial level.[25] The judicial system has established that, in the absence of contrary legislation, patients are entitled to access upon request of their personal medical records. The patient is entitled to personal medical record access in order to examine and copy all information pertaining to administering advice or treatment, including that which has been prepared by other physicians. However, it has also been stipulated that the record itself remains the property of the physician, clinic, or institution that compiles the information. Further, it should be noted that physicians may refuse patient access to records in specific circumstances, but the patient has the right to apply for court intervention, whereby the refusal must be rightfully justified. There is simply no reason to believe that these rulings will be different in the United States.

Freedom of information acts and court cases clearly have implications that relate to HMIS implementation. As these acts become effective, data collected will change, physicians will record different data as patient access becomes more commonplace, and charting of sensitive information will tend to occur less often. Likewise, there will be changes in data collection and data destruction methods to make compliance with patient requests and changes brought about by legislation more efficient, in terms of time and expense, when assembling and reviewing data or being excused from providing the data because they have been destroyed. In the end, there is always an increasing danger of greater risk of potential defamation suits as sensitive information is disseminated and construed as defamatory in some circumstances. Consequently, it will become crucial to recognize the necessary legal obligations in terms of patient information collection. Typically, considerations that will need to be addressed are confidentiality, custody, and administration. Thus, the challenge for health service organizations will be to balance the concerns of individuals and society in the daily administration and release of health information.[26]

In terms of broader issues of privacy, "ownership," property, accuracy, security, and access of health information, Chapter 10 provides further, more detailed discussion.

CONCLUSION

Successful implementation of an HMIS and its continual evolution into the information backbone of health service organizations are the ultimate objectives of the HMISs field. Among the various steps along the path from initial conceptualization to physical operation, the stage when an HMIS resides in the spotlight of organization-wide attention seems to be the physical implementation stage.

This chapter has discussed various concerns to be addressed in HMIS implementation and some general steps involved. It is, however, not expected that managers of all health service organizations follow the same steps and address the same concerns in identical fashion. Rather, it is hoped that the chapter has provided the "essentials" for health managers and planners interested in HMIS implementation or expansion (e.g., an integration of older systems), who will then be able to adapt this global knowledge to schemes suitable to the special environment of each health service organization.

Long-term success of HMIS implementation depends also on factors external to the information system itself. Among these various factors, the organizational influence (that is, the "people influence") has repeatedly been demonstrated to be one of the most dominant. HMIS planners therefore have to pay extra attention to the people aspect in the periodic evaluation and update of the system. Over time, the most successful HMIS is one that responds to both changes in the climate in the organization within which it resides and the global climates of the health service delivery system and the society at large.

CHAPTER QUESTIONS

1. What are some of the critical success factors in HMIS implementation?
2. Why is careful planning so important to the implementation of HMISs?
3. With respect to HMIS staffing, what are some of the major concerns for HMIS planners?
4. Describe some useful tools in HMIS implementation project management.
5. Why is end-user involvement important in HMIS implementation? How can end users be involved in the process?
6. What are some common steps in HMIS implementation? What other issues need to be settled?

NOTES

1. J.E. Toole and M.E. Caine, Laying a Foundation for the Future Information Systems, *Topics in Health Care Financing* 14, no. 2 (1988): 17–27.
2. Ibid.
3. R.W. Zmud, Individual Differences and MIS Success: A Review of the Empirical Literature, *Management Science* 25, no. 10 (1979): 966–979.
4. J. Dearden, MIS Is a Mirage, *Harvard Business Review* 50, no. 1 (1972): 90–99.
5. G. Dickson and J. Simmons, The Behavioral Side of MIS: Five Factors Relating to Resistance, *Business Horizons* 13, no. 4 (1970): 59–71.
6. K. Kropf, San Bernadino County Medical Center Implementation of a Hospital Information System (New York: New York University, 1990): 7–8.
7. M. Staggers, Human Factors: The Missing Element in Computer Technology, *Computers in Nursing* 9, no. 2 (1991): 47–49.
8. J.K.H. Tan, Graphics-Based Health Decision Support Systems: Conjugating Theoretical Perspectives To Guide the Design of Graphics and Redundant Codes in HDSS Interfaces, In *Health Decision Support Systems*, eds. J.K.H. Tan with S. Sheps (Gaithersburg, MD: Aspen Publishers, 1998).
9. R. Lemon and J. Crudele, System Integration: Tying It All Together, *Healthcare Financial Management* 41, no. 6 (1987): 46–54.
10. H. Austin, Assessing the Performance of Information Technology, *Computers in Health Care* 9, no. 11 (1988): 56–58.
11. Ibid.
12. R.J. Feldman, System Evaluation and Implementation Strategies, in *Information Systems for Ambulatory Care*, eds. T.A. Matson and M.D. McDougall (Chicago: American Hospital Publishing, 1990), 67–78.
13. H.W. Ryan, User-Driven Systems Development: Defining a New Role for IS, *Information Systems Management* (Summer 1993): 66–68.
14. S. Gray, DP Salary Survey, *Datamation* 28, no. 11 (1982): 114–128.
15. J. Couger and R. Zawacki, What Motivates DP Professionals, *Datamation* 24, no. 9 (1978): 116–123.
16. K. Bartol and D. Martin, Managing Information Systems Personnel: A Review of the Literature and Managerial Implications, *MIS Quarterly*, Special issue (1982): 49–70.
17. J. Couger and M.A. Colter, *Motivation of the Maintenance Programmer* (Colorado Springs, CO: CYSCS, 1983).
18. J. Baroudi, The Impact of Role Variables on Information Systems Personnel Work Attitudes and Intentions, *MIS Quarterly* 9, no. 4 (1985): 341–356.
19. K.C. Laudon and J.P. Laudon, *Management Information Systems: A Contemporary Perspective* (New York: Macmillan Publishing Co., 1988), 698.
20. C.J. Austin and S.B. Boxerman, *Information Systems for Health Service Administration* 5th ed. (Ann Arbor, MI: AUPHA Press/Health Administration Press, 1998).
21. R.J. Feldman, System Evaluation and Implementation Strategies, 67–78.
22. H.W. Ryan, User-Driven Systems Development, 66–68.
23. R. Lemon and J. Crudele, System Integration.
24. H. Austin, Assessing the Performance of Information Technology.
25. D.M. Robinson, Patient Access to Health Records: New Legal Developments and Implementations, *Healthcare Communication and Computing Canada* (4th Quarter 1992): 54–60.
26. D.M. Robinson, Health Information Confidentiality: Balancing Extremes, *Healthcare Communication and Computing Canada* (3rd Quarter 1991): 8–9.

Part V

Application Cases of Health Management Information Systems

Chapter 12

Epilogue: Health Management Information System Cases

Joseph K. H. Tan

SCENARIO

Since 1996, Synergy Health Network (SHN) has successfully pioneered a digital health network for the research and management of rheumatology and other diseases. Using Clinic™, a distributed database prototype coded in Microsoft Access, and FirstClass, a secure groupware for interchanging data electronically, SHN currently links its research program with a growing number of leading university and community sites across North America and Europe.

At the core of the digital health network is SHN's integrated disease management information system (DMIS). DMIS is designed to perform automatic tracking of data from the various participating sites, to process these data online, and then to provide Web-based integrated reporting back to the participating sites. Specifically, DMIS captures the data in real time; verifies the captured data; and stores, cleans, and reorganizes the data into a meaningful, multidimensional format for online analytical processing and for knowledge discovery using various data mining techniques and multivariate statistical tools. Types of data gathered include patient information (demographics, physician, pharmacy, and insurer information), clinical information (medical history, disease activity, consultation, treatment, laboratory, and diagnostics), and outcomes data (quality of life and resource utilization). The primary intent of this architecture is to ensure that a seamless interface exists between data collection, transmission, and reception among the participating sites.

Today, relevant and timely information has become vital in ensuring first-class quality patient care. With rapid advances in electronic information processing and communications technology, there is need for combining the knowledge on advanced networking and medicine to design secure networks for gathering and disseminating information pertaining to clinical and epidemiological studies of chronic disease. In the case of Synergy, a distributed, networked database model has been employed to enable site participants to span across vast geographical boundaries.

In the next few years, there certainly will be another phase of unforeseen technological advances that will represent fundamental shifts from the current technology and practices. The continuation of this and other trends, including increased scale, concentration, diversification, and specialization (Chapter 2); increased volume of health care data and databases (Chapter 3); increased use of standards for health management information system (HMIS) integration

289

(Chapter 4); increased automation of systems development methodologies (Chapter 5); increased range of HMIS hardware, software, and interface technologies in the marketplace (Chapter 6); increased application of expert and knowledge discovery methods for enhancing automated and intelligent health decision support (Chapter 7); increased linkages among health service organizations through the use of communications and network systems (Chapter 8); increased emphasis on strategic planning and management of HMIS (Chapter 9); increased role and responsibilities of health chief executive officers (CEOs) and chief information officers (CIOs) for health resource management (Chapter 10); and increased participation of health organizational members, management, and third parties in the implementation of HMISs (Chapter 11) are all affecting the health and welfare of individuals, groups, and the society at large.

INTRODUCTION

In this chapter and the rest of Part V, a number of cases that bring together many of the concepts covered throughout the book are introduced. Prior to presenting these cases, it appears useful to provide a conceptual framework for organizing the cases in the context of this entire work. Accordingly, the framework that is chosen for this purpose is the PUSH-PULL framework, discussed in Chapter 1.

THE PUSH-PULL FRAMEWORK REVISITED

For the readers' convenience, a schematic representation of the PUSH-PULL framework, which has been detailed in Chapter 1, is reproduced here (Figure 12–1).

Briefly, the PUSH-PULL framework provides a macro-micro view to HMIS planning, design, and development. The macro context for planning is complex and begins with an assessment of the environment based on a PULL mentality. This strategic planning process is often surrounded by uncertainties that involve an understanding of the complex linkages and levels embedded within and outside the system (e.g., an organization). PULL therefore stands for *p*lanning for *u*ncertain *l*inkages and *l*evels. It is in this strategic context that the critical problem is identified, and for which an HMIS solution or an alternative is envisioned, designed, and developed.

In moving from the macro problem-finding perspective down to the micro problem-solving level, emphasis should be given to forging a clear strategic business–HMIS alignment. At the micro stages, the PUSH mentality comes into play. This involves programming and detailing one or more solutions that would appropriately and uniquely resolve the problem identified in light of the various system (organizational) constraints. If one or more acceptable solutions are found and implemented, the next step is to perform housekeeping, including the evaluation and maintenance of these solutions until such time

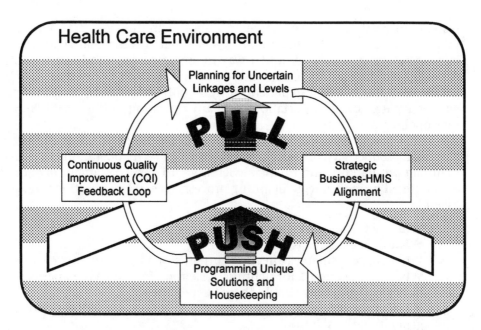

Figure 12–1 The PUSH-PULL Framework for a Macro-Micro Integrated Health Management Information System (HMIS) Approach

that a new challenge is seen to emerge. PUSH therefore refers to *p*rogramming *u*nique *s*olutions and *h*ousekeeping.

From the micro level, a continuous quality improvement (CQI) feedback loop is therefore provided to link back to the macro level. This will ensure that critical problems and/or challenges encountered at the micro level, which deserve to be further studied to uncover their macro level implications, are not neglected. As soon as this process triggers a macro problem serious enough to warrant further attention and action from top management, the entire macro-micro problem-finding and problem-solving cycle is then repeated.

How long it may take a system to move from one end of this cycle to the next will depend chiefly on the urgency and speed of changes experienced both within and outside the system. Yet, in the search for a solution to one problem, a variation of this same solution may then yield interesting insights to another existing, but apparently hidden, problem in the system. At this point, each case will be discussed separately, and the case will be placed in the context of the PUSH-PULL framework. Readers may first want to read the full cases following this chapter's general discussion and then come back to read the summary and brief analysis of the cases discussed here.

Case 1: Emergency Medical Transportation Resource Deployment

Case 1 illustrates the design and use of a computerized dispatch system to enhance the efficiency and productivity of an EMT provider in terms of resource utilization and nonemergency response. In this case, the environmental context for which strategic *planning* was initiated is the change in the reimbursement system currently under way in emergency medical transportation. According to the authors of this case, Schmitz and Corley, this change of budgetary pressures is being experienced by Abbott Ambulance, a not-for-profit emergency medical transportation company operating in the greater St. Louis metropolitan area.

At the macro level, Abbott management saw the problem as the need to "increase productivity or become more efficient in its operations in order to maintain profitability and financial viability." To deal with major *uncertainties* encountered in the strategic planning process, several key questions should be asked.

- Who are the key stakeholders?
- What linkages need to be formed?
- What are key variables affecting current system performance?
- What are the criteria for defining system performance (i.e., performance indicators) and how should these be measured?
- Who, and from what level of the organization, should be involved in generating the solutions?

For example, management in this case might consider the key stakeholders to include health care providers, customers, and third-party payers. Although there is no clear indication in the case description, setting up an advisory committee to form *linkages* between Abbott management and these stakeholders might be desirable to understand more fully the extent of the current problem and to brainstorm strategies and alternative solutions. Key factors, such as source of requests (whether the calls are from health care providers or the general public), nature of requests (whether these calls are for emergency or nonemergency transportation), timing of requests (whether the transportation was scheduled or not), and levels of ambulance capability expected (whether these calls are for basic or advanced life support), should be carefully studied during the planning stage.

It is also noted that consideration had been given to how the system performance is to be measured to guide better the design of a solution. Moreover, personnel from many *levels* of the organization were actively involved in the planning process, including senior management, HMIS department personnel, management from the operations department, and managers from the dispatch department. Hence, an acceptable solution strategy is pursued based on consensus rather than the thinking and work of an individual person or department.

Moving down to the micro-level, more questions would still need to be asked to justify a strategic business–HMIS alignment and *programming* a solution. Examples of questions include:

- What alternative strategies are there to control various types of resource allocation and how should these allocations be prioritized?
- What kind of an HMIS may be used to solve the problem?

- What data should be tracked and monitored to assist the dispatcher in dealing with the complexity of the assignment problem?

Clearly, a strategic HMIS solution, the Computer Aided Dispatch (CAD) system was thought to be a good and acceptable means to assist the dispatcher in assigning vehicles more efficiently and effectively. Data to be collected included the type of trips and pick up time, response time, vehicle drive time and distance, and crew workload.

The *uniqueness* of the Abbott solution might best be seen in the flexibility of the designed solution. Specifically, the CAD system was designed for dealing with nonemergency transportation, but its total calculation included emergency requests. Hence, an assignment for a nonemergency trip could be changed automatically because of an emergency request. Moreover, the CAD system was designed to mimic the hierarchical decision process that dispatchers attempted to follow in their own thinking processes. Finally, there was also the option of a dispatcher overriding the recommendations provided by CAD.

Essentially, the *solution* here was the development of CAD using Lindo, a linear programming language that ran on an IBM AS/400 platform, with the data linked to the dedicated computer used by the dispatcher on a 24-hour-a-day basis. CAD's power supply was also protected through a hospital-grade generator. Within CAD, an electronic database record was used to supply and track information on trips in terms of pick-up location, destination, and pick-up time. Given the request for the trip, CAD then optimized the process by continuously evaluating the pending trips and the available resources before providing the dispatcher with the recommended assignment.

As for *housekeeping*, evaluation, and maintenance of the solution, it is already noted that the dispatcher had the option of doing an override assignment manually by pressing a function key. This "disagree process" would then require the dispatcher to write down the reason for his or her disagreement with the system. Data captured automatically during this process were then used to provide feedback to management and, in some cases, feedback and education to the dispatcher to allow him or her a better understanding of CAD, its logic, and its approach to the solution of the resource allocation problem. CQI of the system was also further achieved by monitoring the performance measures and making fine-tuning changes as needed.

Altogether, the Abbott case illustrates the problem-finding and problem-solving cycle of the PUSH-PULL framework in a resource allocation and assignment problem. Beyond this, Schmitz and Corley note that CAD appeared to provide a more general insight to solving other potential problems existing in other parts of the Abbott system.

Case 2: A Decision Support System for Bed Assignment at Cedar Rapids Medical Center

Case 2 shows how the use and development of a bed scheduling decision support system (DSS) can improve both the quality of patient care and resource utilization within a local hospital. In this case, the environmental contexts for which strategic *planning* evolved were the decrease in patient revenues and the need to make the best use of existing bed capacity at the Cedar Rapids Medical Center (CRMC), a regional hospital in Cedar Rapids, Iowa.

At the macro level, CRMC management saw the problem of patient-bed assignment as a particularly complex task that would have significant effect on quality and outcome of patient care, resource utilization, and the smooth functioning of the hospital. CEO Benson was quick to strike a planning committee to oversee the handling of this problem. The committee members, consisting of an orthopedist, a nursing supervisor, an internal consultant, and others involved in bed assignment, were also active in forming *linkages* with the major stakeholders.

Major *uncertainties* were identified from surveys and personal interviews of the major stakeholders during the strategic planning process. These included:

- a growing patient dissatisfaction with waiting time for admission, transfer, and discharge
- the potential "loss" associated with patient displacement in terms of quality, outcomes, and increased length of stay
- expressed physician concerns over the inappropriate assignment of beds for patients
- the inadequacy of the current piecemeal hospital information system because of incomplete information to help nursing supervisors appropriately assign beds

In this case, it is noted that a significant amount of planning time was given to understanding the current bed assignment process and its strengths and weakness to better guide the design of a solution. Moreover, personnel from many *levels* of the organization were actively involved in the planning process, including physicians, nurse supervisors, internal consultant, HMIS personnel, and others (e.g., senior management). For example, the HMIS department contributed by conducting a feasibility study on the viability of the various options for a new proposed system while top management provided support. Hence, a collegial solution strategy aligning business–HMIS goals was pursued based on group thinking rather than leaving it in the hands of the nurse supervisors who were primarily responsible for this function.

Moving down to the micro-level, *programming* of the solution continued with an identified list of the goals or functional requirements for the proposed bed assignment system (e.g., real-time information, flexibility, user friendliness, full system integration, and so on). Considerations were also given to the different options for HMIS development: prepackaged software, outsourcing, and in-house development.

As for the *uniqueness* of the solution, this is most evidenced in the way the suggested solution accommodated the organization of beds at CRMC. In particular, physicians were interviewed to estimate the disutility or "loss" associated with each displaced patient-day. The linear programming model used would then determine the unique patient-bed assignment that would minimize total system loss.

Basically, the *solution* here is a nursing decision support system (NDSS) that was developed in-house using the prototyping approach. The NDSS used a linear programming model to track and analyze data captured in a bed and patient database. The telephone was used to request demographic and basic information from the patient prior to admission and bar-code labels were used to trap additional information into the system during the admission, transfer, and discharge process.

As for *housekeeping*, evaluation, and maintenance of the solution, it is noted that the initial working prototype represented an improvement over the current system but provided too many choices and requested too much information. A revised NDSS was later completed and CQI of the system was achieved through further testing, training, and documentation.

In this CRMC case, O'Neill and Prater show that the problem-finding and problem-solving cycle of the PUSH-PULL framework could be applied in the area of nursing administration. It should also be possible to revise or customize the NDSS developed at CRMC to other hospital settings.

Case 3: The Radiology Department at Institution-MED

Case 3 outlines several major issues and challenges leading to the evolution of an all-electronic radiology operation for Institution-MED. In this case, the environmental context necessitating strategic *planning* (and change) might be attributed to the apparent inadequacies and inefficiencies inherent in the use of traditional radiology techniques and processes, which resulted in continuing revenue losses.

At the macro-level, Institution-MED's newly hired radiology departmental chair saw the need to move the traditionally operated radiology department into an all-electronic teleradiology operation based on integrated radiology information system/picture archiving and communications systems (RIS/PACS) technology. A total reengineering of the workflow also resulted in the need for a change in basic infrastructure, including equipment, space, and personnel. The chair was active in forming *linkages* with the major stakeholders, including management, radiologists, and referring physicians to make these changes possible.

Resistance to change and acceptance of the new integrated RIS/PACS technology were among the major *uncertainties* encountered during the reengineering and planning process. Some issues and challenges included:

- understanding the effect of the new technology on users and staff
- answering questions about the credibility of reading soft copy images
- training of radiologists to use the new technology
- the extra burden imposed on the ordering physicians with the new procedure

In this particular case, it is noted that the radiology department chair spent a significant amount of time on "marketing" the new technology. In addition, personnel from many *levels* of the organization who were affected included technologists, nurses, radiologists, transcribers, and billing staff. HMIS personnel were asked to take on the responsibility of image storage and image distribution, and the job function of film development in the darkroom was replaced by bar-code reading and computed radiography cassette processing. Moreover, the engineering department also contributed by taking on the responsibility to perform system maintenance and continuous system enhancement.

Moving down to the micro-level, *programming* of the solution rested importantly on identifying and meeting the various requirements of the new integrated RIS/PACS system (e.g., bandwidth requirement, multiple image sources, multiple film printers, multiple viewing workstations, communications and network requirements, and so on). Considerations were also given to the different options for several functions: network wiring, image compression techniques for storage reduction and bandwidth savings, and upgrading of bandwidth support and network.

The *uniqueness* of the Institution-MED solution is best seen in the way security and privacy issues are handled. In particular, security of software and the network against viruses and unauthorized intrusions, the protection and distribution of source codes, and the protection of data and database access were key to ensuring a secure and safe virtual working environment. In addition, the new system features an online help desk intranet service.

Clearly, the *solution* here was the implementation of an integrated RIS/PACS environment to support teleradiology. One major obstacle was the limited online archival of images older than 6 months and reliability of the system, which brings us to the *housekeeping*, evaluation, and maintenance of the solution. Here, note that the teleradiology environment was continuously upgraded as newer and more advanced technology emerged; for example, the automatic downloading of new software versions, the merging of teleradiology operation and PACS, and the shifting of the internetworking technology from a proprietary technology to an industry-standard Internet technology.

In this case, Shieh and Roberson demonstrate how the problem-finding and problem-solving cycle of the PUSH-PULL framework can be applied to the evolution of a traditional radiology environment to an integrated RIS/PACS environment to promote digitized radiology.

Case 4: Delivering Enterprise-Wide Decision Support through E-Business Applications

In Case 4, Kohli and Groot provide a detailed account of the transition from a second generation DSS to a third generation, Web-enabled DSS environment at Holy Cross Health System (HCHS) to deliver enterprise-wide decision support and e-business applications. The environmental context driving strategic *planning* (and change), in this instance, was the processing limitation experienced with the use of the current second generation DSS and the rising cost of its maintenance.

At the macro-level, the HCHS Information Steering Committee and the CIO initiated the sponsorship of the project. A conscious effort was then made to include user participation resulting in the formation of an enterprise-wide DSS users' group (UG). In this way, active *linkages* were formed across HCHS members organizations (MOs) representing the major stakeholders, including acute-care hospitals, extended care facilities, residential facilities for the disabled and older adults, occupational medicine, and community service organizations.

User expectations, product requirements, investment capital, and project prioritization were among the major *uncertainties* encountered during the change management process. Some major barriers and challenges included:

- valuing the utility of the third generation DSS
- having a business understanding of the DSS data
- defining the role of DSSs
- measuring the return on investment for the DSS implementation

A trained internal consultant was assigned to work with the project team. In addition, personnel from many *levels* of the enterprise participated, including management, users (stakeholders), the consultant, and systems people (e.g., the DSS group). For example, the DSS group was responsible for generating knowledge and the DSS, which served as a corporate resource for decision makers at all levels of the HCHS and the MOs. The network and systems people were responsible for matters pertaining to data security and privacy.

Moving down to the micro-level, *programming* of the solution piggybacked on feedback received from current DSS users to drive the sponsorship and various requirements for the third generation DSS. Considerations were also given to the different options for several activities: choice of systems development methodologies, selection of vendor, and use of in-house versus outside consulting services.

The *uniqueness* of the HCHS solution was most obvious in the integration of the third generation DSS with the previous generation tools, or more simply, backward compatibility. In this way, HCHS users could still benefit from the significant past investment in development, training, and support for previous DSS generation tools. Another special feature was the use of automated project management software to aid the monitoring of progress of the current project plan.

Simply, the *solution* was the migration of second generation DSS to a Web-enabled, third generation DSS environment. More importantly, the new system environment featured the creation of a data warehouse that supported online analytical processing on the resulting multidimensional managerial reporting cube. *Housekeeping*, or maintenance evaluation of the new DSS environment, is the responsibility of the decision support services. Other issues given attention in this area included data security and privacy.

In summary, the problem-finding and problem-solving cycle of the PUSH-PULL framework was applied in the HCHS case to a transitional DSS implementation project.

Case 5: Managing a Troubled Health Management Information System Project

This case documents the management and recovery of a troubled HMIS implementation project at Green Valley Hospital (GVH), one of the major teaching and research hospitals in Canada.

The lack of current system integration and the lack of clinical systems were two key drivers for which the challenge of strategic *planning* (and change) was taken up by the hospital administration through the initiation of an organization-wide strategic reengineering effort. The goal of this effort, according to Iacovou and Dexter, was to "treat the patient smarter" by enhancing quality of care, coordination, internal communication, and resource allocation on one hand, and by reducing waste and costs through emphasizing "specific patient costing" and CQI on the other hand. An attempt to align this goal between the key hospital processes and information technology was seen very early in the planning stage.

At the macro-level, senior management (President Smith) brought in Datacom, an external consultant, to help in the development of a comprehensive 5-year strategic information system plan. This plan, based on extensive interviews with GVH users, called for the implementation of an integrated patient administration and care system (IPACS), which should be capable of providing byproduct HMIS guidelines and patient-specific costing information. To meet the plan's objectives, the consultant further assisted in the procurement process.

Major *uncertainties* underlying the entire planning process is GVH's reliance on the approval of and funding from the provincial Ministry of Health for the project, the difficulty of reaching consensus on a suitable vendor, and the frequent turnover of GVH's HMIS managers because of disagreement between senior management and consultants and between users and information technology personnel. In any case, planning and negotiating for the project resulted in active *linkages* being formed between GVH senior management and the consultant, and between GVH senior management and the Ministry of Health. Both the information technology personnel and users felt neglected in the negotiations.

Accordingly, although personnel from many *levels* of GVH, including key users, HMIS staff, and senior administrators, apparently participated in a preliminary review of the vendors, the decision for going with IBAX appeared to rest solely with the president's favor. This was despite clear resistance from the HMIS manager and users, because IBAX was unfamiliar with the Canadian hospital context. In fact, it is noted that the president's strong favor for hiring Datacom and choosing IBAX was primarily because of his past connections with them.

Moving down to the micro-level, *programming* of the IPACS solution ended with a mix bag of results. Whereas the implementation of the two financial applications (i.e., general ledger and accounts payable) were relatively successful with the users, those of materials management, human resources/payroll, accounts receivable, and capital assets tracking modules proved to be quite a disaster. There was strong resistance from users because not only did these applications appear to lack the needed functionality, but also the use of these modules added to user workload. An even more distressful experience was found with the implementation of the two clinical systems, the admission, discharge, transfer system and the operating room application. At this point, the entire IPACS project was placed on hold as GVH sought an alternative solution.

The *uniqueness* of the GVH solution rested in what was done in recovering from the "troubled" IBAX attempt. Following rejection and termination of the IBAX relationship, GVH had to move very quickly to save time and money and be up and running. Fortunately, GVH could fall back on Medsys, the original supplier of GVH's existing admission, discharge, transfer system and one of those vendors whose initial bid for the IPACS project was dismissed. There were many advantages to go back to Medsys, particularly the familiarity of GVH personnel with the vendor, although some departments (e.g., HR and radiology) had decided to acquire their own systems using other third-party vendors.

The *solution* here was therefore the implementation of a mix of solutions, largely with Medsys clinical systems, and partly with third-party vendors in place of the failed IBAX attempt. In terms of *housekeeping*, evaluation, and maintenance, Datacom consultants, who were asked to do a formal audit a year prior to the end of the 5-year plan, provided an overall positive evaluation of the implementation project despite the troubled IBAX experience. President Smith left GVH and the newly installed systems appeared to be working.

In summary, the problem-finding and problem-solving cycle of the PUSH-PULL framework is applied in the GVH case to a troubled and recovered HMIS implementation project.

CONCLUSION

Following this chapter the individual cases contributed by their respective authors are presented. It is hoped that both the students and the instructors will find the questions at the end of these cases useful and meaningful for stimulating class discussions.

Emergency Medical Transportation Resource Deployment

Homer H. Schmitz and Mark L. Corley

INTRODUCTION

As the emergency medical transportation community evolves, it faces many of the same reimbursement difficulties that faced other segments of the health care delivery system as they encountered changes in the reimbursement system. For example, when one looks at the evolution of reimbursement in other health care delivery sectors such as hospitals and physician practices, there is a progression from billed charges to other more restrictive reimbursement mechanisms, usually culminating in some form of capitation.[1] This is a process by which economic risk is systematically shifted from the reimbursement entity to the health care provider. Simultaneously, the total reimbursement to the provider is reduced. This change in the reimbursement mechanism is currently under way in emergency medical transportation and is being experienced both from the government sector and the private sector. As reimbursement becomes more restrictive, paying less per unit of service, as well as paying less by shifting economic risk for the volume of services provided, the result is a need for the emergency medical transportation provider to increase productivity or to become more efficient in its operations in order to maintain profitability and financial viability.

Emergency medical transportation systems have taken various approaches to increase efficiency in their operations. Because resource utilization represents the single largest expense in the budget of an emergency medical system, strategies to control this utilization have become one of the primary targets for improving efficiency. Resource utilization includes the vehicles, their maintenance, and the crews to operate the vehicles. The primary focus of these efforts is to deploy the resources so that they can deliver the most timely and highest quality services possible and to appropriately prioritize the allocation of those resources when there is excess demand.

This case provides a study of the development of a computerized dispatch system that optimizes the use of the resources based on certain predefined parameters.

Abbott Ambulance is a nonprofit company operating in the greater St. Louis metropolitan area, including transportation activities in both Missouri and Illinois. The services offered include basic life support (BLS) and advanced life support (ALS) ambulance transportation and van, paralift, and stretcher van transports. BLS and ALS ambulances transport all patients who may require some level of medical care before or during transport. The vans and paralift vehicles may not transport any person who might reasonably be expected to require such care. Vans and paralifts are operated by a single driver who does not have the training to monitor a sick or injured person. The company operates a fleet of approximately 85 ambulances, 5 vans, and 6 paralift vehicles, and employs approximately 600 people.

The company's range of business activities includes contracts with municipalities to provide 911 primary response activities, backup services, and contracts with various health care organizations to provide a continuum of medical transportation services. In addition, the company receives calls from various health care facilities and from the public to provide both emergency and nonemergency medical transportation.

Abbott Ambulance must respond to a variety of medical transportation needs in the St. Louis metropolitan area. This discussion focuses exclusively on the nonemergency ambulance service, which includes both BLS and ALS transports. These medical transports can have their origin in a call from a health care provider, such as a skilled nursing facility or hospital, for either scheduled or nonscheduled transportation to some other facility for medical services, or a call from the public for either scheduled or nonscheduled transportation.

Given this array of business activities, which can have a large number of combinations for types and priorities relating to transportation requirements, the demand for resources is a complex algorithm with a hierarchy of priorities. It is very difficult for a person to keep track of all of the variables involved without some tools to assist in the prioritization of resource allocation. Therefore, a computer program was developed to assist in these activities.

THE PROBLEM

Given the high volume of business activities and the complex relationship governing the prioritization of the transportation resources, a single dispatcher is unable to manage efficiently and effectively the numerous combinations of resources and requests for service. The factors that must be considered in making the decisions relating to the resource assignments make the problem far too complex for a human being to handle in the tight time constraints required without the assistance of an automated resource allocation system.

TYPES OF TRIPS

The system that was developed at Abbott Ambulance allows for two types of nonemergency trips. To service these two types of nonemergency trips, there are two levels of ambulance capability available for assignment.

- *Code 0* trips are defined as prescheduled trips. They are requests that have been made for nonurgent ambulance service that was requested well in advance of the desired pick-up time for the patient. This type of request is usually for an appointment or transport that is planned for a future date and time.

- *Code 1* trips are not prescheduled and are requests for non–life-threatening circumstances requiring immediate transportation. An example would be a request to transport a patient from a skilled nursing facility to a hospital for evaluation of an elevated body temperature. In this type of trip, it is presumed that the patient's condition is very stable, and there is an agreed upon expectation between the ambulance company and the requester of the service that the next available appropriate ambulance will be sent.

Emergency requests are not assigned within the framework of this component of the dispatch system, but when an emergency request is received, it is handled in the following way. The computer calculates the nearest available ambulance to an emergency request and the dispatcher assigns the call immediately. This does, however, have an effect on the nonemergency system in that the vehicle assigned to the emergency request is therefore unavailable for a nonemergency assignment. The system resource allocations might need to be reconfigured subsequent to an emergency call because the available resources have changed.

LEVELS OF AMBULANCE CAPABILITY

Basic Life Support Ambulance

This ambulance is a vehicle staffed by two emergency medical technicians (EMTs) who have the training to provide basic care and monitoring while transporting the patient. EMTs receive about 4 months of training in basic patient care. The training enables the EMT to monitor patients, assess illness and injury, and provide comfort and maintenance while transporting the patient. This type of crew is not able to perform services at an advanced level, such as administration of intravenous fluids, drug therapy, or monitoring electrocardiograms. Typical services performed by this level of ambulance would be moving nonambulatory patients, administration of oxygen, and monitoring vital signs. It should be noted that this ambulance type is not qualified to transport patients that require the higher level of care provided by an advanced life support ambulance.

Advanced Life Support Ambulance

One EMT and one paramedic staff this type of ambulance. Paramedics receive about 18 months of training in advanced patient care. Training includes anatomy and physiology, emergency cardiology, pharmacology, and advanced skills such as intravenous therapy, electrocardiology, and airway management. They can provide a higher level of patient care, including intravenous fluids administration, drug therapy, and electrocardiogram monitoring. It is important to note that in order to optimize resource utilization, this ambulance type may also be called on to perform trips that are basic life support requests.

Although the dispatch of vehicles to transport emergency patients is obviously part of the total system, the focus of this case is on the transport of non-emergency patients and the allocation of resources to serve those patients. The reason is that requests for emergency services are responded to immediately in terms of assignment of the nearest vehicle and crew that are qualified for the requirements of the trip. Because emergency transports take top priority in the system, whenever there is a request for emergency resources, the system calculates the emergency resource requirements and then recalculates the remaining nonemergency allocations. This is done on a real-time basis, so the recalculations are done frequently throughout the course of a day. As was outlined in previous paragraphs, nonemergency transportation allows for many more options in the decision algorithm, and therefore it represents the most significant challenge in terms of optimizing resource allocation. Assignments for non-emergency trips are frequently changed when a vehicle that was originally assigned for a nonemergency transport is used as the most appropriate resource for an emergency transport.

FACTORS TO CONSIDER IN ASSIGNING RESOURCES

As the resource allocation system was developed, one of the first series of decisions to be made focused on determining what service factors were important to successful operation and efficient resource allocation.

- *Pick-up time.* All trips must be assigned a pick-up time so that both the requester of the service and the provider can plan appropriately. In the case of the Code 0 trips, the pick-up time is the agreed upon time between the caller and the dispatcher. Code 1 trips have a pick-up time defined as the same time that the call was received by the dispatcher.
- *Response time.* In order to measure success, it is important to determine the extent to which the pick-up time is achieved. Thus, a standard of performance was developed and is measured simply by comparing the arrival time of the ambulance to the scheduled pick-up time for the trip. In the case of the Code 0 trip, the system is deemed to be late if the ambulance arrives even one minute after the pick-up time. In the case of Code 1 trips, the system is late if the ambulance arrives more than 30 minutes after the pick-up time. Remember that the pick-up time for a Code 1 trip is the time of the original call. Thus, the standard of no more than 30 minutes after the pick-up time actually means that an expectation is established that the ambulance will arrive within 30 minutes of the original call. It should also be noted that a further consideration relating to pick-up expectations is that the customer generally does not like having the ambulance arrive substantially earlier than the prescheduled pick-up time. The system standard is that the ambulance will not arrive more than 10 minutes early.
- *Vehicle drive time and distance.* This factor is very important in optimizing resource allocation. The system attempts to minimize the driving time and distance of any individual vehicle while traveling to a call. Consideration is also given to minimizing "total system drive time," which is

based on the sum of all the individual vehicle's drive time and distance. It will be shown later that there might be multiple combinations in which a particular vehicle might have the same minimum drive time to a single call. It was decided that, in this case, the system would evaluate those combinations and select for the system the one that had less total drive time.

- *Crew work load.* This consideration is a very important factor in the system relative to employee morale and efficiency across the entire organization. In order to promote good morale among the crew, the system is designed to attempt to evenly distribute work load so that an individual crew is not worked disproportionately more than other crews.

SYSTEM CONSIDERATIONS

The Computer Aided Dispatch system at Abbott Ambulance runs on an IBM AS/400 computer hardware platform. The dispatch system is operated on a dedicated computer. All other business applications run on a second AS/400 so that the dispatch system has full access to all of the available computer resources. Because it must operate 24 hours a day and be extraordinarily reliable, it is supported by an uninterruptible power supply, which is fed by a hospital grade generator. The system architecture provides a database of trips, vehicles, and ambulance staff. Trip information is taken over the telephone by dispatchers, and requests for service are placed in a queue until the appropriate resource is assigned to the call. Each trip in the queue has a pick-up location, destination, and pick-up time in its electronic database record. Given the request for the trip, the system then optimizes the process by continuously evaluating the pending trips and the available resources. It must resolve the trip requests with the available resources in a timely fashion because on-time performance is one of the most important parameters of the system.

Ambulance resources are tracked in the same system. Each vehicle is designated with a vehicle number, vehicle type (ALS or BLS), the time that the vehicle is scheduled to go off duty, number of trips that the vehicle has run during the shift, and its current status and location. Vehicle status refers to the current activity of the ambulance. This could be such things as en route to a call, on the scene of a call, out of service, or posted at a location in anticipation of an assignment. Location is tracked in a sector system, which divides the system's service area into 2.25 mile squares. If a vehicle is moving, its start sector and destination sector are stored to allow calculations that extrapolate its location at any given moment. The system is able to calculate distance and drive time to any given set of pick-up locations that are also assigned to the same sector system.

ASSIGNMENT OF VEHICLES TO TRIPS

For any given set of trips when there are available vehicles to assign, there are usually numerous possible combinations of vehicles for the pending trips. As the number of trips and/or vehicles gets higher, the combinations obviously increase accordingly. At some point, this set of combinations of vehicles and trips becomes too complex for a human being to analyze with speed, accuracy, and attention to important factors. Decisions have to be made quickly and system priorities must be satisfied. Therefore, the computer-aided dispatch system was developed in order to assist the human dispatchers in their responsibilities. Note, however, that a computer-*aided* dispatch system is being described. Ultimately, human dispatchers make the final decisions on assignments. It is possible that the dispatcher is aware of some change in the system that might affect the recommendation made by the computer-aided dispatch system. Authority is granted to the dispatcher to make manual assignments and to document the reason that the system recommendation was not followed.

After extensive discussions with computer programmers and system design staff, the decision was made to attempt to design a system that replicates the hierarchical decision process that dispatchers attempt to follow in their own thinking process. Decisions and assignments were based on a variety of factors that the dispatcher is forced to prioritize "on the fly." As the number of ambulances and trips increased, this task became much more difficult to manage and required some assistance. Thus, the computer-aided dispatch system was developed.

In designing the Abbott Ambulance computer-aided dispatch system, the first step was to establish a set of priorities or system parameters that were ranked from most to least important. These priorities formed the basis for the algorithms that produced the system suggestions for resource allocation. In order of priority, the following parameters were built into the system.

Appropriate Response Times

Of primary importance, and the highest priority, is the customer expectation of appropriate response times. Meeting the agreed upon appointment time is considered to be a primary expectation that must be met.

The standard for Code 0 trips was set to meet the exact prescheduled pickup time. The decision was made that the system must have a zero tolerance for substandard performance.

The system standard for Code 1 trips is based primarily on the recognition of customer expectations, which have been established on a historical basis over a period of years. History has demonstrated that if the vehicle arrives within 30 minutes of the appointed time, there is reasonable level satisfaction on the part of the trip requester. When the actual arrival time is more than 30 minutes after the scheduled arrival, complaints tend to increase.

System Drive Time

System drive time was determined to be next most important among the factors to be considered when allocating resources. This is an important element because increased drive time results in higher costs and reduces the probability for an on-time arrival. In addition, lengthy drive times tend to increase the dissatisfaction of crews.

Work Load Distribution

This element was considered to be important but less so than the previously listed two factors. This condition has little to do with customer satisfaction but plays a significant role in crew satisfaction, which is tied to a sense of fairness based on whether each crew does approximately the same amount of work as others over a period of time.

Assignment of Basic Life Support to Basic Life Support Crews

The final factor that was considered for the resource allocation model was the preference to assign BLS trips to BLS crews. Whenever this can be achieved, it results in a preservation of the higher qualified ALS resources for those times when there might be a higher demand for emergency resources.

THE INFORMATION SYSTEM

The information system was developed using the linear programming language Lindo. This choice was based on its capabilities in managing numerous combinations of system variables and side constraints in a very timely manner. Recall that this system must provide computer-aided advice to the dispatchers in a real-time mode. The system was developed so that the program would look for combinations that met the primary criteria of response times. That is, it would look at the pending trips and the parameters associated with each of the trips and try to match those parameters with the available resources. For example, if a trip requires a pick up in 20 minutes at a particular location, the system would search for vehicles that could satisfy that requirement. Because all vehicles have a measurable drive time to any location, it is possible to test the total fleet to find all vehicles whose drive time would allow it to meet the anticipated pick-up time. If the system finds multiple sets of optimal solutions, it would move on to the next level of criteria. If multiple vehicles would be able to meet the requested pick-up time, the program must accommodate the probability that there would be multiple combinations with an equally desirable outcome. Initially, it would select from among the combinations of the scenario that had the least single drive time for any single assignment. If there were multiple optimal choices at that second level, it would select the combination that had the least total drive time for the entire set of combinations. If there were still multiple optimal choices, then it would select the combination that assigned the trips to the crew with the least number of completed assignments. If, at this level, there were still multiple optimal choices the system minimizes the number of mismatches between ALS vehicles and BLS assignments.

System Performance Auditing

In any kind of quality improvement effort, it is critically important that one be able to determine the results of the changes. This means that it is necessary to measure selected key indicators that would be able to suggest whether the process is being improved or whether improvement is not forthcoming. These indicators would be measured in the time frame before the system was changed and in the time frame after the system was changed. Improvement or deterioration can then be noted. Various statistical indicators can be used to reach conclusions about the changes.

When the computer-aided dispatch program was developed and installed, it was important to obtain feedback from the dispatchers on whether or not they believed that the system worked properly and provided benefits to the organization. An audit system was developed and made a part of the overall system. That subsystem allowed the dispatcher the opportunity to disagree with the recommendations given by the program. After the dispatcher runs the resource allocation program, the AS/400 mainframe sends a data stream to a network personal computer. The actual algorithms are calculated on the personal computer. The AS/400 data stream contains all pertinent information about all available vehicles and all of the trip data that is required to allocate resources. The information includes the pick-up time of the request, the drive time of the vehicle to the pick-up location, the vehicle type, the time the crew is scheduled to go off duty, and the number of runs already completed by that crew.

As was previously noted, if dispatchers disagree with the configuration of the output relating to the resource assignments that are suggested, they press a function key on their computer terminals and are given an opportunity to write the reason for their disagreement. They may then manually assign a vehicle to a trip using their judgment as to the best allocation of resources. At the moment the function key is pressed, another program is invoked that captures all of the data that was used by computer-aided dispatch resource allocation program. A printed report is produced, which is sent to senior data processing and operations management staff for analysis. The report records a printout of all vehicles and their status at the time of the report, a listing of all pending queued trips and the calculations made by the program that documents how each factor affected the final recommendation. This "disagree process" allows the management staff to refine the program if the dispatcher's reason for disagreement adds additional insight to the problem. At the very least, in those conditions where it is determined that the dispatcher's judgment lacked total insight into the problem, this documentation can provide feedback and education to the dispatcher so that he or she has a better understanding of the system, its logic, and its approach to the solution of the resource allocation problem.

System Performance Improvement

Two primary methods measure the system performance improvement provided by the resource allocation system that was developed. These measures are response time to trips and improved efficiencies. Efficiency is measured by the number of crew hours used for a given trip volume. If the same number of trips can be run with fewer crew hours, the total system expense is reduced. This can be achieved most easily by reducing the amount of time spent per trip. It was the conclusion of management that this goal would be more easily achieved if trips could be assigned in the most efficient way possible. These were the primary goals of the system design effort. It was the belief of Abbott Ambulance management that if vehicles could be assigned to trips more effectively, they would be on time for more trips, and that the number of units on duty at any given time could be decreased.

The company measures both factors on a weekly basis. Nonemergency prescheduled trips are measured against a zero tolerance for lateness and for 90 percent response time reliability. Reliability is measured by calculating the maximum lateness on 90 percent of the trips. These standard measures both showed dramatic improvement after the system was in place for only a few weeks.

Code 1 trips are measured against a predefined system goal of 30 minutes. For this category of trips, the reliability improved from almost 45 minutes 90 percent of the time to just under 30 minutes. This means that 90 percent of the time, a medical transport vehicle arrived on the scene of a nonemergency, non-prescheduled trip in 30 minutes or less.

The Code 0 (prescheduled) trip reliability is measured against the agreed upon pick-up time. Measurements made in the time frame before the computer-aided dispatch program was put into use show that, on average, the medical transport vehicle arrived to pick up the patient within 25 minutes of the scheduled time 90 percent of the time. After the program was initiated, the average response time reliability improved to no more than 10 minutes late 90 percent of the time.

The company also benefited from increased efficiency in the system. Abbott Ambulance measures system efficiency as a ratio of trips to unit hours. Because of the improved response time and resulting decrease in average trip time, the trip-to-unit-hour ratio improved from approximately 0.32 to 0.34, which is approximately a 6 percent improvement. A trip-to-unit-hour ratio of 0.32 suggests that 3.125 unit hours are required per trip (1/.32). A ratio of 0.34 requires 2.94 unit hours per trip (1/.34). The cumulative reduction of unit hours per week with an average weekly volume of 1,200 trips is over 200 hours. In a system the size of Abbott Ambulance, the savings could be as much as $500,000 annually.

Participants in the design, programming, and implementation of the system included representatives from all departments affected by the new program. The information systems department was represented by the management information systems manager, who was also responsible for the design and programming requirements on the AS/400 system. A programmer who was experienced in personal computer programming developed the data links between the AS/400 and the personal computer environment that runs the actual planning program. Management from the operations department was involved in the process to help answer questions about the effect of the program on the crews, including modifications to the employee schedule. Managers from the dispatch department participated to ensure that all of the appropriate considerations were included in the program and to ensure that the employees were properly trained in the use of the system. This was particularly important as it relates to understanding the feedback mechanisms that were built into the system.

Future considerations for programs that follow the same basic decision making process are currently in the planning and programming stages. The same basic process, using the current system architecture, can be useful in several other areas of the company's operation. This could include systems to assist managers in the design of crew schedules based on an analysis of the historical volume data and programs that would allow the dispatcher the ability to allocate ambulance resources geographically in the service area in anticipation of calls being received.

CONCLUSION

Emergency medical services are in the process of coming under the same kind of reimbursement and budgetary pressures that have been experienced in other parts of the medical care delivery system. As the emergency medical services sector works through these changes, there is no reason to believe that it will not approach the change in much the same way as have other health care organizations. This will include the application of management techniques to operational problems, which are designed to provide greater efficiency and effectiveness on the part of the provider.

This case describes a computerized approach to assist in a more effective dispatching of vehicles, which results in a more efficient allocation of organizational resources. In this particular instance, it also provides a competitive advantage because it results in an improved product. This improved product is based on more timely and reliable vehicle arrivals when they are requested, resulting in higher customer satisfaction.

Because the core system with its resource database has been successfully installed, it is expected that the system will experience additional enhancements, resulting in the potential to gain even more operational efficiencies for the organization.

A properly designed information system provides the opportunity to serve the entire organization. Broadly speaking, the function of an information system is to increase the knowledge or reduce the uncertainty of the decision maker about some future state or event. This applies to all of the functions of management, not just the one for which the information system was designed.

This system was designed to increase the efficiency and effectiveness of the operations of Abbott Ambulance. The system's function is to increase the knowledge or reduce the uncertainty of the dispatcher about the optimum allocation of the organization's resources. However, this does not mean that the information accumulated by the system should be limited to operational uses. Given the availability of the information within the system, other parts of the organization can contemplate uses for the information. When this interdepartmental information use can be achieved, it is the mark of a well-designed information system and usually results in a synergistic effect on all parts of the organization.

CASE STUDY QUESTIONS

1. When changes are made to a process, it is necessary to measure the results of the change. Statistical inference techniques are a way to determine with more precision whether the changes are meaningful. Please discuss what tests might be used under these conditions and why they are used.
2. Do you believe that it is important to provide the "disagree process" for the dispatchers so that they can change the computer-aided resource allocation suggestion? Why or why not?
3. Certain measures of efficiency improved for Abbott Ambulance. Do you believe that the conclusions drawn are valid? Why or why not?
4. Given the successful installation of the system, with its resultant database, what enhancements would you suggest for the current system?

NOTE

1. C. Campbell, H. Schmitz, and L. Waller, *Financial Management in a Managed Care Environment* (Albany, NY: Delmar Publishers, 1998).

A Decision Support System for Bed Assignment at Cedar Rapids Medical Center

Liam O'Neill and N. Jane Prater

By the summer of 1996, Cedar Rapids Medical Center (CRMC) was under siege. Inpatient revenue had decreased by $5 million (3 percent) in the last year, and the number of acute-care beds had been reduced from 650 to 620. Owing to attrition and a hiring slowdown, the number of full-time support staff had decreased by 8 percent, and among the 3,000 employees that remained there was talk of forming a union.

BACKGROUND

CRMC is a regional hospital in Cedar Rapids, Iowa. Founded in 1893, it had grown from 35 beds to become one of the leading hospitals in Eastern Iowa. Its medical staff consists of 1,000 physicians and dentists, most of whom are specialists. In 1995, the hospital treated approximately 24,000 inpatients and 190,000 outpatients. The local population included a high percentage of older persons, and the hospital received almost half of its net patient revenue through Medicare.

Chief executive officer Christopher Benson had been chosen to lead the hospital in 1995. Although currently in a period of contraction, Benson recognized that opportunities existed to create a leaner, more efficient organization. To achieve this goal, he had pursued three basic strategies.

1. a shift in emphasis from inpatient to outpatient
2. the formation of strategic alliances with medical group practices and other providers
3. the outsourcing of support functions, such as laundry and food service

Benson had achieved some early successes by implementing changes such as electronic claims processing, which had reduced the average time in accounts receivable from 53 to 31 days. In terms of day-to-day operations, a constant challenge was how to make the best use of existing capacity without increasing the strain on the nursing and other staff that were already stretched thin.

BED ASSIGNMENT PROCESS

The process of assigning patients to beds had important implications for both quality and resource utilization and was critical to the smooth functioning of the hospital. A number of factors had contributed in recent years to make patient-bed assignment a particularly complex task. In the early 1980s, CRMC had a general surgery unit that treated a broad range of patients. Since then, patient care had become more specialized, and CRMC now maintained separate units with specialty-trained nurses geared toward specific patient populations. This high degree of customization meant that there was a lack of bed substitutability when units reached their maximum capacity. Thus, there was a potential "loss" associated with patient displacement in terms of quality, outcomes, and increased length of stay. In addition, units were organized to provide progressive patient care, in which changes in the patient's condition was marked by movement from one bed to another. For example, the obstetrics division contained labor rooms, delivery rooms, postpartum beds, maternity beds, and newborn nurseries.

INVESTIGATION AND SYSTEMS ANALYSIS

In November 1996, Benson appointed a planning committee to examine the bed assignment process. The committee, led by James Evans, an orthopedist, included nursing supervisor Miranda Smith, internal consultant Brian Roche, and others involved in bed assignment. Top management had grown weary of paying the high fees of external consultants and had decided to develop their own "in-house" consultants. Roche had started as a management engineer and was later trained in general management and communications in order to work on various interdepartmental projects throughout the hospital.

The group's first step was to conduct surveys and personal interviews of the major stakeholders. This information is summarized below.

- *patients:* Some patients were dissatisfied with waits of up to 3 hours in the Emergency and Trauma Center (ETC) before being admitted. Other patients were dissatisfied with what they perceived as unnecessary transfers, especially as they approached discharge.
- *physicians:* The main concern of physicians was that their patients be assigned to the "right unit, and the right level of care," especially for those requiring intensive care (monitored beds). Some asked how they could help improve the process. Others complained of having to walk to other units to see their patients.
- *nurse supervisor:* Nursing supervisors bore most of the responsibility for patient-bed assignment because it was their job to find a bed for each patient. The nature of patient care meant that decisions had to be made quickly and typically with incomplete information. The current system placed a heavy burden on these decision makers.

The hospital's information system consisted of a wide area network and several local area networks for departments such as laboratory and pharmacy.

One problem was that each component seemed to have been added in a piece-meal fashion, with little consideration given to long-term strategy or how these components fit together. Although each module served its own purpose, there was poor integration between modules. For example, when ordering patient meals, nurses had to enter the data in two separate locations.

Nursing supervisors had easy access to terminals through which they could monitor bed status. However, this data was often hours old and thus of little practical use. Instead, they relied on the telephone to locate available beds on other units. Thus, bed assignment was currently done on an ad hoc, patient-by-patient basis, with little emphasis given to long-term planning or a systems perspective.

For the second meeting, Roche had prepared the flowchart in Figure C2–1. Beds were organized around three levels: nursing divisions, units, and levels of care. Each nursing division, such as surgery and pediatrics, consisted of autonomous units and generally provided all levels of care. The housed outpatient unit, also known as custodial care, was reserved for patients who were otherwise ready for discharge but for whom other circumstances, such as transportation difficulties, prevented their immediate release. A "blocked transfer" occurred when a patient was ready to be transferred but no beds were available. The group determined that there was a constant bottleneck (i.e., capacity shortage) in the housed outpatient unit that caused frequent blocked transfers.

Nursing supervisor Smith prepared the flowchart of the current process (Figure C2–2). The first step in admissions process is the physician's assessment of the patient's clinical needs. Smith is then notified to admit the patient onto the unit. If all goes well and the unit has sufficient capacity in terms of beds and nursing staff, the patient is admitted to the unit. Otherwise, Smith has to decide whether to transfer an existing patient to make room for the new patient or to send the new patient to another unit. This is closely related to the triage concept, in which patients with the most urgent clinical needs receive the highest priority.

Once the capacity of the unit has been exceeded, Smith must use her clinical judgment to determine the next best option. If no beds are available in the entire division, the patient is sent to another division. This type of displacement occurs infrequently and only as a last resort, because it tends to create significant logistical difficulties.

To illustrate, she provided the following example. A call is received from the Surgical Intensive Care Unit (SICU) requesting a monitored bed for patient Jones. Neuroscience is the only unit with the nursing expertise to treat Jones. Because all of the monitored beds are currently occupied, Smith assesses the nursing requirements of each patient and discusses with a physician the possible discontinuation of monitors. If a bed cannot be made available in this way, Jones would remain in the SICU until a bed opens up.

One strength of the existing system was that it allowed the nursing supervisor great flexibility and discretion in the bed assignment process. The system's major weakness was that it did not provide the decision maker with adequate support in the form of complete and timely information. The current system had evolved with the implicit assumption that every bed assignment was unique and therefore unable to be processed in a uniform manner.

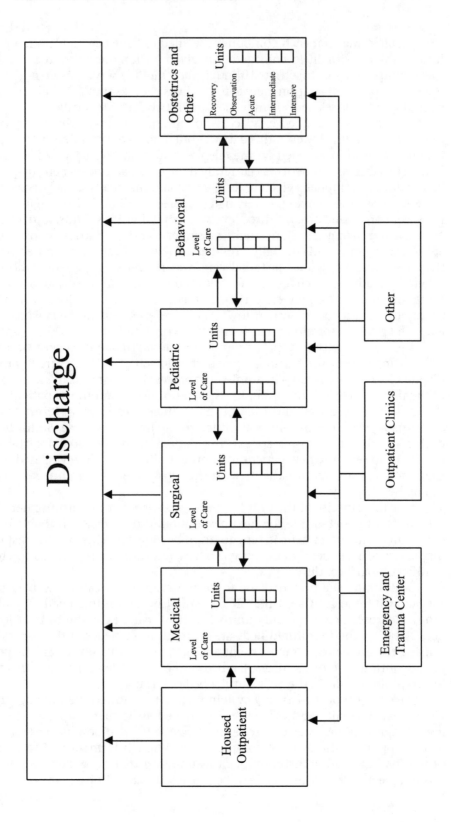

Figure C2–1 Flow of Inpatients through Cedar Rapids Medical Center

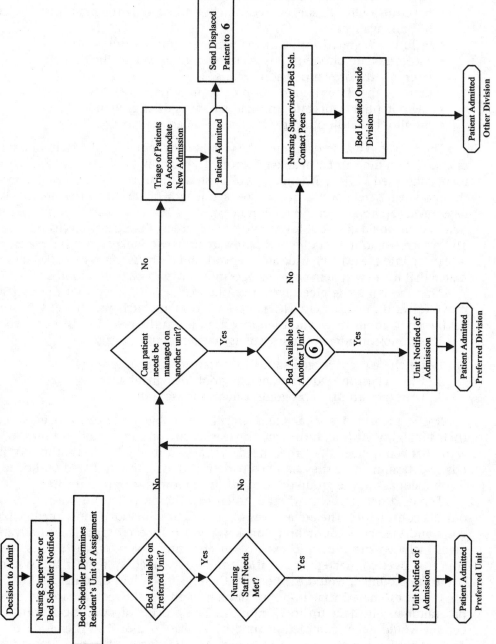

Figure C2–2 Current Admission Process: Neuroscience Unit

With current problems identified, the group then determined the goals or functional requirements of the proposed bed assignment system. The proposed system should

- provide real-time information on current bed status
- be flexible enough to allow nurse supervisors to exercise clinical judgment
- have an easy-to-use interface to facilitate data capture
- have the ability to suggest second choice bed assignments if first choice bed not available
- be fully integrated with existing patient information system
- accommodate phone-in physician referrals as well as the ETC
- reserve beds for planned admissions
- monitor the status and location of displaced patients
- flag potential errors and unusual patient-bed assignments
- monitor bed utilization for long-term capacity planning

The next step was to determine the viability of the proposed system in terms of completion time and available resources. The information systems (IS) department conducted a brief economic feasibility study in which they determined that the proposed system would reduce average length of stay by an estimated 0.5 days, saving approximately $3 million in expenses. It was not clear how much the new system would cost, but it was likely to be far less than the projected savings. The system would not require new hardware or network expansion but could be integrated into the existing wide area network and client/server system. It was estimated that the new system could be operational within 12 to 18 months.

After receiving the green light from Benson, Evans urged that the project move forward immediately. He had seen too many such promising ventures get buried in committees and then forgotten when the next "crisis" occurred.

The group considered three systems development options:

1. purchase prepackaged admissions-transfer-discharge software
2. write a customized program using outside consultants
3. write a customized program using in-house staff

Roche identified several commercially available packages and explored their suitability. Although this was the least costly option, he did not find software that could meet all of their needs. He also contacted several other hospitals to determine how they handled patient-bed assignment. Based on Roche's recommendation, the group decided not to explore this option further.

The next decision was whether to entrust the project to in-house staff or outside consultants. The advantages of outsourcing included more predictable costs and greater accountability on key performance criteria. The disadvantages included the time and expense of choosing a vendor, high costs, and concerns over connectedness of the vendor-developed system. If the system had to be modified, would the hospital then be dependent on outsiders?

It was estimated that in-house development would require two or three programmers and take up to 12 months. The process of selecting an outside vendor would delay completion time by at least 6 months. Therefore, they decided to develop the system in-house. Another factor they considered was the long-term effects on the in-house staff of outsourcing part of the IS function. In May 1997, the group submitted its final recommendations to Benson, including projected timeline and resource requirements.

SYSTEMS DESIGN AND IMPLEMENTATION

With the strong support of executive management, the IS department assumed control of the project. After reviewing the published literature, Roche determined that the bed assignment problem could be formulated as a linear program, where the objective was to minimize the total loss incurred from patient displacement subject to capacity constraints.[1-3] He interviewed several physicians and asked them to estimate the disutility or "loss" associated with each displaced patient day (Table C2–1). The biggest loss occurred when a patient was displaced across nursing divisions, especially in the early stages of care. Using several test cases, Roche then developed a linear programming model to determine the unique patient-bed assignment that would minimize total system loss. This mathematical model could then be integrated into a bed assignment decision support system. A decision support system (DSS) differs from an ordinary management information system in that it integrates the decision maker's own insights with the use of mathematical models to solve semistructured and complex problems.[4]

The existing bed tracking system was operational in nature in that it was designed primarily to report rather than analyze data. To facilitate data capture, bar code labels would be integrated with patient records that could be scanned by nurses upon bed assignment. This was deemed a critical component of a fast and responsive user interface that would meet the needs of the nursing staff. The system's data requirements included a patient and bed database. The patient database would contain the following fields:

- patient identifier (name and Social Security number)
- age, gender
- tentative diagnosis (reason for admission)
- probable time of arrival
- chief complaint: planned treatment and expected length of stay
- comorbid illnesses

Table C2–1 Disutility (Loss) Associated with Displaced Patients: One Physician's Assessment

New Patient Bed Assignment	Loss Resulting from One Displaced Patient Day
1. Unit +, Level of care +	0
2. Unit +, Level of care −	20
3. Unit −, Level of care +	15
4. Unit −, Level of care −, Division +	30
5. Division −, Level of care +	90
6. Division −, Level of care −	100

Note: +, first choice; −, second choice.

- level and acuity of care (acute, observation, recovery, custodial)
- admitting staff specialty and subspecialty

The first four of these variables could be obtained by phone before the patient arrived at the hospital. The remainder would need to be determined by a physician.

By December 1997, the group had developed a working prototype DSS. Nursing supervisor Smith and others were involved in testing the new system to determine how well it met the group's functional requirements. The consensus was that the DSS represented an improvement over the current system but was not without problems. First, the new system took too long, sometimes more than 5 minutes, to complete the assignment process. Second, it provided too many choices and requested too much information.

The IS group went back to work on streamlining and simplifying the current prototype. This phase took longer than expected, and it was clear they would not be able to meet the May 1998 deadline. The Midwest had recently experienced a nursing shortage that had hit CRMC particularly hard. As such, many of the problems originally addressed by the planning committee months ago had only gotten worse.

The IS group ultimately decided to go with a simpler, pared-down version of the DSS that maintained many of the features of the original. The revised DSS could complete a majority of bed assignments in under 2 minutes and was finally ready for rollout in July. However, there was still additional work to be done in terms of testing, training, and documentation. The hospital would maintain parallel systems for 6 months, after which the old module would be retired. The new system went online in August 1998.

CASE STUDY QUESTIONS

1. Describe the bed assignment process.
2. What is the role of an "internal consultant"? How does this differ from that of a traditional management engineer or IS specialist?
3. Describe some of the obstacles to developing the new system in terms of both technical and organizational factors. Which are more difficult to overcome?
4. What are relevant issues in using in-house staff versus external consultants?
5. How would the DSS be an improvement over the existing process in terms of the patient Jones' example? What are the implications of this "blocked transfer" in terms of both quality of care and cost to the hospital?
6. The systems development lifecycle consists of several steps, including investigation, analysis, design, implementation, and maintenance. Choose any step and describe how it applies to this case.
7. It is now 12 months later. How do you foresee the experience of this hospital with its new bed assignment system?

NOTES

1. D. Clerkin, P. Fos, and F. Petry, A Decision Support System for Hospital Bed Assignment, *Hospital and Health Services Administration* 40, no. 3 (1995): 386–400.
2. M.A.Cohen, J.C. Hershey, and E. Weiss, Analysis of Capacity Decisions for Progressive Patient Care Hospital Facilities, *Health Services Research* 14 (1980): 145–160.
3. S. McClean and P. H. Millard, A Decision Support System for Bed-Occupancy Management and Planning Hospitals, *IMA Journal of Mathematics Applied in Medicine & Biology* 12 (1995): 249-257.
4. J.K.H. Tan with S. Sheps, *Health Decision Support Systems* (Gaithersburg, MD: Aspen Publishers, 1998).

The Radiology Department at Institution-MED

Yao-Yang Shieh and Glenn H. Roberson

INTRODUCTION

The radiology department has an important role in the provision of primary diagnostic services, which are essential for modern health care.[1-7] In general, the radiology department is responsible for functions such as patient scheduling, billing, image acquisition, film/image processing, presentation, film tracking, file room management, diagnostic dictation, transcription, report sign-off and distribution, inventory control, quality assurance, and so on.

The radiology department of this case study is associated with a teaching facility with 360 beds that oversees a level-one trauma program. To facilitate discussion, "Institution-MED" will be used to refer to this teaching facility. Before the reengineering effort was initiated in 1994, this department could be characterized by the list below.

- It had no leadership. The radiology chair was vacant for several years, and almost all the radiologists left. The radiology operation was a joint effort of several autonomous groups: technologists, nurses, radiologists, transcribers, and billing staff.
- It had no resident program. It needed a teleradiology operation to cover after-hours operation.
- It had a loss of revenue because of loss of films, and subsequent dissatisfaction from patients was quite significant.
- The local patient base has a high percentage of indigent patients. In the light of shrinking federal and state subsidies, new revenue sources such as teleradiology were needed.
- A new radiology department building was under construction. This provided a golden opportunity to jump on the bandwagon of digital imaging and communications in medicine (DICOM).
- Managers had little insight into the performance of employees, bottlenecks, critical paths, patient satisfaction, turn-around times, and quality control.
- Educational programs had been abandoned.

MOTIVATION OF REENGINEERING INTO AN ALL-ELECTRONIC RADIOLOGY OPERATION

The new department chairperson who took the office in 1994 was convinced that a new radiology department based on integrated radiology information system/picture archiving and communications system (RIS/PACS) technology was the only way to succeed after reviewing a series of issues listed below:

- There was an absence of systems to monitor department-wide activities. There was no easy way of showing activities of interest, including, but not limited to, the total number of procedures and images being done in the past week or past month, turn-around time, and outstanding unread cases at the end of the day.
- The loss of films was a notorious problem that embarrassed the radiology department. The recall of patients to retake X-rays created frustration and serious discomfort for the patients. The referring physicians complained about the long latency before they could get diagnostic reports from radiologists.
- The radiologists felt that the preparation of seminars to teach medical students in the traditional way was very time consuming and needed to be improved. Traditionally, each radiologist created a personal library of slides, each of which depicted an interesting case study. The process of searching through the ever-expanding collection of slides, selecting slides relevant to the seminar at hand, and subsequently inserting them back to the pile of slides was a tedious and enormous, if not impossible, effort.
- Outside hospitals that could not afford full-time resident radiologists requested support in terms of timely reading of radiographic exams. These hospitals typically had contracts with a local radiologist who came once or twice a week to read. This kind of operation was certainly not acceptable in case of an emergency requiring immediate treatment. Furthermore, consultation to specialty radiologists was also desired when local radiologists encountered cases beyond their capabilities.

The biggest problem encountered initially was resistance to change. Many radiologists preferred to stay with films that they were familiar with. They tended to raise many questions to challenge the credibility of reading soft-copy images. Furthermore, the PACS demanded that any procedure to be conducted needed a specific current procedural technology (CPT) code from the ordering physician, who saw this as an extra burden to his or her already heavy workload. It took the determination of the new department chairperson and persistent negotiation and persuasion to win the support from radiologists and from referring physicians.

IDENTIFICATION OF REQUIREMENTS

The daily operation of the radiology department involves two kinds of data—text data and image data. Text data consist of demographic data and clinical data, such as procedures conducted, diagnostic reports, treatment, and so on. Traditionally, the data exchange occurs between a centralized main-frame/minicomputer, where the Hospital Information System (HIS) resides, and a net of dumb terminals. This is the most cost-effective way because of the low volume of data involved and the low cost of dumb terminals. Image data are radiographic image data. Before the era of laser printers, image data were stored in analog form on an image cassette, which was developed in a dark-room. The data communication between the source (image acquisition modal-ity) and the destination (film) was done by the so-called sneakerware.

After the proliferation of laser printers, the printout of films for digital modal-ities such as computed tomography (CT) and magnetic resonance (MR) started to become popular. Such printout requires a point-to-point data link between digital modalities and the dedicated laser printer. Now, it is an ubiquitous network that needs a tremendous increase of bandwidth. Figures C3–1 and C3–2 show the workflow for film-based operation and PACS-based operation, respectively.

Before the implementation of the RIS/PACS integration, the data commu-nication requirements consisted of a star-net of dumb terminals with the HIS computer as the hub for text data, and dedicated point-to-point imagery data link for each digital modality. When it comes to the displaying of images on CRT screens, dumb terminals are not powerful enough to do the job. Com-pared with text data, the required bandwidth is about two orders of magnitude higher. Furthermore, the PACS requires that multiple image sources, multiple film printers, and multiple viewing workstations be able to communicate with one another. An all-connecting network rather than point-to-point linkage is the only practical method of communication. Consequently, the network bandwidth is expected to be very high to support bandwidth sharing by multi-ple users at the same time.

The new workflow affects the human staffing requirement more in the change of required skill than in the number of personnel. Staff for some old functions is reduced; whereas staff for new functions is created. The responsi-bility of image storage and image distribution is shifted from the file room to the information systems group. The job function of film development in the darkroom is replaced by bar-code reading and computed radiography (CR) cas-sette processing. Instead of having films hung on the view boxes by techni-cians, the radiologists have to retrieve images directly through computers.

During the transition period of initial deployment, there needs to be enough training personnel to make sure all users are properly trained. After the formal training period expires, a help desk has to be maintained to answer questions and fix problems in the field. Of course, an engineering staff is needed to do system maintenance and continuous system enhancement.

PRIVACY, SECURITY, AND OTHER ISSUES

The privacy of the patients' confidential data is protected by password authentication. As long as an individual has the right of accessing clinical data of a particular patient, the system provides no mechanism of preventing him or her from disclosing confidential data verbally or in writing. However, the ethics code of Institution-MED represents a legal obligation for each employee.

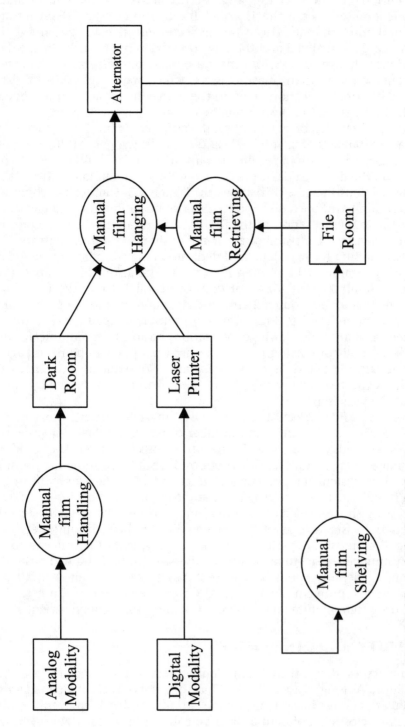

Figure C3–1 Workflow of Film-Based Operation

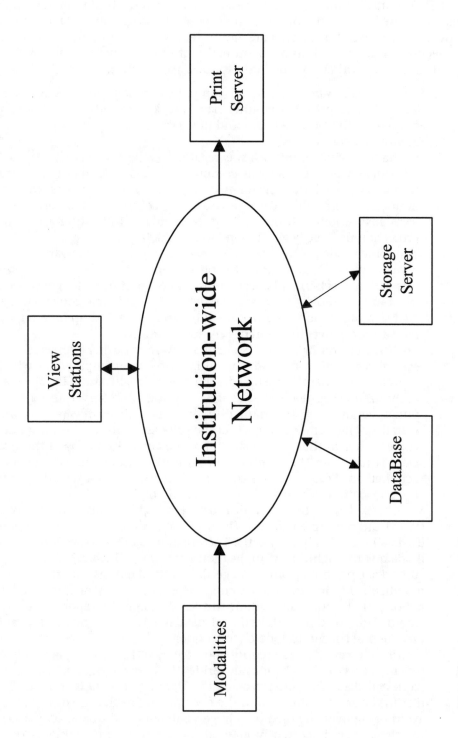

Figure C3–2 Workflow of PACS-Based Operation

Because Institution-MED is a teaching/research institute, radiographic images are used frequently for research purposes. Demographic data associated with any image used for research are always removed to maintain anonymity.

Security is the protection of the integrity of information against potential threats. It can be further classified into following categories:

1. *Security of hardware.* The server computers are kept in a secure room that only authorized personnel have the key to enter. The room is equipped with smoke detector and fire alarm system.

2. *Security for software code.*

    –In the past, virus protection was regarded as the responsibility of each individual computer user. The computer services department of Institution-MED played the role of instilling the virus awareness and announcing a virus alert. Because viruses are being developed on a daily basis, Institution-MED has decided to provide an institution-wide virus protection package beginning in January 2000.

    –The source code for the PACS has been managed by a software version control system. It keeps track of software modifications for team projects with a check-in and check-out mechanism. It provides good documentation of project history and strict control of source code access, as well as modification. The whole source code is backed up on a regular basis to computers in different physical locations.

    –The distribution of the PACS client software is further protected by a special registration mechanism initiated by the computer on which the client software is installed. The special registration involves an authorized account number assigned by the PACS server and a computed signature of the hard disk on which the software was first installed. The former ensures that the software is one of the authorized copies; whereas the latter ensures that the authorized copy of the software is run from the computer of its initial installation. If someone acquired an illegal software copy, he or she would not be able to run the application from his or her own computer.

3. *Security for data.* Patients' clinical data are highly critical and are controlled and monitored closely. The user is not allowed to access or modify data in the database directly. The only mechanism to access or modify data is through utility application programs, which are available to authorized personnel only. Image data and diagnosis reports are not modifiable. Modification to diagnosis reports can only be initialized by radiologists through addendum so that the previous report is still on record. Full backup of the clinical database is done once a day, and incremental backup is done once an hour.

4. *Security of access.* Access security is protected at two levels—access control and access audit. The former verifies the user's right of accessing the requested data. The latter records the transaction details into the log files for future investigation in the event an access flaw is suspected. To avoid being overwhelmed by a large volume of audit data, only access to critical data is currently audited. Access from off-campus is done strictly through integrated services digital network (ISDN) and dedi-

cated T1/fractional T1 lines. The setup of call for ISDN requires verification of an encrypted password.

5. *Security of network and communication.*

   –The network wiring was migrated from shared Ethernet wiring to switched ATM (asynchronous transfer mode) and switched Ethernet wiring about a year ago. The switched wiring scheme greatly reduces the risk of being tapped illegally. All network switch cabinets and routers reside in secure locked rooms.

   –Currently, the RIS/PACS is operated within the Institution-MED intranet, which is inaccessible from the outside, and is therefore quite secure. It is likely that the PACS will extend its service beyond Institution-MED in the future by attaching the PACS server directly to the Internet. By that time, the security will need to be strengthened, although Institution-MED already has a firewall to discourage hackers.

   –To avoid the controversial debate and potential legal risks involved with image compression, only lossless compression is used at Institution-MED.

   –A RIS/PACS view station provides an easy way of exploring the Internet. Proper use of this capability embedded in the view station can increase user productivity. There were instances when the Internet connection was abused and inappropriate sites were accessed. Because some of the users are managed as a user group account rather than as individual user accounts, it is not easy to pinpoint who actually abused the system.

EVALUATION OF THE SYSTEM ON-SITE

Usefulness of the System

The system's usefulness was measured by determining how the quality of service improved after the integrated RIS/PACS was put in place. Three areas of improvement are significant.

1. It virtually eliminates the chronic problem of lost films. In the past, film loss meant repeating radiographic procedures, extra cost of film, additional personnel time, and delayed diagnostic reports to referring physicians.

2. It saves radiologists physical trips to intensive care units. Radiologists can retrieve images from their offices, thus providing diagnoses in a timely manner.

3. It provides radiologists a convenient mechanism for collecting valuable cases for teaching purposes. They do not have to go out of their way to earmark cases manually.

Availability of the System

As a result of the limited online archival capability of the PACS, images older than 6 months are stored offline on tape and cannot be retrieved for online viewing. The reference frequency of images drops exponentially with time. Images older than 6 months represent below 10 percent of requests. In these cases, old films have to be retrieved from the file room for comparison purposes. Nevertheless, the situation is improving as the online storage is increased. This archival problem will disappear when the proposed permanent tape archival is installed.

Sometimes there is unavailability because of system malfunction. Causes for system malfunction include (in descending order of occurring frequency) network breakdown, computer breakdown, human errors, and software bugs. Realizing the importance of a high-bandwidth network backbone, Institution-MED and its associated teaching hospital have separately initialized a major network upgrade. Because of the complexity of the upgrade and lack of coordination between these two institutes, the upgrade has been quite an unstable process. Computer breakdown resulted from poor projections of load growth with time, which led to gradual slowing of response and eventually no response from the overloaded servers. Fortunately, this kind of problem demonstrated recognizable patterns and can be fixed by adding more computing power and storage capacity. Human errors can result in images being stored under a wrong name or medical record number. This kind of error often occurred when the HIS computer was down and clinical data had to be entered manually.

USE, ACCEPTANCE, AND REVISION OF THE SYSTEM

The system has been used as a complement to the traditional film system rather than as a replacement during regular hours mainly because of the lack of a permanent archival. The radiologists can choose either film or soft-copy for reading, depending on the availability and convenience. The system also has been used by a number of outside clinics, who refer significant numbers of patients to Institution-MED. Furthermore, the teleradiology functionality of the system has been used extensively for after-hours coverage.

The system has been regarded as permanent. Radiologists and physicians have come to realize that it is a very important resource. Whenever they cannot get the film easily and quickly, they turn to the PACS for help. The teleradiology functionality of the system has been accepted as the standard way of after-hours coverage.

The integrated RIS/PACS evolves continuously. Major enhancements are listed below.

1. The teleradiology operation and PACS have been merged into one system. Consequently, radiologists can access images of local hospitals and remote clinics from the same view station.
2. The underlying inter-networking technology has shifted from proprietary technology toward industry-standard Internet technology. The deployment of view stations has become simpler and simpler by taking advantage of the ubiquitous presence of the Internet.
3. The distribution of new software has become simplified. At the early stage of deployment, it was a significant effort to keep software up to date. This problem has been greatly relieved by automating the new

software download. Every time the user starts the PACS software, a comparison of its version number is checked to see if it is the latest release. If not, the user is prompted to download the latest release by a few clicks.

4. System monitoring and management by means of agent technology has become simplified. Personal computers report their status periodically so that a system manager can monitor the system from a single point.

5. Frequently asked questions and their answers are posted as an online help desk and can be accessed by users.

CASE STUDY QUESTIONS

1. Compare the workflow of a film-based radiology operation versus an all-electronic operation.
2. In your opinion, what are the significant benefits of transforming a radiology department from film-based to all-electronic?
3. Generally speaking, there are three approaches to implement a PACS. What are they?
4. What is the major difference in system requirements for a traditional RIS versus a PACS?
5. Who are the major stakeholders of the radiology operation? List primary concerns of each stakeholder.
6. Security threats are both natural and intended. Make a list arising from natural disaster and another list arising from intended attack.
7. Does the biggest threat to an enterprise information system come from internal employees or external hackers?

NOTES

1. G.H. Roberson and Y.Y. Shieh, *Radiology Information Systems, Picture Archiving and Communication Systems, Teleradiology—Overview and Design Criteria* 11, no. 4 (1998): 2–7.
2. R.L. Arenson, Use of Computers in Radiology, *The Radiologic Clinics of North America* 24 (1986): 1–133.
3. H.K. Huang, *Elements of Digital Radiology* (Englewood Cliffs, NJ: Prentice-Hall, 1987).
4. R.L. Arenson, D.P. Chakraborty, S.B. Seshadri, and H.L. Kundel, The Digital Imaging Workstation, *Radiology* 176 (1990): 303–315.
5. J.R. Cox, E. Muka, G.J. Blaine, et al., Considerations in Moving Electronic Radiography into Routine Use, *IEEE Journal on Selected Areas on Communications,* 10 (1992): 1108–1120.
6. E.L. Siegel, Economic and Clinical Impact of Filmless Operation in a Multifacility Environment, *Journal of Digital Imaging* 11, no. 4 (1998): 42–47.
7. J.K.H. Tan, *A Model for Achieving Total Quality-Management Information Technology Infrastructure within an Integrated Delivery System* 11, no. 4 (1998): 35–41.

Delivering Enterprise-Wide Decision Support through E-Business Applications

Rajiv Kohli and Henry J. Groot

INTRODUCTION

This case study presents an implementation of a Web-enabled decision support system (DSS) at Holy Cross Health System (HCHS). HCHS is a national organization with hospitals, called member organizations (MOs), in various markets across the United States. HCHS MOs have combined beds of over 4,000, employ about 20,000 people, and have a total operating revenue of approximately $1.5 billion. Some MOs have been providing health care for over 100 years. The MOs provide a range of services including acute-care hospitals, extended care facilities, residential facilities for the disabled and older adults, occupational medicine, and community service organizations.

DSSs are computer systems designed to help improve the effectiveness and productivity of managers.[1] DSSs deliver models that can be used to systematically evaluate policies and alternatives.[2] Conventional hospital information systems help meet the challenge by providing data necessary for policy formation and outcome measurement. However, integrating those systems with DSS can help managers gain insight into the operations, consider alternatives, and develop business strategies.

Operationally, the DSS at HCHS is used for resource allocation decisions, many of which use the costs and time for day-of-stay level patient data. Such decisions improve the cost-efficiency of patient care delivery. For example, an analysis indicated that patient test results from the laboratory to the emergency department were being provided late, causing longer wait times for patients. The redesigned process linked a printer in the emergency department to the laboratory system, where results were printed as soon as the test was completed in the laboratory. At the managerial level, DSSs provide information, such as department-level costs and high-cost items, which managers use to contain costs, and look for ways to better integrate services with other departments. For example, using activity-based costing, the registration department manager found that too much time and costs were being incurred in registering patients. Therefore, the manager reengineered the patient registration process by linking the registration system with the medical records system and accessing previously collected patient information. Strategically, the

DSS at HCHS is used to make pricing and contracting decisions and merger/ acquisitions planning.[3] By modeling a contract using existing costs, HCHS managers decide whether they should enter into a contract or if an existing contract should be renegotiated. There have been instances when a HCHS MO has declined to enter into a contractual arrangement following an expected loss from the modeled contract. DSS data at HCHS have also been used for strategic decisions on discontinuing services or starting new ones.

OVERVIEW OF DECISION SUPPORT

Our first generation DSS, which was developed as a flat file–based case management system, operated from 1983 through 1989. The primary driver for creating the case management system was the federal Medicare diagnosis-related group (DRG)–based prospective payment system (PPS), under which the Health Care Financing Administration (HCFA) would reimburse a predetermined amount for categories of diseases. The PPS meant that we had to better manage our patient care process. The DSS was primarily designed to support patient billing departments at MOs through value-added processes such as cost accounting, high-level expected reimbursement, and patient classification by DRG, services, and markets. At the request of remote users, the reports from the DSS were executed in batch mode and were mailed to the requesting user. The turnaround time was 3 days for standard reports and 1 week for ad hoc or customized reports. Our first generation DSS contained only inpatients.

Our second generation DSS, which operated from 1990 through 1999, was a hierarchical database with indexed files and an improvement over the flat file DSS in the first generation. It also had user controlled reporting capabilities available through a wide area network (WAN) linking all our MOs with the corporate office. This was interfaced each night with MO information systems to accept updated patient financial and clinical information. We processed the data and updated the predefined files each night. The MOs produced reports and performed analyses against these files to support their operational, managerial, and strategic decision making. The DSS resided in a mainframe computer consisting of a hierarchical database with proprietary query tools and value-added applications such as cost accounting, claims management, and "what-if" reimbursement modeling. In addition, it also had an expanded data set that included data from physician offices, home health centers, patient satisfaction, and severity-based clinical models. Our second generation DSS added our patient records resulting in a 10-fold increase in the volume of data. This required efficient report generation and remote printing at users' local printers.

The primary technical drivers for the migration to the second generation DSS at HCHS were the acquisition of T1 leased lines and a database. The business drivers were the changes in the reimbursement structure such as multi–per diems and payer-defined case rates heralding the age of managed care. Our first generation DSS could not calculate expected reimbursement from some complex managed care contracts.

With such expanded capabilities and an extensive historical database, why should HCHS plan for yet another migration? What limitations were we experiencing with the second generation DSS? What expectations did our DSS users have? What would our DSS developers like to see in third generation DSS?

The second generation DSS, with its hierarchical database, had reached processing limitation leading to performance issues such as increase in time in executing reports and processing of complex analyses. Further, as HCHS home grown applications became complex, the maintenance costs began to rise. At the same time, it was getting harder for HCHS to retain technical personnel who were developing skills in more advanced technologies such as online analytical processing (OLAP) and relational OLAP. The DSS user exposure to the Internet and its ease of access were raising expectations of how the DSS should provide data. The Internet browser, with its minimum training requirements, has become the standard of a computer user interface, thereby adding to the urgency to migrate to the third generation DSS.

The technology of the second generation also had reached the upgrade and maintenance zenith. Similarly, the software choices with the operating system had their limitations. The users also had matured in their expectations of data access and presentation. They expected advanced data manipulation capability through which they could change the data displays according to their analytical preferences. Table C4–1 shows HCHS migration from the second generation DSS (legacy systems) to the third generation data warehouse DSS.

IMPLEMENTATION

As is the case with most technology-based projects, implementation is the key to the success of DSSs and is largely dependent on how well one manages the managerial and implementation issues. These issues include soliciting continued high-level sponsorship of the project, managing change, demonstrating quick successes through rapid application development, considering outsourcing as an alternative, integrating existing tools, maintaining data standards, and coordinating project management.

Sponsorship

Generally speaking, the sponsorship of a project should come from the information systems and the business leadership. We find that often the sponsorship in technology-oriented projects comes from only information systems (IS) senior management. While IS sponsorship is required, the sponsorship from the business users is equally important. The literature on information technology implementation suggests that user sponsorship is a proxy for anticipated usage of the system and a determinant of system success.[4] On the other hand, when the user sponsorship is absent or not solicited, the users perceive that the technology is being implemented without proper understanding of the business requirements.

At HCHS, prior to proposing the transition to the third generation, we ensured that the information steering committee and the chief information officer sponsored the project so that necessary resources could be obtained. Following the sponsorship, the success of the DSS depended on the actual

Table C4–1 Characteristics of the Three Generations of Decision Support Systems

Characteristics	First Generation	Second Generation	Third Generation
Period	1983–1989	1990–1999	2000–present
Technology	Flat files reporting on mainframe	Hierachical database with indexed files on mainframe	Relational database Web-enabled
Applications	Case management	Activity-based costing Contract modeling Severity adjustment, Patient satisfaction	Physician profiling system Online reporting Activity-based costing Contract modeling Severity adjustment Patient satisfaction
Connectivity	None, single site	User access through wide area network	User access through wide area network and intranet
Strengths	Support standard costing Patient classification into services, diagnosis-related groups, markets	User access and control Accurate costing Support for managed care Integrated modules	Greater user access and control User friendly graphical interface Efficient reporting Greater portability of data though Web-enabled tools Improved security
Limitations	Remote reporting Delay in user data access Inpatients only	Character based Poor user interface Time consuming to execute reports	None

usage. The DSS, by nature, supports a number of decision makers, most of who have to be motivated to use the data for improved decision making. Therefore, the extent to which the DSS can support business decision making is limited only by user creativity. Although this is a favorable situation for any information system, the undefined set of users leads to a fragmented clientele base. We find our user base spread across clinical, financial, and operations departments and various levels of HCHS member organizations. Hence, the unclear business domain made it difficult to get our users involved in the development of a third generation DSS.

We solicited sponsorship and support from our diverse users through a DSS users group (UG). The DSS UG was created at HCHS to bring together users from various application areas across the MOs to share their use of DSS data in evolving business decision-making situations. We conducted monthly conference calls, invited DSS users, and arranged annual meetings to provide the developers with an opportunity to demonstrate the DSS enhancements. Our DSS UG also served as a forum for feedback from users and built much-needed sponsorship.

Managing Change

The management of change is a critical factor in making any significant change, particularly one that affects the nature of work. Change management also requires cultivating and managing realistic expectations of all parties involved. One such change in health care also affecting HCHS has been the shifting economics of hospital services. Constriction of revenue resulting from managed care is driving the scarcity of capital for investment into information technology. This change requires that HCHS investment be made in technologies or systems that will be used effectively. Such a change requires a shift in the thinking of the users, who in the past may have supported investment in information systems just because it is "nice to have."

Change management also requires prioritizing projects that require allocation of human and financial resources. Therefore, users of the DSS have to follow a methodology to prioritize those projects that are critical to the business functions. Such prioritization can lead to delaying or limiting the scope of existing projects. HCHS subscribes to a managing organizational change (MOC) methodology to support any major change in business practice resulting from the process redesign or information systems implementation. The MOC methodology prescribes assigning a trained internal consultant to the project team to work with the sponsor and the change agent. The MOC consultant assesses the capacity of change among the team members and guides the change process to its successful conclusion.

Rapid Application Development

The rapid pace of change in businesses, especially health care, requires quick actions in response to market conditions. In the same vein, when the response requires developing an information system, the traditional systems, analysis, and design methodologies are not suitable because of the time involved in implementing an information system. Our business situations require quick development of the next generation DSS, even if it is not the complete system with all its features.

The IS literature provides examples of rapid applications development (RAD), and another similar approach involving the users called joint application development (JAD), as substitutes for the complete systems analysis and design. We applied RAD and JAD approaches to develop the third generation DSS. The consultants and developers of previous DSSs worked closely to build a data model in a relational database. Once the data model was finalized and a prototype DSS developed, key users were invited to test the DSS and provide input. Under RAD at HCHS, projects and deliverables have been planned in 90-day increments. We have found such an approach to be cost-effective and one that meets user expectations.

Outsourcing

RAD is of increasing importance because of increasing pressures on the IS department from outsourcing application vendors. Outsourcing is an increasingly popular option for organizations that prefer to strengthen their core competencies and find it difficult to invest resources in the development of information systems. Outsourcing vendors, on the other hand, can invest large amounts of resources that can then be spread over a greater number of customers. Therefore, vendor-provided application software can be a viable alternative to internally developed applications.

HCHS considered outsourcing the DSS development as a viable option. In partnership with a leading vendor, HCHS cooperated to develop the next generation DSS. Prior to adopting the DSS as a health system standard, HCHS chose one of its hospitals as a pilot site. The vendor-developed DSS consisted of advanced data manipulation tools and a member-centered data model to accommodate the managed care driven market. However, after 2 years of partnership to develop the next generation DSS, there is still no corporate-wide DSS that can be implemented. Therefore, HCHS decided to develop in-house the third generation DSS.

Integrating Existing Tools

To the extent possible, HCHS is integrating the third generation DSS with the previous generation's tools. In the software industry, this is referred to as backward compatibility. There is a significant investment in development, training, and support for these tools that, if abandoned, can lead to business disruption. This is particularly the case for reports created in the previous generation DSS that are executed periodically for mandatory reporting or business decision making.

Although the need for backward compatibility may appear to contradict with the change management discussion above, it is an attempt to manage risk of business disruption even if it implies that some data manipulation tools will be less than optimum. Further, the HCHS OLAP, which runs the multidimensional managerial reporting or MR Cube (Figure C4–1), will benefit from the third generation DSS by producing synergistic business value for users of both systems.

Data Standards Migration

Maintaining data standards implies that the meaning of a data field is consistent among applications and across various hospitals. For instance, an admit date can mean different things under different conditions. It can mean the date when the patient registered for a procedure, the date when a patient was admitted for observation, or a date when the patient was admitted as an inpatient following an observation period. Any of these explanations of admit date would be acceptable as long as they are consistently applied across the organization and users understand the accepted definition. If the definition of admit

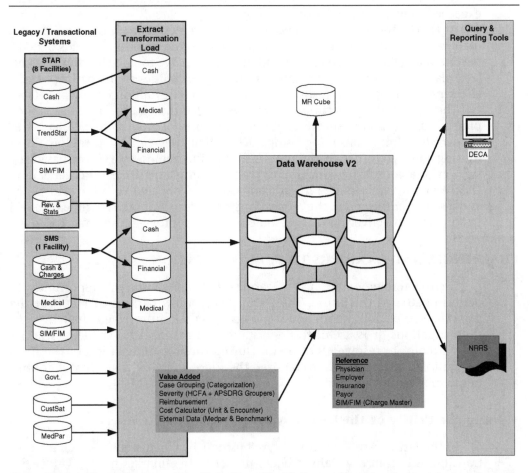

Figure C4–1 The Migration of the Holy Cross Health System Decision Support System from the Legacy System (Second Generation) to the Web-Enabled Data Warehouse (Third Generation)

date is not predefined and acted on, it could vary the length of stay for patients and therefore lead to inaccurate financial and clinical outcomes.

Adherence to data standards is critical in using preexisting reports, in applications such as cost accounting and reimbursement modeling, and in benchmarking quality of care outcomes across hospitals of HCHS. Data standards have been a challenge for HCHS from the first generation of the DSS. Migration to the third generation DSS is both an opportunity and a challenge to revisit and assert data standards.

Project Management

Among all the implementation issues, project management is perhaps the most decisive determinant of project success. It is the glue that holds together all the above mentioned issues. Past studies have indicated that most IS projects fail because of lack of control and a weak project plan. KPMG conducted a study of over 100 projects deemed to have failed and found that two thirds exceeded their schedules by over 30 percent.[5]

At HCHS, we manage the DSS and other projects using automated project management software. The use of project management software yields benefits beyond managing the project at hand. It is an effective tool to structure the project, plan for resources, and communicate responsibilities to the participants. It also serves as a means for justifying the resource consumption for the project.

The steps in the project plan and the estimated time frames are an asset for a project. Organizations spend significant amounts of money to purchase this "knowledge" from consulting companies so that they can avoid the pitfalls of missing some steps or scheduling unrealistic timeframes. HCHS purchased the services of a consulting company to plan and implement the third generation DSS. We created a baseline project plan that was compared with the actual time and resource at the end of the project. Any deviations from the baseline plan will be studied to effectively manage resources and to improve future project plans.

CHALLENGES AND BARRIERS TO IMPLEMENTATION

Each IS implementation is a learning experience and an opportunity to perform better in the future. There are usually a few barriers that impede the smooth IS implementation, and some issues remain unresolved challenges. In such situations, it is useful to understand and manage the challenges rather than attempt to resolve all of them. During the implementation of the third generation DSS, HCHS has recognized the following challenges that it continues to manage.

Valuing the Utility of the Decision Support System Resource

In the last decade, the health care business has seen significant changes in transitioning from a socialist welfare model to free market model. Under the socialist welfare model, the health care providers were reimbursed for any type of service provided for a sick person with little or no emphasis on efficiency or quality outcomes. The free market approach holds health care providers account-able for the efficiency of operations, quality of clinical outcomes, and patient satis-faction. To this extent, the health care providers also share in the risk of cost over-runs with the payers. Traditionally employers or insurers have taken on this risk.

Given such fundamental shift in the business, compounded by an aging population and accelerating growth in information technology, generating information for control and decision making has become indispensable. How-ever, the management approach of many health care decision makers has not kept pace with the changing business. They see little value of data analysis to establish norms, benchmark their operations against others' outcomes, or examine productivity.

HCHS is responding to this challenge by educating current and potential users of DSS data through presentations at various clinical and financial meetings and demonstrating to them the value a DSS can bring to decision making. It is equally important to educate the physicians within hospitals who may not neces-sarily use the DSS but have a significant effect on the outcomes stored in a DSS. The director of the DSS and internal DSS consultants regularly meet with physi-cians and administrative decision makers to demonstrate, with examples drawn from their data, how they can influence clinical, financial, and quality outcomes.

Another approach being practiced is to develop "hybrid" managers. Hybrid managers are from clinical or financial departments of an MO who are trained in the use of DSSs. These managers then work with their peers and demon-strate the strategic use of the data through practice. We hope that the hybrid managers will act as emissaries for the DSS as a corporate resource.

Understanding the Data

The DSS, like other IS, is a tool that is effective only when the business context is well understood. We find that one of the most challenging aspects of the DSS implementation has been and continues to be the business under-standing, or lack thereof, of the data within the DSS. The data in the DSS are highly specialized and sometimes complex. A DSS user has to invest in under-standing the meaning of the DSS fields and the values that these fields can assume.

Further, there are calculated fields within the DSS that result from manipu-lating other fields. For example, the variable cost of a chargeable item is calcu-lated using the field's departmental expenses from the general ledger, total units of the item consumed from the order entry system, and relative value units from the cost information system. The decision maker using DSS data should understand the relationships in this calculation. For instance, a charge-able item that costs $20 in one week can cost $20.50 in the next week. This can occur in the first week of a new quarter in which the departmental expenses have increased or the units of output have decreased, or both. The change in the per-unit cost affects departmental productivity, profitability, and perhaps budgeting. Similarly, the users have to understand that traditional statistical analysis is often not appropriate for ordinal data values. For example, arith-metic mean is not appropriate for the values in the Zip code field.

DSS analysts manage this challenge by educating users on the intricacies of calculations and the periodicity of data through a number of ways, such as one-on-one training for new users, periodic refresher courses at each of the hospitals, and training classes at the annual DSS UG conferences.

Evolving Role of Decision Support Services

With the changing user expectations and the market dynamics, the role of the DSS has been evolving into a provider of applications, called an application service provider, in addition to a provider of data for decision support. The user expectations from the DSS have grown significantly from the time when it was a database for storing patient billing information to the present where it is considered as a strategic business system. The DSS assists in policy formulation and validation, contract evaluations, business process redesign initiatives, and cost control. As the data complexity has increased, the technology and the tools for analytical support have also grown. The user expectations of the DSS have evolved and they expect the DSS to be accessible from remote locations at all times. These expectations have augmented the DSS's responsibility to be service oriented and technically astute. This is a challenge when HCHS has made a policy decision to focus on its core competencies and stay out of the software development business.

DSS managers perceive their responsibility of generating knowledge and the DSS serving as a corporate resource for decision makers at all levels of the HCHS and the MOs. To this effect, the DSS group has equipped itself with the technology and skills required to accomplish its responsibilities with a customer service orientation.

Measuring Return on Investment

In the era of cost cutting and improving efficiency, the IS departments have to justify the investment in information technology. The issue of information technology payoff has been debated for decades in studies that have reported mixed results. The lack of conclusive evidence of payoff has been termed the "information technology paradox."[6]

Although in some instances information technology investment is a competitive necessity and can be technically complex and intangible in nature, the senior management still expects justification of the investment. The DSS has faced similar responsibilities to justify its continued investment. Although intuitively the role of the DSS is crucial to the competitiveness of HCHS, the DSS has regularly sought feedback from the users on how they use the DSS. The feedback from decision makers helps provide the justification for the value of the DSS. More recently, there have been efforts to examine the payoff from the DSS quantitatively by analyzing 3 years of monthly actual DSS usage data at each of the hospitals. The results indicate that the DSS does lead to an improvement in organizational efficiency and quality, particularly when combined with organizational business process redesign initiatives.[7] Other studies using DSS data in clinical settings have indicated that using DSS data can help improve clinical care by predicting adverse outcomes,[8] and that after adjusting for severity, there were no significant differences between the cost and efficiency of primary care physicians and medical subspecialists.[9]

Data Security and Privacy

Although the most sensitive patient-related information resides at the hospitals, the DSS also contains patient-related and competitive information, the confidentiality of which is of paramount importance. Security checks and validations begin from the site of the user. The HCHS commitment to maintaining security and privacy of patient and physician information is driven by the Catholic tradition of maintaining the "dignity of the person" also reflected in its mission statement. In addition, the Health Insurance Portability and Accountability Act of 1996 (HIPAA) requires that health care organizations protect the privacy of patient information.

In electronic transfers of data, HCHS uses packet switching through public networks in which the data is encrypted twice, once prior to leaving the hospital and again by the telecommunications provider through the frame relay. Further, HCHS ensures security within its systems as well the databases. As indicated in Figure C4–2, first-level security is enforced when a user accesses the password-protected local area network (LAN). In some cases, the users have to use a workstation at a predefined location in addition to the password to access the LAN. Next, the user workstation has to be authorized to communicate through the WAN.

The second-level security is enforced at the corporate office through a firewall. Only authorized users are allowed to go through the firewall. Once the user request to access an application is passed through the firewall, the login server verifies the user name and password. Following this verification, the user's authorization for applications is checked to verify whether the user is a valid DSS user, and if so, which modules are authorized for the user. Once within the DSS application, the security extends to the database level, such as read only, read and write, calculate; and to the field level, such as the department and accounts that can be accessed. For instance, the manager of the pathology laboratory should be able to look at the costs of the pathology laboratory department and at the salaries of those individuals who directly report to him or her. Within the DSS, the patient lookup is by the medical record number as opposed to the patient name. Each database and network access is recorded in a log file that is periodically reviewed by network management personnel. Any questionable access is reported to the department manager for follow-up action.

CASE STUDY QUESTIONS

1. What can HCHS do to prepare for anticipating market changes and staying ahead of the business needs?
2. How can HCHS impart training to users on the analytical and proper utilization of the data?

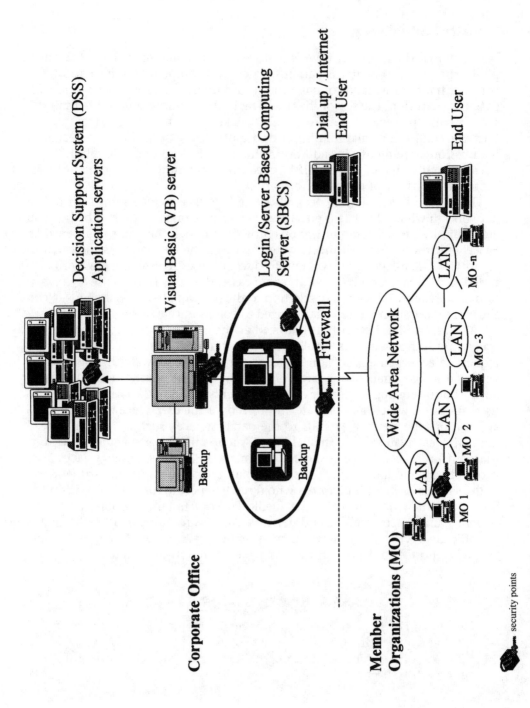

Figure C4-2 Holy Cross Health System Information Systems Network Architecture and Security Points

3. Prepare an implementation plan for the next generation of the DSS application. Who would you involve in your project team and what expertise would they bring?
4. How would you go about measuring the return on investment for the investment in the DSS?
5. How do you respond the growing demand for a "true" enterprise model in the very nonintegrated reality of health care information technology?

NOTES

1. P. Keen, Value Analysis: Justifying Decision Support Systems, *MIS Quarterly* 5, no. 1 (1981): 1–15.
2. G. Forgionne and R. Kohli, HMSS: A Management Support System for Concurrent Hospital Decision Making, *Decision Support Systems* 16, no. 3 (1996): 209–229.
3. R. Kohli, J.K.H. Tan, D. Ziege, F. Piontek, and H. Groot, Integrating Cost Information with Healthcare Decision Support Systems. *Topics in Healthcare Information Management* 20, no.1 (1999): 80–95.
4. F. Davis, Perceived Usefulness, Perceived Ease of Use, and User Acceptance of Information Technology, *MIS Quarterly* 13, no. 3 (1989): 319–340.
5. KPMG, Canada, What Went Wrong? Unsuccessful Information Technology Projects, (1995); http://audit.kpmg.ca/vl/surveys/it_wrong.htm.
6. E. Brynjolfsson, The Productivity Paradox of Information Technology, *Communications of the ACM* 35, (December 1993): 66–77.
7. S. Devaraj and R. Kohli, Information Technology Payoff in the Healthcare Industry: A Longitudinal Study, *Journal of Management Information Systems*. In press.
8. E. Zarling, F. Piontek, and R. Kohli, The Utility of Hospital Administrative Data for Generating a Screening Program To Predict Adverse Outcomes, *American Journal of Medical Quality* 14, no. 6 (1999): 242–247.
9. E. Zarling, F. Piontek, R. Kohli, and J. Carrier, The Cost and Efficiency of Hospital Care Provided by Primary Care Physicians and Medical Subspecialists, *American Journal of Medical Quality* 14, no. 5 (1999): 197–201.

Managing a Troubled Health Management Information Systems Project

Charalambos L. Iacovou and Albert S. Dexter

THE HOSPITAL

Green Valley Hospital (GVH) was established in 1897 by the Sisterhood of the Holy Cross. Today, GVH is among the major teaching and research hospitals in Canada. GVH provides care for about 200,000 patient days per year using a facility of about 550 beds. Its annual revenue exceeds $160 million and is increasing by about 9 percent annually. Sixty percent of the patients serviced by GVH live in Oxford, a major Canadian city where the hospital is located. GVH currently employs about 3,200 staff; about 500 of them are physicians.

Five senior executives—the president and chief executive officer (CEO) and four vice presidents—manage the administration of the hospital. The vice president of medicine is responsible for the medical and research activities of the hospital. The vice president of patient services is in charge of the nursing and lab staff. The vice president of finance is responsible for the financial operations of the hospital. The vice president of administration manages the auxiliary staff and services.

During the late 1980s, the Canadian health care sector faced severe budget cuts because of adverse economic conditions. The provincial government initiated a series of budget reductions and introduced stricter cost-control measures in public organizations, including hospitals. At the same time, it was planning the implementation of a "regionalization policy" to further reduce costs and improve the quality of the province's health care services. Under this new policy, the decision making and oversight responsibilities were transferred from the individual hospital boards of directors and the provincial Ministry of Health (MOH) to regional boards. These boards were responsible for allocating funds to the various health care providers in their regions and for overseeing their operations. The membership of the regional boards consisted of both elected and appointed officers. According to the MOH, the shift of responsibility to the boards would enable the regions to remove duplication, to increase synergies through better coordination, and to better prioritize fund allocations because of their localized knowledge.

To prepare the hospital for this transition and to improve its strategic position, GVH hired Donald Smith as its new president and CEO in 1988. Smith had recently gone through a similar transition at another Canadian hospital. Soon after his hiring, the new president placed a new senior management team in place and restructured the senior management portfolio. As part of this restructuring, he abolished the position of the vice president of administration and created two new positions—vice president of corporate services and vice president of professional and support services. One of the major goals of this new management team was the radical reengineering of the operations aiming to improve the quality of care and efficiency. Based on his previous experience, Smith firmly believed that the deployment of sophisticated health management information systems (HMISs) could significantly enhance the ability of the hospital to achieve its strategic goals.

MANAGEMENT INFORMATION SYSTEMS DEPARTMENT

Until the early 1980s, information technology received little attention and support from GVH's senior management. All of GVH's computer applications were designed to support the hospital's accounting and financial processes and provided no support to the clinical staff. These applications were developed in-house on an ad hoc basis through informal cooperation between interested users and the four computer professionals (two computer operators and two programmers) employed by the hospital. All applications resided on the sole IBM mainframe computer owned by the hospital.

The first attempt to introduce planning in the development of GVH's information systems (IS) took place in 1983. The administration of the hospital hired Arthur Andersen to conduct an IS needs review. Based on that review, the consultants recommended the acquisition of a patient admission, discharge, and transfer (ADT) system to computerize the hospital's basic patient management functions. A number of interested users, assisted by the Arthur Andersen consultants, developed a request for proposal (RFP) for such a system and began considering several alternatives. As a user explains, this process was cut short by the provincial MOH:

> At the time, we thought that we would like to choose SMS [as the vendor]. However, that fell through the floor when Medsys, a newly developed hospital information systems organization, came into the market and the then deputy minister said "thou shalt," and the sweetener was that if we took this particular software it'd be free. It was hard to argue with free, as we didn't have a lot of money. So our people said "fine," and a few of us got the job of implementing the Medsys ADT system.

To manage the implementation of the new system and establish a formal management information systems (MIS) department, the hospital hired its first MIS director, Ian Crooks, in 1985. The MIS department was placed in the portfolio of the vice president of finance because virtually all existing applications were supporting the hospital's financial operations. Despite this attempt to formalize the MIS department, the new director introduced little planning in its operations.

Our new MIS director was one of these really sort of laid-back guys who wasn't high on formal processes. He basically said to people like me "what do you need?" And we said, "Gee I think we need X." And he said "okay" and a month later he'd have somebody working on it. It was wonderful. We ended up with an operating room booking system that is still being used—he got that from a free tape from another hospital. He said "let's see if we can make this work" and we did. In a similar fashion, we built our own in-house relief booking system to manage our casual staff because we couldn't get anybody to agree to buy one. So one of the programmers built a little system in about a month. We put it in 1985 and we're still using it. I trained somebody on it yesterday. We also built an ambulatory care scheduling system and other applications. So most of our systems we did just ad hoc. But we got somewhere.

Under Crook's leadership, the MIS department continued to act in a largely ad hoc fashion with little senior management support and involvement until the arrival of the new president. Because of the conflicting styles of President Smith and Crooks, the MIS director quit in 1988. A participant explained the conflict between their management styles:

Ian was pretty good at ad hoc response, and when people asked for something, they got it. But there was no integrated way of going out and seeking input, and there wasn't a lot of direction. So when Don Smith came, he said we "need direction" and he brought in a consulting group to work with us. And Ian basically decided that he wasn't all that keen with the direction because there was a whole lot more structure and formality being put into place and that wasn't his style. He was a doer, he wanted to get on with it, he didn't want to sit around in meetings forever. He was not really your strategic, political kind of person. And he was not about to play political games with Don. And the more the people wanted him to play games, the quieter Ian would get, and that's why he quit.

To replace Crooks, a new MIS director, Doug Carpenter, was hired. Carpenter's management style was more formal than that of Crooks and was congruent with the president's management philosophy. Carpenter initiated a number of formal processes and established an organizational structure in the MIS department (Figure C5–1). By 1989, the department employed nine full-time-equivalent staff and had a budget of $1 million.

PROJECT BACKGROUND

By the late 1980s, GVH had developed a large number of stand-alone applications to support the administrative and financial operations of the hospital. Despite this, the hospital's administration and clinical staff were dissatisfied with the existing information systems for two reasons.

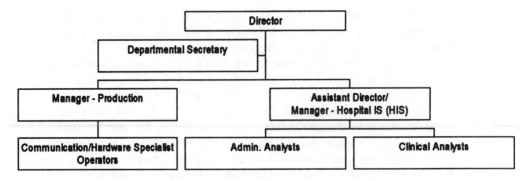

Figure C5–1 Management Information System Organizational Chart

1. *Lack of integration.* Because of the ad hoc approach that was used in early IS developments at GVH and the lack of a formal IS planning process, the various departmental systems were not integrated. Although this lack of integration was not a major concern in the past, the pressure from the provincial government to better control costs, eliminate waste, and improve patient care made integration highly desirable.

We wanted to improve patient care and felt that we needed to connect the systems together in order to do our business better. We didn't like the idea that we were putting all this patient demographic data into computers in multiple departments. We felt that this duplication and waste were just no longer acceptable, that even if they were systems supplied by different vendors there had to be integration. And the units were writing and rewriting things, and this was the beginning of budget cutbacks. We'd gone through one set of budget cutbacks, which started to drive this whole process. We knew that it was only going to get worse through time. So we had to do something to become more efficient and improve patient care.

2. *Lack of clinical systems.* Virtually all of GVH's existing systems were exclusively developed to support the hospital's financial and administrative functions. The lack of clinical systems to support the medical staff impeded their ability to provide high-quality care to the patients consistently. For example, all communication between the medical staff and the support units in the hospital, such as the admitting department, laboratory, and dietary unit, was paper-based (and often in batch mode), making coordination and the allocation of resources very difficult. The following comment by a medical staff member illustrates the difficulties caused by the lack of effective communication systems.

It used to be we did all the discharges at 10 in the morning, so the world thought the patient was gone when, in fact, many times the patient was still there in his bed until five o'clock at night when the family came to pick him up. Meanwhile, newly admitted patients were arriving and were being sent to the still-occupied beds. This made our jobs very difficult. We needed a solution that would allow us to do the discharges and transfers in real time as they happened.

To rectify this situation, the new management team initiated a strategic reengineering effort. The goal of this effort was to "treat the patient smarter" by improving care quality, internal communication, coordination, and resource allocation and by reducing wastage and costs by emphasizing specific patient costing and continuous quality improvement. A new director of resource management, Martha Kelly, was hired to lead hospital-wide projects focusing on this reengineering effort. In addition, a renewed emphasis was placed on IS development. The following comment illustrates the close coupling between information technology and the key hospital processes.

We wanted to implement process improvements and find ways of treating the patients smarter. We began by evaluating the care that different physicians provided to the patients. If you look at what different physicians do, you will realize that they treat their patients differently because they all learned at different places. From beginning to end, that process of treatment performed by only one physician may be good. But when a different physician tries to look after another's patients, you usually get problems with patients because he tries to look after the patient the way another doctor would, and things are missed. Even when treatments are clinically effective, you may have problems with the cost of the specific treatment. Even though a treatment may have been the best at one point in time, there may be a newer way of doing the same thing that is less expensive. Or, it could be that the newer way is more expensive and yet is not proven to be more effective.

So the physicians began examining the way they did their business. They said, "Okay, for all of these kinds of treatments, let's put guidelines in." They went through all the literature, went through all of their processes, and determined optimum procedures. For example, they put guidelines in for how often and under what circumstances they have a patient's blood gasses checked when a patient is on a respirator. In such cases, they need to monitor the patient carefully because they don't want to give him or her too much oxygen because it can cause brain damage. So you want to make sure that you're monitoring frequently enough. They found out that whenever certain things happened you may need to perform some sort of a procedure, but you don't just do it because you "want to make sure." In the last 10 years there have been so many lawsuits and malpractice allegations that physicians have over time increased the checking that they do just because they're concerned.

So, to move forward with that kind of change, we needed to provide sophisticated computer support. We discovered through this process that you could only implement so many guidelines in a manual method. To do this you really need to have a computer as a source of reminders for people, particularly in a teaching hospital like GVH. We have staff who are residents and are new every year and we have nursing students who rotate every 6 weeks. So there's a huge overhead administratively to make sure that these guidelines that we've implemented are passed on to all the new people coming in so that we don't lose ground.

To aid the hospital in the development of a comprehensive IS strategy that would support and implement the reengineering initiatives, Smith hired Datacom Consulting. Smith had developed a good working relationship with Datacom at his previous position, where a major IS implementation supported by Datacom was in progress. After an initial review, Datacom identified a strong dissatisfaction with the services provided by the MIS department and pointed out that the fragmented and unstructured nature of the existing systems could not adequately support the new initiatives. To rectify this situation, a strategic information systems (SIS) planning session was initiated in March 1988. After a series of meetings and interviews with the users, the consultants drafted a 5-year SIS plan.

Among the plan's major objectives was the "implementation of an integrated MIS capable of providing by-product MIS guidelines and patient-specific costing information." Specifically, this new integrated system was to provide "as good as or better" functionality to each of the departments supported by stand-alone applications while enhancing patient care and nursing unit management, integrating financial and patient care information, and providing electronic links to some of the existing systems used by the pharmacy, lab, and other departments. The plan identified a number of specific applications that would be implemented as part of the SIS implementation.

Soon after the completion of the SIS plan, GVH, with the help of Datacom, initiated a procurement process to meet the objectives of the plan. The goal of this process was to identify a commercially available "turnkey" integrated patient administration and care system (IPACS) that could be fully implemented within 4 years. To identify such a system, an RFP was prepared and sent to five hospital IS vendors. All five replied with proposals. After a preliminary review and considerable debate among key users, IS staff, and senior administrators, three of the proposals (including one by Medsys) were classified as unsatisfactory because they lacked needed functionality. The remaining two vendors were invited to provide more detailed proposals and conduct on-site product demonstrations.

During the evaluations of the two proposals, there was strong disagreement about the ability of the proposed systems to meet the needs of the hospital. Specifically, the president favored the system proposed by IBAX.[1] The majority of the users opposed IBAX's proposal because they did not feel it would satisfy their needs. According to GVH's senior management, IBAX's proposal was particularly attractive for three reasons:

1. It was the least expensive among all submitted (being priced at $5.2 million).
2. It supported flexibility and scalability.
3. It promised extensive customization of Baxter's existing software products to fit the needs of the Canadian health care sector.

Given the recent entry of IBAX into the Canadian marketplace, the GVH executives felt that there was strong pressure for IBAX to create a first-class Canadian system.

In its proposal, IBAX admitted that this was their first large-scale Canadian hospital implementation. They wanted to use GVH as the basis for the development of a definitive large-scale hospital product for the Canadian market. In order to do that they had to move in two steps. First, the base product would be given some generic major enhancements to bring it up to larger hospital scale and Canadian scale. And then there were some specific customizations for GVH. Even though the scale of modifications was extensive, the company appeared to have the financial depth to undertake this, given that Baxter was behind it.

According to the users, however, IBAX's proposal suffered from serious shortcomings. The users were not convinced that the proposed systems would offer the needed functionality because the IBAX products were developed for and marketed toward the U.S. health care industry, whose operations and requirements differ significantly from those of the Canadian health care sector. In addition, many users felt that the existing, in-house–developed applications provided better functionality than the various IBAX software modules. The MIS manager also expressed concerns about the technology used in the Baxter systems. These systems were developed using RPG3[2] and the AS400 IBM machines to satisfy the needs of medium-sized hospitals. Although IBAX promised to customize their systems to fit the needs of larger tertiary hospitals such as GVH, the MIS director felt that the limitations of the original technology would make such customizations difficult.

To alleviate the concerns of the users and the MIS director, IBAX conducted intense discussions with the hospital staff to better identify their needs. It also provided GVH staff with the opportunity to conduct on-site reviews of two Canadian sites that were implementing IBAX systems. Based on these discussions and visits, the users identified a number of necessary customizations. As a result, IBAX revised its original proposal to reflect the specific requirements of the GVH staff. The revised proposal was distributed to the department managers for review.

In September 1989, all involved department managers prepared memos summarizing their evaluations. All managers expressed serious concerns about the proposed systems and did not endorse the proposal. Some of them, who conducted their own on-site evaluations by contacting their colleagues at other hospitals implementing IBAX's systems, identified several concerns with the systems and IBAX's support services in their memos. The following extract from one of these memos indicates the seriousness of their concerns.

> The adequacy with which their efforts will meet our needs must be believed in blind faith, as there is nothing to see and no guarantee that what we require will, in fact, be possible . . . I have grave concerns that the basic product, despite enhancements, falls short of our requirements.

Despite these concerns with the proposed systems, less than a month after the managers' feedback was received, the senior administration of the hospital tentatively selected IBAX as the preferred vendor for implementing IPACS. This caused a great deal of dissatisfaction among involved users and IS staff. In response to this decision, the second MIS director, Doug Carpenter, resigned.

According to the understanding between GVH and IBAX, the finalization of the agreement was conditional on successful contract negotiation, approval by the provincial MOH, and receipt of the required provincial government funding. During the subsequent negotiation phase, IBAX staff conducted about 50 additional on-site users interviews. Over 120 detailed custom enhancements were identified and documented in the final draft of the proposal, increasing the cost of the proposal by $700,000. During these negotiations, the senior administration of the hospital submitted the proposal to the hospital board and the provincial MOH. As this was the first full-scale IS implementation in the province, the project received significant political support by the provincial government. By December 1989, the hospital had received the approval of both the board and the ministry.

In January 1990 at a public signing ceremony, a "master agreement" for the 5-year implementation of the IPACS project was formalized between IBAX and GVH. According to the agreement, IBAX was to implement a number of financial and clinical applications for the hospital. The financial applications would be based on the Software 2000 application suite and Baxter's material management software.[3] The clinical systems, mostly patient management applications, would be based on Baxter's software, which was developed and marketed in the United States. A number of applications (including the hospital's laboratory, pharmacy, radiology, and ICU systems) were excluded from this agreement because their users felt that IBAX's systems were inferior to their existing systems.

To implement the proposed system, GVH was to acquire the needed hardware from IBM. The hardware included an AS/400 model B70 computer with 96 MB of memory and eight communication lines, seven 800-MB disks, 106 dumb terminals, 56 workstation printers, and two high-speed printers. The implementation of IPACS was to last 5 years, from 1990 to 1995, and cost about $5.9 million.

IPACS PROJECT HISTORY

To prepare for the development of IPACS, a number of changes took place within the MIS department. Two project managers (one for the financial and other administrative systems and the other for clinical systems) and network staff were hired to complement the existing skills base. In addition, the department was restructured to better accommodate the needs of IPACS. The department's new structure is shown in Figure C5–2. Finally, a search for new MIS director was initiated in early 1990.

The two project managers worked closely with end users to form informal planning committees for each of the applications. The purpose of these teams was to provide feedback to IBAX consultants, evaluate the development progress, and assist in the training of other users. Many physicians, clinical support staff, and clerical personnel became heavily involved in this process. All of them, however, continued to perform their regular duties.

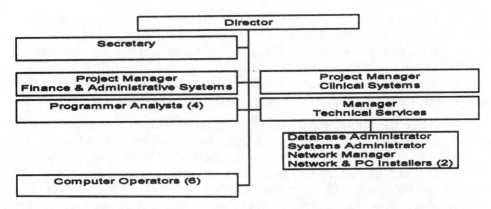

Figure C5–2 Management Information System Organizational Chart (1996)

To prioritize the development of the various applications, GVH and IBAX decided to begin the implementation of the financial systems before initiating the development of the clinical systems. This was done for two reasons. First, the financial applications, which were based on the Software 2000 suite, required fewer modifications and customizations than Baxter's clinical systems. Second, the existing financial systems were in a bad shape. As one administrator put it:

> Our finance software was a disaster. It was a very old system that was just hopeless. It crashed more than it ever ran. And so everybody agreed that it was a pretty high priority. We realized that we couldn't run a business if we didn't have the right financial information. Managers need that kind of information. We needed the GL and other functions to work and to be reasonably timely. So all of us, clinical personnel and everybody else, said "that's great, fine, go ahead and we won't worry about the clinical stuff for a while."

The first part of 1990 was devoted to the implementation of two applications: general ledger (GL) and accounts payable (AP). Because of the highly standardized nature of these applications, their implementation required minimal customization. Both applications were operational by the middle of 1990, and their users were relatively satisfied with them.

After the completion of the first two applications, the IPACS project team shifted its focus on the implementation of the materials management application. This application was part of the Baxter program suite. Because of a number of issues raised by finance and accounting personnel, its implementation proved to be more difficult than those of the previous two applications.

> The staff identified a lot of problems in the system. Even though the materials management people who were involved with the system were ready to go live, the finance people were not willing to accept it. They didn't like the way moving average price was calculated, they didn't like the way entries were posted to the general ledger, they didn't like a lot of other things. So we called in some more

IBAX consultants and we said, "This isn't going to work and we cannot go live." We had several meetings with them. They actually took two of us down to Florida to help them come up with the necessary functions and calculations. This delayed the delivery of the application and created a lot of resistance among users who felt that the customizations were not satisfactory.

While the implementation of the materials management application was in progress, a new MIS director, Andrew Divon, was hired. In addition to managing the MIS department, Divon was charged with the overall responsibility of the IPACS project. At the same time, the MIS department was moved from the portfolio of the vice president of finance to that of the vice president of corporate services. Incidentally, there was a major reorganization at IBAX at the same time. Its CEO was dismissed by the senior of administration of Baxter Systems.[4] This had a serious implication for GVH.

The original commitments between IBAX and GVH were both contractual and personal to a degree because there was a strong personal relationship between the CEO of IBAX, the CEO of GVH, and a couple of the local IBM senior staff. They had a very good relationship that made for easy smoothing out of any wrinkles that occurred. After these management shakeups, we did not have that anymore.

By the early part of 1991, the materials management application was put into operation and the implementation of three financial applications—human resources/payroll, accounts receivable (AR), and capital assets tracking (CAT)—was initiated. The users strongly resisted the introduction of the AR and CAT modules because they did not provide the needed functionality. These applications also created additional workload for the users because a number of processes that were previously performed by the existing applications would have to be performed manually after the introduction of the IPACS modules.

While GVH and IBAX were negotiating a solution to the AR and CAT introduction issues, the implementation of two clinical systems (OR and ADT) was also initiated. Despite earlier promises by Baxter to highly customize these two products, the actual customizations did not meet the needs of the clinical staff. A participant described the reception of the OR application by the nursing staff:

So IBAX says "we're going to bring in OR-star"—that was the product that they were touting. Well, the people in the OR took one look at it and said, "No, this won't work." They felt that it didn't match what was in the RFP. The users felt that the OR application was not going to work and was not, in any way, better than what they had at the time. It was worse than what they had! We said, "We don't want this system until you can provide us with a decent wait list system." As you know, in Canada, wait listing is really important. Our government requires information about our average waits, about every patient who has surgery. They want to know what was the longest wait, what was the shortest wait, and a whole bunch of other junk that we have to send to the ministry. This new system didn't even have a wait list because in the States wait lists aren't an issue. So they took that system, they merely changed the date format, they put it in military time, and that was all the customizing they did! So the people in the OR were not happy. The staff and the nurses in the OR are "one breed of cat." I mean, you just don't fight with them. And they said absolutely no! I mean they would have scalped anybody that would have tried to change their system. That's how strongly they felt. So they basically said, "Sorry, count us out. We refuse. We'll stay with what we got. Get out of here. We're not going to have anything to do with it."

The ADT application suffered from similar functionality shortcomings and was rejected by the involved users as well. In addition, there were a number of technical problems associated with the ADT software.

The version of the product that was due to be delivered in 1991 was delivered behind schedule. When it arrived, it was immediately tested exhaustively by our staff and by our users. That was the first sign of trouble. The users came to me in revolt and said that the system that they'd been delivered was awkward, cumbersome, not very Canadianized, and not as functional as the system they had already. The systems that GVH was using at that time were considered to be outdated systems. However the users demonstrated that the new Baxter product was more labor intensive to use. Even though it contained a lot more information, it was missing some of the essential information that they needed. Baxter's system was functionally rich, particularly if you were a U.S. hospital—there was a lot of front-end accounting and patient accounting going on.

At the same time there were some technical hitches with it. The technical staff had deep concerns about the quality of the code of the product. Because it was RPG3, which perhaps was not the most up-to-date language, the modifications that were made to this product made it run in a very machine-intensive fashion. Luckily we had a good-size machine, and we were not too concerned. We were, however, concerned with the fact that the way modifications were made left a lot of redundant code in the system. Because the product was so old, the people who were updating it and enhancing it did not want to disturb any of the base product; they would simply go around it rather than eliminate it. So we had, in fact, huge software files, much of which was redundant code that was left in there because to take it away might bring the whole thing down.

By the middle of 1992, the implementation of the ADT program came to a virtual standstill. As one project participant recalls:

We had gotten to the point where we did all the conversion preparation. We got ready to move all of the data over, but we were still waiting for the update in the features. We knew we couldn't proceed without a specific list of features being met, and that was the code that we were waiting for. IBAX was supposed to be rewriting the front end, but they hadn't come back to us to get the specifications. We had a long list of detailed specs for a lot of the functionality changes, but we were never asked for them. This was where the red flags where raised.

The inability to develop a satisfactory ADT application had serious implications for the whole IPACS project because most of the other applications were dependent on the data that was to be captured and stored in ADT. Frustrated IS staff and users approached the executives of GVH and demanded a resolution to this situation. The newly hired MIS director and the vice president of corporate services put the IPACS project on hold and initiated discussions with IBAX in order to find a solution. IBAX conducted a presentation at GVH recommending the replacement of the systems under development with a suite of brand new systems that were about to be announced by Baxter. According to a project participant, their recommendations did not impress the GVH staff:

> The presentation itself was very slick, but it was very clear that they had such a hefty user base to support and limitations in terms of their working capital that we could not really expect to see any of the new systems for 2 years. So, we went to the new CEO of Baxter, who was a good turnaround artist, and explained that we had been given these contractual agreements and assurances by IBAX's previous senior management. He did not commit the typical mistake of assuring that they would meet all of our requirements. He said he'd get back to us once his people had taken a look at it.

> It took about 4 to 5 months for that to happen because it took a while for the new management team to get established. They came back to us and said, "In all honesty, we cannot do this. It's not businesslike and it may not even be technically feasible, and there is strong concern on our part about creating such a unique environment for GVH that would result in extremely high long-term costs." They were not prepared to allocate the staff to do it. They had a large base of generic users from the United States, and for the amount of money that we had been contracted to pay, they could not deliver the systems.

After a detailed review of the project status and lengthy negotiations between Baxter, IBM, and GVH, the three parties reached a mutual agreement in 1992. According to the "termination agreement," IBAX was to return all payments made by GVH for the software after subtracting about half of the project's incidental expenses. In return, GVH would state that Baxter had completed all of their contractual obligations.[5] Even though IBM did not refund any of the payments made for the hardware, it agreed to let GVH exchange the hardware that was not needed because of the project's cancellation.

The cancellation of this project left GVH in a major predicament. Although it had upgraded some of the financial systems using Baxter's and Software 2000's applications, none of the legacy clinical systems were upgraded, leaving the clinical staff with almost no computerized support. In addition, because GVH was planning on having its ADT system replaced, it had not kept up with its vendor's release updates. Consequently, the vendor was about to stop supporting GVH's ADT system. Perhaps the most critical aspect of the project's cancellation was the fact that the widely publicized implementation of the SIS, which was initiated 3 years ago, had consumed over $2 million with virtually no results!

THE RECOVERY PROJECT

Because of the political pressure to complete the implementation of the SIS plan within the original budget and time schedule (by the end of 1995), the managers began prioritizing the SIS activities. They asked each user department to promptly review the current state of their systems and rank their needs in terms of replacing them. In addition, the users were asked to review the original RFP and update it to better reflect their current needs. This process was described by one of the managers.

> I'm told to look at the old RFP that we'd done for IPACS to see if it's still valid and add what we absolutely have to have. We weren't allowed to go "blue-skying" here. But, if there were some things we felt we absolutely had to have, given the reality of the 90s, then we would be allowed to add some of that. So I worked with one of the IS project managers and we did this new RFP and I went back to users and asked them for feedback. So, we incorporated the newly identified requirements and clarifications as a supplement to our original RFP. We did this for all of the applications.

At the same time, GVH invited four hospital system vendors—including the supplier of its existing ADT system, Medsys—to demonstrate their current software solutions. GVH's senior administration quickly decided to examine the possibility of selecting Medsys to be the supplier of the new systems. GVH submitted the revised RFP to Medsys and gave it the "first right of refusal." This was done for several reasons.

- By selecting Medsys, GVH did not need to replace all of its existing systems because Medsys had supplied a number of them, including ADT. This would allow GVH to selectively upgrade and replace critically needed applications in a piecemeal fashion while retaining existing functioning applications. Thus, GVH would be able to keep the cost and implementation time of the recovery project to a minimum. A participant explained the rationale behind this decision.

> We didn't go out to the market because the idea was that if Medsys would meet our requirements and our needs, either with its existing or planned applications, then it would save us a lot of money because we wouldn't have to buy a new ADT system. We could continue to struggle along with the other systems until we'd found something better.

- Medsys had recently announced the development of new hospital systems with significantly enhanced functionality (compared to the previous generations of Medsys applications). Its new products included new patient management software and new clinical workstation systems. They were based on a client/server architecture, allowing their integration with GVH's existing and other third-party applications. This was quite beneficial for GVH.

We knew that we couldn't replace the ADT and the lab system and a number of other systems for financial reasons. We'd have to keep them because they were providing not everything we needed, but they did function and we really needed to look at where we were going to go with our clinical systems. We didn't look elsewhere because we didn't have the dollars to buy another system that would require a different ADT or a different whatever. We needed a system that could integrate with what we already had because that was the limit of our resources. By that time we had implemented a number of interfaces between our stand-alone applications, and Medsys had also produced interfaces between their different systems, and we were now operating with a better functioning client/server architecture. We had interfaces to pharmacy, to lab, and were working on a few other things. So we felt we were in a very good position even though we hadn't moved forward with the Baxter systems.

- Medsys was a local vendor and was very interested in working with GVH to fully develop its new software. Medsys offered to use GVH as one of its two beta testing sites, allowing the users to provide feedback and direction to their future software development efforts. The GVH staff favorably received this opportunity for their participation in the software design process.

One of the advantages with having gone with Medsys is we had a lot of input into that prototype, and we continue to do so. A number of our staff participated in a couple of design sessions when Medsys was originally building their order-entry product. After a 2-day meeting, based on our feedback they threw the whole thing out and started over using some of the newer technology and concepts. This made us feel very good about the process. Our physicians also had a lot of input. They were able to go and sit down with the developers and walk through the screen inch by inch and field by field and say "yes, that will work" or "no, it won't." As a result, this was a very friendly clinical system. I think that one of the reasons why health care hasn't adopted the technology the way the retail industry has is because it hasn't been useful. The technology has got too many limitations to be useful for the kind of work that we do. I have to say I borrowed this one from a physician friend of mine, but "physicians and nurses do not think linearly." What we do is pattern recognition. Unless the systems can support this kind of thinking, they are not very valuable to us.

After receiving Medsys's response to the new RFP, a newly established clinical systems advisory committee[6] conducted a user review. Based on the review, the committee concluded that "the proposed systems provide for most of GVH's requirements and do it in an acceptable way." An agreement to implement the systems was signed between Medsys and GVH in 1993. According to the agreement, the Medsys patient care system was to be implemented utilizing the residue of funding left from the cancellation of the IBAX contract.

The implementation of the Medsys clinical systems began with the lab communication and ADT systems. This decision was explained by one of the managers.

> Lots and lots of the literature says that you should give clinical people applications that provide immediate tangible benefits. Well, one of the biggest benefits that people want is lab results. Physicians want to look up lab results on the wards; that's one of the biggest benefits that they see. We also considered establishing a similar link with radiology, but radiology didn't have a system, so what were we to communicate with? The only really good clinical departmental system we had was in the lab, so it was logical to say "all right, the first phase of the Medsys project would be the lab." We'd give the clinical staff the lab results first using a lookup function to get used to the technology and keyboard without having to worry about screwing things up, so that's what we did. We implemented that first. We then also said because we now have a network connection in the wards we'll do the discharges and the transfers on the nursing unit. That's been problematic. The problem is when you're faced with looking after patients or updating a computer system, guess which the nurse does first. . . . So we have a bit of a problem with the updates, and that drives admitting crazy.

While implementing the various Medsys applications, a number of departments, such as human resources and radiology, decided to acquire their own systems using third-party vendors. As the available funds were extremely limited, stand-alone business cases were developed to justify the acquisition of these applications. For example, the human resources department was able to justify the acquisition of a new payroll system by estimating the savings that the hospital would receive from insourcing its payroll operations from a service bureau. In most cases, the integration of these systems with the other hospital systems was facilitated by client/server–based interface engines.

In 1994, about a year before the conclusion of the 5-year SIS plan, President Smith commissioned Datacom again to conduct a formal audit of the whole SIS implementation. The consultants conducted interviews with the users and MIS staff from March until July. At the same time, the MIS department prepared its own "audit and progress report," reviewing the existing IS portfolio. This report was incorporated in the consultant's audit.

The Datacom consultants reviewed the status of 26 applications that were included in the original SIS plan. Out of the 26, seven of them were fully completed, 10 of them were being implemented (or being reworked due to the

IBAX failure), and the remaining nine were not initiated or faced major implementation issues. Their review stated that the majority of the financial systems had been upgraded or replaced. Several of the clinical systems, on the other hand, continued to face critical shortcomings. As part of their audit, Datacom also reviewed a number of additional systems that were not part of the 5-year SIS plan, including 11 unfunded, unintegrated LANs.

The summary of their audit was published in a 50-page report. Parts of the report were selectively disseminated within the hospital during the fall of 1994. According to the report, the review identified strong dissatisfaction with the project, which was explained as follows:

> In the 5 years since the formulation of the IS strategy, the environment has changed dramatically. Over the same period, many of the management and physician staff involved in planning the strategy approved by the board had ceased working at GVH before the termination agreement was reached with IBAX. As a consequence, management and medical staff charged with implementing the IBAX and subsequently the Medsys solutions are, in a substantial number of instances, twice removed from the original "buy-in" decision. Clearly, a firm institution-wide recommitment to a new information system plan is needed.

Overall, the review provided a positive evaluation of the SIS implementation project. It stated that "based on the independent review and user feedback, foundation financial systems have by and large been satisfactorily replaced/upgraded and base clinical foundation systems have been successfully implemented in the relatively short 2-year interval since the failed IBAX implementation effort was terminated." Furthermore, the consultants predicted the successful conclusion of the incomplete applications that were part of the original IPACS project. Based on their review, they deemed IPACS to be a success.

> The MIS department has implemented essentially all of the functions enumerated in the strategic plan and then some and has remained within the 5-year one-time cost and operating budgets contemplated in 1990. . . . Assuming that all implementation objectives stipulated for the end of 1994 and currently in progress are met, this budget will have been adhered to in all material respects. Accordingly, it is important that the hospital declare a (well-deserved) success and get on as soon as possible with formulating a new plan responsive to new needs.

Finally, the consultants recommended the following:

- the creation of a concomitant IS organizational realignment as there exists "too much friction, distrust, and poor communicating"
- the celebration of the SIS implementation success "instead of carping about what it (wrongly) perceives others have achieved better or sooner"
- the restructuring of the IS steering committees

- the integration and coordination of IS with other key functions, such as resource utilization management, patient costing, and patient care
- a workshop to discuss and develop a new SIS plan

Despite the optimistic predictions of the Datacom consultants, not all of the originally specified applications were completed in 1995. In 1995, the MIS director left the hospital. Martha Kelly, the director of the Quality Data Center, assumed the responsibilities of the MIS director and directly reported to the president. Kelly also oversaw health records, admitting, and quality utilization management of the organization. Kelly explained this reorganization.

> Most of the stuff I worked at for the last 5 years has to do with redesigning the way we deliver clinical care. It was the feeling of the CEO that because of the decisions that were made about organizational restructuring, the person who was leading the system redesign issues should also be heavily involved in influencing information systems development. These areas were too disconnected, so IS could potentially go off in one direction and not meet the business needs. I don't know anything about IS, but I know the business really well, and there was a sense that that was what was required. We needed the leadership of someone who knew the business and knew where the business needed to go.

As part of this new organizational change, Kelly created an extensive committee structure with heavy user involvement to decentralize decision making. This structure consisted of a number of committees and integrative working groups. A manager commented on the value of this new structure.

> I think this structure will ensure that some of these high-level decisions aren't made in isolation. For example, if the patient care working group comes up with some sort of system they want to bring, they've got to get the blessing from the infrastructure working group to make sure from a technical side everything is there and it will work. Then, it's got to go to the top management working group to get their approval. Decision making has improved a lot.

Some users, however, did not share this view.

> It is more difficult to make decisions now. It's slower and usually involves two, three, or four meetings. We now have a whole bunch of committees. While that at least will help us make sure that there is some kind of input or some kind of involvement of more people in the organization, it's cumbersome. We now have this enormously complex structure. There's an information management advisory group to senior management. And then under that there's a clinical group. There's a records group. And there's a technical group. Sure, at least we're getting somewhere and are trying to set some technical standards. It used to be that the MIS department would decide

out of the middle of nowhere to move us all to Microsoft Office, for example. Maybe that was the best decision, but they didn't ask anybody. We now have an education group to take care of these changes. This group, however, hasn't had a meeting for a while. And we've got a research group. So, we've got all these groups that are all related to information management. We're still trying to figure out how to get on with fully implementing the Medsys systems. We have a meeting once a month with this clinical-something working group, and the process keeps going on with no end in sight.

In 1996, the board of GVH dismissed Smith, who initiated the SIS plan. By then, most of the IPACS applications, including lab order entry, the new ADT, triage, and a new patient costing system were working. Furthermore, a number of additional systems, which were not part of the original IPACS project, were being developed at GVH.[7] Several of the original IPACS applications, however, including the clinic administration, patient scheduling, and nursing systems were not fully implemented. A project participant commented on the overall impact of the IPACS project on the current state of IS at GVH:

A failure like this could happen again, and it wouldn't be very different because we are working in a political area. When you've committed a heck of a lot of money to a project, you tend to want to save it rather than pull the plug when something goes wrong. Well, sometimes it's better to pull the plug, yet you still feel that if I put in that little extra effort, a little bit more money, I'll make it work, so you always have to contend with that as well. There is so much commitment and momentum you cannot stop. And the other thing is that this was the president's solution, as everyone seems to think, but without him making some very strategic decisions, we wouldn't be as computerized today as we are. Okay, he might have made a bad decision, but he got GVH rolling and he got money committed to computerize and he really put GVH on the map.

CASE STUDY QUESTIONS

1. What HMIS solutions have been proposed (discuss them in terms of infrastructure, hardware, software, and peopleware solutions), and what organizational problems were these solutions intended to resolve?
2. Discuss the human–computer "interaction" occurring in the various organizational problem-finding and problem-solving stages in the case. What were the major factors leading to the HMIS implementation troubles?

3. How was the "crisis" perceived and overcome? Do you agree with the way the recovery had been performed? Can you suggest alternative strategies that could have been pursued to turn these troubles into "blessings"?
4. What are critical success factors in this case? Comment on the key barriers to successful HMIS implementation relevant to the GVH case.

NOTES

1. Ibax was a joint venture between IBM and Baxter Systems. The purpose of this venture was to "sell computer software to hospitals and physicians" in the "$6 billion American market for health care information services." Even though Baxter Systems was based in the United States, a new Canadian company, Ibax, with about 40 employees was formed to serve the Canadian market. Ibax was currently implementing a major IS project at St. Mary's Hospital, which was Smith's previous employer. Many users attributed Smith's strong support toward the Ibax proposal to his Datacom and Ibax connections at St. Mary's and became quite resentful. To protest Smith's favoritism, they nicknamed GVH "St. Mary's North" and were bringing President's Choice grocery bags to work!

2. RPG3 is a "punch-card emulator" programming language that was a developed in the 1970s. This language was developed to help migrate applications from a punch card environment to a newer data entry environment. Because Baxter's systems were written in RPG3, the applications had certain technical peculiarities limiting their ability to be easily customized and integrated with other applications.

3. This was a third-party software suite that was to be customized by Ibax to fit the needs of GVH and the Canadian health care sector in general.

4. Three months after this incident, the senior management team of Baxter Systems (who fired the Canadian CEO of Ibax) was fired as well (by Baxter's administrators).

5. Six months after this agreement was signed, Baxter Systems closed down Ibax's Canadian operations.

6. This was one of three committees established by the new MIS director to coordinate the implementation of the various systems and improve the cooperation between MIS and the rest of the hospital. The other two committees were the business systems steering committee and the senior steering committee.

7. By 1996, there were 54 systems and 25 networks within GVH. Thirty systems and 15 networks were under the responsibility of the MIS department while the individual departments managed the rest.

Index

About the Contributors

Joseph K. H. Tan, PhD, is an Associate Professor of Health Informatics in the Faculty of Medicine at the University of British Columbia (UBC) in Canada. He is an associate of the UBC Institute of Health Promotion Research, the UBC Center for Health Services and Policy Research, and the UBC Center for Integrated Computer Systems Research. He has served as an editor and co-editor of special journal issues, as a member of editorial boards for a number of health information and business journals, and as a conference coordinator, track and session chair, and reviewer of various academic and professional associations at local, national, and international levels. He is well-published in the field of health management information systems and health decision support systems. More recently, he has been appointed as a member of the British Columbia Health Information Standards Council and elected as Vice President of Management in the Health Technology Sector in INFORMS. Dr. Tan also has taught in various international settings and is actively involved in promoting collaborative and online health informatics education program delivery.

Monica Adya, PhD, is an Assistant Professor of Information Systems at the University of Maryland Baltimore County (UMBC). Her research interests are in the areas of intelligent decision support systems, business forecasting, judgment and decision making, knowledge elicitation, and knowledge discovery in medical databases. Her dissertation work and most of her current work is in the use, refinement, and extension of rule-based systems for forecasting. She has published in *Information Systems Research, International Journal of Forecasting,* and *Journal of Forecasting.*

Ashok Bhatkhande, MD, DPH, is the Director (Administration) at the Breach Candy Hospital in Bombay, India. He is also a faculty Associate in the Department of Health Policy and Management at the School of Hygiene and Public Health at Johns Hopkins University in Maryland. He has 22 years of teaching experience in public health, health care administration, and health economics. He has represented the Indian private health care sector at various national and international meetings. He also has 15 years of experience as a Chief of Operations at leading private hospitals in Bombay. During this period he has developed and implemented software applications for managing hospitals.

Mark L. Corley is the Vice President of Operations for Abbott Ambulance, Inc. He has almost 30 years of experience in emergency medical service, ranging from emergency medical technician, paramedic, supervisor, and instructor. At Abbott he is responsible for ambulance operations, the communications center, fleet maintenance, and information systems. His management duties include responsibility for over 500 employees operating more than 100 ambulances. He was instrumental in the system design of several computer programs in use at Abbott, including the computer-aided dispatch system, the crew scheduling program, and a newly designed system that is being used to post ambulances in anticipation of calls based on historical volume patterns.

Albert S. Dexter, MBA, PhD, is a Professor of Management Information Systems at the Faculty of Commerce and Business Administration at the University of British Columbia. He has published more than 100 articles in many journals, including *Accounting Review, Business Quarterly, Journal of Accounting Research, Journal of Business Administration, Management Information Systems Quarterly, Management Science,* and *Marketing Science,* among others. He received his MBA from Harvard University and his PhD in Accounting and Management Information Systems from Columbia University.

Guisseppi A. Forgionne, PhD, MBA, MA, is a Professor of Information Systems at the University of Maryland Baltimore County. He also has served as a Department Chair at UMBC, Mount Vernon College, and Cal Poly Pomona. He has published 24 books and approximately 125 research articles and has consulted for a variety of public and private organizations on decision support systems theory and applications. Dr. Forgionne has received several national and international awards for his work. He received his MA in Econometrics and his MBA and PhD in Management Science and Econometrics.

Aryya Gangopadhyay, PhD, is an Assistant Professor of Information Systems at the University of Maryland Baltimore County. His research interests include electronic commerce, multimedia databases, data warehousing and mining, and geographic information systems. He has authored and co-authored two books, numerous papers in journals such as *IEEE Computer, IEEE Transactions on Knowledge and Data Engineering,* and *Journal of Management Information Systems,* as well as presented papers at many national and international conferences.

Henry J. Groot, MS, is the Director of Information Resources at the corporate offices of Holy Cross Health System Corporation. His accomplishments include positioning the decision support function to support the decision makers in multiple business units and clinical settings and to support their information needs by increasing use, understanding, and application of information for analysis and reporting. The deployment of decision support has spanned across disciplines such as finance, corporate development, utilization and quality assurance, and operations. Mr. Groot received his MS in Management Information Systems from Purdue University. His work has been published in *Healthcare Informatics* and *Topics in Healthcare Information Management.*

Charalambos L. Iacovou, PhD, is an Assistant General Manager of Management and Information Services at the Cyprus Popular Bank and a Research Fellow at the McDonough School of Business at Georgetown University. His current research focuses on the management of troubled information systems projects, the adoption of information technology by small organizations, and the role of trust in electronic commerce. His papers and cases have appeared in *Annals of Cases on Information Technology Applications and Management in Organizations, Journal of Information Technology,* and *Management Information Systems Quarterly.* He received his PhD in Management Information Systems from the University of British Columbia.

Rajiv Kohli, PhD, is the Project Leader of Decision Support Services at the corporate offices of Holy Cross Health System. He is also an Adjunct Assistant Professor at the University of Notre Dame. Dr. Kohli's research interests include assessing the information technology investment payoff, process innovation, and the effectiveness of enhanced decision support systems in health care. Dr. Kohli's research has been published in *Decision Support Systems, Journal of Management Information Systems, Journal of Association for Information Systems,* and *Information Processing & Management,* among other journals. Dr. Kohli is a recipient of the Teaching Recognition Award from the University of Maryland University College. He received his PhD from the University of Maryland Baltimore County.

Liam O'Neill, PhD, is an Assistant Professor in the Sloan Program of Health Management at Cornell University, where he teaches health information systems and health statistics. His primary research interests concern the strategic and operational use of quantitative methods in health care. He has acted as a consultant in the area of health care management engineering and has published scholarly articles in *Anesthesia & Analgesia, Health Care Management Science, Management Science,* and *Naval Research Logistics.* He received his PhD in Operations Management from Pennsylvania State University.

N. Jane Prater, RN, BSN, is a Nurse Manager at the University of Iowa Hospitals and Clinics. She has over 13 years of experience in managing inpatient units, both in private hospitals and academic medical centers. She received her BSN from the University of Illinois and is a currently pursuing an MSN at the University of Iowa with a concentration in nursing and business management.

Wullianallur Raghupathi, PhD, is a Visiting Professor of Information Systems in the Graduate School of Business at Fordham University in New York City. His teaching and research interests include strategic uses and implications of health care information systems, enterprise resource planning systems, electronic commerce, and software process improvement. He has published over 15 journal articles as well as numerous conference publications. He received his PhD in Information Systems from the University of Texas at Arlington.

Glenn H. Roberson, MD, is a Professor, Vice Chairman, and Chief of the Neuroradiology Section at the University of Alabama at Birmingham. Previously, he was Professor and Chairman of Radiology at Texas Tech University

School of Medicine, where he developed an intranet site to house electronic medical record systems for radiology departments. His research interests include clinical neuroradiology and digital imaging. He received his MD from the University of Texas Southwestern Medical School.

Homer H. Schmitz, PhD, is a Professor in the Department of Health Administration at Saint Louis University and is President and Chief Executive Officer of Abbott Ambulance, Inc., an emergency medical service company with approximately 600 employees. For over 32 years he has accumulated extensive executive experience in managing the operations, information systems, planning, and finances of various sectors of the health care market, including a 450-member multispecialty physician practice, a managed care organization with over 250,000 enrollees, and a 500-bed acute care teaching hospital. Dr. Schmitz is a nationally recognized author and lecturer in health care management. He has authored or co-authored four books and over 70 articles in technical and professional journals. He has lectured at over 80 national and international meetings and seminars and has had numerous national and international health care consulting assignments.

Yao-Yang Shieh, PhD, is a Professor in the School of Medicine at Texas Tech University Health Sciences Center and is in charge of the Picture Archiving and Communication Systems (PACS). His research interests include medical informatics, medical imagery analysis and processing, teleradiology, and PACS. His research has been published in the *Journal of Digital Imaging, Diagnostic Imaging,* and *ACME Transactions,* among others. Dr. Shieh is a 1998 recipient of the Certificate of Merit award from the Radiology Society of North America. He received his PhD from Purdue University.

J. Michael Tarn, PhD, is an Assistant Professor of Computer Information Systems at Western Michigan University. He specializes in multidiscipline research involving info-communication systems, strategic management, modern organizational theory, and electronic commerce. His recent research has contributed to the theoretic modeling of organizational expansion and the development of integrative management support systems. His areas of expertise are telecommunications and network management, integrative systems design, international management information systems, chargeback decision support systems, client/server database design, business forecasting, and critical systems management. He received his PhD in Information Systems from Virginia Commonwealth University.

H. Joseph Wen, PhD, is an Associate Professor of Management Information Systems at the New Jersey Institute of Technology. He has 15 years of information systems design experience on decision support systems, executive information systems, and client/server databases. He has published 56 papers in academic journals, books, and national conference proceedings. Dr. Wen has received over $6 million in research grants from various state and federal funding sources for information systems analysis and design. He received his PhD from Virginia Commonwealth University.